THE PACIFIC BASIN SINCE 1945

The Postwar World
General Editors: A.J. Nicholls and Martin S. Alexander

As distance puts events into perspective, and as evidence accumulates, it begins to be possible to form an objective historical view of our recent past. *The Postwar World* is an ambitious series providing a scholarly but readable account of the way our world has been shaped in the crowded years since the Second World War. Some volumes will deal with regions, or even single nations, others with important themes; all will be written by expert historians drawing on the latest scholarship as well as their own research and judgements. The series should be particularly welcome to students, but it is designed also for the general reader with an interest in contemporary history.

Decolonization in Africa, Second Edition
J.D. Hargreaves

The Community of Europe: A History of European Integration since 1945, Second Edition
Derek W. Urwin

Northern Ireland since 1945, Second Edition
Sabine Wichert

A History of Social Democracy in Postwar Europe
Stephen Padgett and William E. Paterson

'The Special Relationship': A Political History of Anglo-American Relations since 1945
C.J. Bartlett

Rebuilding Europe: Western Europe, America and Postwar Reconstruction
D.W. Ellwood

Central Europe since 1945
Paul G. Lewis

International Relations since 1945. A History in Two Volumes
John Dunbabin
   The Cold War: The Great Powers and their Allies
   The Post-Imperial Age: The Great Powers and the Wider World

Modern Indonesia: A History since 1945
Robert Cribb and Colin Brown

Peace Movements: International Protest and World Politics since 1945
April Carter

The Bonn Republic: West German Democracy, 1945–1990
A.J. Nicholls

THE PACIFIC BASIN
SINCE 1945

2nd Edition

ROGER C. THOMPSON

Longman

An imprint of **Pearson Education**

Harlow, England · London · New York · Reading, Massachusetts · San Francisco
Toronto · Don Mills, Ontario · Sydney · Tokyo · Singapore · Hong Kong · Seoul
Taipei · Cape Town · Madrid · Mexico City · Amsterdam · Munich · Paris · Milan

Pearson Education Limited
Edinburgh Gate
Harlow
Essex CM20 2JE

and Associated Companies throughout the world.

Visit us on the World Wide Web at:
www.pearsoneduc.com

First published 1994
Second edition published 2001

ISBN 0582-42387-2 PPR

British Library Cataloguing-in-Publication Data
A catalogue record for this book is available from the British Library

Library of Congress Cataloging-in-Publication Data
Thompson, Roger C., 1941–
    The Pacific Basin since 1945 / Roger C. Thompson.—2nd ed.
      p. cm.
    Includes bibliographical references and index.
    ISBN 0–582–42387–2 (limp)
      1. Pacific Area—Politics and government.   2. United States—Foreign relations—
Pacific Area.   3. Pacific Area—Foreign relations—United States.   I. Title.

    DU29.T48   2000
    990—dc21
                                                      00–059798

10 9 8 7 6 5 4 3 2 1
05 04 03 02 01

Typeset in Baskerville MT 11/13pt by 35
Produced by Pearson Education Asia Pte Ltd.
Printed in Singapore

CONTENTS

Illustrations viii
Abbreviations ix
Preface xii
Editorial Foreword xiii

Introduction 1

1. Postwar Asian Reconstruction and Political Changes,
    1945–1949 3
    Reconstructing Japan 3
    The Cold War comes to East Asia 9
    China, the US and the USSR 11
    Dividing Korea 15
    Contest for control of Vietnam 20
    Struggle for independence in Indonesia 25
    Outbreak of insurrection in Malaya 31
    The Huk rebellion in the Philippines 35
    Conclusions 38

2. Containing the Advance of Asian Communism, 1950–1960 40
    The Korean War 40
    Repercussions of the Korean War 48
    China, the US, USSR and Taiwan 50
    Colonial Remnants in China: Macau and Hong Kong 53
    Japan and the Korean War 55
    Continuing conflict in Vietnam 56
    Suppression of rebellion in the Philippines 65
    Defeating insurgency in Malaya 67
    Opposition to the US–Japan Security Treaty 69
    The US, the USSR and Indonesia 70
    Conclusions 71

3. Confrontation and Cooperation in East and Southeast Asia,
    1961–1968 73
    The Kennedy Administration and Vietnam 73
    The US, China and the USSR 79
    Indonesia and Irian Jaya 80
    Confrontation 82
    Malaysia expels Singapore 86

The Johnson Administration and Vietnam 87
Other nations and the Vietnam War 99
Conclusions 105

4. Détente, Disengagement and Invasion in East and
    Southeast Asia, 1969–1979 106
    Searching for an end to the Vietnam War 106
    US moves towards China and the USSR 114
    Ending the Vietnam War 115
    Indonesia's invasion of East Timor 123
    ASEAN, Cambodia, Vietnam and China 127
    The US and East Asia 133
    Conclusions 138

5. Independence for some Pacific Islands, 1945–1980 139
    Postwar reconstruction and islander aspirations to 1949 139
    Slow Polynesian roads to independence 142
    Pushing independence for Papua New Guinea 147
    Independence for the Solomon Islands and Vanuatu 151
    Opposition to independence in the French Pacific 155
    Struggle for independence in New Caledonia 157
    Pacific outposts of the American Empire 162
    Melanesians under Indonesian rule 166
    Independent Pacific Island states 168
    Conclusions 173

6. Arresting Communism in Latin America, 1945–1979 174
    The CIA and Guatemala 174
    The Alliance for Progress era 176
    Crushing Marxism in Chile 181
    The Nixon/Ford administrations, Peru and Central America 185
    The US and Mexico 187
    The Carter administration and Latin America 188
    Latin America and the wider Pacific Basin 190
    Conclusions 192

7. Asian Economic Expansion and Strategic Change,
    1980–1990 194
    Japan's new economic order in the Pacific Basin 194
    Japan and the American defence network 206
    The US, the USSR and the East Asian strategic balance 209
    The Cambodian conflict 220
    The ASEAN states 224
    Conclusions 227

8. Conflicts and Coups in the Islands, 1980–1990 229
    The coups in Fiji and their consequences 229
    Papua New Guinea (PNG) 234
    New Caledonia 239
    French Polynesia 244
    Other Pacific nations and the French presence in the Pacific 246

Australasia and the US 247
The US and the Pacific islands 249
Australia, Indonesia and the islands 251
Conclusions 252

9. War and Cooperation in the Western Hemisphere,
   1980–1990... 254
   The US crusade against Nicaragua.. 254
   The US and the long war in El Salvador 260
   US relations with other Central American States and Panama 263
   The US and other American nations 267
   The Americas and the Pacific Basin 272
   Conclusions 276

10. The Post-Cold War Pacific Basin since 1991 277
    Japan's relations with the US and Russia 277
    The two Koreas and international powers 280
    China, the US and Taiwan 285
    China, Hong Kong and Macau 289
    China's relations with Russia and Japan 290
    The ASEAN states 292
    The East Asian economic crisis 295
    Indonesia, East Timor and Australia 298
    Australasia, the US and the Pacific Islands 301
    North America and APEC 306
    Central and South America 308
    Conclusions 312

Conclusion 313
Further Reading.. 317
Maps 327
Index 337

ILLUSTRATIONS

PLATES *between pages 162–3*

MAPS
1 The Pacific Basin 328–9
2 Southeast Asia 330
3 North and South Vietnam 331
4 Eastern China, Korea and Japan 332
5 Central America 333
6 Papua New Guinea 334
7 Fiji 334
8 New Caledonia 335

ABBREVIATIONS

AFTA	ASEAN Free Trade Agreement
AMG	American Military Government in South Korea
ANZUS	Australia, New Zealand, United States Security Treaty
APEC	Asia-Pacific Economic Conference
ARENA	*Alianza Republicana Nacionalista*
ARF	ASEAN Regional Forum
ARVN	Army of the Republic of Vietnam
ASEAN	Association of Southeast Asian Nations
BMA	British Military Administration in Malaya
BRA	Bougainville Revolutionary Army
CCP	Chinese Communist Party
CER	Closer Economic Relations (Australia and New Zealand)
CDGK	Coalition Government of Democratic Kampuchea
CDP	Christian Democratic Party of Chile
CEP	*Centre d'Expérimentation du Pacifique*
CIA	United States Central Intelligence Agency
COSVN	Central Committee Directorate for South Vietnam
CSR	Colonial Sugar Refining Company
DPRK	Democratic People's Republic of Korea
DRV	Democratic Republic of Vietnam
EEC	European Economic Community
FI	*Front Independantist*
FLNKS	*Front de Libération Nationale Kanak et Socialiste*
FMLN	*Farabundo Marti Frente de Liberación Nacional*
FNSC	*Fédération pour une Nouvelle Société Calédonienne*
FSM	Federated States of Micronesia
GDP	Gross Domestic Product
GNP	Gross National Product
IAEA	International Atomic Energy Agency
JCS	United States joint Chiefs of Staff
KMM	*Kesatuan Melayu Muda*
KMT	Kuomintang
KPA	Korean People's Army

KPMP	*Kalipunan Pambansa ng mga Magsaska sa Pilipinas*
KPNLF	Khmer People's National Liberation Front
LDP	Liberal Democratic Party
MAAG	Military Assistance and Advisory Group in Vietnam
MACV	Military Assistance Command Vietnam
MCP	Malayan Communist Party
MFN	Most Favoured Nation
MPAJA	Malayan People's Anti-Japanese Army
MRLA	Malayan Races Liberation Army
MRP	*Mouvement Républicain Populaire*
MSC	Malaysian Solidarity Convention
NAFTA	North American Free Trade Agreement
NATO	North Atlantic Treaty Organization
NEI	Netherlands East Indies
NIC	newly industrialising countries
NFP	National Federation Party
NHNP	New Hebrides National Party
NLF	National Front for the Liberation of South Vietnam
NSC	United States National Security Council
OAS	Organization of American States
OPM	*Organisasi Papua Merdeka*
PALIKA	*Parti de Libération Kanak*
PAP	People's Action Party
PAVN	People's Army of Vietnam
PDC	Christian Democratic Party (El Salvador)
PKI	Indonesian Communist Party
PKM	National Peasants' Union
PKP	Philippines Communist Party
PLA	Chinese People's Liberation Army
PLAF	Vietnamese People's Liberation Armed Force
PNG	Papua New Guinea
PNI	Indonesian Nationalist Party
PRG	People's Revolutionary Government of South Vietnam
PRK	People's Republic of Kampuchea
RDPT	*Rassemblement Démocratique des Peuples Tahitiennes*
ROK	Republic of Korea
ROKA	Republic of Korea Army
RPCR	*Rassemblement pour la Calédonie dans la République*
RVN	Republic of Vietnam
SAR	Special Administrative Region
SCAP	Supreme Commander of the Allied Powers in Japan
SDF	Self Defence Force of Japan

SEAC	South East Asia Command
SEATO	South East Asia Treaty Organization
SLN	*Société le Nickel*
UC	*Union Calédonienne*
UDT	Timorese Democratic Union
UFC	United Fruit Company
UMNO	United Malay National Organisation
UN	United Nations
UNA	United Nations army
UNO	*Unión Nacional de Opositora*
UNTCOK	United Nations Temporary Commission on Korea
URNG	*Unión Revolucionaria Nacional Guatemalteca*, Guatemala
US	United States of America
USI	United States of Indonesia
USSR	Union of Soviet Socialist Republics
VCP	Vietnamese Communist Party

ABBREVIATIONS USED IN FOOTNOTES

ABC	Australian Broadcasting Corporation
ASDSC	Australian National University Strategic and Defence Studies Centre
CIDM	*Commission Internationale D'Histoire Militaire: ACTA No. 14 Montreal, 16–19 viii 1988*
CO	Colonial Office
FEA	*The Far East and Australasia: A Survey and Directory of Asia and the Pacific*
FRUS	*Foreign Relations of the United States*
OECD	Organisation for Economic Co-operation
OMSIT	*OECD Monthly Statistics of International Trade,* January 2000
PIYB	*Pacific Islands Yearbook*
PP	*The Pentagon Papers* (Senator Gravel Edition)
PRO	Public Record Office
UGVW	*The U.S. Government and the Vietnam War: Executive and Legislative Roles and Relationships*
YITS	*Yearbook of International Trade Statistics*

PREFACE

In writing the first edition of this book there were numerous people to thank for their assistance, especially Peter Dennis who recommended me to the editors of the series and arranged for me special study leave at a crucial stage of the writing process; Elizabeth Greenhalgh who proof read and indexed the book; and Jeffrey Grey, Sewart Loan and Stephen Henningham who assisted me in various ways. The staff of the Australian Defence Force Academy Library allowed me to borrow at one time an enormous array of books and journals. My children and wife also supplied valuable support. For the second edition of the book, I was again well supported by the excellent library at the Australian Defence Force Academy as well as the libraries of the Australian National University. The University of New South Wales again granted me a valuable time of study leave. Again I was well supported by my wife, Sheila, through the intense process of writing this edition.

EDITORIAL FOREWORD

The aim of this series is to describe and analyze the history of the World since 1945. History, like time, does not stand still. What seemed to many of us only recently to be 'current affairs' or the stuff of political speculation, has now become material for historians. The editors feel that it is time for a series of books which will offer the public judicious and scholarly, but at the same time readable, accounts of the way in which our present-day world has been shaped since the Second World War. The period which began in 1945 has witnessed political events and socio-economic developments of enormous significance for the human race, as important as anything which happened before Hitler's death or the bombing of Hiroshima. Ideologies have waxed and waned, the industrial economies have boomed and bust, empires of various types have collapsed, new nations have emerged and sometimes themselves fallen into decline. While we can be thankful that no major armed conflict occurred between the so-called superpowers, there have been many other wars, and terrorism emerged as an international plague. Although the position of ethnic minorities improved in some countries, it worsened dramatically in others. As communist tyrannies relaxed their grip on many areas of the world, so half-forgotten national conflicts re-emerged. Nearly everywhere the status of women became an issue which politicians were unable to avoid. The same was true of the global environment, apparent threats to which have been a recurrent source of international concern. These are only some of the developments we hope will be illuminated by this series as it unfolds.

The books in the series will not follow any set pattern; they will vary in length according to the needs of the subject. Some will deal with regions, or even single nations, and others with themes. Not all of them will begin in 1945, and the terminal date may vary; as with the length, the time-span chosen will be appropriate to the question under discussion. All the books, however, will be written by expert historians drawing on the latest research, as well as their own expertise and judgement. The series should be particularly welcome to students, but it is designed also for the general reader with an interest in contemporary history. We hope that the books will stimulate scholarly discussion and encourage specialists to look beyond their own particular interests to engage in wider controversies.

History, and especially the history of the recent past, is neither 'bunk' nor an intellectual form of stamp-collecting, but an indispensable part of an educated person's approach to life. If it is not written by historians it will be written by others of a less discriminating and more polemical disposition. The editors are confident that this series will help to ensure the victory of the historical approach, with consequential benefits for its readers.

A.J. Nicholls
Martin S. Alexander

INTRODUCTION

If we continue the war, Japan will be altogether destroyed. Although some of you are of opinion that we cannot completely trust the Allies, I believe an immediate and peaceful end to the war is preferable to seeing Japan annihilated. As things stand now the nation still has a chance to recover.[1]

Thus spoke Emperor Hirohito on 8 August 1945, in making the pronouncement which persuaded his evenly divided Cabinet to seek the peace that came with Japan's surrender six days later to the United States (US). His analysis was correct. Japan was saved from further destruction by fire and atomic bombs and from Russia's eleventh hour entry into the Pacific War by the belief that Japan could trust the US to support its reconstruction. Indeed, when Hirohito died in 1989, Japan had peacefully achieved, with American assistance, an economic dominance in the Pacific Basin far greater than acquired by military conquest in the years to 1945.

Japan's re-emergence after the Second World War as an economic power in the Pacific Basin is an important theme of this book. Another major theme is the way the US became involved in contesting the expansion of communism in the Pacific Basin, with participation in two major Asian wars. The profound influences of these wars on Pacific Basin affairs are analyzed. The struggles by former colonies in Asia to achieve independence and the ways in which these contests became intertwined with US fears of communism are discussed. Ways in which the US combated imagined and real threats of communism in Latin America and the relationships of those struggles to the maintenance of US hegemonic control are explored in terms of the Pacific rim nations of the Western hemisphere. Attempts by the new nations of Asia, the Pacific and the American Pacific rim republics to cooperate together are considered. This second edition also adds a new chapter on the influences of the post-Cold War era of the 1990s. The emphasis of the book is on international relations rather than internal histories of the various nations, although attention is paid to the latter where necessary for a full understanding of relevant issues. Attention also is given to some developments before 1945 where necessary to explain postwar events. The terminating

---

1   The Pacific War Research Society, *Japan's Longest Day* (London, 1968), 70.

date in this new edition is 1999, though there is mention of some important events early in 2000 before the end time of the writing, 10 May 2000.

The Pacific Basin is defined as those countries on the rim of the Pacific Ocean and its subsidiary seas, such as the Sea of Japan and the Gulf of Thailand, and the islands within those waters. At times the definition is arbitrary. The Timor Sea adjoins the Indian Ocean, but Timor is included in the book because it was part of Indonesia. Only a small portion of Honduras touches the Pacific Ocean, but its inclusion makes Central America an entity for the book. The arbitrary nature of the geographic division is indicated by the exclusion of Laos, though it is part of the former French colonies of Indochina, except for its influence on the Vietnam War. Bolivia, though one of the Andean nations is also excluded because, like Laos, it is landlocked. Canada has faced the Atlantic in its international affairs much more than the Pacific and therefore is not extensively treated.

In citation of names, modern-day local usage is preferred, except where Westernized versions have dominated in English language literature. An example of the latter is citing two of the Vietnamese Ngo brothers by their first names: Diem and Nhu. It should be noted that in Asian languages family name comes first and that in Latin America the principal family name is usually placed second as in Salvador Allende Gossens.

Great emphasis in this book is given to US policies in the Pacific Basin. This is partly because of the pervasive impact of the US on the region and the English language sources used. However, in this new edition significant use has been made of publications in the 1990s that have revealed important new information, especially about Russian foreign policy, but also about the policies of China and North Vietnam.

The book is based principally on published works. Its main value is as a synthesis of the many, especially recent, publications about aspects of Pacific Basin history. The aim is to provide the reader with the most up-to-date interpretations, to indicate major differences of opinion among historians and to provide an interpretation that should not be regarded as the only explanation of events. Some published and archival primary source material has been used. The author also has drawn on some of his own experiences of relevant historical events and the memories of other participants.

The author does not claim complete objectivity, for such an ideal is impossible. He writes from a liberal political perspective. He is a citizen of a Pacific Basin nation, Australia, that has had some wider regional influence, though often as a supporter of a greater power, Britain or the US. He has travelled extensively in the Pacific Islands and to some of the rim countries and writes from knowledge gained from many years of teaching US, Pacific and Southeast Asian history. He acknowledges the assistance of colleagues with greater knowledge of other parts of the Pacific Basin.

CHAPTER ONE

Postwar Asian Reconstruction and Political Changes, 1945–1949

Before 1941 the Western Pacific Basin had been dominated by the imperial powers: Britain, France, the Netherlands, Japan and the United States (US). Japan overran most of these colonies during the Second World War, which stimulated indigenous nationalist groups, some working with Japan to gain independence, others assisting the allies against Japan. As a result, the situation in East and Southeast Asia at the time of Japan's surrender in 1945 was inevitably complex. Major questions were whether the Western colonists could hope to regain control of their former colonies; what was to be the future of defeated Japan; and how far would the head of the victorious coalition, the US, remain involved in the area in the face of new threats of communist expansion.

Reconstructing Japan

Japan's surrender on 14 August 1945 presented the US with a unique opportunity to shape the future of its former rival in the Pacific. Since 1943 planning had been carried out by experts in the American State Department on Japan for a de-militarized democracy such that Japan could no longer threaten its neighbours or world peace. They approached the subject comprehensively, and they knew that reform would need the cooperation of new or previously suppressed leadership groups in Japan.[1]

---

1 Robert E. Ward, 'Presurrender Planning: Treatment of the Emperor and Constitutional Changes', in Robert E. Ward and Sakamoto Yoshikazu (eds), *Democratizing Japan: The Allied Occupation* (Honolulu 1987), 1–41.

Control of detailed planning and implementation of policies for Japan's future, however, was left to an army general, Douglas MacArthur. Before the war he had been politically exiled to organize the defence of the Philippines so as to remove a threat to President Franklin Roosevelt's re-election chances. But MacArthur had generated great self-publicity and popularity from his command of the American army in the Pacific, which, with allied assistance, had rolled back the Japanese military tide. Roosevelt's successor, Harry Truman, dared not dismiss MacArthur and was also keen to keep a potentially strong political rival well outside the US. So MacArthur received the Japanese surrender and was in a natural position to head the occupation force in Japan. MacArthur, in turn, saw an opportunity to write his name in history as the creator of democracy for seventy million Japanese, which also might serve future political ambitions.[2]

In Japan MacArthur became the Supreme Commander of the Allied Powers (SCAP), an acronym applying also to the planning organization he headed, and which was American in almost all but name. He acted as a grand proconsul. He hardly ever strayed outside his daily journeys in Tokyo from the American Embassy to his official headquarters. The only real constraints placed on MacArthur by Washington before 1948 resulted from the wartime planning, especially the State–War–Navy Coordinating Committee's (SWNC) document SWNC-228, which was cabled to him in October 1945. It outlined major features of a proposed democratic government with the emperor as a constitutional monarch. While it did indicate the final shape of the new Japanese constitution, MacArthur was determined to maintain freedom of control in implementation of the reforms. Indeed, until 1948 this was permitted by the administration in Washington, whose foreign policy attention was directed much more to European than to Asian affairs.

MacArthur established a broad policy agenda for his staff. It was summed up in his statement on 11 October 1945: 'The emancipation of women; the encouragement of the unionization of labor; the opening of schools to more liberal education; the abolishment [sic.] of systems which through secret inquisition and abuse have held people in constant fear; the democratization of Japanese economic institutions to the end that monopolistic industrial controls be revised.'[3] Detailed planning for the implementation of these principles was left to SCAP personnel.

---

2 Michael Schaller, *Douglas MacArthur* (New York 1989), chs 2, 9–10; Michael Schaller, *The American Occupation of Japan: The Origins of the Cold War in Asia* (New York 1985), ch. 2; and Theodore Cohen, *Remaking Japan: The American Occupation As New Deal* (New York 1987), ch. 4.
3 Quoted in Carol Gluck, 'Entangling Illusions – Japanese and American Views of the Occupation', in Warren I. Cohen (ed.), *New Frontiers in American East Asian Relations: Essays Presented to Dorothy Borg* (New York 1983), 198.

By 25 April 1946, 1,550 American military personnel and civilians had been engaged for SCAP operations. They were a disparate set of people usually appointed with minimal or no screening. But they included many qualified recruits from the large number of American soldiers in Japan, many of whom were former civilians, and from expert teams that MacArthur requested from the US. Few SCAP members had previous knowledge of Japan.[4]

Some more junior members of SCAP had important influence because the separate planning sections enjoyed significant autonomy. An example was an idealistically minded twenty-two year old American college graduate, Beate Sirota, who was fluent in Japanese because of a pre-war childhood in Japan with her Austrian parents. SCAP's Civil Rights Committee gave her the task of drafting measures to improve the status of Japanese women. She collected information in Tokyo libraries about women's rights in European constitutions and contacted liberal-minded Japanese women. Consequently, the Japanese constitution outlawed, in article 14, any 'discrimination in political, economic or social relations because of race, creed, sex, social status or family origin', and also, in article 24, made marriage dependent 'on the mutual consent of both sexes', declaring 'the essential equality of the sexes' in all respects. As well as being revolutionary in a society in which women were subordinate to men, these clauses were more progressive than legal rights in the US.[5]

There were other radical clauses in the Japanese constitution, the final draft of which was made public on 6 March 1946. It extended Anglo-American human rights, in a Westminster-style government with a constitutional emperor, by including 'the right to maintain the minimum standard of wholesome and cultural living', 'academic freedom', and the right of workers to collective bargaining. Article nine also declared Japan's renunciation of war and the maintenance of armed forces.

SCAP's reforming arm stretched further into Japanese society. All land held by absentee landlords and other property above ten acres was bought by the government and sold to tenant farmers on easy credit terms. This reform, established on Australian advice, aimed to reduce the large class of tenant farmers who might become the seedbed for radical revolution, as well as to break the power of Japanese landowners. Its success was measured by a reduction in the land worked by tenant farmers from 46 to 10 per cent by the end of the allied occupation. The Home Ministry, the central pillar of the pre-war national bureaucracy, was abolished and local government

---

4 Cohen, *Remaking Japan*, ch. 4.
5 Susan J. Pharr, 'The Politics of Women's Rights', in Ward and Sakamoto (eds), *Democratizing Japan*, ch. 8. John Dower, *Embracing Defeat: Japan in the Wake of World War II* (London 1999), 365–7.

became elective. Compulsory education was extended from six to nine years, and greater emphasis was given to individual skills and learning. New rights for workers allowed rapid unionization. Eighty-three *zaibatsu* companies, which had dominated the pre-war economy, were targeted to be broken up, and anti-trust laws were passed. Another major program to break the power of the pre-war leadership was the purging of over 200,000 former military officers and high officials of government and business. Twenty-five were tried for war crimes, most receiving long jail sentences; seven of them were executed in December 1948.

Japanese reaction to these reforms was mixed. Though Emperor Hirohito's command had impelled Japanese armies to lay down arms and the people to accept peace, the first postwar Japanese Cabinet resigned on 16 October 1945 when faced with SCAP's directive to free political prisoners and to start the purge of military and civilian officials. With MacArthur's agreement former foreign minister Shidehara Kijurō, who had resigned over the Manchuria incident of 1931, became prime minister. His Cabinet worked on a draft of constitutional reform, which retained much of the Meiji constitution. But SCAP insisted on its own version. Japanese Cabinet members were shocked, particularly about the status of the emperor and the renunciation of war. But Hirohito accepted the change in his position, telling the Cabinet: 'If that is what they want, I see no reason not to accept it.'[6] MacArthur also had clearly stated that the constitution was non-negotiable. The Japanese government duly approved the SCAP constitution, though one Cabinet official wrote: 'thus the draft Constitution, reeking of defeat was born. Unable to contain my feelings of rage, I secretly wept.'[7] However, in a few areas the Japanese Parliament was able to influence the constitution, such as extending compulsory education from primary to middle school years.[8]

Though the constitution was certainly not the free expression of the Japanese people, there was significant public support for SCAP's policies. Former Japanese liberals, educated women, union leaders and others saw the American occupation as an opportunity to create a new Japan freed from the militarism and despotism of the recent past. Many of the reforms, especially of land and labour, had been proposed in Japan prior to the war but had been blocked by the dominance over the government of the military and the socio-economic elite. General public acceptance of SCAP's sweeping constitutional changes was assisted by the way the Japanese population, initially very fearful about the occupying American army, welcomed the generous and easy-going attitude of most American soldiers. There was

---

6   Quoted in Masumi Junnosuke, *Postwar Politics in Japan, 1945–1955* (Berkeley 1985), 61.
7   Shirasu Jiro, quoted in ibid., 66.
8   Koseki Shichi, *The Birth of Japan's Postwar Constitution* (Boulder 1998), 183–8.

some freezing of this good will when puritanical military officers closed down the brothels provided for American servicemen and banned over-night visits to Japanese homes. But soldiers found other ways to enjoy the company of Japanese women. On balance, wrote Theodore Cohen, one of the SCAP officials who married a Japanese woman, relations between the occupying Americans and the Japanese generally encouraged public accept-ance of the radical reforms.[9]

In fact MacArthur was idolized by many Japanese like another god emperor. Little more than a year after his arrival in the country, a booklet in Japanese outlining his biography had sold 800,000 copies. Noting this phenomenon, Japanese newspaper editor Itakura Takuz commented: 'The Japanese people have long been plagued by the mistaken idea that govern-ment is something to be executed by some deity, hero or great man', and he lamented that the transference of this worship to MacArthur was 'the worst enemy of democracy'.[10] But many of his compatriots still clamoured even to catch a glimpse of the great man. MacArthur also earned the approval of many Japanese people for intervening personally to save the country from mass starvation in 1946 resulting from the war-ravaged and inflation-racked economy. He did this by diverting to Japanese civilians surplus army food supplies that became available with the decline in the number of American servicemen in the country from 600,000 to 200,000, a reduction made possible by the peaceful Japanese reception of the occupation. He then used his immense popularity and stature in the US to push Congress into grant-ing Japan much more financial aid than the administration had intended.

However, the increased aid to Japan encouraged a movement within the American government to halt MacArthur's reform program. He was accused of damaging Japan's chances for economic recovery and financial self-sufficiency. Important members of the administration, such as the intel-lectual director of the State Department's Policy Planning Staff, George Kennan, agreed that America's own prosperity and military security re-quired economic recovery in Western Europe and Japan. Their recipe for Japan was to halt the dismantling of the *zaibatsu*, to stop the economic reparations imposed on Japan after the war and to introduce other policies to promote economic growth. Army Under Secretary William H. Draper Jr, who had overall responsibility for the occupation, affirmed after a visit with Kennan to Japan in March 1948 that SCAP had turned the country

---

9 Makote Iokibe, 'Japan Meets the United States for the Second Time' and Herbert Passin, 'The Occupation – Some Reflections', in *Daedalus*, Summer 1990, 91–129. Cohen, *Remaking Japan*, ch. 7. For a critical discussion of prostitution see Dower, *Embracing Defeat*, 120–38.

10 Quoted in Cohen, *Remaking Japan*, 53.

into an economic 'morgue'. Kennan even claimed that MacArthur's policies had opened Japan to communist influence.[11]

MacArthur strongly resisted this attempt to control and change his policies. He had no quarrel with America's emphasis on strategic containment of international communism, but he saw China, not Japan, as the place to hold the line against it. He also vigorously defended his *zaibatsu* program as necessary for removing the power of the Japanese old guard. Nor did he desire to see any diminution in his authority, especially because he had ambitions to become the Republican Party candidate in the 1948 presidential election.

On 6 April 1948, however, MacArthur suffered a decisive political defeat when he won less than a third of the Republican Party convention delegates for his home state of Wisconsin. Opposition in Washington to his economic policies grew. In October 1948 Truman approved a directive to MacArthur to terminate reparations, to eliminate most restrictions on Japanese industry and to promote Japanese exports in the context of wage control and a balanced internal budget. After his surprising election win in November, Truman dispatched banker Joseph Dodge to Tokyo to implement the new approach. The result was that most of SCAP's attack on the *zaibatsu* collapsed. In the end only eleven companies were broken up; the anti-monopoly law was limited merely to regulating the effects of monopoly holdings; and new cartels led by many pre-war Japanese business leaders were encouraged in the name of economic growth. New laws were passed in Japan restricting the rights of unionists, such as preventing public servants from striking; and there was a purge of communists and other radicals from union ranks. The whole process has been labelled by Japanese historians, and more lately by American revisionists, as a 'reverse course'.

There has been a debate about the extent of the 'reverse course'. The revisionist historian Howard Schonberger argued that 'the signals of closer American collaboration with Japanese conservatives and the business class were unmistakable'. SCAP's Labor Division chief, Harry Cohen, agreed that after 1948 a new alliance emerged 'between the conservative and big business elements' of Japan and the US. More recently John Dower claimed: 'Driven by Cold War considerations, the Americans began to jettison many of the original ideals of "demilitarization and democratization".'[12]

There were, indeed, major limitations to the effect of the reforms in Japan. Women's rights in the constitution did not overcome the social prejudice against women's equality. At the end of the 1990s most Japanese

---

11   Schaller, *MacArthur*, 145. See also William S. Borden, *The Pacific Alliance: United States Foreign Economic Policy and Japanese Trade Recovery, 1947–1955* (Madison 1984), ch. 2.
12   Howard B. Schonberger, *Aftermath of War: Americans and the Remaking of Japan, 1945–1952* (Kent 1989), 282. Cohen, *Remaking Japan*, 459. Dower, *Embracing Defeat*, 525.

women still did not receive equal pay for the same work as men or equal career opportunities. The universal voting rights did not prevent the conservative Liberal Democratic Party (LDP) from being constantly voted into office into the 1990s. One of the most successful reforms was the renunciation of war but, under later American pressure, Japan created its own powerful 'self-defence' force.[13]

But how far the so-called 'reverse course' weakened the reforms of the early American occupation of Japan is questionable. Historians, such as Carol Gluck and Robert E. Ward, point to the fact that, by the time of the new directives from Washington in 1948, there were clear signs that SCAP was travelling in the same direction, especially in the move to stifle emerging communist influence in labour unions after MacArthur banned a general strike planned for 1 February 1947. In this case a brake was being applied to radical Japanese exploitation of SCAP's reforms. Also Richard Finn, one of the junior members of SCAP and later director of Japanese affairs in the State Department, affirms that MacArthur's suppression of left-wing unions was in line with his general policy of encouraging a moderate labour movement.[14] Furthermore, MacArthur admitted to Kennan in March 1948 that he thought the 'reform measures . . . were almost completed'.[15] Japanese international relations scholar, Sakamoto Yoshikazu, agrees that SCAP's reforming agenda was limited and was virtually completed by the end of 1947. Thus the influences of the Cold War and American concern to boost Japan's economic growth were not necessarily pushing SCAP in any new reactionary direction in 1948.[16]

The Cold War comes to East Asia

The Cold War had a profound influence on future Pacific Basin affairs and it was starting to develop in Asia by the end of 1945.[17] The entry of the

13 See Masumi, *Postwar Politics*, chs 4–5; Merion and Susie Harries, *Sheathing the Sword: The Demilitarisation of Japan* (New York 1987); and Janet E. Hunter, *The Emergence of Modern Japan: An Introductory History Since 1853* (London 1989).

14 Richard B. Finn, *Winners in Peace: MacArthur, Yoshida, and Postwar Japan* (Berkeley 1992), 142–3. See also Gluck, 'Entangling Illusions', 199–207.

15 Quoted in Robert E. Ward, 'Conclusion', in Ward and Sakamoto, *Democratizing Japan*, 408.

16 Sakamoto Yoshikazu, 'The International Context of the Occupation of Japan', in Ward and Sakamoto, *Democratizing Japan*, 69.

17 See Marc S. Gallicchio, *The Cold War Begins in Asia: American Policy and the Fall of the Japanese Empire* (New York 1988); and Robert L. Messer, 'American Perspectives on the Origins of the Cold War in East Asia, 1945–1949', in Akira Iriye and Warren Cohen (eds), *American, Chinese and Japanese Perspectives on Wartime Asia 1931–1949* (Wilmington 1990), 243–68.

USSR into the Pacific War, six days before the Japanese surrender, raised in Washington the spectre of Soviet domination of Korea, Manchuria and perhaps even northern China. Truman was much less willing to accept such a prospect than was Roosevelt, who had signed the Yalta Agreement of February 1945 between Britain, the US and the USSR. Under its terms the Soviet Union was promised the Japanese Kurile Islands and southern Sakhalin, control of Manchuria's railways and of Port Arthur, and internationalization of the Manchurian port of Dalian (Darien). In return Stalin had pledged to support the Kuomintang (KMT) government and to guarantee to enter the war against Japan within three months of the defeat of Germany.

Though he had been Roosevelt's Vice-President, Truman had not been party to his former chief's foreign policy thinking. Nor did he have any foreign affairs background. Therefore he was willing to listen to State Department officials who had been critical of Roosevelt's alleged open-handed policy towards Russia. They advised Truman to take a harder line, especially as they claimed that the USSR was already violating the Yalta Agreement in Eastern Europe. Truman also was given confidence in the potential success of this changed direction by America's possession of the atomic bomb.[18]

The Truman administration's suspicion of the USSR was heightened when its leader Joseph Stalin, demanded control of Dalian. He also proposed to confiscate Japanese industry in Manchuria as 'trophies of war', which the US regarded as vital for China's economic recovery. So when Japan signalled on 10 August its desire to surrender, Truman authorized the dispatch of American troops to northern China and to Southern Korea. However, the Soviet Union's entry into the war necessitated a division of Korea; and the shortage of available American military manpower, in view of the needs of the occupation of Japan, precluded the US from hindering the USSR's activities in Manchuria.[19]

Stalin, in turn, distrusted American intentions in China. His suspicion had been aroused by a suggestion by the American Ambassador in Moscow, Averell Harriman, that the USSR should announce its support for free trade in Manchuria and this was reinforced by the American troops sent to northern China.[20]

---

18 Messer, 'American Perspectives', 251–2.
19 Gallicchio, *The Cold War Begins*, chs 4–5.
20 Niu Jun, 'The Origins of the Sino-Soviet Alliance', in Odd Arne Westad (ed.), *Brothers in Arms: The Rise and Fall of the Sino-Soviet Alliance, 1945–1963* (Stanford 1998), 55.

China, the US and the USSR

China's relations with the US and the USSR in the immediate post Second World War era heralded major confrontations in the Eastern Pacific Basin in subsequent years. The alleged purpose of the 53,0000 marines Truman sent to China after the end of the Pacific War was to assist in transporting nationalist troops into the north in order to supervise the Japanese surrender, which was being carried out by the wartime American military adviser to the KMT, Lieutenant-General Albert Wedemeyer. But the rapid troop movement was designed primarily to prevent the Chinese Communist Party (CCP) from extending its control in northern China. Over 400,000 KMT troops were transported to northern China in American planes and ships. Also almost $450 million in American lend lease aid went to nationalist China in the two months after the Japanese surrender. Additional military equipment was sold to KMT leader Chiang Kai-shek's forces for a fraction of its true value. Moreover, the American marines allowed nationalist troops to operate against communist Chinese forces by guarding communication lines, resulting in some clashes between American and CCP troops.

These actions by the Truman administration continued a bias in favour of the KMT that had been developing in the last year of the Roosevelt administration under the influence of Wedemeyer and the US Ambassador in China, Patrick Hurley. This preference had occurred despite Roosevelt's policy of working towards a coalition of the KMT and the CCP to rule postwar China. But Hurley and Wedemeyer had underestimated the power of the CCP, which by the end of the war controlled about a fifth of China extending from its base at Yenan in the northwest. They also overestimated the support of the CCP by the USSR. Stalin had no confidence in a CCP victory and was concentrating instead on extracting wealth from Manchuria. Initially, Soviet troops failed to cooperate with the CCP's attempts to expand its influence in northeast China. However, after the landing of American troops there, the USSR allowed a flow of arms and communication facilities to the CCP, restricted nationalist forces entering Manchuria and allowed disguised CCP units to attack them.[21]

In late 1945 America therefore stood on the brink of heavy military involvement in the Chinese civil war on the side of the KMT. However, the Truman administration accepted alternative advice from John Carter

---

21   Westad, *Brothers in Arms*, 55–6. Sergei N. Goncharov, John L. Lewis and Xue Liai, *Uncertain Partners: Stalin, Mao and the Korean War* (Stanford 1993), 10–12.

Vincent, director of the State Department's Office for Far Eastern Affairs and a former American diplomat in China, that 'involvement in civil strife in China would occasion serious difficulties for us without compensating advantages'.[22] General demobilization of the American army was another good reason to withdraw US troops from China. Nor had the Truman administration abandoned Roosevelt's policy of seeking a KMT–CCP coalition.

Then on 27 November, Hurley suddenly resigned. He blamed Truman, the State Department and alleged subversive communists in their midst for his resignation. 'See what a son-of-a-bitch did to me', yelled the outraged Truman.[23] Hurley's accusations generated Republican Party criticism of Truman's China policy, which prompted the President to choose as a special envoy to China, a man far above politics: war hero, General George Marshall.

That appointment muted criticism in the US of the administration's China policy for a time but did nothing to solve the dilemma of two parties competing for control of China's government. Instructed to seek a negotiated settlement of the civil war, Marshall arrived in the nationalist wartime capital of Chongqing in December 1945. There he was welcomed by the KMT government and by CCP negotiators, who were led by Zhou Enlai. They successfully negotiated a truce, which was implemented in January and February 1941. However, by mid April 1946 the civil war had recommenced. Despite Marshall's threat to cut off financial aid, initial KMT military successes put Chiang in no mood to resume negotiations. A switch in Soviet policy towards the CCP also influenced the renewed outbreak of warfare. The USSR had been supporting a negotiated agreement and had blocked CCP troops from gaining control of major Manchurian cities, which was a major reason why the CCP had agreed to negotiate with its enemy. But, by the spring of 1946, Soviet negotiations with the nationalists had broken down over issues of economic cooperation and Stalin was angered by nationalist government-sponsored anti-Soviet demonstrations. Consequently, as Soviet troops started to withdraw from Manchuria, he gave a green light for the CCP to go on the offensive.[24]

---

22 Vincent to Byrnes, 12 November 1945, in Ernest R. May (ed.), *The Truman Administration and China, 1945–1949* (Philadelphia 1975), 63.

23 Quoted in John M. Blum (ed.), *The Price of Vision: The Diary of Henry A. Wallace, 1942–1946* (Boston 1973), 519.

24 Niu Jun, 'Origins of the Sino-Soviet Alliance', 57–60. Goncharov, Lewis and Xue, *Uncertain Partners*, 12. For American policy in China to 1946 see Michael Schaller, *The US Crusade in China, 1938–1945* (New York 1979); Bevin Alexander, *The Strange Connection: US Intervention in China, 1944–1972* (New York 1992) and Xiaoyuan Liu, *A Partnership for Disorder: China, the United States, and Their Policies for Postwar Disposition of the Japanese Empire, 1941–1945* (Cambridge 1996).

At first the fighting was centred in Manchuria, where the KMT held the cities and the CCP most of the countryside. But, though the American-armed nationalist troops were better equipped and initially more numerous, they were underpaid, poorly fed and abysmally led. Moreover, their government, whose officials were enriching themselves at the expense of an economy running riot with inflation, was losing its last shreds of public support. KMT troops were soon routed from easily defended positions. By November 1948 communist forces, well armed with captured American weapons and with ranks swollen by defecting nationalist soldiers, had conquered Manchuria and were driving into northern China. In the subsequent campaign, in which the KMT lost over 500,000 troops, the CCP captured Beijing and Tientsin in January 1949. In May 1949 they crossed the Yangtze River and entered Shanghai. The game was up for the crumbling nationalist regime, whose members were depositing their riches offshore in Taiwan. On 1 October 1949 the CCP's leader, Mao Zedong, proclaimed the Chinese People's Republic in Beijing. In December Chiang Kai-shek and his henchmen fled to Taiwan with the remnants of their shattered army.[25]

The Truman administration tried to wash its hands of this unfolding disaster. An arms embargo on China had been declared after the recommencement of the civil war; and a disillusioned Marshall returned to Washington in January 1947, damning both the KMT and the CCP for ruining his efforts to establish a coalition government. There was strong support within the State Department for abandoning the doomed nationalist regime. Overpopulated and underdeveloped China was not viewed as important in the Cold War. Western Europe, the Middle East and Japan were much more significant regions in American eyes for resistance to Soviet expansionism. Furthermore, defence appraisals viewed the islands from Japan through Okinawa to the Philippines as forming an adequate western Pacific defence perimeter for the US.[26]

But the Republican Opposition did not accept this strategic logic. Searching for political weapons to fight the coming 1948 election, Republicans saw the abandonment of an anti-communist regime in China to advancing red hordes as very useful heavy artillery with which to bombard the administration. There was plentiful ammunition, such as Hurley's denunciation of

---

25   See Steven I. Levine, *Anvil of Victory: The Communist Revolution in Manchuria, 1945–1948* (New York 1987), ch. 4; Lloyd Eastman, *Seeds of Destruction: Nationalist China in War and Revolution* (Stanford 1984), ch. 7; E.R. Hooton, *The Greatest Triumph: The Chinese Civil War 1936–49* (London 1981), chs 3–7.

26   Lester J. Foltos, 'The New Pacific Barrier: America's Search for Security in the Pacific, 1945–47', *Diplomatic History*, 13, 1989, 317–42.

communist subversion in the State Department and a noisy pro-Chiang Kai-shek lobby in America. A leader of the Republican campaign was congressman Richard Nixon, who railed against the 'apologists for the Chinese communists in the US, both in and out of the State Department'.[27]

Faced with this barrage of criticism and fearful of USSR support for the CCP, Truman and Marshall, now US Secretary of State, were unwilling completely to abandon the KMT. So the arms embargo was lifted in May 1947. In the next month 100,000 rounds of rifle ammunition were sold to the nationalist government at 10 per cent of cost price. However, Marshall also sent General Wedemeyer to China to impress on the KMT the need for significant reforms and to assess whether anything was worth salvaging. Wedemeyer found much in nationalist China to criticize, but his strong anti-communist predisposition induced him to recommend large-scale military and economic aid to the KMT government, including a team of 10,000 officers and troops as military advisers.[28]

Wedemeyer's recommended level of support for the KMT was too much for Marshall and Truman. It invited American military participation in a war in distant Asia, with the threat of a military response from the USSR, which was geographically much better placed to intervene. Indeed, impressed by growing success of CCP forces, the USSR in early 1948 significantly increased assistance to them. Especially helpful was repair of railroads by Soviet experts, which greatly assisted CCP offensives. Nevertheless, Chinese sources claim that Stalin called for the CCP advance to stop at the Yangtze because he feared the US might be provoked to militarily intervene in China, thus causing a third world war. But the Truman administration no longer believed that Chiang would survive as leader of China, though political pressure in America was maintaining financial aid for him in the form of the China Aid Act of April 1948, which granted $125 million.[29]

A problem was that many Republicans refused to accept that the KMT was a lost cause and during 1949 maintained the political attack on the administration's China policy. The government responded by releasing in August the 'China White Paper', which contained many of the documents about America's relations with China during the past decade. The aim was

---

27 Quoted in Gordon H. Chang, *Friends and Enemies: The United States, China, and the Soviet Union, 1948–1972* (Stanford 1990), 26.

28 William Stueck, *The Wedemeyer Mission: American Politics and Foreign Policy During the Cold War* (Athens, Ga. 1984), chs 1–2, 4.

29 Ibid., ch. 5. Niu Jun, 'Origins of the Sino-Soviet Alliance', 62–3. John Garver, 'New Light on Sino-Soviet Relations: The Memoir of China's Ambassador to Moscow, 1955–62', *The China Quarterly*, no. 122, June 1990, 303. Brian Murray, *Stalin, the Cold War and the Division of China: A Multi-Archival Mystery* (Washington 1995), 5–6.

to justify its view that no American intervention could have saved the KMT. Dean Acheson, who became Secretary of State in January 1949, privately remarked of Chiang Kai-shek: 'I arrived just in time to have him collapse on me.'[30]

To many members of the State Department the logical step therefore was to recognize the communist government in China. But Truman had decreed that the US should 'be most careful not to indicate any softening toward the communists but to insist on judging their intentions by their actions'.[31] Nor had the 'China White Paper' abated the intense political criticism in America about the so-called 'loss of China', and the Truman administration was concentrating on mobilising support for Western Europe. So, despite Britain's decision to recognize the CCP government in January 1950, the US adopted a wait and see policy. Furthermore, Zhou Enlai had been alienated by Hurley's policies in 1945 and there was no chance of communist China seeking any rapprochement with the US in 1949. This split between the new potentially powerful communist state in the Western Pacific Basin and the US had the potential to significantly widen the impact of the Cold War in that region. Also the Chinese victory and the, albeit vacillating, Soviet support for China during the Civil War had created the conditions for the signing of a Sino-Soviet security treaty by Stalin and Mao Zedong in Moscow in February 1950.[32]

Dividing Korea

Another early result of the Cold War, which had a major influence on subsequent Pacific Basin affairs, was the creation of two separate countries in Korea. Initially, at the Yalta Conference, Roosevelt and Stalin had agreed to a Soviet–American–British–Chinese trusteeship over Korea as preparation for ultimate independence. The trusteeship idea was Roosevelt's preferred method for containing the USSR by admitting it into an American-led club of nations. This policy appreciated the realities of Soviet military strength in border regions like Korea. However, the news of the successful testing of the atomic bomb, secretly given to Truman while attending the Potsdam

---

30   Dean Acheson, *Present at the Creation* (New York 1969), 257.
31   Quoted in Chang, *Friends and Enemies*, 35.
32   Thomas J. Christensen, *Useful Adversaries: Grand Strategy, Domestic Mobilzation, and Sino-American Conflict, 1947–1958* (Princeton 1996), ch. 4. Warren I. Cohen, 'Conversations with Chinese Friends: Zhou Enlai's Associates Reflect on Chinese-American Relations in the 1940s and the Korean War', *Diplomatic History*, 11, 1987, 283–9. Jian Chen, *China's Road to the Korean War* (New York 1993), 38–50.

Conference in July 1945, convinced him to seek American control of the peninsula if Japan could be induced to surrender before Russia entered the war. The declaration of war by the USSR, and its manifest ability to occupy the whole of Korea before any American troops could arrive, upset this aim. So, Truman suggested to Stalin a division of the Soviet and American military zones along the 38th north latitude parallel, hastily chosen because it roughly divided the country in half and was north of Korea's capital city, Seoul. Stalin agreed to this proposal because he wished to avoid any confrontation with US in the Far East and looked forward to a settlement that would create a united Korean government friendly to the USSR.[33]

The Americans had a poor understanding of Korea. While there was a historic division of the peninsula between the populous South and the much more rugged North, the 38th parallel was an arbitrary line that separated the minerals, electric power and heavy industries of the North from the light industries and agricultural production in the South, which had a population – estimated at 15.8 million in May 1945 – about twice the size of the North.[34] Korea was also in a chaotic state. Conscripted from farms to serve in factories, mines and the Japanese army, Korean peasants had been exposed to an outside world unknown to their parents, and many had become dissatisfied with traditional rural society. Korean landlords and bureaucrats were only partially modernized in their attitudes. The Japanese autocracy had stifled all forms of Korean protest, which, with the end of the war, were released like the contents of a suddenly opened pressure-cooker.[35]

The American commander of the occupying 24th US Corps, Lieutenant General John Hodge, was a tough soldier with little understanding of politics or administration. Selected to head the occupation only because his corps was the most readily available, he had no prior knowledge of Korea. His political advisers had been briefed only on the trusteeship proposal, not about an American military occupation. Korea was an afterthought in American wartime planning which had concentrated on Japan.

The American Military Government (AMG) in South Korea relied for advice, in fact, on the tiny minority of Koreans who spoke English and who belonged mainly to the wealthy classes. So the AMG sided with business leaders and landowners in opposition to the Korean People's Republic, which was proclaimed on 6 September by the Committee for the Preparation

---

33 Bruce Cumings, *The Origins of the Korean War*, vol. I (Princeton 1981), ch. 4. James Irving
    Matray, *The Reluctant Crusade: American Foreign Policy in Korea, 1941–1950* (Honolulu 1985),
    chs 1–2. Kathryn Weathersby, *Soviet Aims in Korea and the Origins of the Korean War,
    1945–1950: New Evidence from Russian Archives* (Washington 1993), 6–11.
34 Cumings, *Origins of the Korean War*, vol. I, 60.
35 Ibid., chs 2–3.

of Korean Independence, a coalition of communists and other left-wing leaders under the leadership of the centre-left Yŏ Un-hyŏng. This coalition was supported by numerous locally based people's committees, mostly spontaneously formed to oppose all who had collaborated with the Japanese. Hodge had no understanding of the popular basis of this unrest, blaming it on Soviet-backed communists whereas the Soviet Union was rejecting appeals for help from communists in South Korea. The AMG also used former Korean members of the colonial bureaucracy and police force who were condemned by most Koreans as collaborators. But criticism of Hodge in Washington was muted by the fact that the Truman administration shared his aim to stop the spread of Soviet influence in Korea.[36]

The Truman administration, however, was still committed to the international trusteeship ideal for the whole of Korea as a means of containing Soviet expansion. A meeting of British, American and Soviet foreign ministers in Moscow in December 1945 agreed to create a provisional, democratic Korean government, to be determined by an American–Soviet Joint Commission in Korea. The Soviet Union's agreement was based on a continued wish for a united Korea but one that would not act against the USSR's strategic and economic interests.[37]

There was strong opposition in South Korea to the Moscow agreement, especially from seventy-year old Syngman Rhee. He had been imprisoned in 1898 by the Korean monarchy for pro-constitutional agitation. On his release in 1904, he had travelled to the US, gained a Ph.D. degree, and stayed in that country for most of his subsequent life until 1945. A shrewd but obstinate man, he was the self-styled leader of Korean exiles in the US and had long and unsuccessfully badgered State Department officials to support Korean independence under his control. On his return to Korea in October 1945 Hodge gave him a red carpet reception, looking to him to lead the disorganized local right-wing groups, which had been weakened by their previous collaboration with the Japanese.[38]

This AMG favouritism towards Rhee and others on the right, who dominated a Representative Democratic Council instituted in February 1946, pushed left-wing leaders and communists to stir up popular opposition to the American occupation. They promoted a general strike on 24 September 1946, which was followed by violent incidents known as the October people's resistance. This was suppressed by the police and by right-wing youth groups. More than 200 policemen and as many as 1,000 civilians

---

36   Ibid., chs 3–6, 8. Matray, *The Reluctant Crusade*, ch. 3. Melvyn P. Leffler, *A Preponderance of Power: National Security, the Truman Administration and the Cold War* (Stanford 1992), 88–90.
37   For Russian policy see Weathersby, *Soviet Aims in Korea*, 13–16.
38   Cumings, *Origins of the Korean War*, vol. I, ch. 6.

were killed; much of the country's rice crop was destroyed; many left-wing leaders were imprisoned; and most of the people's committees collapsed. Hodge wrongly regarded the left-wing protests as Soviet inspired.[39]

The Truman administration was able to reopen negotiations with the USSR about Korea after another foreign ministers' conference in Moscow in April 1947. But discussions in the joint commission in Korea stalled over the Soviet insistence that Rhee and Korean conservatives could not join any provisional Korean government on the grounds of their opposition to trusteeship. Indeed, Rhee and his supporters were agitating against trusteeship and in favour of South Korean independence. This included a campaign of terror against Rhee's political opponents in which Yŏ Un-hyŏng was assassinated.

Washington decided to quit Korea in 1947 in the face of the failure of the Joint Commission negotiations and the refusal of the Republican-controlled American Congress to approve financial aid for South Korea on top of large financial assistance to Greece and Turkey. The Joint Chiefs of Staff (JCS) declared Korea of no strategic value. The 45,000 American troops there would be no match for Soviet military power and 'could well be used elsewhere'.[40] The violent actions of Rhee and his henchmen also ensured that the trusteeship ideal was unworkable. Therefore Washington turned to the United Nations (UN) to conduct elections in Korea that would lead to an independent government, with the expectation that the USSR would object so that the election would only take place in the South. The Truman administration hoped that free elections in the South might encourage American Congressional approval for economic aid and that the UN would give the country a legitimate status, which the USSR would find difficult to overturn. Then South Korea might have a viable future.[41]

The government in North Korea opposed elections in its territory. There, USSR forces from the start of the occupation had organized communist political and social structures. Stalin handed local power to a leftist–communist alliance led by Kim Il-sung, who had been born in Pyongyang, the future capital of North Korea, in 1912 and had been a Soviet-backed leader of anti-Japanese guerrillas in Manchuria. His government implemented radical land reform on the CCP model and allowed initial popular

---

39   Ibid., ch. 10.
40   Quoted in Richard Whelan, *Drawing the Line: The Korean War, 1950–1953* (Boston 1990), 44.
41   William Whitney Stueck, Jr, *The Road to Confrontation: American Policy toward China and Korea, 1947–1950* (Chapel Hill 1981), ch. 3. Matray, *The Reluctant Crusade*, 123–4. Bruce Cumings, *Origins of the Korean War*, vol. II, (Princeton 1990), 65–8.

participation in decision making through people's committees, though power was soon firmly in the hands of Kim's central government with background Soviet military control.[42]

The UN Temporary Commission on Korea (UNTCOK), with delegates from eight countries, most of which had close defence and economic ties with the US, could only operate in the South. There, escalating violence, with leftist attempts to disrupt the election process and rightist intimidation of political opponents, resulted in nearly 500 deaths in five months and imprisonment of over 10,000 people resulting from an administration crackdown on the left wing – not the right. Hodge asked to be relieved of his post because of Rhee's hostility towards him. But Hodge's successor, General John Coulter, who was second-in-command of the AMG, regarded Rhee as leading the only viable political force. Rhee and his right-wing allies, who fielded three quarters of the candidates and clearly intimidated voters, in fact controlled the election. UNTCOK, which was greatly constrained in its freedom of observation by an election committee dominated by the right wing, declared the election on 9 May 1948 to have demonstrated a reasonable degree of free expression. But the delegates from Australia, Canada and Syria refused to participate in the charade.[43]

Thus, with the connivance of the AMG, the unscrupulous and dictatorial Syngman Rhee became the president of the Republic of South Korea (ROK) with international blessing. The US then withdrew its army, the last troops leaving in June 1949. There had been a Soviet military withdrawal from North Korea in the previous December. But Soviet officials remained to watch over Kim's government. Defeated in its aim for a united friendly Korea, the Soviet Union was ensuring its control over North Korea to fulfil the strategic aim of protecting a USSR border and to ensure Soviet exploitation of North Korea's wealth in economic resources, such as the mineral monazite which contained thorium, which was valuable for the USSR atomic bomb construction. To protect this asset, the Soviets left behind them ninety-three Second World War vintage aircraft, plus tanks and artillery. Also over 80,000 North Koreans were serving in the CCP army in the Chinese Civil War. Rhee was keen to achieve unity by forceful subjugation of the North. But Washington refused to provide him with arms to wage an aggressive war, giving only enough to equip 65,000 soldiers to defend the country and suppress insurgents, plus a 500-strong American military advisory group.

---

42 Cumings, *Origins of the Korean War*, vol. I, ch. 11; vol. II, ch. 9. Weathersby, *Soviet Aims in Korea*, 12–13. Sydney A. Seiler, *Kim Il-song 1941–1948: The Creation of a Legend, The Building of A Dream* (Lanham 1994), chs 6–7.

43 Cumings, *Origins of the Korean War*, vol. II, 70–8. Matray, *The Reluctant Crusade*, 134–49.

The American government was suspicious of Rhee's intentions and wanted no open-ended military commitment.[44]

Indeed, in 1949 the ROK was in a parlous state. The economy was in a mess, with the North denying power resources. There was a shortage of technicians, high unemployment and rampant inflation. American occupation had established a climate of press censorship, arbitrary arrest and political violence which Rhee continued to exploit after independence. He also faced leftist guerrilla groups, which were being brutally suppressed by his army. The favouritism of the AMG from the start towards Rhee had ensured that he would be victorious and wrecked any hope of a negotiated settlement with the USSR for a united Korea.[45]

Contest for control of Vietnam

Vietnam was the region in the Western Pacific Basin that experienced the longest actual war of the Cold War era. On 2 September 1945 Ho Chi Minh proclaimed the independence of Vietnam in Hanoi, the capital of the Indochina province of Tonkin. Born in 1890 in central Vietnam, he left in 1912 as a merchant steamer's cabin boy and settled in France, where he joined the French Communist Party. He moved via Russia to Canton in China, where in 1930 he organized the Indochina Communist Party. It participated in nationalist revolts in 1930–31, which were brutally crushed by French military power. Considered a gentle man with a warm personality, Ho was a master organizer. As well as a communist, he was a fervent nationalist whose first aim was the liberation of his homeland. From headquarters in a cave near the Chinese border, he founded in May 1941 the Vietminh (Front for the Independence of Vietnam), which aimed to arouse support among rural Vietnamese by advocating independence and broad 'democratic' reforms, but which played down land reform in order to gain wider support. The Vietminh were assisted greatly by the way French rule was discredited by the easily achieved Japanese military occupation in 1940–41. The suddenness of the Japanese surrender and a spontaneous popular

---

44   Matray, *The Reluctant Crusade*, ch. 8. Peter Lowe, *The Origins of the Korean War* (2nd edition, London 1997), ch. 3. Cumings, *Origins of the Korean War*, vol. II, 445–6. Weathersby, *Soviet Aims in Korea*, 21–3.
45   Okonogi Masao, 'The Domestic Roots of the Korean War' in Yonosuke Nagai and Akira Iriye (eds), *The Origins of the Cold War* (New York 1977), 299–320. Cumings, *Origins of the Korean War*, vol. II, chs 6–8.

uprising in Hanoi gave Vietminh troops, commanded by a gifted general, Vo Nguyen Giap, the chance to seize power in August 1945, with the tacit support of China, which had been designated at the Potsdam Conference to occupy Indochina north of the 16th latitudinal parallel.[46]

The Vietminh also had been able to exploit a growing national consciousness among the Vietnamese, who before the war were seventeen million of the twenty-two million population of Indochina. Ninety per cent of the Vietnamese were smallholding peasants, half of whom owned less than a hectare of land, with consequent widespread indebtedness to money lenders and losses of land to Vietnamese and Chinese land holders. Vietnamese peasants also had been heavily taxed by the French administration. It did supply them with physical security, improving health services and education and some benefits of economic development. But such benefits were dissipated by the 1930s depression. Few Vietnamese had the right to vote and then only in the colony of Cochin China. This colony and the rest of Indochina, which had a mixture of control ranging from protectorates over indigenous kingdoms to direct French rule, was administered by a governor general. He was supported by 36,000 French subjects, who were mostly soldiers and administrators, and who maintained overall economic control and racial superiority over the 'natives'. The subordination of the Vietnamese people was fertile ground for the work of Vietminh leaders, who mostly came from the small Vietnamese middle class.[47]

Some American support for the Vietminh was indicated on independence day in Hanoi by Ho's quotation from the American Declaration of Independence, by the presence at the ceremony of four American army officers and a diving salute to the crowd by two American warplanes. Roosevelt had opposed the restoration of French colonialism in Indochina because he viewed France as an exploitative colonial power and because Vichy France had allowed the Japanese occupation. His hope was for international control of the region and, though this was strongly opposed by Britain, he kept that option open. Truman did not have the same faith in international control and was concerned to support France as a bulwark against communist expansion in Europe. So he did not oppose the resumption of French rule in Indochina. However, his administration

---

46 Anthony Short, *The Origins of the Vietnam War* (London 1989), ch. 1. Jaques Dalloz, *The War in Indo-China 1945–54* (Dublin 1990), chs 1–2. Lloyd C. Gardiner, *Approaching Vietnam: From World War II Through Dienbienphu 1941–1954* (New York 1988), ch. 2. Greg Lockhart, *Nation in Arms: The Origins of the People's Army of Vietnam* (Sydney 1989), chs 2–3.

47 Dalloz, *War in Indo-China*, ch. 1. David G. Marr, *Vietnamese Tradition on Trial, 1920–1945* (Berkeley 1981), chs 1, 7–10. William J. Duiker, *Vietnam: Revolution in Transition* (2nd edition, Boulder 1995), 30–43.

rejected French requests to provide transportation for troops to enable a quick return to Indochina.[48]

France, however, received British support in Vietnam south of the 16th parallel. Occupation of that area had been assigned at Potsdam to the British South East Asia Command (SEAC), which to some American critics meant 'Save England's Asian Colonies'. The SEAC commander of the 20th Indian division, Major-General Douglas Gracey, was determined not to recognize any Vietminh authority. He took no notice of Vietminh representatives waiting to greet him, when he flew into Cochin China on 13 September. In the region's anarchical climate, with factional struggles, looting and anti-French violence, Gracey established curfews and press control, re-armed French soldiers interned by the Japanese and moved to disarm Vietminh police in the capital city, Saigon. In consultation with the acting French High Commissioner, Gracey supported on the night of 23 September a successful surprise attack, by re-armed and recently landed French troops, on Vietminh-held public buildings and outposts in Saigon. This was denounced as an act of war by the Vietminh nationalist front in the city.[49]

Violence escalated with arbitrary attacks on Vietnamese people by French soldiers. The Vietminh responded with attacks on French civilians and fought against the reinforced French troops. But France was able to restore significant control in Cochin China and Annam by the end of 1945.[50]

In March 1945 the provisional government in France had promised 'appropriate liberty' for Indochina within a new French Union without defining what the term meant. One definition was provided a year later when, on 6 March 1946, Ho Chi Min signed an agreement with Jean Sainteny, the French government's political representative in Hanoi. Sainteny was concerned to prevent Vietnamese violence against French personnel still awaiting evacuation and was conscious that the Vietminh had substantial control in Tonkin. So he conceded recognition of 'the Republic of Vietnam as a free state with its own government, parliament, army and finances, forming a part of the Indo-China Federation and the French Union'. He said later that though the government was 'Communist-led' it contained 'as many nationalists as Communists'. Ho agreed to membership

---

48 David G. Marr, *Vietnam 1945: The Quest for Power* (Berkeley 1995), 261–70, 532–9. George C. Herring, 'The Truman Administration and the Restoration of French Sovereignty in Indochina', *Diplomatic History*, 1, 1977, 97–117. William J. Duiker, *US Containment Policy and the Conflict in Indochina* (Stanford 1994), 36–40. Peter Dennis, *Troubled Days of Peace: Mountbatten and South East Asia Command, 1945–46* (Manchester 1987), 25–33.

49 Dennis, *Troubled Days of Peace*, 33–46. Peter M. Dunn, *The First Vietnam War* (London 1985), ch. 8. Dalloz, *War in Indo-China*, 58.

50 Dennis, *Troubled Days of Peace*, ch. 3. Dunn, *First Vietnam War*, ch. 8.

of the French Union, to accept French advisers, to guarantee France's economic and cultural interests and to a future referendum about the status of Cochin China and Annam. He also agreed to welcome the arrival of French troops in Tonkin. Ho signed this accord in recognition of the important role of the French in negotiating the withdrawal of 200,000 Chinese occupying soldiers, who were engaging in significant plunder and whose commanders had pretensions to incorporate northern Vietnam into China. But he faced the absence of recognition of his Democratic Republic of Vietnam (DRV) by any other nation, including the USSR, which was more concerned to support communists in France. Also Vietnam was beyond the reach of Soviet power.[51]

This accord was short-lived, especially because France was determined to retain control of the economically richest region – Cochin China. This was the main reason for the failure of negotiations in April 1946 between Vietminh leaders led by Giap and the French High Commissioner, Admiral d'Argenlieu, who distrusted the Ho-Sainteny agreement. A visit by Ho and other Vietminh leaders to Paris in June–July produced no solution to the impasse. The decline of the political power of the Socialists meant that the French government was now led by the Catholic *Mouvement Républican Populaire* (MRP), which was keen to restore France's war-shattered national pride, for which a colonial empire was seen as important.[52]

Back in Vietnam an inevitable explosion caused the war to flare up in the North. A French attempt to seize a junk carrying suspected smuggled fuel, and its recapture by Vietminh militiamen on 20 November 1946, was seized upon by the hawkish French commander, General Jean Valluy, with the approval of d'Argenlieu, to teach the Vietminh a lesson; even though the incident stemmed from the French administration's breaking of the Ho-Sainteny agreement by taking control of the administration of Vietnam's customs policies. Three days later, after a two hour ultimatum to the Vietminh to evacuate the Tonkinese port of Haiphong, the city was mercilessly bombarded by a French cruiser killing at least 1,000 people, most of them civilians. Ho still sought negotiations. On 15 December he sent an appeal to a new Socialist government in France, but the French administration in Saigon delayed transmission of the cable. With no reply

---

51   Martin Shipway, *The Road to War: France and Vietnam, 1944–1947* (Providence, RI 1996), 59–62, 164–74. Dalloz, *War in Indo-china*, 68–70. Interview with Jean Sainteny in Michael Charlton and Anthony Moncrieff, *Many Reasons Why: The American Involvement in Vietnam* (Ringwood 1979), 29. Douglas Pike, *Vietnam and the Soviet Union: Anatomy of an Alliance* (Boulder 1987), 29–31. Vladislav Zubok and Konstantine Pleshakov, *Inside the Kremlin's Cold War: From Stalin to Krushchev* (Cambridge, Mass. 1996), 57.

52   Shipway, *Road to War*, chs 7–9.

from Paris, Ho ordered Giap with some 60,000 troops to prepare for war. On 19 December 1946, a Vietminh uprising in Hanoi was sparked by an attack on the city's power station, though it is unknown whether that signal was fired by French *agents provocateurs* or by dissident Vietminh hardliners or on the order of Giap. The Vietnam War had begun.[53]

Giap's mostly inexperienced army, however, was no match for well-trained French troops, who by September 1947 had a strength of 115,000, supported by heavy artillery and air power. They expelled the Vietminh from Hanoi and other Tonkin towns, and forced Ho, Giap and his men into the mountainous interior. But because France needed to fight another colonial war, in Madagascar from March 1947, and because Vietminh guerrillas were still at large in Cochin China, the French military command in Vietnam had insufficient power to crush the Vietminh completely. Failing in positional warfare in 1946, the Vietminh had evolved an offensive guerrilla strategy using village and regional units and extensive tunnel systems.[54]

The French effort to crush the Vietminh was influenced by political changes in France. In 1947 the French right wing used the Vietnam War and the Cold War in general to force communists from the Socialist Party-led government. However, in opposition the Communist Party did not whip up any anti-war movement because at this stage the USSR was indifferent to the Vietnam conflict despite vague promises made to a Vietminh delegation to Moscow in November 1947. The Socialists, who were divided on the Vietnam question, lost popular support over industrial unrest in France during 1947; and in a political re-shuffle in November the overseas ministry came under the control of the MRP.[55]

The main MRP policy for Vietnam was an attempt to construct an alternative indigenous regime in Vietnam by turning to Bao Dai. He was the French-educated former king of Annam whom the Japanese in 1945 had appointed as puppet emperor of Vietnam. He had abdicated under Vietminh pressure after the Japanese surrender and was living in Hong Kong when he was approached by the French administration to become its tame emperor. However, when his rule was proclaimed on 2 July 1949, the independence of his state was significantly restricted in military, diplomatic and economic spheres. Nor was Bao Dai's return to Vietnam greeted with

---

53   Ibid., ch. 10. Short, *Origins of the Vietnam War*, 49–56.
54   Dalloz, *War in Indo-China*, 95–102. Lockhart, *Nation in Arms*, 183–93. Pierre Brocheux, *The Mekong Delta: Ecology, Economy, and Revolution, 1860–1960* (Madison, Wis. 1995), 198–200. Cecil B. Currey, *Victory at any Cost: The Genius of Viet Nam's Gen. Vo Nguyen Giap* (Washington 1997), 135–41.
55   Edward Rice-Maximin, *Accommodation and Resistance: The French Left, Indochina and the Cold War, 1944–1954* (New York 1986), chs 4–5. Oleg Sarin and Lev Dvoretsky, *Alien Wars: The Soviet Union's Aggressions Against the World, 1919–1989* (Novato, Calif. 1996), 88.

much popular enthusiasm, and his status was clearly revealed when he did not reside in Norodom Palace in Saigon, now the French High Commissioner's residence. Instead Bao Dai and a European concubine retreated to the hill resort of Dalat, where he liked to hunt tigers. Nevertheless, the French government could now proclaim the creation of a Vietnam nation, which might be the focus of a nationalist alternative to the Vietminh.

However, in 1949 other world governments, including the US, were hesitant to recognize Bao Dai's regime in Vietnam because of its limited independence and doubts about his playboy image. With the emerging Cold War, in which France's role in Western Europe was regarded as crucial, Ho Chi Minh's communism was viewed with increasing disfavour in Washington. By 1948, it was widely believed there, without any evidence, that he was being supported by the USSR. But the US was also critical of France's unwillingness to extend political rights to the Vietnamese and through 1949 was maintaining neutrality in the Indochina War.[56]

Nevertheless, during 1949 a change was occurring in American foreign policy thinking that foreshadowed future support for the French in Vietnam. The Cold War was not progressing well. Despite the extensive Marshall Plan aid for Europe, the British economy was faltering and France faced major domestic turmoil. Ominously, in September Truman announced that the USSR had exploded an atomic weapon, and in October the CCP won control of China. Consequently, the American State Department started developing, for the first time, a comprehensive plan for halting communist advances in Southeast Asia by supporting anti-communist forces. Such a policy would have the added advantage of taking pressure off France and Britain, who were fighting wars against communist guerrillas. This was a policy development that was to greatly extend intervention by the major power in the Eastern Pacific Basin into its Western region.[57]

Struggle for independence in Indonesia

Holland, however, did not receive American support for a desperate struggle to crush a nationalist rebellion in the Netherlands East Indies (NEI). On

---

56 Robert D. Schulzinger, *A Time of War: The United States and Vietnam, 1941–1975* (New York 1997), 31–9. George McT. Kahin, *Intervention: How America became Involved in Vietnam* (New York 1986), 3–30; Short, *Origins of the Vietnam War*, 62–79. Duiker, *US Containment Policy*, ch. 3.

57 Andrew J. Rotter, *The Path to Vietnam: Origins of the American Commitment to Southeast Asia* (Ithaca 1987), ch. 5. Leffler, *Preponderance of Power*, 312–40.

that southwestern edge of the Pacific Basin, Indonesian nationalists had taken the same opportunity, as had the Vietminh in Tonkin, to exploit the sudden power vacuum created by the Japanese surrender in 1945. On 17 August Achmed Sukarno proclaimed the inauguration of the Republic of Indonesia in Jakarta, as the capital city was later to be renamed.

In contrast to Vietminh leaders, Sukarno and his co-leader, Muhammed Hatta, were not communists. Sukarno, born in Java in 1901, had read Marxist literature, but during his Dutch language schooling at Surabaya he was strongly influenced by a group of Indonesian nationalists who rejected Marxist and Islamic ideology. Their focus was merely independence from Dutch rule, to which Sukarno added an indomitable belief in his own destiny like the great men of history he avidly read about. He became the founding chairman of the Indonesian Nationalist Party (PNI) in 1928, which quickly suffered from Dutch repression. He was jailed in 1930 and, after an early release, was exiled in 1933 along with other nationalist leaders, including Hatta. Under an earlier 'ethical policy', Dutch colonialism had provided European education to a generation of Indonesian leaders, who were then politically suppressed by a more conservative regime in the 1930s. That administration stifled any expressions of Indonesian nationalism and even more moderate requests for Indonesian participation in government. Consequently, by 1942 there was widespread urban hostility towards Dutch rule. Many rural Indonesians had been quiescent under Dutch control, but they were suffering severely from the effects of the economic depression in the 1930s.[58]

In 1942 the Japanese, who easily overcame Dutch resistance, freed and returned to Java nationalist leaders to much popular acclaim. The Japanese proclaimed the ideal of Asian brotherhood, though they ruthlessly exploited Indonesian labour. By late 1944, under the threat of American attack, Japan firmly promised Indonesian independence. In May 1945 an indigenous convention approved an Indonesian constitution, based on five principles of nationalism, humanitarianism, democracy, social justice, and belief in a God who transcended all religions. This wartime experience gave a massive confidence boost to nationalist leaders and greatly increased their potential popular support.[59]

---

58 M.C. Ricklefs, *A History of Modern Indonesia* (2nd edition, Stanford 1993), chs 14–15. Colin Wild and Peter Carey, *Born of Fire: The Indonesian Struggle for Independence* (Athens, Ohio 1988), chs 10, 11, 13. Robert Cribb (ed.), *The Late Colonial State in Indonesia: Political and Economic Foundations of the Netherlands Indies 1880–1942* (Leiden 1994).

59 Theodore Friend, *The Blue-Eyed Enemy: Japan Against the West in Java and Luzon, 1942–1945* (Princeton 1988), chs 4–5. Shigeru Sato, *War, Nationalism and Peasants: Java under the Japanese Occupation 1942–1945* (St Leonards, NSW 1994), chs 3–7.

The Dutch government was even keener to reoccupy NEI than the French in Indochina. The NEI, the centrepiece of the Dutch colonial empire, was before the war the Netherlands' fourth largest market and fifth greatest source of imports, supplying essential raw materials, especially rubber, tin and oil. Even more important was the transfer to Holland of profits from Dutch companies in the colony, which, along with interest on and redemption of loans and pensions, and wages of Dutch employees in Indonesia, contributed an estimated 14 per cent of the Dutch national income in 1938. After being occupied by Germany during the Second World War, the Netherlands saw reoccupation of the NEI as a means of salving national pride; and foreign exchange from Indonesian earnings was badly needed to balance Holland's huge postwar balance of payments deficit.[60]

However, though the US government had a more benign view of Dutch than of French colonialism, allied shipping priorities had frustrated Netherlands plans to establish in Australia an armed force of sufficient strength to reoccupy the NEI. An NEI government in exile had been located in 1942 in Australia and was joined in March 1945 by the re-appointed governor of NEI, Hubertus van Mook. He had very limited military power to re-establish Netherlands control in the archipelago. Nor had he sufficient information about wartime conditions to shake a widely held Dutch delusion that, apart from a few nationalist agitators, Indonesians would welcome the Dutch return. In reality, Laurens van der Post, a British military attaché in Java, knew 'how widespread and strident [was] the evidence of militant nationalism'.[61]

As with the French in Cochin China, the Netherlands had to rely on the British SEAC for initial support in Indonesia. But information from advance personnel there convinced SEAC's commander, Admiral Lord Louis Mountbatten, that his men could face hostility from the Indonesian Republic, which had a potentially large army, well armed with Japanese weapons, though lacking in training. Therefore, Lieutenant-General Sir Philip Christison, the commander of the occupying British force, announced that his task was only to disarm the Japanese, to rescue prisoners of war and to maintain law and order in main cities.[62]

A difficulty for the Netherlands was that neither Mountbatten nor the British government believed there was a military solution to the problem of the Indonesian Republic, certainly not one to be undertaken by British

---

60 Pierre van der Eng, 'Marshall Aid as a Catalyst to the Decolonization of Indonesia', *Journal of Southeast Asian Studies*, 19, 1988, 336. Ricklefs, *History of Modern Indonesia*, 146–7.
61 Dennis, *Troubled Days of Peace*, 66–77. Laurens van der Post, *The Admiral's Baby* (New York 1996), 210
62 Dennis, *Troubled Days of Peace*, ch. 5. Greg Poulgrain, *The Genesis of Konfratasi: Malaysia Brunei Indonesia 1945–1965* (London 1998), 36–7.

forces. This would also set a bad example and stretch military resources at a time when there was turbulence in neighbouring Malaya. Therefore, negotiation with Indonesians was the only recourse. Indeed, British troops faced armed Indonesian resistance, especially in Surabaya, where two brigades of the 5th Indian division, supported by naval firepower and air attacks, took three weeks from 10 November 1945 to establish British control of the city against Indonesians equipped with Japanese machine guns, artillery and tanks. However, the failure of initial negotiations, conducted under British pressure between the Dutch and representatives of the Indonesian republic, further military clashes between British troops and Indonesians, as well as criticism from British officers about 'trigger happy' Dutch, also convinced Mountbatten by April 1946 to withdraw and hand over the control that SEAC had achieved in Java and Sumatra to Holland. Also in Eastern Indonesia Australian occupying forces quickly allowed the Dutch to resume control.[63]

Nevertheless, negotiations were revived. The Indonesians offered a compromise by insisting only on sovereignty over the islands with substantial Indonesian control: Java, Madura and Sumatra. Under strong British pressure, supported by the US, the Dutch government accepted this partition proposal in the Linggajati agreement of November 1946. Under its terms the Republic and the Netherlands pledged to cooperate to create by 1 January 1949 a federal United States of Indonesia (USI) in which the Indonesian Republic and the Dutch-held islands would be sovereign states with the Dutch queen as symbolic head.

On both sides, however, there were many leaders who rejected that compromise. With nationalist sentiment disrupting efforts to consolidate Netherlands control in eastern Indonesia, and a Dutch wish to appropriate more of the wealth of Java and Sumatra to compensate for the cost of NEI reconstruction, the Netherlands government decided to use the 100,000 troops it had established on Java to assert its authority over the Indonesian Republic in a euphemistically named 'police action'. Launched on 20 July 1947, it consisted of major military thrusts from the Dutch centres on Java. These advances succeeded in capturing all of Java's deep-sea ports plus Sumatra plantations and oil and coal installations. Indonesian military forces lacked training, coherence of command and the sea and air power that supported the Dutch troops.

The 'police action', however, aroused strong opposition in the UN led by newly independent India and by Australia, where the Labor government had

---

63   William H. Frederick, *Visions and Heat: The Making of the Indonesian Revolution* (Athens, Ohio 1988), 182–296. Dennis, *Troubled Days of Peace*, chs 9–10.

swung from initial support for the restoration of Dutch rule in Indonesia to advocacy of a negotiated solution, which Holland was now seen to be rejecting. Furthermore, the US supported negotiations. The Netherlands had the misfortune of not being a major European power like France. Nor was the Indonesian Communist Party (PKI) involved in the Indonesian republican government, which had pledged not to interfere with foreign investment. Holland was pressured to accept a cease-fire on 4 August, without achieving the conquest of Java. Washington also took the lead in UN sponsored Indonesian–Dutch negotiations, which led to an agreement signed on the US warship *Renville* in January 1948. The Renville agreement recognized a cease-fire along the so-called van Mook Line, which connected points of the most-advanced Dutch incursions into Republican territory, even though it enclosed many Republican-occupied areas.[64]

The Dutch moved to create new states out of the captured territory so that the USI could outvote the Republic of Indonesia. But in those states there was much sympathy for the republican cause. The Indonesian Republic in turn faced political instability caused by dissension with the Renville agreement. It also suffered from economic distress caused by the Dutch blockade, an influx of as many as six million refugees and high inflation generated by the government's printing of money to meet costs. In west Java there was a popular revolt led by a Dutch-educated Islamic mystic, S.M. Kartosoewirjo. More seriously, the PKI was organizing strikes and peasant take-overs of properties. By mid September there were violent clashes between communist and government forces leading to a PKI uprising in the town of Madiun, which was crushed by the Indonesian army resulting in the deaths of the PKI's leader, Musso, and at least 8,000 PKI supporters. Meanwhile post-Renville negotiations between the Dutch and the republicans were breaking down, especially over the Netherlands strategy to create more USI states. There were also frequent clashes between Dutch and Indonesian troops along the long van Mook line, and there were Indonesian raids within the Dutch zone which had been infiltrated by guerrilla bands.[65]

The Netherlands government's response to these clashes and the stalling of USI negotiations was to launch on 18 December 1948 the second 'police

---

64   Anthony Reid, *The Indonesian National Revolution 1945–50* (Melbourne 1974), 111–14. Margaret George, *Australia and the Indonesian Revolution* (Melbourne 1980), chs 3–8. Ken Buckley, Barbara Dale and Wayne Reynolds, *Doc Evatt: Patriot, Internationalist, Fighter and Scholar* (Melbourne 1994), ch. 20. Robert J. McMahon, *Colonialism and Cold War: The United States and the Struggle for Indonesian Independence, 1945–49* (Ithaca 1981), chs 2–6.
65   Robert Cribb, *Gangsters and Revolutionaries: The Jakarta People's Militia and the Indonesian Revolution 1945–1949* (Sydney 1991), ch. 11. Reid, *Indonesian National Revolution*, 124–47.

action'. A majority of Dutch Cabinet ministers were hoping to eliminate the Republic. With 99,000 troops in Java and unchallenged air support, the Dutch army considered it could easily defeat the opposing disorganized forces. Indeed, airborne paratroops landing at the Republic's capital of Yogyakarta captured the republican Cabinet. But Indonesian military leaders and most of their soldiers escaped. In fact, while capturing key republican positions and major towns, the Dutch forces failed to defeat the Indonesian army. It dispersed and engaged in guerrilla attacks on military posts, lines of communication, plantations and even towns well into the Dutch rear.[66]

The second 'police action' not only failed in its objectives, it also raised another storm of international protest in which the US took strong action. The suppression of the Madiun uprising had given the Republic of Indonesia good anti-communist credentials. So pressure, including a threat of suspension of Marshall Plan aid, was placed on Holland to halt the military campaign and return to the negotiating table. Though the threat about Marshall Aid money was symbolic rather than actual, since most of it had already been committed, there was a realization in Holland of a potential future threat to aid money as well as of strong international opposition. Also the Netherlands could escape from the financial obligation to support Indonesia's economic recovery if it became independent and Dutch economic interests were protected. Therefore a cease-fire was announced to take effect on 11 August. From 23 August to 2 November there was a round table conference between Dutch and Indonesian representatives in The Hague at which a Republic of the USI was recognized with Sukarno as president and Hatta as prime minister. The new state accepted responsibility for the NEI's debt, which was set, after much haggling, at forty-three billion guilders, much of it being the cost of the 'police actions'. Guarantees were given for the protection of Dutch investments. The status of West New Guinea (Irian Jaya) was postponed for later negotiations. On 27 November 1949 the Netherlands transferred sovereignty of the rest of NEI to the new Indonesian Republic which, with its seventy-eight million people and 1.9 million square kilometres of land, was to become a major Southwestern Pacific Basin power.[67]

---

66 M.H. Groen, 'Dutch Armed Forces and the Decolonization of Indonesia: The Second Police Action (1948–1949), A Pandora's Box', *War and Society*, 4:1, 1986, 79–104. Salim Said, *Genesis of Power: General Sudirman and the Indonesian Military in Politics 1945–49* (Singapore 1991), ch. 5.
67 Van der Eng, 'Marshall Aid as a Catalyst', 338–52. Ine Megens, *American Aid to NATO Allies in the 1950s: The Dutch Case* (Amsterdam 1994), 25–35. For a recent overview of the Indonesian revolution see Robert Cribb and Colin Brown, *Modern Indonesia: A History since 1945* (London 1995), ch. 2.

Outbreak of insurrection in Malaya

In Malaya, another communist uprising became linked to the Cold War in the Southwestern Pacific Basin. In contrast to the Dutch in Indonesia, the British return to Malaya after the Second World War was generally welcomed by its indigenous people, despite Britain's humiliating defeat by the Japanese in 1941–42. The Malays had become a minority: 43.5 per cent of the population of 5,848,910 in the 1947 census, compared with 44.7 per cent Chinese and 10.3 per cent Indians. Before the war Malays had been largely shielded from Western influences by British protection of their mostly subsistence peasant and hierarchical Muslim society. The British administration ruled through the traditional sultans in two sets of Federated and Unfederated States alongside the three Straits Settlements colonies covering the first areas of British commercial penetration – Singapore, Malacca and Penang. Many members of the Malay aristocracy had become English language-educated public servants. Although a sense of nationalism had been growing in the Malay community, the main nationalist organization, the Malay Association, was conservative and loyal to the British crown. A more radical young Malay union, the Kesatuan Melayu Muda (KMM), was formed in 1938 by Ibrahim Yaacob. It advocated a pan-Malay union with Indonesians, but it failed to receive significant popular support. The Chinese and Indians had been brought to work in the colony's rubber plantations and tin mines, and the Chinese had become prominent in commerce. Among the Chinese there was pressure for equal rights. Though by 1931 some 31 per cent of the Chinese were locally born, they had no citizenship rights outside the Straits Settlements, not even possessing the British subject status of foreign-born Indians.[68]

From 1942 to 1945 Malays generally were quiescent under Japanese rulers. The Japanese preferred to work with established public servants rather than with the KMM, which was perceived as having little public support. The Japanese brutally mistreated the Chinese, encouraging many of them to support a resistance movement, the Malayan People's Anti-Japanese Army (MPAJA). This was the armed wing of the predominantly Chinese Malayan Communist Party (MCP), which had been formally established in 1932. The MPAJA received British military support during the war and, when the Japanese surrendered, it resisted appeals from the KMM to join in opposing a British return. A frustrated Ibrahim Yaacob left with

---

68   See William R. Roff, *The Origins of Malay Nationalism* (New Haven 1967) and Victor Purcell, *The Chinese in Malaya* (Kuala Lumpar 1967).

other KMM leaders to fight for Indonesian independence. However, the MPAJA used the four-week time gap before the British arrived in the mainland capital of Kuala Lumpur to murder Malay collaborators, provoking retaliatory Malayan attacks on the Chinese. Communal violence continued during 1945, and the British Military Administration's (BMA) order for the surrender of all arms was only partially obeyed, leaving many weapons in MCP members' hands. The war had thus generated in Malaya open racial conflict. Furthermore the BMA, which contained only a minority of people with knowledge of the country, brought disrepute to British authority. It failed to curb the minority of British soldiers who indulged in plunder and rape; it was ineffective in controlling the communal violence; it created mass poverty by declaring Japanese money worthless; and it fostered corruption and black marketeering.[69]

Remaining KMM supporters tried to exploit resultant popular discontent by launching a radical Malay Nationalist Party. But most Malays refused to support it. They were much more agitated by a British proposal to reorganize the Malay states and two of the Straits Settlements – not strategically important Singapore – into a Malayan Union. The objectionable features of this plan were the stripping of the powers of the traditional rulers, who had religious as well as social and political status; the centralizing of power in Kuala Lumpur; and the granting to non-Malays of equal citizenship rights. These reforms were the result of pre-war British discussions about citizenship rights for non-Malays and a wartime shift in Colonial Office preferences towards the Chinese, who had opposed the Japanese occupation and whose loyalty could be claimed by China. Granting them full citizenship rights also was seen as the only basis for welding together a future independent Malaya in which there was no place for special protection of Malays or of their sultans.[70]

Mass Malay protests resulted in the formation in May 1946 of the United Malay National Organisation (UNMO), which attracted much popular support. Its opposition to the Malayan Union was peaceful but so widespread that Britain decided to back down. This policy reversal was also influenced by the lukewarm approach to the union by Indians and Chinese and by a

69 Cheah Boon Kheng, *From PKI to the Comintern, 1924–1941: The Apprenticeship of the Malayan Communist Party* (Ithaca 1992), 18; Richard Stubbs, *Hearts and Minds in Guerilla Warfare: The Malayan Emergency 1948–1960* (Singapore 1989), 11–16; Cheah Boon Kheng, *Red Star Over Malaya: Resistance and Social Conflict During and After the Japanese Occupation, 1941–1946* (Singapore 1983), 294–5. Khong Kim Hoong, *Merdeka!: British Rule and the Struggle for Independence in Malaya, 1945–1957* (Selangor 1984), ch. 2.
70 Albert Lau, *The Malayan Union Controversy 1942–1948* (Singapore 1991), chs 1–4.

concern to stem any anti-British movement among the Malays. Independence was still considered well into the future for politically inexperienced Malays; and the colony's tin and rubber exports, which were rapidly recovering from wartime damage, were major earners for Britain of scarce American dollars. So in 1948 the Malayan Union was replaced with the Federation of Malaya Agreement. It restored the power of traditional Malay rulers and retained universal citizenship rights but made them more restrictive by, for example, lengthening the required periods of residence for non-Malays from five to fifteen years. This victory firmly established UNMO's popular support among Malays, many of whom were now dubious about the British connection.[71]

The MCP vociferously opposed the Federation Agreement. It had organized a series of strikes in 1946, exploiting working-class grievances about food shortages and low wages. The BMA responded with military pressure against strikers and arrests of strike leaders, causing the MCP to adopt a lower profile and concentrate on organizing public support. Though gaining little influence in the Indian and Malay communities, it won significant Chinese support, assisted by the nationalistic nature of Chinese language education in Malaya since the 1920s and continuing low wages and high food prices. Nor was there an alternative strong Chinese political association.

However, on 10 May 1948 the MCP central committee decided to authorize armed struggle. This decision was influenced by the lack of wider community support, by British administration pressure on Chinese trade unions, by the inspiration of the CCP victories in China and, especially, by the unmasking in 1947 of its Secretary General, Loi Tek, as a wartime collaborator with the Japanese. He was also a British Special agent who had been architect of the MCP peace strategy, and he absconded with most of the party's funds, leaving more radical leaders in charge. The result was a growing escalation of violent incidents culminating in the murder of three British planters on 16 June 1948 by members of the MCP's Malayan Races Liberation Army (MRLA).[72]

The British administration was soon convinced that this armed uprising was part of a USSR supported anti-colonial strategy since it coincided with the outbreak of a communist-led revolution in Burma and the abortive Madiun uprising in Indonesia. But the British could provide no evidence. Indeed, as with Vietnam at this stage, Stalin displayed no interest in Malaya.

---

71 Ibid., chs 6–9. Stubbs, *Hearts and Minds*, 27–8. Khong Kim Hoong, *Merdeka*, ch. 3.
72 Stubbs, *Hearts and Minds*, ch. 2. John Coates, *Suppressing Emergency: An Analysis of the Malayan Emergency, 1948–1954* (Boulder 1992), 12–18.

Furthermore, by 1951 the British administration in Malaya was discounting external assistance to the MCP, and the only evidence was the arrival that year of some Chinese army officers.[73]

A major source of support for the insurgency – men, food and information – was the large community of Chinese squatters, who had been driven from urban centres into rural districts by economic hardship during the 1930s depression and had been neglected by the government. The areas they occupied were vast forest reserves, Malay reservations and especially European plantations that had fallen into disuse during the war. Their number was unknown to the government; an estimate was 300,000 in 1948.[74]

The first MRLA objective was destruction of the economy and of government authority. Targets were mines, plantations and communications including assassinations of owners, managers and public officials. Operation-centres were camps hidden in jungle but close to squatter areas. The initial insurgent strength was about 2,300 front line men, who grew to a peak of 7,292 in 1951. Their early weapons were those not surrendered by the MPAJA in 1945.[75]

The British administration declared a state of emergency after the murders of 16 June. Initially its force to combat the insurgents consisted of 9,000 Malay police and ten infantry battalions, seven of them Gurkhas and three British but with poor training for the task of combating guerrilla warfare. Soon army reinforcements arrived plus armoured cars, artillery and aircraft. The army, used to pursuing and destroying insurgents, at times shooting Chinese suspects indiscriminately, was ineffective against insurgents in a jungle environment. The police had the more difficult job of maintaining security. Their numbers increased to 16,220 by 1950, but many of the hastily trained recruits treated members of the Chinese community with open brutality. To 1950 the campaign was controlled by the Commissioner of Police with advice from military commanders. Major improvements had been made to the police force after the arrival in 1948 of the British Police Commissioner in Palestine, Colonel W.N. Gray. New regulations gave the administration sweeping powers of arrest and control of transport and food distribution, and in 1949 the Chinese squatter problem was addressed with regulations empowering resettlement. That year 6,343 squatters were detained and 9,062 Chinese were repatriated to China. These

---

73   Pike, *Vietnam and the Soviet Union*, 28–32. Zubok and Pleshakov, *Inside the Kremlin's Cold War*, 75. R.B. Smith, 'China and Southeast Asia: The Revolutionary Perspective, 1951', *Journal of Southeast Asian Studies*, 19, 1988, 97 100.

74   Anthony Short, *The Communist Insurrection in Malaya 1948–1960* (London 1975), ch. 7.

75   Ibid., ch. 4. Robert Jackson, *The Malayan Emergency: The Commonwealth's Wars 1948–1966* (London 1991), ch. 2.

were preliminary measures to combat the insurgency, but they suffered from coordination problems; and the use of force was increasing sympathy in the Chinese community for the rebels. The insurrection in Malaya was to remain a major problem for the anti-communist cause in the Southwestern Pacific Basin.[76]

The Huk rebellion in the Philippines

Across the South China Sea, in the Philippines, insurgency also flared up after the end of the Pacific War, which became interpreted as another communist challenge. American colonialism had been more benevolent than French or Dutch rule in Southeast Asia, and in 1934 the Philippines were promised independence from 1946. Admittedly, a major reason for that promise was pressure within the US Congress to rid the country of an economic burden and to stop immigration of Filipinos and the free importation of Philippines produce, especially sugar. American sugar interests, at the beginning of US rule of the Philippines, had combined with anti-imperialists and anti-trust minded progressives to impose strict limits on American land holdings and a fifty year limit on American corporations. In 1938 the 8,700 Americans in the Philippines population of sixteen million were mostly military personnel and public servants. In 1916 literate Filipinos were given the right to vote for an almost wholly elected congress, with the US retaining power only over defence and foreign affairs. In 1936 the colony was given Commonwealth status with its own elected president. By then nearly all public servants were Filipinos and educational opportunities were far greater than in any other colony in Asia. Nearly half the population was literate. However, though big church estates were broken up and sold to the people, there were no measures to stop the accumulation of wealth by Filipino landowners and their dominance over the political system.[77]

Indeed, there was growing popular dissent in the 1930s on the large central plain of the most heavily populated island, Luzon. That region's population of 1,389,000 in 1939 was almost double its level in 1903, creating an acute land shortage problem at a time when landlords were becoming commercially minded and placing more pressure on the predominantly tenant farming population. Under the influence of American education and

---

76 Ibid., ch. 3. Stubbs, *Hearts and Minds*, ch. 3. Coates, *Suppressing Insurgency*, ch. 2.
77 Norman G. Owen, *Prosperity Without Progress: Manila Hemp and Material Life in the Philippines* (Berkeley 1984), ch. 7. David Wurfel, *Filipino Politics: Development and Decay* (Ithaca 1988), 8–12.

capitalism, the older Spanish-based traditional society of mutual obligations between peasant and landlord was rapidly disappearing. Peasants reacted with acts of violence, which grew after the stagnation of the sugar industry from 1936 caused by American sugar quotas. But the violence only prompted repression by landowners and their local authority allies. There were also strikes and the formation of peasant political organizations. The small Philippines Communist Party (PKP) had little to do with this dissent because of government oppression and because its base was urban.[78]

During the Pacific War, however, a PKP leader, Luis Taruc, became the head of the main anti-Japanese resistance on Luzon, the *Hukbalahap* (Huk) movement. He was a central Luzon tenant farmer's son, who had received an English-language education to college level, which gave him a love of American history. Too poor to finish college, he returned to his home district to work as a tailor, and he became a socialist leader until his party merged in 1938 with the PKP. Taruc was not an ideological Marxist. There were some committed communists in the Huk leadership, but they were neither a majority nor a controlling influence. By September 1944 the Huks had over 10,000 guerrillas armed mainly with captured Japanese weapons. They were not supported, and at times were actively opposed, by the official American resistance organization. Its members had been commanded to lie low and concentrate on gathering intelligence for MacArthur's army, which invaded the islands in force in August 1944 and was widely welcomed by Filipinos. The Americans re-established the Philippines Commonwealth government, giving the Huks no chance to launch a social revolution. Indeed, they were only a small minority of the Philippine resistance movement, and their activities were confined to central Luzon.[79]

Though the Philippines became an independent republic on 4 July 1946, it gave, under American negotiating pressure, major concessions to the US. Ninety-nine year leases were conceded for twenty-two military and naval base sites. Ironically, economic constraints – such as free trade, pegging the Philippine peso to the American dollar and parity for American investors in the republic – paved the way for much more American economic expansion into the new nation than was possible when it was US territory. The investment parity provision aroused much Filipino opposition and was only accepted because of a narrow electoral victory in April 1946 by the conservative pro-American Liberal Party. Smear tactics and money power

---

78 Benedict J. Kerkvliet, *The Huk Rebellion: A Study of Peasant Revolt in the Philippines* (Berkeley 1977), chs 1–2. Eduardo Lachica, *The Huks: Philippine Agrarian Society in Revolt* (New York 1971), chs 3–4. John A. Larkin, *Sugar and the Origins of Modern Philippine Society* (Berkeley 1993), ch. 6.

79 Kerkvliet, *The Huk Rebellion*, ch. 3. Friend, *Blue-Eyed Enemy*, chs 8–9.

assisted this victory. There was also a subsequent unseating from the Congress of elected representatives from central Luzon because of alleged fraud and terror to allow the government to achieve the three fourths majority necessary to pass a constitutional amendment committing the Philippines to free trade with the US.[80]

The expulsion of six elected members of the National Peasants Union (PKM) was one of the grievances that sparked the armed Huk uprising in mid 1946. The Huks, though fighting alongside the invading Americans, had been rejected by the postwar regime, which ordered them to surrender their arms and employed violence against those who refused. Despite this pressure many weapons were successfully hidden. The Huks were victims of the hostility of the official American guerrillas and of landowners and other members of the governing elite, which included pardoned wartime collaborators. The communists in their midst rendered Huks unacceptable to Americans. This rejection, the restoration of the power of landowners, and repression of peasants and the PKM, including murders, were other sparks igniting rebellion in central Luzon.[81]

The Huk insurrection grew in strength. Precise numbers of guerrillas are unknown, but there were at least 5,000 in central Luzon by late 1948. So in size they matched the insurgents in Malaya and had a popular base of support among the tenant farmers in that region. Their weapons came from wartime caches plus captured arms and ammunition and weapons stolen for them by civilian employees at American bases. However, the rebellion failed to expand outside central Luzon because there was not the same history of peasant radicalism in other regions, nor the same high proportion of tenant farmers. There were also cultural differences. Even in central Luzon there were problems of manpower and food supplies. PKM support for the rebellion also diminished under government repression, which increased the dominance of communist leaders, although Taruc and other Huk leaders remained non-Marxist.[82]

The rebellion was sustained by the Philippine government's use of violent repression, rather than attempting to redress peasant grievances. The use of troops, aircraft and artillery to support local constabulary resulted in many civilians being killed or arrested for allegedly supporting the rebels. As one witness recalled: 'The mailed fist policy meant open season on all suspected Huk and PKM. And, of course, this also meant trouble for people

80 Friend, *Blue-Eyed Enemy*, ch. 11. H.W. Brands, *Bound to Empire: The United States and the Philippines* (New York 1992), 227–36.
81 Kerkvliet, *The Huk Rebellion*, ch. 4.
82 Ibid., ch. 5.

who were not directly involved.'[83] Evacuation of peasants caused much economic hardship. The American government, which readily believed the Huks were communists, provided by mid 1948 $72.6 million in military aid to equip 22,000 constabulary troops and 33,000 regular army soldiers. But in 1949 the rebellion was continuing to grow in a country recovering from great wartime damage and with a political system dominated by its socio-economic elite. It remained a thorn in the side of the anti-communist cause in the Pacific Basin into the 1950s.[84]

Conclusions

By 1949 the Western Pacific Basin had been dramatically reshaped since 1945. Much stronger postwar forces of Asian nationalism had achieved victory in Indonesia, had been granted success in the Philippines but faced French resistance in Indochina. The outbreak of the Cold War had compromised the nationalist cause by forcing a division in Korea and by increasing the resolve of Western world powers to resist the independence movement in Vietnam. The communist victory in China now cast a huge shadow over the future prospects for Western interests in the region. The US was being deflected from a primary concern about halting the advance of communism in Europe into a decision to start lending its support to anti-communist causes in the Western Pacific Basin. This reconsideration had already halted the process of socio-economic reform in Japan. It had prompted pressure on Holland to grant independence to the Republic of Indonesia and to allocate financial support for the campaign against the Huk rebellion.

The American objectives in the Western Pacific Basin were mixed. 'The reverse course' in Japan has been used as evidence that the US primary objective was to promote 'Open Door' economic imperialism. This theory can be supported by American approval of the Indonesian Republic, which pledged to protect foreign investment, and by the imposition on the independent Philippines government of policies to assist expansion of American capital there. But it is too simple to say that American foreign policy decision makers such as Truman, Kennan and Acheson were acting at the behest of American capitalists. They all shared the 'corporationist' view that American ideas and values were good for other countries. This was

---

83 Quoted in ibid., 194.
84 Ibid., 188–203.

demonstrated by the planning for the occupation of Japan and by opposition to the corruption and elitism of Chiang Kai-shek. But also much of postwar US foreign policy was influenced by 'realist' assessments of American power and security influences. Such realities conceded control of Manchuria to the USSR; they influenced the handing over to SEAC of responsibility for Southeast Asia; and they prompted the withdrawal from Korea in 1949. Reasons for increasing American involvement in the Western Pacific Basin from 1950 will be examined in the next chapter.

CHAPTER TWO

Containing the Advance of Asian Communism, 1950–1960

In the Western Pacific Basin in 1950 the US faced a major communist advance in Korea, an increasingly difficult French struggle to suppress the communist-led insurgency in Vietnam and the growing Huk rebellion in the Philippines. The British government also was combating an increasingly militant communist insurgency in Malaya. The attempts to suppress these rebellions, which presaged major communist victories in the Cold War, are major themes in this chapter. Also discussed are the wider influences of the Korean War in the Pacific Basin, US moves to contain communist China, other aspects of US anti-communist policies in Asia and Sino-Soviet relations.

The Korean War

At 4 a.m. on Sunday 25 June 1950, the army of the Democratic People's Republic of Korea (DPRK) started a series of attacks across the 38th parallel. The US State Department did not receive confirmation of newspaper reports about this until six and a half hours later, Saturday 9.26 p.m. American eastern standard time. The issue was then referred quickly by the US to the UN. Convened in emergency session on the Sunday afternoon, its Security Council approved a US resolution, which declared the North Korean attack 'an act of aggression', ordered a withdrawal of DPRK forces from South Korea and authorized member states to assist in 'the execution of this resolution'. Only Yugoslavia, which abstained from voting, expressed opposition. Crucially, the USSR, one of the five nations with a power of veto in the council, was not present because Stalin had been boycotting the UN since mid January for its refusal to transfer Nationalist China's seat to the People's Republic of China. Washington was attempting to force the DPRK to retreat without American military intervention. However, the rapid advance of the better-equipped, larger and more experienced North Korean People's Army (KPA) into South Korea provoked, under UN authority, a speedy American commitment of air and naval power and then ground forces to prevent a complete DPRK victory.[1]

The US was not acting under any treaty obligation to the ROK. Administration personnel had made public statements minimizing the importance of South Korea, much to Rhee's consternation. Such speeches, however, were not intended as signals that America would abandon a country to which that year it had granted $120 million in aid; in which there was America's largest overseas embassy; and which was being assisted by a sizeable mission of US military advisers. South Korea was seen to be an important supplier of rice to Japan and a market for the Japanese exports that were being encouraged under the new program for Japanese economic recovery. Rather, the American public statements were designed to deter the ROK from expecting US support for any aggressive move against the DPRK.[2]

The American decision to seek UN support for military assistance to the ROK was made in the context of increasing Cold War intensity in Europe and Asia. The communist take-over in Czechoslovakia in 1948 and the Russian blockade of Berlin in 1948–49 had signalled to the US a dangerous threat of Soviet expansionism into Western Europe. In Asia, the communist victory in China presented new problems for the region because it was widely believed in America that the CCP and the USSR were close allies. This belief had been spelt out in NSC-68, a re-evaluation of US foreign policies and strategic plans by the Departments of State and Defense, which was submitted by the National Security Council (NSC) to Truman on 7 April 1950. There were also the continuing insurgencies in Burma, Malaya, Vietnam and the Philippines that allegedly were actively supported by the USSR. Therefore, the attack on non-communist South Korea by the DPRK was seen as another Soviet-inspired aggression that must be resisted similarly to the Russian blockade of Berlin. Not to do so would raise echoes of Munich in 1938, especially given the virulence of the growing Republican Party attack on the 'loss' of China and the alleged softness of

---

1   See Glenn D. Paige, *The Korean Decision* (New York 1968). James Irving Matray, *The Reluctant Crusade: American Foreign Policy in Korea, 1941–1950* (Honolulu 1985), ch. 10.

2   Bruce Cumings, *The Origins of the Korean War*, vol. II (Princeton 1990), ch. 13. Ronald McGlothlen, 'Acheson, Economics, and the American Commitment in Korea, 1947–1950', *Pacific Historical Review*, 58, 1989, 23–54.

the administration towards communism that was being fuelled by the Alger Hiss and other spy scandals.[3]

In reality, the Korean War was no part of a Soviet grand plan for mastery of the world. However, it is now clear that Stalin, although initially reluctant, not only approved the North Korean attack but also sent military advisers to help plan it and extra arms and equipment to increase KPA capability. Though he feared that the US might intervene, there was contrary evidence based on the American military withdrawal from South Korea and the American public statements about its strategic unimportance. Also, Stalin's intelligence advice was that the South Korean army would be no match for the KPA, which was being reinforced by over 50,000 North Koreans who had served in the Chinese communist army. Furthermore, Kim Il-sung assured Stalin that an attack on the South would provoke a pro-North Korean revolution there. Another motive for his support for Kim's plan was the Sino-Soviet treaty and the successful development of Soviet nuclear power. These developments gave him a new confidence that the USSR could improve its strategic position in East Asia after the humiliating back down over Berlin and the defection from the Soviet camp by Tito's Yugoslavia. Moreover, if the Soviet Union did not support the eager Kim, China might do so and damage the USSR's revolutionary credibility in the communist world. Stalin did not trust Mao Zedong, fearing that he could be another Tito. Indeed, probably an underlying reason why Stalin withdrew from the UN after its failure to seat communist China was to ensure China's inability to participate in UN affairs. Furthermore, avoiding any commitment to China was probably the major reason why Stalin refused to listen to the advice of his representative at the UN, Jacob Malik, to return to the UN and veto the Security Council response to the US request for action against North Korea. If the US intervened in Korea under a UN mandate, there would be no declaration of war. Therefore if China became involved in the conflict there would be no 'state of war' requiring USSR adherence to the Sino-Soviet security treaty.[4]

Indeed, Stalin further manoeuvred to protect the USSR if the US intervened. He told Kim Il-sung in Moscow in April 1951: 'If you should get kicked in the teeth, I shall not lift a finger. You have to ask Mao for all the

---

3   Peter Lowe, *The Origins of the Korean War* (2nd edition, London 1997), chs 5–6.
4   Andrei Gromyko, *Memoirs* (London 1989), 102. Vladislav Zubok and Konstantine Pleshakov, *Inside the Kremlin's Cold War: From Stalin to Krushchev* (Cambridge, Mass. 1996), 54–64. Kathryn Weathersby, *Soviet Aims in Korea and the Origins of the Korean War, 1945–1950* (Honolulu 1993), 23–6. William Stueck, *The Korean War: An International History* (Princeton 1995), 33–5. Sergei N. Goncharov, John L. Lewis and Xue Liai, *Uncertain Partners: Stalin, Mao and the Korean War* (Stanford 1993), 10–12.

help.' Kim dutifully travelled to Beijing in mid May. Mao disapproved of Kim's invasion plan, preferring to concentrate on achieving unity in China. But he could not publicly oppose Kim's burning desire to achieve the unification of Korea. Also, Mao was hoping for Soviet support for China's aim of conquering Taiwan. Actually, Kim assured Mao that no Chinese military support would be needed if the US did intervene. Kim expected a quick victory before any effective American force could prevent it.[5]

Certainly, there was a wildfire advance by the KPA into South Korea. However, American troops from Japan arrived in time to assist remnants of the ROKA to defend a small area around the southeast port of Pusan. Many South Koreans, alienated by Rhee's policies, either did not resist or actually welcomed the invaders. But there was no revolutionary uprising. Also by early September America's Far East Commander, MacArthur, directed a UN army (UNA) of 83,000 Americans plus a British Commonwealth brigade comprised of British troops from Hong Kong, who were soon joined by an Australian battalion. With the addition of surviving ROKA divisions, MacArthur now had 180,000 troops to set against the 98,000 strong KPA. With the reluctant permission of the JCS, MacArthur used this advantage in a successful amphibious landing on 15 September at Inchon on the west coast of South Korea close to Seoul, which was occupied by 28 September. The main KPA supply line had been severed. This disaster for the DPRK, along with a UNA break out from the Pusan perimeter, caused a headlong KPA retreat across the 38th parallel.[6]

The subsequent decision to switch the UNA from containment of the DPRK attack to a roll-back attempt to reunite Korea under noncommunist rule was uncontroversial in the US. The shock of the initial KPA success, and then the euphoria aroused by MacArthur's dramatic counter-stroke, had aroused widespread public support for an advance across the 38th parallel. Nor did the administration need any urging to do this, especially because stopping at the border would boost the Republican Party attack on its policy towards communism at a time of imminent mid-term congressional elections.[7]

The US roll-back decision also discounted any threat of Russian or Chinese retaliation. The USSR had responded to the American intervention

5 Goncharov, Lewis and Liai, *Uncertain Partners* (quotation 145).

6 For good short histories of the war see Burton I. Kaufman, *The Korean War: Challenges in Crisis, Credibility and Command* (Philadelphia 1986); and Callum A. MacDonald, *Korea: The War Before Vietnam* (New York 1986). For a recent bibliography of literature on the war, see Paul M. Edwards, *The Korean War: An Annotated Bibliography* (Westport 1998).

7 Gordon H. Chang, *Friends and Enemies: The United States, China and the Soviet Union, 1948–1972* (Stanford 1990), 77–80.

in the war with proposals in the UN for a joint Soviet–American effort for peaceful reunification of Korea, which the US had brushed aside. China warned that it would not tolerate an American military advance into North Korea. But this was dismissed in Washington as bluff on the assumption that neither China nor the USSR wanted a general war with the US. Also, the US, with British support, achieved a big majority in a vote in the UN General Assembly on 7 October, which authorized the UNA to cross the border. This decision avoided the need for endorsement by the Security Council, to which the USSR had returned. The US, and the other nations, which had been persuaded to support the extension of the war, had deluded themselves that they could safely remove the artificial border.

But China was not bluffing. On 4 August, at a meeting of the CCP Politburo, Mao warned that if 'the US imperialists win the war they will become more arrogant and will threaten us'. He therefore considered that China would have to come to North Korea's aid.[8] In preparation, large-scale reinforcements boosted the strength of Chinese forces on the Manchuria–Korea border to more than 250,000 troops. On 4 October a special enlarged Politburo meeting in Beijing reviewed the pros and cons about entering the war. There was opposition on the grounds that China, with minimal industrial strength and no significant navy or air force, would be fighting the world's greatest military power. But Mao Zedong insisted that a war with the imperialistic US was inevitable and that to allow an American presence on the Yalu River would pin down a large Chinese force while the US had freedom to attack from Taiwan or through Vietnam. A war against the US also would help quell dissidents in China by demonstrating the government's strength. Furthermore, the USSR was urging China to intervene. Not to do so, Mao warned his colleagues, would remove prospects of Soviet support for China against a direct American threat. Moreover, Stalin was willing to provide the PLA with major war materiel and air support, being happy to assist China to fight a war with the US that the USSR strongly desired to avoid.[9]

Therefore, on 14 October, the first PLA 'volunteers' started crossing the Yalu River into Korea. This move occurred six days after UNA troops entered the DPRK and after American planes conducted bombing raids up to the Yalu, which included dropping some bombs on the Chinese side. Ironically, on the next day on Wake Island in mid Pacific, MacArthur

---

8   Shuguang Zhang and Jian Chen (eds), *Chinese Communist Foreign Policy and the Cold War in Asia: New Documentary Evidence, 1944–1950* (Chicago 1996), 157

9   Shuguang Zhang, *Mao's Military Romanticism: China and the Korean War, 1950–1953* (Lawrence 1995), 71–84. Jian Chen, *China's Road to the Korean War* (New York 1993), 137, 181–9. Goncharov, Lewis and Xue, *Uncertain Partners*, 168–96.

assured Truman, at their first-ever meeting, that there was no danger of Chinese intervention in the war.[10]

At first the PLA launched probing attacks on UNA and ROKA units as they fanned out into the northern part of the DPRK after capturing Pyongyang on 20 October. But MacArthur and his generals discounted the danger because the PLA units pulled back after initial sharp engagements. UNA forces continued to advance along a wide front, with one American regiment reaching the Yalu River on 21 November. MacArthur had exceeded his instructions in using American troops so close to the Chinese border. But the JCS was unwilling to challenge his military reputation, which had been heightened by his success at Inchon. On 15 November, the Chinese military commander, Peng Dehuai, responded sadly to the failure of his warning attacks: 'All we seem to have accomplished is to convince the Americans that Chinese troops have not entered Korea in any strength.' Therefore there was 'no alternative but to teach the imperialists a lesson', he said as he bent over a relief model to explain to his generals how he intended to encircle the American Ninth Army group and destroy it.[11]

Therefore, when MacArthur launched an offensive on 24 November to achieve complete control of North Korea, his widely dispersed 150,000 strong armies were counter-attacked by the PLA, which now had 300,000 troops in North Korea plus 80,000 survivors of the KPA. Furthermore, Peng achieved comprehensive surprise because he moved his troops forward under cover of darkness, and the low level of PLA technology with little radio contact had protected it from American electronic surveillance. Within four days, the UNA and the ROKA were in headlong retreat out of North Korea.

In response to this sudden Chinese success, MacArthur wanted to widen the war, using air power – possibly atomic bombs – and a naval blockade of China as well as unleashing the Chinese nationalist troops on Taiwan to attack the Chinese mainland. But Truman's administration had tried to contain the war from the beginning, by ordering the 7th fleet to patrol the Formosa Strait between Taiwan and China in order to prevent an attack across it from either side. Because Washington believed the USSR was supporting China, the weight of government opinion was against any move that might bring the USSR into the war. Such a global contest would place America at a great disadvantage with a rearmament program only in its

---

10 Kaufman, *Korean War*, 90–1.
11 Dean Acheson, *Present at the Creation* (New York 1969), 456. MacDonald, *Korea*, 57–9. Russell Spurr, *Enter the Dragon: China's Undeclared War Against the US in Korea, 1950–51* (New York 1988), 169.

early stages and a subsequent inability to stop any Soviet advance in Europe while fighting China.[12]

However, the US government was equally determined to preserve the ROK. To allow a complete Chinese victory would threaten the whole American policy to contain communist expansion in the Western Pacific Basin and might induce a loss of Japanese confidence in the US. Nor did Truman wish to add the 'loss of Korea' to the Republican propaganda's lost China theme. So he rejected a plea from Prime Minister Attlee of Britain for agreement to a cease-fire in Korea in return for seating China in the UN and reaching a solution about Taiwan.[13]

Fortunately for Washington, the Chinese onslaught ran out of steam after taking Seoul and pushing the UNA south of the Han River. The major problem was the need for Chinese units to stop periodically and regroup to cope with the PLA's primitive communications system and the difficulties of an ever-extending and inefficient supply line. American air power and increasing American artillery strength also hampered the Chinese advance. Then on 25 January 1951 a new American field commander, the hard driving General Matthew Ridgway, launched a UNA counter-offensive using the principle of maximum use of tanks, artillery fire and air strikes against selected Chinese targets – a 'meat grinder' strategy. Seoul was recaptured on 15 March.

On 11 April, Truman stunned the American nation by sacking MacArthur, replacing him with Ridgway. It was the culmination of an emerging fundamental policy difference between the president and his Far East Commander, who continued to advocate widening the war to the Chinese mainland. He had communicated that opinion on 20 March to the minority Republican leader of the House of Representatives, who obligingly read the letter to Congress on 5 April, which clinched the case for MacArthur's dismissal. He returned to America to a hero's welcome and made public speeches, using his gifted verbosity, to condemn the government's limited war policy in Korea as 'appeasement', which the Republicans gleefully reiterated.[14]

The war in Korea was heading for a stalemate. Initially the UNA forces faced the most massive Chinese attack of the war launched on 22 April.

---

12 Rosemary Foot, *The Wrong War: American Policy and the Dimensions of the Korean Conflict, 1950–1953* (Ithaca 1985), 101–30. For the US quarantine of Taiwan see Thomas J. Christensen, *Useful Adversaries: Grand Strategy, Domestic Mobilization, and Sino-American Conflict, 1947–1958* (Princeton 1996), 133–7.

13 Rosemary Foot, 'Anglo-American Relations in the Korean Crisis. The British Effort to Avert an Expanded War, December 1950–January 1951', *Diplomatic History*, 10, 1986, 43–57.

14 Steuck, *The Korean War*, 178–84.

Though the UNA suffered over 7,000 casualties, huge Chinese losses and army disorganization allowed the UN command to launch a successful counter-offensive. The Chinese army was pushed north of the 38th parallel. This achievement influenced a revised American Far Eastern policy, NSC-48/5, which now sought a peace that would preserve the ROK. To force China to the peace conference table, this policy statement endorsed strong military pressure against Chinese forces in Korea and encouragement of anti-communist elements in China, but no widening of the military conflict. Pressure from America's European allies contributed to the decision for peace negotiations, which the USSR supported.[15]

Stalin's initial response to American intervention in the Korean War was surprise and alarm. The Inchon landing and the subsequent collapse of the KPA induced a sense of panic that the USSR would be drawn into a war with the US. So, Stalin instructed Malik at the UN to pursue all channels for a potential peace settlement. Soon, however, the Soviet peace moves were suspended with the rapid Chinese advance. Stalin now was looking forward to the 'complete defeat of the American troops'. But, with the successful American counter-attack, Stalin, in consultation with Mao, renewed Soviet support for a peace settlement. China agreed to this in recognition of military difficulties but also resolved to keep fighting during armistice talks in order to keep open any military option.[16]

American negotiations with the Chinese began on 10 July 1951 at Chinese-held Kaesong on the 38th parallel and soon shifted to the nearby village of Panmunjom. But the talks proved long and difficult. Stalin was in no hurry to reach a settlement. The longer it took, the more American forces would be tied down in Korea and would be no threat in Europe. Also, this was a great opportunity to collect intelligence about American military technology and capacities. Furthermore, continuing conflict between the US and China ensured Chinese dependency on the USSR. China's government believed that the US could be forced to make more concessions if Americans became tired of the war. China's objectives were to push UN troops back to the 38th parallel and a settlement that would result in the withdrawal of all 'foreign' forces from Korea. Another negotiating impasse was the American insistence on voluntary non-repatriation to China by Chinese prisoners of war. At times there were heavy clashes between soldiers eyeing each other across intermittently declared cease-fire zones. There was a continuing air war over North Korea between the

---

15   Foot, *The Wrong War*, 131–6. Kaufman, *The Korean War*, ch. 6.
16   Kathryn Weathersby, 'Stalin, Mao, and the End of the Korean War', in Odd Arne Westad (ed.), *Brothers in Arms: The Rise and Fall of the Sino-Soviet Alliance, 1945–1963* (Stanford 1998), 93–101 (quotation 93).

American air force and alleged Chinese planes that were mostly Soviet-supplied and piloted. But Stalin ensured that no Soviet pilots or planes would fall into enemy hands by limiting their involvement to a defensive area behind Chinese lines.[17]

This stalemate frustrated US military commanders and many members of the American public. A majority in the 1952 election voted for a Second World War hero, General Dwight Eisenhower, as Republican Party president. He had promised to end the war on 'honorable terms'. However, there was more fierce fighting with the Chinese and attempts to seize military vantage points in North Korea, despite war weariness in China, which was spending 60 per cent of its revenue on the war. Rhee also stalled the peace process by an unwillingness to accept the inevitability of a divided peninsula. But the USSR played a decisive hand after Stalin's death on 5 March 1953. The new collective Soviet leadership was determined to end the Korean War. China had no option, since without Soviet material support it could not continue fighting the US. On 27 July 1953 an armistice was finally signed ending the war without the achievement of China's negotiating aims.[18]

Repercussions of the Korean War

The influences of the Korean War along the East Asian rim of the Pacific Basin were profound. In Korea, it solidified the peninsula into two nations viewing each other with continuing hostility. South Korea continued to be propped up by more than 50,000 American troops to ward off any future attacks and by a $700 million aid package. Eisenhower was committed to disengage from Korea. He also introduced a 'new look' defence policy, which called for big cuts in the army from its inflated Korean War strength, with a reliance on the armies of US allies backed by a mobile US reserve and massive nuclear superiority to deter Soviet or Chinese aggression. But Eisenhower's administration was locked into promising continuing assistance to the ROK by Rhee's intransigence over the armistice negotiations and

17   Ibid., 100–7. Zhang, *Mao's Military Romanticism*, ch. 9. Jon Hallion, 'Air Operations in Korea: The Soviet Side of the Story', in William J. Williams (ed.), *A Revolutionary War: Korea and the Transformation of the Postwar World* (Chicago 1993), 149–70.
18   Kaufmann, *The Korean War*, chs 7–9. Stueck, *The Korean War*, ch. 9. Weathersby, 'Stalin, Mao and the End of the Korean War', 108–9. Zhang, *Mao's Military Romanticism*, 232–46.

the need to persuade him to attend a conference in Geneva in April 1954 between the USSR, the US, Britain and France to establish peace in Korea. Truman also had turned a blind eye to Rhee's use of thuggery and intimidation in 1952 to force the South Korean Assembly to agree to constitutional amendments that consolidated his presidential power. He then used this advantage to suppress or frighten away opponents in a presidential election in which he won five million of seven million votes. Truman's administration knew that any move to replace Rhee would be interpreted by conservatives in the Republican Party as communist inspired. Furthermore, Washington saw no viable alternative to Rhee as leader of South Korea. Also the war had devastated the South Korean economy with property losses estimated at $2 billion which equalled its Gross National Product (GNP) in 1949. North Korea's losses were of a similar magnitude and 10 per cent of the Korean population had been killed, wounded or were missing.[19]

America's relations with China also were greatly influenced by the Korean War. From the war's outset, the US imposed a trade embargo on China. It has been argued that the Eisenhower administration was trapped into maintaining implacable hostility towards Red China because of public outrage at the sudden Chinese attack on American forces in North Korea and the humiliation of the subsequent retreat by American forces. This hostility, along with Senator Joe McCarthy's witch-hunt for alleged communists in the State Department, resulted in the dismissal of China experts from the department. The result was an alleged failure to miss the signs of Sino-Soviet conflict in the subsequent decade. However, more recently declassified US documents demonstrate that the administration was aware of Chinese–Soviet divisions. It has been suggested that a policy of maximum pressure was placed on China to force Beijing to seek assistance from the USSR which might impose strains on the relationship.[20]

Sino-Soviet relations had improved during the Korean War. China received valuable airforce support and other military assistance from the USSR, though not as much as desired. During the early 1950s there was significant Soviet technical assistance in the form of machinery, industrial technology and education for Chinese students in Moscow. Also, Nikita

---

19 Henry W. Brands, Jr, 'The Dwight D. Eisenhower Administration, Syngman Rhee, and the "Other" Geneva Conference of 1954', *Pacific Historical Review*, 61, 1987, 59–85. Edward C. Keefer, 'The Truman Administration and the South Korean Political Crisis of 1952: Democracy's Failure?', *Pacific Historical Review*, 60, 1991, 145–68. Steuck, *The Korean War*, 361.

20 David Allan Mayers, *Cracking the Monolith: US Policy Against the Sino-Soviet Alliance, 1949–1955* (Baton Rouge 1986), chs 4–5. Chang, *Friends and Enemies*, chs 3–6. Rosemary Foot, *The Practice of Power: US Relations with China since 1949* (Oxford 1995), 119–25.

Khrushchev, who soon emerged after Stalin's death as the new leader of the USSR, welcomed cooperation with China along with his search for peaceful coexistence with the West. But continuing hostility between China and the US did indeed start to place strains on the Soviet–Chinese relationship.[21]

China, the US, USSR and Taiwan

The ongoing conflict between the US and China was heightened by America's support for Chiang Kai-shek's nationalist Chinese regime in Taiwan. It had received new strategic status for the US during the Korean War as a potential threat to China and as an offshore defence base. From 1951 to 1957, $683 million in economic assistance and $1.47 billion in military aid flowed from the US to Taiwan.[22]

On that mountainous island of 36,000 square kilometres, which had been a Japanese colony from 1895 to 1945, the nationalists had established the structure of their former government of China as an outward sign of resolve to return to the mainland. Consequently, Taiwan's national assembly was controlled by the KMT, which was dominated by mainlanders, with Chiang Kai-shek as a virtual president for life. The 80 per cent of the population who were Taiwanese had no say in this political arrangement, though they were given democratic control over local government. The Taiwanese were ethnically Chinese, but their long separation from the mainland had given them a distinctive outlook and separate culture. Also, relations with the 'mainlanders' had been soured by initial postwar nationalist rule. Taiwanese who had enjoyed significant economic progress under repressive Japanese rule found themselves after 1945 under equally oppressive but more corrupt masters who plundered the island's resources for their own wealth and for the needs of the nationalist mainland regime. A consequent Taiwanese riot in February 1947, which developed into an incipient rebellion, was brutally crushed by nationalist troops, leading to the death of or unexplained disappearance of over 100,000 Taiwanese, especially community leaders. The now leaderless and traumatized Taiwanese retreated into the quiescent and

---

21   Chang, *Friends and Enemies*, 79–80, 203–4. Deborah A. Kaple, 'Soviet Advisors in China in the 1950s', in Westad (ed.), *Brothers in Arms*, 117–30. Sergei Goncharenko, 'Sino-Soviet Military Cooperation', in Westad (ed.), *Brothers in Arms*, 145–9. Odd Arne Westad, 'The Sino-Soviet Alliance and the United States', in Westad (ed.), *Brothers in Arms*, 171–5.
22   Chang, *Friends and Enemies*, 160–2.

apolitical mode with which they had reacted to the Japanese conquest of their island.[23]

The flash point between the US and China was the nationalist retention of three small island groups close to the Chinese mainland. They were Jinmen (Quemoy) guarding the entrance to the Chinese port of Xiamen (Amoy); Mazu (Matsu) lying on the approach to the port of Fuzhou (Foochow); and the Dachen Islands to the North. The nationalists regarded these islands as potential launching pads for their much-vaunted ambition to return to the mainland. Starting on 3 September 1954, China launched a heavy bombardment of Jinmen, with continuing artillery strikes and air raids on the islands and massing of Chinese troops opposite them. The nationalists responded in kind, stationing a large proportion of their forces on the islands. This communist Chinese bellicosity was influenced by Mao's continued fear that the US intended to attack China and by recent US negotiations with Chiang Kai-shek for a mutual defence treaty.[24]

The US government became involved in the nationalist defence of China's offshore islands because of a conviction in Washington that their loss would be a devastating blow to the shaky prestige of Chiang Kai-shek's regime. Eisenhower's administration did place successful pressure on Chiang to withdraw in January 1955 from the Dachens, which were beyond warplane range from Taiwan. But, in the process, a secret promise was given to him that the US would oppose a Chinese invasion of Jinmen and Mazu. On 28 January 1955 the American Congress also gave the administration a free hand to use force to protect Taiwan and 'related positions and territories'. Eisenhower and his Secretary of State, John Foster Dulles, who had served the Truman administration as a special diplomatic envoy to Japan, planned in fact to use atomic weapons against China if the islands were attacked. Blunt warnings of this prospect were delivered to Beijing. There was dissent within the NSC about risking a war with China, but Eisenhower and Dulles presumed that the USSR would not intervene to support Beijing. They were convinced by the new Khrushchev regime's efforts to remove sources of dissension between America and the USSR. Indeed, the most plausible reason why China stepped back from the brink by refraining from launching any invasion of the islands was absence of Soviet support. In turn, Soviet faith in the reliability of China, which was viewed in Moscow as having pursued a counterproductive policy, had been shaken. The American position was more than inspired brinkmanship, as

---

23 Thomas B. Gold, *State and Society in the Taiwan Miracle* (New York 1986), 44–64. Mei-ling T. Wang, *The Dust that Never Settles: The Taiwan Independence Campaign and US–China Relations* (Lanham, N.Y. 1999), ch. 2.
24 Westad, 'The Sino-Soviet Alliance', 173.

biographers of Eisenhower have suggested. It was a firm American game-play that preserved peace in the Western Pacific Basin only because China backed off.[25]

Beijing made another threat against Jinmen and Mazu with a bombardment commencing on 23 August 1958. This move again provoked an American determination to resist any Chinese attack. However, Mao was not seeking a war with the US or even an invasion of those islands. His main motives were to demonstrate to the USSR China's foreign policy independence and to enhance mobilization of his new economic program, the Great Leap Forward. Indeed, this move reflected new tensions in the Sino-Soviet relationship emerging from a visit by Soviet premier, Nikita Khrushchev to Beijing in late July 1958. His conversation with Mao had centred on Chinese demands for more aid from the USSR and on Soviet plans for greater military cooperation. Khrushchev promised extra resources, but Mao was very unwilling to agree to unified command of a new submarine fleet and to joint construction of military communication facilities in northern China. Nor did Mao inform Khrushchev of any intention to attack Jinmen and Mazu. After the attack began, Moscow did warn Washington that the USSR would support China with nuclear weapons against nuclear attack by the US. But Soviet officials recognized the Chinese independence motive. Andrei Gromyko, the Soviet Foreign Secretary, rushed to Beijing in early September to demand an explanation. He later wrote that he was 'flabbergasted' when Zhou and Mao 'showed a willingness to accept the possibility of an American nuclear attack on China'. Gromyko warned them that there 'definitely' would be no 'positive response' from the USSR. The Kremlin also started to remove special military advisers from China. Beijing defused the crisis by suspending the bombardment of Jinmen and Mazu. But Mao was unrepentant, declaring: 'the islands are two batons that keep Khrushchev and Eisenhower dancing, scurrying this way and that'. Cracks had widened in the Sino-Soviet alliance.[26]

The alliance started to split in 1959. In late June Khrushchev informed China that he was unilaterally suspending Sino-Soviet nuclear cooperation in the cause of a nuclear free East Asia. Mao retorted by condemning, in an inter-party circular, Kremlin thinking as 'right-deviationist'. His hostility

---

25 Robert Divine, *Eisenhower and the Cold War* (New York 1981), 61–70; Stephen E. Ambrose, *Eisenhower: The President* (New York 1984), 245. Chang, *Friends and Enemies*, ch. 4. John Garver, 'New Light on Sino-Soviet Relations: The Memoir of China's Ambassador to Moscow, 1955–62', *The China Quarterly*, no. 122, June 1990, 305–6. Westad, 'The Sino-Soviet Alliance', 173.
26 Westad, 'The Sino-Soviet Alliance', 176. Andrei Gromyko, *Memoirs* 251. Zubok and Peshakov, *Inside the Kremlin's Cold War*, 220–6.

probably was exacerbated by a forthcoming trip by Khrushchev to the US. On his return, Khrushchev visited Beijing in October 1959 to commemorate the tenth anniversary of the Chinese revolution. Details of his conversations with Mao are unknown. But their acrimony was demonstrated by Khrushchev's subsequent complaint: 'To Mao there are no laws, no lasting agreements', and by Mao's denunciation that 'Khrushchev is very infantile. He does not understand Marxism and Leninism, [and] he is easily cheated by the imperialists.' However, a longer term negative impact of the 1958 Taiwan crisis, for the US as well as for the USSR, was China's realization of a need to develop its own nuclear weapons.[27]

Colonial Remnants in China: Macau and Hong Kong

Despite the complete mainland victory of the communist forces in China in 1949, no moves were made by Beijing to take over the vestiges of European empires in China: Portuguese Macau and British Hong Kong. Victorious Chinese troops easily could have stormed across Hong Kong's frontier in 1949, but instead the PLA stopped short of the border. The CCP central committee had decided to solve diplomatically remaining colonial problems from the past, announcing that it would honour all China's international treaties. This policy also covered Macau, even though this relic of long distant Portuguese imperialism had become a haven for KMT refugees.[28]

There had been discussions between Britain and the Chinese nationalist government about the future of Britain's Hong Kong island colony and the New Territories on the mainland, which had been leased by Britain in 1898 for ninety-nine years. This British enclave in China represented the days of China's diplomatic weakness. However, though the pre-war nationalist government had voiced the need to overturn 'unequal treaties', it was unwilling to provoke conflict with Britain. China at that stage was seeking international respectability and soon was facing the major problem of Japanese expansionism. After the end of the Japanese occupation of Hong Kong in 1945 there was no significant nationalist Chinese opposition to the

---

27   Zubok and Peshakov, *Inside the Kremlin's Cold War*, 228–9. Westad, 'The Sino-Soviet Alliance', 177. See also John W. Lewis and Xue Litai, *China Builds the Bomb* (Stanford 1988).
28   Steve Tsang, *Hong Kong: An Appointment with China* (London 1997), 66–70. Geoffrey C. Gunn, *Encountering Macau: A Portuguese City-State on the Periphery of China, 1557–1999* (Boulder 1996), 153–4.

return of British colonial authorities. Ironically, Hong Kong had been a safe haven for the CCP during the Chinese Civil War. But the CCP made it clear that it regarded both Hong Kong and Macau as remnants of the unequal treaties imposed on China by outside imperialist powers, which would require correction in the future.[29]

After China entered the Korean War, tension developed between Hong Kong and its huge neighbour. A burgeoning commerce between them was stifled by the UN embargo on trade on goods that could assist China's war effort. Hong Kong's exports to China fell from HK$1.6 billion in 1951 to HK$520 million in 1952. This was a major economic burden for Hong Kong's population. It had been swollen by refugees from communist China, rising from 600,000 in 1945 to nearly 2.2 million by 1952 in a land area of only 1,074 square kilometres, which had no raw materials and needed to import most of its food and even water. People living on rooftops were witnesses to resultant poverty. When a fire in December 1951 destroyed over a thousand squatter shacks, CCP newspapers accused the British administration of deliberately starting the conflagration in order to allow the extension of Hong Kong's airport. The British administration reacted by banning a Hong Kong communist newspaper and prosecuting editors for seditious circulation of Chinese lies. Beijing fulminated against 'savage and despotic' British rule in Hong Kong and vowed the territory's liberation 'one day'. However, such propaganda was not converted into action, and after the Korean War there were renewed flows of Chinese goods and people across Hong Kong's border.[30]

There was also tension during the Korean War between Macau and China. Initially, Macau was a conduit for smuggling of petroleum and war materials to China. But in 1951 the US successfully pressured Portugal to comply with the UN trade ban on China, which in turn pressured Portugal to suppress cross-border smuggling, resulting in two interchanges of gunfire across the frontier in July 1952. Consequently, Macau's food supplies from China were cut off. But diplomacy resolved this crisis in the next month. Later Chinese pressure succeeded in the cancellation of celebrations of four centuries of Portuguese rule in Macau planned for 1957.[31]

There was further tension between China and Hong Kong over a British attempt to impose quotas on Chinese immigrants, which provoked a savage

---

29　Kevin P. Lane, *Sovereignty and the Status Quo: The Historical Roots of China's Hong Kong Policy* (Boulder 1990), 41–70.

30　Ibid., 70–1. Jon Woronoff, *Asia's 'Miracle' Economies* (London 1986), 143. Theodore Geiger and Frances M. Geiger, *The Development Progress of Hong Kong and Singapore* (London 1975), 68.

31　Gunn, *Encountering Macau*, 154–5.

riot in 1956 that left fifty-nine people dead. A result was Chinese condemnation of British collusion with 'cold blooded murderers' from Taiwan.
A consequent meeting between Zhou and Hong Kong's Governor in Beijing
resulted in a continued Chinese commitment not to challenge British rule
and a British agreement not to use the territory as a military base or source
of subversion against China and to protect Chinese officials there.[32]

During the 1950s a legacy of the Korean War trade embargo with China
was an industrial take-off in Hong Kong led by the textile industry. This
was assisted by the influx into the colony after the communist victory in
China of many Shanghai mill owners bringing with them machinery and
skilled workers. Facilitating the industrial growth was the creation of new
markets in Asia for cotton goods, resulting from the wealth generated by the
Korean War, plus markets in Britain and the US. By 1959 35 per cent
of the colony's domestic exports were products of its textile industry, the
beginnings of major economic growth in this small Pacific rim territory.
Hong Kong also was becoming a valuable conduit for China's trade with
the outside world.[33]

Japan and the Korean War

The Korean War proved a salvation for the Japanese economy, which had
been struggling under the effects of domestic inflation and an American
imposed austerity plan to enhance Japanese exports. MacArthur and the
Japanese Prime Minister, Yoshida Shigeru, a pre-war diplomat who escaped
the postwar purge, were able to reactivate Japanese production of military
materiel to supply American forces in Korea, justified on the grounds
of providing for an 'emergency'. Japan's propinquity to the war zone and
still underutilized industrial capacity not only assisted America's suddenly
overstrained armaments production but also provided a decisive boost to
the Japanese economy. Between 1950 and 1954 Japan supplied close to
$3 billion worth of war-related supplies, which economic historians acknow-
ledge was the decisive ingredient in the postwar re-creation of Japan's
industrial might. Japanese technicians also were used in Korea to man harbour
facilities, power plants and essential industries. Some forty-six Japanese ships
manned by members of the former Japanese Imperial Navy served in Korean

---

32   Lane, *Sovereignty and the Status Quo*, 71–4.
33   Geiger and Geiger, *Development of Hong Kong*, 68–74.

waters. About 2,600 Japanese seamen and dockers supported the Inchon landing.[34]

The Korean War also was the catalyst for the signing of peace treaties with Japan, which ended the American occupation. The threat to East Asian security presented by the outbreak of the war and the consequent enhanced strategic importance of Japan brought the need for a peace treaty to the fore. The US administration speedily resolved to send Republican Senator Dulles to negotiate with the nations formally involved in the occupation of Japan for a peace treaty, which he discussed with a wide range of groups in Japan, negotiating in particular with Yoshida. The result was a conference which began on 5 September 1951 in San Francisco and which was attended by delegates from fifty-two nations, including Japan. Three days later these nations, with the exception of the communist states – the USSR, Poland and Czechoslovakia – signed the Peace Treaty that formally ended the military occupation of Japan. A second, important part of this process was the signing of a Japan–US mutual security treaty, which established an alliance of equal partners and which was to have a major influence on future Pacific Basin affairs. Japan regarded the treaty as a guarantee of independence under US military protection. This peace treaty process was also a catalyst for the Australia, New Zealand, United States Security Treaty (ANZUS). Australia and New Zealand were particularly fearful of rearmament in Japan. They also had provided military assistance to the US in the Korean War and were seeking an American guarantee for their security in the new Cold War environment.[35]

Continuing conflict in Vietnam

In early 1950 the US became concerned about advancing communism in the Southeast Asia portion of the Pacific Basin. This region was now regarded in Washington as an area for Japanese trade expansion, which would stimulate Japan's economic growth. Britain had become worried about the growing

---

34 William S. Borden, *The Pacific Alliance: United States Foreign Economic Policy and Japanese Trade Recovery, 1947–1955* (Madison 1984), 145–7. Reinhard Drifte, 'Japan's Involvement in the Korean War', in James Cotton and Ian Neary (eds), *The Korean War in History* (Atlantic Heights 1989), 120–34. Michael J. Green, *Arming Japan: Defense Production, Alliance Politics, and the Postwar Search for Autonomy* (New York 1995), 31–41.

35 Michael M. Yoshitsu, *Japan and the San Francisco Peace Settlement* (New York 1983), chs 3–5. Richard B. Finn, *Winners in Peace: MacArthur, Yoshida, and Postwar Japan* (Berkeley 1992), ch. 19. John Welfield, *The Postwar International Order and the Origins of the Japanese–American Security Treaty* (Canberra 1982). W. David McIntyre, *Background to the ANZUS Pact: Policy-Making, Strategy and Diplomacy, 1945–55* (Basingstoke 1995), ch. 13.

power of the Vietminh in Vietnam in terms of combating the communist insurgency in Malaya. London expressed this concern strongly to Washington. Communism in Vietnam also was seen as a potential threat to American efforts to promote Japanese trade to Burma, where there was a major communist insurgency, and to Thailand, which was being viewed as a domino that might fall to communism with communist victories in Indochina. Furthermore, France's efforts to defeat the Vietminh, which cost 167 million francs in 1949, were placing severe burdens on the economy of that important Western European nation. Moreover, paying attention to combating communism in Vietnam would help deflect the growing Republican attack on alleged communist sympathizers within the State Department. This was especially the case after the DRV's announcement of its recognition by the USSR and by Communist China in January 1950 as the only legitimate government in Vietnam.[36]

Therefore, in February 1950 the US recognized the Bao Dai government in Vietnam. With news of Chinese arms flowing to the Vietminh and the successful Chinese invasion in April 1950 of nationalist-held Hainandao Island, Truman authorized on 1 May $10 million in aid for the French war effort against the Vietminh. On 5 June Congress approved $23.5 million to French Vietnam, the largest amount in an economic aid package for Southeast Asian countries. Despite initial scepticism about Bao Dai, Truman's administration had accepted, without further analysis, assurances that France was working towards the creation of an independent country under that ruler, who was little more than a French puppet.[37]

After the communist victory in China, France was starting to lose the war in Vietnam's northern province of Tonkin. Before 1950 the French had controlled towns and lines of communication, and there was an ebb and flow struggle with elusive Vietminh guerrillas in the countryside. But in 1950, with Chinese assistance, the Vietminh were pressing against French outposts in northern Tonkin, causing a strategic withdrawal of French troops there, which in turn opened the northern border over which Vietminh soldiers were moving to and from Chinese camps. There they were being trained and armed with modern weapons to add to those captured from the French. Also the government in Paris was unable to increase the number of French soldiers in Vietnam, who were never much more than 100,000 throughout the war, because of the demands on a volunteer army in other

---

36   Andrew J. Rotter, *The Path to Vietnam: Origins of the American Commitment to Southeast Asia* (Ithaca 1987), chs 6–8.

37   Ibid., 166–79. Gary R. Hess, *The United States' Emergence as a Southeast Power, 1940–1950* (New York 1987), 355–6. Anthony Short, *The Origins of the Vietnam War* (London 1989), 78–84.

colonial territories and for European defence. It was illegal to send overseas French soldiers doing compulsory military service.[38]

American aid for the French military effort in Vietnam increased sharply after the outbreak of the Korean War to $450 million in the fiscal year 1951. The result was a strengthening of French control in southern Vietnam, where Vietminh guerrillas were distanced from Chinese aid. In January 1951 Giap decided, against Chinese advice, to deliver a coup de grâce in the Red River Delta. He failed because most of his troops were not yet ready for battle against French forces operating on interior lines with well-prepared defences.[39]

However, France was unable to suppress the rebellion in the Vietnamese countryside, despite escalating American aid, which by 1953 was paying for over 60 per cent of French military expenditure in Vietnam. Efforts, under American pressure, to increase the Vietnamese proportion of the French army were limited by French reluctance to rely on Vietnamese officers. The American administration urged more aggressive war plans. But a new French commander, General Henri Navarre, could do little with the need for so many of his troops to protect French-held positions from guerrilla attacks. He did look, however, for a showdown with the Vietminh by placing a strong garrison in the Dien Bien Phu valley in Western Tonkin, which was also designed to stop Vietminh incursions across the nearby border into Laos.[40]

The battle of Dien Bien Phu, which began on 13 March 1954, reflected Navarre's gross underestimation of Vietminh capabilities. The 12,000 French troops on the valley floor left control of the surrounding hills to enemy forces, in order to entice them to attack a well-defended position. The sixteen by eight kilometre width of the valley was regarded as adequate protection because of allegedly superior French firepower. However, since the end of the Korean War, the Vietminh army had received artillery from China, some of it captured from the Americans in that war. The French artillery in the battle was outnumbered by nearly four times as many Vietminh guns, which were of equal or better capability and were sited in much less-exposed firing positions. With this tactical advantage, the 47,000 Vietminh attackers were able to seize two forward French outposts that

38 Jaques Dalloz, *The War in Indo-China 1945–54* (Dublin 1990), 104–27. Greg Lockhart, *Nation in Arms: The Origins of the People's Army of Vietnam* (Sydney 1989), 225–9.
39 Lockhart, *Nation in Arms*, 230–42. Dalloz, *The War in Indo-China*, 132–3. George C. Herring, *America's Longest War: The United States and Vietnam 1950–1975* (3rd edition, New York 1996), 26–9.
40 George McT. Kahin, *Intervention: How America became Involved in Vietnam* (New York 1986), 42. Dalloz, *War in Indo-China*, 158–62. Robert D. Schulzinger, *A Time for War: The United States and Vietnam, 1941–1975* (New York 1997), 56–9.

commanded the valley's one airport, making inaccurate parachute drops the only source of French supply. Then, with the assistance of trenches creeping towards the remaining French lines and human wave assaults, the defenders were pounded into submission on 7 May 1954.[41]

Dien Bien Phu was not as decisive a battle as has been claimed. It had not dislodged the French from any other major position in Vietnam, while the Vietminh had expended much energy in winning the battle. Also, before it began, the French government was seeking a negotiated end to the war. A victory at Dien Bien Phu would have allowed the government to negotiate from a position of military strength.[42]

Another significance of the battle was pressure applied by Paris on Washington to intervene with air strikes against the attacking Vietminh. Such American intervention, including possible use of nuclear weapons, was supported by Admiral Arthur Radford, the chief of the JCS. Dulles opposed unilateral American intervention because of a fear that China might respond and that there would be another 'Korean War'. Intervention could only be achieved by 'united action' with Britain, France and other Asian countries, which he found on a visit to Britain and France was impossible to achieve. Also the Eisenhower administration knew that it would not win support in Congress to embark on unilateral intervention, which could well involve American soldiers in another Asian war so soon after the Korean War. However, the NSC was authorized to prepare a contingency plan for American military intervention if China entered the war.[43]

In fact the war between France and the Vietminh was resolved by a peace conference in Geneva, beginning one day after the fall of Dien Bien Phu, and also attended by Britain, the US, the USSR and China. The two communist powers pressured Ho Chi Minh to agree to a division of Vietnam to the bitter disappointment of many of Ho's colleagues. Khrushchev was pursuing his policy of peaceful existence with the West. China was concerned about prospects of American military intervention and had no wish, so soon after the exhausting Korean War, to be embroiled in another war with the US. After much negotiation, an agreement was signed on 20 July to divide Vietnam at the 17th parallel north latitude. Assisting this agreement was the appointment of a new French premier on 17 June,

---

41   For accounts of the battle from the Vietminh side see Lockhart, *Nation in Arms*, 252–63 and Peter Macdonald, *Giap: The Victor in Vietnam* (New York 1993), chs 10–11.
42   Dalloz, *War in Indo-China*, 168–75.
43   Melanie Billings-Yun, *Decision Against War: Eisenhower and Dien Bien Phu, 1964* (New York 1988), chs 4–6. William J. Duiker, *US Containment Policy and the Conflict in IndoChina* (Stanford 1994), ch. 5. Richard H. Immerman, *John Foster Dulles: Piety, Pragmatism and Power in US Foreign Policy* (Washington 1999), 87–93.

Pierre Mendès-France, who made a public commitment to achieve peace in Indochina within one month. The division of Vietnam was to be only temporary. The Geneva Agreements provided for free elections for a national government to be held in both sections of Vietnam within two years and to be supervised by representatives from a Western, a non-aligned and a communist country: Canada, India and Poland. A cease-fire also was established in Cambodia and Laos, which became fully independent.[44]

The US administration's participation in the Geneva Conference was negative. Eisenhower and Dulles were distrustful of negotiations with communists. Also they had no wish to be condemned at home, as was the Truman administration, for being soft on communism. Dulles revealed his uncompromising attitude during his short stay in Geneva by publicly snubbing Zhou Enlai. Washington believed that only a military solution imposed by Western powers could stop an eventual communist take-over of the whole of Vietnam and probably the rest of Indochina. The final agreements were better than expected, but Washington refused to sign them, pledging only not to 'disturb' their provisions and reserving the right to take necessary future action.[45]

Dulles's preferred option was to establish a collective security arrangement for protecting Southeast Asia from further communist advancement. The result was the formation in Manila in September 1954 of the South East Asia Treaty Organization (SEATO). The treaty's signatories – the US, France, Britain, Australia, New Zealand, Thailand, Pakistan, and the Philippines – agreed to consult and cooperate with each other against communist subversion or open attack and to provide a defensive umbrella over the states of Indochina. The Philippines saw the treaty as a means of reinforcing US commitment to its own defence, though it would have liked a guarantee included in the treaty. Thailand, in the past, had followed a 'bending in the wind' policy of conciliating more powerful nations in order to preserve its own independence. But in November 1947 there had been a military coup led by Field Marshall Plaek Phibunsongkhram. He sought military aid from the US in order to provide his army with modern weapons. Initially reluctant, the US responded positively in late 1949 with its new concern about Southeast Asia. The Thai government's response was a growing alignment with the US demonstrated by Thailand's offer of 4,000 troops to assist the beleaguered UN army early in the Korean War and a

---

44 Iya V. Gaiduk, 'The Soviet Union and Veitnam, 1945–75', in Peter Lowe (ed.), *The Vietnam War* (New York 1998), 133–6, Jian Chen, 'China and the Vietnam Wars, 1950–75', in Lowe (ed.), *The Vietnam War*, 158–62. Kuo-kang Shao, *Zhou Enlai and the Foundations of Chinese Foreign Policy* (New York 1996), 187–8. Herring, *America's Longest War*, 39–45.
45 Immerman, *John Foster Dulles*, 92–5.

contribution of 40,000 tons of rice for South Korean relief. Consequently, as well as economic assistance, US military aid to Thailand was worth $56 million by 1953. Therefore, Thailand was keen to join SEATO, though there was disappointment in Bangkok that the treaty was not a more cast-iron American guarantee of Thailand's security. The US Senate passed the SEATO treaty by a very big majority, a sign of the American political consensus about the Cold War.[46]

The US also decided to support the regime of a new ruler in the southern Republic of Vietnam (RVN), Ngo Dinh Diem. He was a French-educated Roman Catholic in a predominantly Buddhist country, who, since 1921, from the age of twenty, had been a civil servant and in 1933 was Bao Dai's secretary of the interior. Diem soon resigned from that post because of French interference. But his nationalist credentials were compromised by his collaboration in 1945 with Japanese authorities. He spent most of his subsequent time in Europe and the US, though displaying nationalist sentiments. He became Bao Dai's premier in June 1954, assisted by influential US friends. Not consulted in the making of the Geneva Agreements, Diem loudly denounced them as signing away more than half his country; and he turned to the US for support. Convinced that Diem represented a hope of establishing a strongly anti-communist South Vietnam, the US willingly supplied financial assistance, particularly to resettle some 900,000, mostly Catholic, refugees from the North, plus military aid for the South Vietnamese army. This financial assistance was worth $322.4 million in the fiscal year 1955–56.[47]

Diem was little better than Bao Dai as a focus for a viable anti-communist regime in Vietnam. His Roman Catholic religion and reliance upon the urban elite were poor qualifications for winning the support of Buddhist peasants. His wartime collaboration and subsequent absence overseas weakened his nationalist image in comparison with Ho Chi Minh, the leader of the long independence struggle against the French. The US recognized that Diem would have little hope of winning the projected 1956 election against Ho.

So, Diem was allowed to subvert the Geneva Agreements by demanding free elections and free speech in each zone before reunification elections

---

46   Ibid., 96–115. H.W. Brands, *Bound to Empire: The United States and the Philippines* (New York 1992), 258–9. Daniel Fineman, *A Special Relationship: The United States and Military Government in Thailand, 1947–1958* (Honolulu 1997), parts 1–3.

47   Lloyd C. Gardiner, *Approaching Vietnam: From World War II Through Dienbienphu 1941–1954* (New York 1988), 292–3. Short, *Origins of the Vietnam War*, 190–1. Carl A. Thayer, *War by Other Means: National Liberation and Revolution in Viet-Nam 1954–60* (Sydney 1988), 123. Ronald H. Spector, *Advice and Support: The Early Years of the US Army in Vietnam 1941–1960* (New York 1985), chs 12–15.

were held, and then to renege on those terms in the RVN. In 1955, voters were given a referendum choice between himself and Bao Dai as Chief of State, which was fraudulently organized to give Diem 98 per cent of the vote. Elections for a RVN national assembly in 1956 were heavily influenced by the government's firm control of the press and suppression of opponents, which ensured that only three of the assembly's 123 members were a genuine opposition. Diem's dictatorial pretensions had already by 1955 provoked a severe internal crisis, when he alienated three powerful politico-religious sects, the Cao Dai, a syncretic religion based on elements of Catholic Church order, the millenarian Buddhist Hoa Hao, and the mafia-style Binh Xuyen. But with a fund of $12 million secretly supplied by the US Central Intelligence Agency (CIA) Diem bought off key Cao Dai and Hoa Hao leaders, integrating some of their troops into his army, which then crushed a Binh Xuyen revolt. American advisers in Saigon at the time urged Washington to abandon Diem, but the surprise victory of the RVN army (ARVN) in the civil strife convinced Dulles that he should continue to support the nation, which was kept alive with economic and military aid. From 1955–56 to 1959–60 this assistance was worth $1.584 billion and fostered dependency rather than internal economic development.[48]

Diem paid only lip service to democratic values. There was a widespread campaign of violence and oppression against the regime's political opponents administered by Diem's ruthless brother, Nhu. The French-trained chief of the ARVN's General Staff, Tran Van Don, commented that Diem and Nhu 'resorted to arbitrary arrests, confinement in concentration camps for undetermined periods of time . . . and assassinations of people suspected of communist leanings. Their use of Gestapo-like police raids and torture were known and decried everywhere.' Furthermore, their 'repression spread to people who simply opposed their regime'. A later American Defense Department analysis concluded that the government's 'Communist Denunciation Campaign thoroughly terrified the Vietnamese peasants and detracted significantly from the regime's popularity.'[49]

Under American pressure, Diem's government did legislate to redistribute land, much of it abandoned during the first Vietnam War, to landless peasants, who formed 80 per cent of the population of the Mekong Delta. But former landlords now living in urban areas were given the right to

---

48 Herring, *America's Longest War*, ch. 2. Thayer, *War by Other Means*, 123. William S. Turley, *The Second Indochina War: A Short Political and Military History, 1954–1975* (Boulder 1986), 13–15.

49 Tran Van Don, *Our Endless War: Inside Vietnam* (San Rafael 1978), 66. *The Pentagon Papers: The Defense Department History of United States Decisionmaking on Vietnam*, vol. I (Senator Gravel Edition, Boston 1971) (*PP*), 255.

impose rents on peasants who occupied the vacated land, which often exceeded the government's 25 per cent maximum rate. There was also corruption and inefficiency in the administration of the land reform, including preference for Catholic refugees from the North. Consequently, only 10 per cent of the landless South Vietnamese became property owners. Diem also took away the traditional right of villagers to elect their own village chiefs, fearing that Vietminh people would win, and appointing instead mostly Northern Catholics.[50]

Diem's regime therefore created fertile ground for a communist-led resistance movement in the RVN. Initially the Vietnamese Communist Party (VCP), which had led the struggle against French rule, accepted the call from Geneva for a cease-fire. The party looked forward confidently to an imminent DRV take-over of the whole country in national elections and therefore stood aloof from the civil strife in the RVN in 1955. However, Diem's campaign of violent repression against the VCP, drove the party underground. As many as 90 per cent of the party's cells had been destroyed by mid 1956 with tens of thousands of cadres killed or jailed and tortured. The party concentrated on rebuilding its rural strength by exploiting peasant grievances against the inequities of land reform and the imposition of authoritarian and often corrupt village officials. The VCP still faced much ARVN violence, which provoked some violent responses by its members. But the party renounced at this stage an armed uprising, influenced by its North Vietnamese members. In the DRV, the VCP was concentrating upon rebuilding the war-ravaged countryside, which included coping with a severe threat of famine, for which deliveries of rice from the USSR and China were valuable. The VCP in the North also was facing problems involved in land reform which, it later admitted, involved excessive government repression.[51]

In 1959, however, the VCP decided to launch an armed struggle to overthrow Diem's regime and reunite Vietnam. The 15th VCP Central Committee Plenum in January 1959, resolved to establish a National Front for the Liberation of South Viet-Nam (NLF) to be controlled by the party's South Vietnamese central committee and to be supported by a 'liberation army'. A member of Vietnam's Foreign Ministry at the time, Nguyen Khac Huynh, explained, 'we had given up a strategy of purely political struggle, which could not succeed due to Ngo Dinh Diem's brutal tactics against our people'. Also by 1959 North Vietnam had achieved some economic stability

---

50 *The Pentagon Papers*, vol. I, 67–9. Thayer, *War by Other Means*, ch. 6. Kahin, *Intervention*, ch. 4.
51 Thayer, *War by Other Means*, chs 2–7. Ngo Vinh Long, 'South Vietnam', in Lowe (ed.), *The Vietnam War*, 67–8.

with a record harvest in the previous year and had established good relations not only with the USSR and China but also with Laos and Cambodia
and non-aligned Burma and India. China, the USSR and communist Eastern European countries were providing aid worth over US$570 million
from 1955 to 1960, though this was less than half the level of US aid to the
RVN. However, Nguyen commented: 'Our greatest difficulty was gaining
support from the Soviet Union and China for our new policy of struggle for
reunification . . . It took all of Ho Chi Minh's great skills to obtain support
from both Moscow and Beijing for Resolution 15.'[52]

North Vietnam had confidence in an uprising in the South. Many party
members there had long been calling for a general rebellion, and some,
particularly in the highlands and in the Mekong Delta, had been maintaining
armed struggle and local violence, which was spreading. Indeed, Hanoi
faced the danger of losing control of a growing popular revolt in the South.
To avoid US military retaliation against the DRV, it was decided to rely
mainly on South Vietnamese resources, including Southerners returning
from the North. The struggle was to be directed by the Southern NLF,
which was launched by the VCP in December 1960, though it included
non-communist nationalists. Insurgent violence initially targeted rural
government officials – 1,400 were assassinated or kidnapped by the end of
1960. This violence was designed to destroy government influence in rural
areas, where armed guerrilla units, which in February 1961 were called the
People's Liberation Armed Force (PLAF), were being organized. These
insurgents, who were contemptuously called Viet Cong by their opponents,
already numbered 16,000 by the end of 1960, according to US intelligence.[53]

By August 1960 there was serious concern in Washington about 'the
stability and effectiveness of President Diem's government', as expressed in
a State Department Special National Intelligence Estimate. It noted that in
South Vietnam there was not only increasing PLAF activity; there was also
criticism among intellectuals 'and to a lesser extent in labor and business
groups' about the 'pervasive influence' of the government's Can Lao party
controlled by Nhu. It was silencing dissidents with political arrests, beatings,
torture and murders. The report condemned 'Diem's virtual one-man rule
and the growing evidence of corruption in high places'. It further acknowledged that the government lacked 'positive support among the people in

52 Thayer, *War by Other Means*, ch. 8. Robert S. McNamara, James G. Blight and Robert K.
    Brigham, *Argument Without End: In Search of Answers to the Vietnam Tragedy* (New York 1999),
    93.
53 Thayer, *War by Other Means*, ch. 9. Ken Post, *Revolution, Socialism and Nationalism in VietNam*,
    vol. II (Aldershot 1989–90), chs 5, 9–10. Ngo Vinh Long, 'South Vietnam', in Lowe (ed.),
    The Vietnam War, 69–70.

the countryside'. This was principally because of the 'ineptitude and arrogance of many local and provincial officials . . . the harshness with which many peasants have been forced to contribute their labor to government programs, and the unsettling economic and social effects' of a resettlement program to enhance government authority. However, Diem dismissed his critics as 'dupes of the Communists', and was concentrating on a military solution to the problems. Yet the seven ARVN divisions, which were assisted by a 675 strong American Military Assistance and Advisory Group (MAAG), had been trained and deployed mostly to resist 'an overt attack from North Vietnam'. In General Tran's view the Americans 'put us in the same mold as Koreans' and trained the ARVN to fight another Korean War.[54]

Nevertheless, the State Department report concluded that 'these adverse trends are not irreversible', if Diem could take measures to protect and win the support of peasants and to 'reduce the corruption and excesses of his regime'. There was a strong but blind faith within the Eisenhower administration that, with more time and continued American support, Diem's regime could survive as a bulwark against the tide of advancing communism.[55]

Suppression of rebellion in the Philippines

The Truman and Eisenhower administrations in the 1950s had more success in their support for the suppression of the communist-led insurrection in the Philippines. In 1950 the Huk insurgents in central Luzon had grown in number to at least 12,000 chiefly because of the brutality of the government's attempts to defeat them. The alliance since 1948 between the communist PKP and the peasant-based Huks had improved the insurgency's organizational base. The Huks demonstrated their strength with two waves of daring raids in April and August 1950 on towns and barrios. Their best prize was the seizure of 80,000 pesos from the Lugun provincial treasury in Santa Cruz. This offensive strategy was the idea of the professionally educated and Marxist brothers Joseph and Jesus Lava, who had taken over direction of Huk policy from Taruc. But the Lavas mistakenly believed that a financial crisis in the Philippines would create a genuine revolutionary climate that would soon lead to the downfall of the Liberal Philippines government,

---

54 'Short-Term Trends in South Vietnam', 23 Aug. 1960, *Foreign Relations of the United States (FRUS), 1958–1960*, vol. I: Vietnam (Washington 1986), 536–41. Don, *Our Endless War*, 149.

55 David L. Anderson, *Trapped by Success: The Eisenhower Administration and Vietnam, 1953–1961* (New York 1992), 196–7.

whereas outside central Luzon Filipino peasants generally remained apathetic to the Huk cause.[56]

Furthermore, the Philippines President, Elpidio Quirino, took an important step, at American behest, when in September 1950 he appointed Ramon Magsaysay as Secretary of the Department of National Defense. The son of a school-teacher, Magsaysay had been born in 1907 among peasants of central Luzon. A commerce graduate, he served with US backed guerrillas during the Second World War and afterwards became a Liberal member of Congress and chairman of the House Committee on National Defense. In 1950 he travelled to the US to request assistance for the financially harassed government and returned with $10 million as an emergency grant with promises of more money to come.[57]

Magsaysay, as defence secretary, demanded a free hand in order to introduce drastic army reforms aiming to remove the military brutality that had driven peasants to join the Huks. He was successful in giving the army new zeal to pursue Huk groups without stealing from or otherwise mistreating peasants. There were still some military excesses, but the new approach coupled with offers of amnesty for Huk guerrillas, which were rigorously honoured, started to thin their ranks. Former Huks also contributed to army intelligence. Appreciating the socio-economic reasons for the peasant-based Huk support, Magsaysay convinced the government that it should implement agrarian reforms, which forced landlords to allow peasants to keep more of the harvest. Rural development projects were introduced, and financial assistance was given to former insurgents to settle on land away from central Luzon, especially on Mindanao. Magsaysay's own adherence to a simple life style and his willingness to travel to talk with peasants made him a very popular leader.[58]

The military and economic reforms implemented or inspired by Magsaysay and his personal popularity were the most important reasons for the decline of the Huk insurgency after 1950. The reforms greatly improved the government's image among central Luzon peasants. The military reforms also resulted in much better targeted military pressure against the Huks, though there was still some poor army discipline. Assistance came from the Joint United States Military Advisory Group, which by 1952 consisted of

---

56 Eduardo Lachica, *The Huks: Philippine Agrarian Society in Revolt* (New York 1971), 123–30. Benedict J. Kerkvliet, *The Huk Rebellion: A Study of Peasant Revolt in the Philippines* (Berkeley 1977), 203–33.

57 Lawrence M. Greenberg, *The Hukbalahap Insurrection: A Case Study of a Successful Anti-Insurgency Operation in the Philippines, 1946–1955* (Washington 1987), 79–81.

58 Ibid., 82–95.

thirty-two officers and twenty-six soldiers to give military advice and administer American military aid. It also was committed to support economic reform on the basis of a correct American Embassy analysis that the Philippine government had lost the trust of most of the central Luzon peasant population. The American assistance program used people who had familiarity with the Philippines, and it drew upon a reservoir of Filipino good will towards Americans who had liberated their country from the Japanese and quickly granted them independence. American financial aid, which from 1951 to 1956 amounted to $500 million, was a vital factor in the defeat of the insurrection because it enabled the implementation of the important economic and military reforms. The close relationship between American capital investment and the Filipino ruling classes assured a high degree of compliance with American supported reforms, which greatly eased the way for the implementation of Magsaysay's reform agenda. With declining peasant support and increased government military pressure, the Huks were reduced by 1956 to a few small half-starved bands. Only a few survived by 1960. However, Magsaysay, who was president from November 1953 until killed in an aircraft crash in March 1957, failed to implement fundamental reform of the landlord-dominated society of central Luzon, and this stored serious problems for the future.[59]

Defeating insurgency in Malaya

Defeating the communist insurgency in Malaya was more difficult. Although MRLA insurgents after 1951 never numbered more than 6,000 – about half the largest number of Huks – they operated over a much larger area than central Luzon and had the protection of a more jungle-covered and mountainous terrain. The MRLA had more definite targets: British personnel, the economic infrastructure and the security forces. Furthermore, they were more tightly disciplined than the Huks, with the assistance in 1951 of some Chinese army officers who infiltrated Malaya. A high point of MRLA success was the ambushing and killing of the British High Commissioner, Sir Henry Gurney, on 6 October 1951. That year the insurgents killed 504 government security men and 533 civilians, many of whom were managers and workers on rubber estates and at tin mines. A new strategy to

---

59 Kerkvliet, *The Huk Rebellion*, 233–48. Amanda Doronila, *The State, Economic Transformation, and Political Change in the Philippines, 1946–1972* (Singapore 1992), 103–6.

drive out the British was the killing of wives and children of British planters and miners.[60]

In 1951, however, 1,077 MRLA members were killed, the highest number to that year, which was a result of increasing government efficiency and pressure. Improvements started with the arrival in Malaya in April 1950 of Lieutenant-General Sir Harold Briggs, a retired wartime divisional commander. Appointed the director of all operations against the MRLA, he quickly perceived that a major fault of previous efforts had been the absence of a coordinated plan.

The Briggs plan provided the basis for government operations for the rest of the Emergency. A major aim was to deny supplies and intelligence to the MRLA, which involved relocating Chinese squatters into 'new villages'. Given no choice, by the end of 1951 385,000 people had been shifted to 492 of these settlements. Initially poorly protected and serviced, the new villages were being improved during 1952 with new government revenue generated by a boom in rubber and tin prices. This prosperity was caused by the Korean War, which proved an economic salvation for Malaya. The Briggs plan also targeted the 60,000 Sakai aboriginal people in the mountains, many of whom had been coerced by the MRLA to provide food and guides. Jungle forts were constructed to bring the Sakai under British protection and to provide medicine and trading opportunities. Another important initiative of the Briggs plan was to coordinate all sources of intelligence under one director and an intelligence committee. Information played an increasingly important role in apprehension of insurgents. Close cooperation between small groups of troops and police further improved operations against MRLA squads with larger military forces blocking insurgent sources of supply. A very tight control of food supplies, to the extent of searching villagers and workers, was a major part of the program.[61]

Gurney's assassination also provoked more British financial support for the anti-MRLA campaign. General Sir Gerald Templer, the British Director of Military Intelligence, arrived to succeed Briggs, who retired in November 1951. Templer employed mass leaflet drops and broadcasted messages from aircraft in a successful psychological campaign to entice insurgents to surrender. Rewards were increased for the capture of those who kept fighting. Such methods alongside greater military pressure contributed to a downhill run in MRLA fortunes after 1951. However, to combat fewer than 6,000 guerrillas, 40,500 overseas troops were used in 1952, made

---

60 Robert Jackson, *The Malayan Emergency: The Commonwealth's Wars 1948–1966* (London 1991), 38–41. Short, *The Communist Insurrection*, ch. 12.
61 Short, *The Communist Insurrection*, chs 15–17. Richard Stubbs, *Hearts and Minds in Guerilla Warfare: The Malayan Emergency 1948–1960* (Singapore 1989), ch. 4.

up of seven British, seven Gurkha, one African and one Fijian battalions, which were joined in 1955 by one from Australia. There were also 28,500 Malay troops and police supported by 39,000 Special Constables along with the much larger Home Guard. By the end of 1956 the MRLA had shrunk to an estimated 2,063. Fighting still continued, but by 1960 the MRLA, a pale shadow of its former self, had been driven to the Thai border area. Furthermore, the surviving insurgents were being suppressed by the Malayan government, which had achieved the independence that had been delayed by the Emergency and was granted in 1957 when the insurgency largely had been defeated.[62]

Important in the defeat of the MRLA was a new government approach after 1951 to attempt to win more Malay and Chinese support. Significant for this process was a commodity price boom generated by the Korean War, which greatly increased government revenue to spend on the new measures to combat the MRLA and brought widespread prosperity to the people of the colony. Ironically, an MRLA policy decision in 1951 to compete for popularity by stopping attacks on the civilian population also improved government morale and increased Malay support for the government cause. The MRLA was further restricted to the Chinese minority in Malaya for its support and by lack of any direct line of communication with a friendly nation which so benefited the Vietminh in Tonkin. The Huks also had been limited by geographic isolation and minority peasant support. Consequently the MRLA and the Huks suffered from growing arms and ammunition shortages that were the opposite experience of the Vietminh. However, both the Philippines and Malayan governments needed to change their policies in 1950–51 to seek support from their civilian populations in order to gain supremacy over the insurgents, an approach not really adopted by the French in Vietnam.[63]

Opposition to the US–Japan Security Treaty

Communists were blamed in Washington for provoking anti-US demonstrations in Japan in 1960. The demonstrators, however, were mainly members of the Japanese Socialist Party and other non-communists concerned about the signing of a revised security treaty between Japan and the US. The new treaty was long desired by leaders of the Japanese government to

---

62   Stubbs, *Hearts and Minds*, chs 5–8. Jackson, *The Malayan Emergency*, chs 5–8, 13. Larry E. Cable, *Conflict of Myths: The Development of American Counterinsurgency Doctrine and the Vietnam War* (New York 1986), 82.

63   Stubbs, *Hearts and Minds*, ch. 9.

change the terms of the 1952 treaty that gave the US the freedom to move military forces in and around Japan without any guarantee to defend that nation. The new treaty still permitted US military bases in Japan but required consultation with Japan for deployment of forces from them or introduction of nuclear weapons. It also obliged America to defend Japan against foreign aggression. Japan was required to cooperate in its own self-defence and was not required to pay for American defence costs in Japan. Japanese critics complained that the treaty would obligate their country to develop armed forces and would make Japan a target in any future American war with China or the USSR, which both denounced the treaty. There was also public concern about such threats after the shooting down of an American U2 spy-plane over the USSR when it was known that U2 planes were based in Japan. The LDP Prime Minster, Kishi Nobusuke, contributed to the crisis by ramming the treaty through the Japanese Diet without enough time to debate the issues. A result of the violent demonstrations was the cancellation of a projected visit by Eisenhower to Japan in June 1960. Kishi was forced to resign during the protests, which were also directed against him as a previous member of Tojo's wartime Cabinet. But the LDP easily won national elections later in the year and thus preserved the alliance between Japan and the US.[64]

The US, the USSR and Indonesia

The US also was concerned about growing communist influence in the important Southwest Pacific Basin country of Indonesia. With its large population and its economic wealth in rubber, tin, oil and other resources Indonesia was regarded as a vital sector of non-communist Southeast Asia. During the 1950s the communist PKI made a spectacular comeback from its decimation in 1948. Under the youthful and pragmatic leadership of D.N. Aidit, the PKI sought to become the largest political party. In the 1955 election it achieved 16 per cent of the vote, only 6 per cent behind the leading party, the PNI. The PKI was kept out of government by a coalition of the other three main parties. However, resultant internal divisions in Prime Minister Ali Sastroamidjojo's Cabinet encouraged President Sukarno to call for 'guided democracy', rather than party competition, which the PKI supported. Also in 1956–57 army rebellions in Sumatra and in Sulawesi

---

64 Michael Schaller, *Altered States: The United States and Japan since the Occupation* (New York 1997), chs 8–9.

were threatening to fragment the nation. In this crisis atmosphere, with the support of the national army, Sukarno proclaimed martial law and introduced 'guided democracy', under which the PKI moved to improve its position. It was able to exploit a crisis in November 1957, when a motion calling on the UN to support negotiations about Irian Jaya failed to receive the necessary two-thirds majority in the General Assembly. In the resultant furore in Indonesia about Western influence in the UN, all Dutch properties were seized and Dutch personnel were expelled from Indonesia; and PKI and PNI unions started taking over the abandoned Dutch enterprises. In local Java elections the PKI was out-polling the PNI.[65]

The US was alarmed at growing PKI influence. Indeed, from October 1957 American arms were being supplied to the rebels in Sumatra and Sulawesi with the aim of either overthrowing the government in Jakarta or radically changing it. Also CIA pilots flew planes which bombed Indonesian forces. But early in 1958 Indonesian army and air force action crushed the rebellions and on 18 May Indonesia captured an American pilot, Allen Pope, on a bombing mission over Ambon. US–Indonesian relations were seriously damaged. The Philippines, Nationalist China, Thailand, Malaya and Singapore all provided bases for American actions to aid the rebels, and Australia gave secret vocal support. One of Sukarno's responses – imposing a ban on activities of the KMT in Indonesia – gave the PKI a chance to increase its support in the local Chinese community. Furthermore, Sukarno turned to Eastern Europe and the Soviet Union for arms supplies and for economic development projects. For these purposes Khrushchev supplied a credit of $US 117.5 million in 1959 and another $US 250 million on a visit to Jakarta in January 1960. Eisenhower left to his successor a serious concern about communist influence in Indonesia.[66]

Conclusions

By 1960 the Western Pacific Basin had become a major battleground in the Cold War between the communist world and the US led anti-communist coalition. A stalemate had been preserved after the expenditure of much

---

65   M.C. Ricklefs, *A History of Modern Indonesia* (2nd edition, Stanford 1993), chs 18–19. Rex Mortimer, *Indonesian Communism under Sukarno: Ideology and Politics 1959–1965* (Ithaca 1974), chs 1–4.

66   Ricklefs, *History of Modern Indonesia*, ch. 18. R.A. Longmire, *Soviet Relations with South-East Asia: An Historical Survey* (London 1989), 53–7. Audrey R. and George McT. Kahin, *Subversion as Foreign Policy: The Secret Eisenhower and Dulles Debacle in Indonesia* (Seattle 1995), 120–6, 148–52, 155–8, 169–95.

blood and money in the Korean War. That war, however, had beneficial consequences for the non-communist cause in providing the impetus for a peace treaty with Japan, by giving a crucial boost to the Japanese economy and by generating extra wealth in Malaya for defeating the communist insurgency there, which in turn allowed the granting of independence to Malaya and to Singapore. British military power remained in the region to protect its former colonies and its surviving outpost in East Asia, Hong Kong. In Vietnam, France, despite strong American financial backing, lost the struggle to hold the free world line in northern Indochina, leaving the US to support South Vietnam. However, US pressure on China by supporting the KMT regime on Taiwan had helped to widen growing cracks in the Soviet–Chinese alliance. Japan had become a major bastion for American power in East Asia, though not all its citizens were happy about the American alliance. Also in North Vietnam, a decision was made to launch a major communist-led insurrection in South Vietnam. Furthermore, the Soviet Union was financing an increase in the military muscles of Indonesia, where the Communist Party was growing in influence. The Western Pacific Basin was to remain a major Cold War battleground in the 1960s.

CHAPTER THREE

Confrontation and Cooperation in East and Southeast Asia, 1961–1968

The biggest issue in the Pacific Basin in the 1960s was the war in Vietnam in which a communist-led insurgency struggled against US supported South Vietnam. This conflict gradually involved and affected many other Pacific Basin countries. The war also generated new economic wealth for Japan and other East and Southeast Asian nations, setting some on a road of increasing economic growth. The nature of that war, the international involvement in it, and its wider influences are the major themes of this chapter. Another subject relates to the ending of colonial empires in the Southwestern Pacific Basin. This was Indonesia's campaign to annex Dutch New Guinea and its Confrontation against the new Malaysian federation. But the end of Confrontation ushered in a new era of cooperation in Southeast Asia.

The Kennedy Administration and Vietnam

John F. Kennedy, who in January 1961 at forty-three years of age became the first American president born in the twentieth-century, had based much of his presidential campaigning for the Democratic Party on the theme that the US was losing world power. He complained that Eisenhower's Republican administration had presided over a decline in the size of US armed forces, had allowed the development of an alleged new Soviet missile supremacy and had failed to prevent an outbreak of communist expansionism in regions such as Cuba, Indochina and the African Congo. Kennedy called for 'New Frontier' policies to get the country moving again.

However, Kennedy sought a new flexibility in US relations with the USSR. He wished to move away from dependence on the Eisenhower administration's threat of massive nuclear retaliation, though ironically his mistaken belief in Soviet nuclear supremacy started a nuclear arms race between the two powers. Kennedy sought to increase America's conventional military power so that his government could respond in low-key ways to communist expansionism. He also had a strong political reason to beat an anti-communist drum given previous Republican campaigns against alleged Democratic Party softness about communism.[1]

Along with wider world problems of alleged Soviet expansionism, Kennedy was briefed by Eisenhower about a threat to the independent kingdom of Laos in Indochina. Plane loads of arms had been arriving there from the USSR for North Vietnamese-supported Pathet Lao rebels. Kennedy seized on this Soviet threat in his inaugural address to Congress and in other public statements. This public indignation masked in fact heavy involvement by the CIA in equipping and training a rival army, which was also aiming to seize power in Laos. There was a clear threat of direct US–USSR military confrontation, which caused Kennedy to reluctantly accept a Soviet proposal for a cease-fire in May 1961 in preparation for a peace conference in Geneva in 1962. That was followed by a Soviet withdrawal from Laos.[2]

However, the Laos scare directed Kennedy's attention to Diem's regime in South Vietnam, which was struggling to suppress another alleged Soviet-backed communist insurgency. Washington also had become alarmed about a well-publicized speech by Khrushchev in Moscow on 6 January 1961 expressing Soviet support for national wars of liberation, though the rhetoric was mostly directed at bolstering USSR communist world leadership credentials in the growing split with China. The Kennedy administration was further warned by its people in South Vietnam that the PLAF was winning the struggle against the ARVN, which could be reversed with better support for Diem. The MAAG in Saigon had submitted a counterinsurgency plan, which advocated American financial aid to increase the size of the ARVN and the Vietnamese Civil Guard, which Kennedy endorsed. He authorized an additional $42 million to the existing $70.9 million in military aid, 100 extra personnel for the MAAG and 400 Special Forces troops to train ARVN soldiers in counterinsurgency tactics. Kennedy also appointed a new ambassador, Frederick Nolting, a career diplomat serving with NATO

---

1   Thomas G. Paterson, 'John F. Kennedy's Quest for Victory and Global Crisis', in Thomas G. Paterson (ed.), *Kennedy's Quest for Victory: American Foreign Policy, 1961–1963* (New York 1989), 3–23.
2   Interview with Roger Hilsman in Michael Charlton and Anthony Moncrieff, *Many Reasons Why: The American Involvement in Vietnam* (Ringwood 1979), 78. Short, *Origins of the Vietnam War*, 227–35. Orrin Schwab, *Defending the Free World: John F. Kennedy, Lyndon Johnson, and the Vietnam War, 1961–1965* (Westport 1998), 5–6.

in Paris, who knew little about Vietnam. His instructions were to give more support to Diem and oversee 'a stepped-up' program of military assistance to the ARVN, which had some focus on economic development.[3]

Kennedy did receive contrary advice from within his administration. George Ball, the Under Secretary for Foreign Affairs, considered that sending more military advisers to the RVN 'would gradually involve us in a military contest'. He privately warned Kennedy that 'if we go down that road we might have within five years, 300,000 men in the rice paddies and jungles of Vietnam . . . impossible terrain in which to engage our forces'. But Kennedy insisted: 'That will never happen.'[4]

In fact Kennedy was fending off strong advice for much more US support for South Vietnam. Vice-President Lyndon Johnson went to Vietnam to show the American flag and brought back in May 1961 a recommendation for a 'major effort' to assist the struggle there against communism rather than 'throw in the towel' and signal to the world that 'we . . . don't stand by our friends'. General Maxwell Taylor, Kennedy's military adviser, and Walt Rostow, an economist and special foreign security affairs adviser, also visited the RVN and produced a joint report advocating increasing US military aid, sending more military advisers and despatching 8,000 US soldiers under the cover of flood relief aid in the Mekong Delta. Kennedy resisted sending any American troops, but he agreed to increase the number of military advisers. By the end of 1962 there were 11,000 of them plus 300 US military aircraft and 120 American helicopters in South Vietnam.[5]

This escalation of US involvement in South Vietnam was a significant decision by Kennedy's administration. William Bundy, the Assistant Secretary for Defense and International Affairs at the Pentagon, explained the major reason: 'I think it was the sense that you had to stand firm in this area, that otherwise the idea of Communism as the wave of the future would have a very great effect.' The Defense Secretary, Robert McNamara, later commented: 'We believed that if the South Vietnamese domino fell, then all of Southeast Asia – Thailand, Indonesia, Malaya, the Philippines, even Japan – could be at risk.' The administration also had

---

3   Anthony Short, *The Origins of the Vietnam War* (London 1989), 236–46. George C. Herring, *America's Longest War: The United States and Vietnam 1950–1975* (3rd edition, New York 1996), 73–8. Interview with Frederick Nolting in Charlton and Moncrieff, *Many Reasons Why*, 70–1.
4   Interview with George Ball in Charlton and Moncrieff, *Many Reasons Why*, 78.
5   Congressional Research Service, Library of Congress, *The US Government and the Vietnam War: Executive and Legislative Roles and Relationships (UGVW)* (Washington 1985), Part II, 45. John Newman, *JFK and Vietnam: Deception, Intrigue and the Struggle for Power* (New York 1992), 130–9. Lawrence Bassett and Stephen E. Pelz, 'The Failed Search for Victory: Vietnam and the Politics of War', in Paterson (ed.), *Kennedy's Quest for Victory*, 240–1.

confidence in the ability of American economic and military power to conquer communist expansionism. Furthermore, there was an important political motive. When in September 1963, in the face of grave problems confronting Diem's government, Kennedy was asked if he would reduce aid to South Vietnam, he said 'no' because 'strongly in our mind is what happened in the case of China . . . We don't want that'.[6]

But South Vietnam was in a more parlous state than Kennedy envisaged. By 1961 over half of its villages had come under NLF influence. Insurgent violence was an important reason. In Long An province near Saigon, during the week of Tet in January 1960, twenty-six village chiefs and other government supporters were murdered, which subsequently caused many of Diem's officials in the province to resign or flee; and part of the land in Long An was being redistributed by NLF-established peasant committees. NLF control of the countryside had deprived the government of much of its taxation revenue, causing heavy reliance on American aid. Indeed, many formerly fatalistic peasants had been radicalized by their experience of the eight years of the first Vietnam War. Also, as Tran Van Don admits, the NLF in urban areas succeeded in enlisting the help of non-communist 'progressive intellectuals, liberal bourgeois and frustrated nationalists' who 'had been harassed previously, or jailed by President Diem's overzealous secret police'. Furthermore, the first Vietnam War had given many members of the PLAF significant experience of guerrilla warfare. Hit-and-run tactics and sophisticated methods of deception, such as long underground communication tunnels, were well developed.[7]

There were also limits to the quality of the Kennedy administration's knowledge about South Vietnam. Taylor admitted that on his visit he 'found very quickly that the information we were getting back in Washington was highly unreliable'. Nolting remained convinced that the increased American assistance 'began to reverse the tide of Communist success' in 1962. But in a letter to the State Department in July 1961 he admitted that it was difficult to discern if the war against the PLAF was 'getting better' but stressed a need to 'create a new and winning psychology'. He therefore

---

6   Interviews with Maxwell Taylor and William Bundy in Charlton and Moncrieff, *Many Reasons Why*, 72–5, 69. Robert S. McNamara, James G. Blight and Robert K. Brigham, *Argument Without End: In Search of Answers to the Vietnam Tragedy* (New York 1999), 22. *Public Papers of the Presidents of the United States, John F. Kennedy, 1963* (Washington 1964), 659.

7   Jeffrey Race, *War Comes to Long An: Revolutionary Conflict in a Vietnamese Province* (Berkeley 1973), 113–34. James Walker Trullinger, Jr, *Village at War: An Account of Revolution in Vietnam* (New York 1980), 85–90. Bassett and Pelz, 'Failed Search for Victory', 81. Tran Van Don, *Our Endless War: Inside Vietnam* (San Rafael 1978), 81. William S. Turley, *The Second Indochina War: A Short Political and Military History, 1954–1975* (Boulder 1986), 39–40.

wrote: 'I have taken a much more optimistic line in conversations with other diplomats and with the press here.' He became a victim of his own deception as indicated by his continued faithful support during 1963 of Diem, whose popularity in South Vietnam was fast diminishing.[8]

Indeed, Nolting's estimate of an improving war situation in 1962 belied the dismal performance of the ARVN. Lieutenant-Colonel John Paul Vann, who arrived in Vietnam in 1962 to act as senior American adviser to an ARVN division, quickly noted how: 'Petty jealousies among battalion and regimental commanders take precedence over, and detract from, the primary mission of closing with and destroying the enemy.' Officers used the artillery and aircraft supplied by the US to bombard villages indiscriminately on the mere suspicion of a PLAF presence. The torturing and killing of prisoners also revolted him. He could think of no worse ways to fight a war.[9]

Kennedy was keen on the idea of developing more effective methods of combating communist-led insurgencies and applying them in South Vietnam. However, recommended policies using unconventional small group action coupled with economic aid for indigenous social development were subverted by US army conventional warfare doctrines that concentrated on search and destroy missions using massively superior American fire power. Washington also persuaded Diem to introduce a strategic hamlet system, duplicating the successful scheme adopted during the Malayan emergency, as a non-military option to counter the insurgency. However, the strategic hamlet program was not the answer to the NLF insurgency. Vietnamese peasants were far more rooted to their home villages than were Chinese squatters in Malaya. Also, a large number of the strategic hamlets were incapable of being protected from determined guerrilla attack, especially because insufficient efforts were made to rid the hamlets of PLAF members living inside them. Nor was there a coordinated anti-insurgent campaign as in Malaya. Indeed, many hamlets were deprived of promised resources by the corrupt management of the program.[10]

Nor, compared with the Philippines, was there effective indigenous leadership to support counterinsurgency programs. Diem was not the Magsaysay

---

8 Interview with Taylor in Charlton and Moncrieff, *Many Reasons Why*, 72–3. Frederick Nolting, *From Trust to Tragedy: The Political Memoirs of Frederick Nolting, Kennedy's Ambassador to Diem's Vietnam* (New York 1988), 43, 147.

9 Neil Sheehan, *A Bright Shining Lie: John Paul Vann and America in Vietnam* (New York 1988), 91, 101–10.

10 Schwab, *Defending the Free World*, 40–4. Cable, *Conflict of Myths*, ch. 11. Eric M. Bergerud, *The Dynamics of Defeat: The Vietnam War in Hau Nghia Province* (Boulder 1991), 33–8. Louis A. Wiesner, *Victims and Survivors: Displaced Persons and Other War Victims in Viet-Nam, 1954–1975* (Westport 1988), ch. 3.

of South Vietnam. Diem and Nhu had no intention of giving up any power by implementing the democratic and social reforms that Nolting urged. They believed the US needed them more than the reverse, a misconception fostered by Nolting and by other Americans.

The day of reckoning came on 1 November 1963 when South Vietnamese army units attacked the presidential palace, from which Diem and Nhu fled, to be murdered the next morning by ARVN soldiers. An important background to this coup were Buddhist riots in May 1963 in Hue, the diocesan seat of another of Diem's brothers, Roman Catholic Archbishop Ngo Dinh Thuc. Buddhist priests had been forbidden by Catholic city officials to celebrate Buddha's birthday in the same public manner that the jubilee of Thuc's ordination had been celebrated in the previous month. Though the Catholic Minister of the Interior overturned the decision, it had already sparked off long-standing Buddhist grievances about the mono- polizing of RVN public positions by Catholics. In the two months after the riot, there were five successive self-immolations by Buddhist monks calling for the overthrow of Diem; and anti-government elements, includ- ing the NLF, used Buddhist protests to further their own anti-Diem cause. This dissent finally convinced the Kennedy administration of the need for change in Saigon. So Nolting was replaced by a Republican Party leader, Henry Cabot Lodge, in a bipartisan display of American concern for the RVN's future. There was still nervousness in Washington about backing a coup that might not succeed. On 30 October Lodge was told that if he 'should conclude that there is not clearly a high prospect of success' he should dissuade the plotting generals. But Lodge considered that 'after our efforts not to discourage a coup' any such pressure would be futile, and anyway he was 'not convinced that the coup was going to fail'. Indeed, on 27 October he had given the go-ahead signal to them.[11]

Kennedy himself was assassinated three weeks later. There has been a debate about whether, if he had survived, Kennedy would have in 1964 moved to withdraw from South Vietnam.[12] This hypothesis has no good evidence to support it and belies the increasing American involvement in the RVN during his administration. Kennedy had left there 16,700 American

---

11 George McT. Kahin, *Intervention: How America became Involved in Vietnam* (New York), ch. 6. Robert D. Schulzinger, *A Time for War: The United States and Vietnam, 1941–1975* (New York 1971), 113–23. Moya Ann Ball, *Vietnam-on-the Potomac* (Westport 1992), 70–7. *FRUS, 1961–1963*, vol. iv: Vietnam August–December 1963 (Washington 1991), 484–90, 500–1. Anne E. Blair, *Lodge in Vietnam: A Patriot Abroad* (New Haven 1995), 65–70.

12 See John Newman, *JFK and Vietnam*, 319–25, 359–66, 400–11, 423–7; Robert McNamara, *In Retrospect* (New York 1995), 95–7; William J. Duiker, *US Containment Policy and the Conflict in IndoChina* (Stanford 1994), 307–8; Schulzinger, *A Time for War*, 122–3; Kevin Ruane, *War and Revolution in Vietnam, 1930–75* (London 1998), 59–61.

military personnel who were permitted to engage in battle alongside the ARVN units they advised. He had financially supported an increase in ARVN and Home Guard forces to over 200,000 men. Yet the NLF insurgency was growing stronger, boosted by a DRV decision in 1963 to step up its support. US intelligence acknowledged that more than 90 per cent of the PLAF were Southerners; most of its recruits from the North were Southern returnees. But the Americans were making the strategic mistake of encouraging the ARVN to direct its energies to defending South Vietnam's borders in order to cut off DRV aid to the PLAF. Also many ARVN divisions were kept from the conflict to provide protection for Diem. The US administration had not appreciated the depth of anti-government feeling in the countryside. The State Department's Paul Kattenburg said, after his return from a fact-finding mission to Vietnam, that he listened to an NSC meeting on 31 August 1963 attended by Johnson, Secretary of State Dean Rusk and other major decision makers. 'There was not a single person there that knew what he was talking about . . . They didn't know Vietnam . . . They simply didn't understand the identification of nationalism and Communism and the more this meeting went on . . . I thought "God, we're walking into a major disaster".'[13]

The US, China and the USSR

Influencing the increased military commitment by the Kennedy administration to the RVN was a fear of active Chinese support for the communist revolution in South Vietnam. Bundy explained: 'the idea of China as a menace grew particularly from the time of the Sino-Indian conflict in the fall of 1962 which seemed (and I think exaggeratedly) an example of the Chinese being ready to move hard in peripheral areas'. In fact China was not actively encouraging the DRV's revolutionary policy in South Vietnam. After joining with the USSR to impose the partition of Vietnam at Geneva in 1954, China's major priority was to avoid another debilitating contest with the US and to develop its underdeveloped economy. China, however, did provide significant military aid to North Vietnam from 1956 to 1963 including over 10,000 artillery pieces, twenty-eight naval vessels and 1.8 million military uniforms. A motive for this assistance was to maintain influence in the region in the face of the growing split between Beijing and Moscow and to demonstrate Chinese support for wider world national liberation struggles.

---

13 Turley, *Second Indochina War*, 40–8. Interview with Paul Kattenburg, 16 February 1979, in *UGVW*, II, 161.

The Soviet Union also provided some military aid to the DRV; but that financial commitment was only half the level of China's. Also the USSR was not actively supporting the revolution in South Vietnam.[14]

The Kennedy administration knew of the widening split between China and the USSR. However, that knowledge did not encourage any American move towards China. The Democratic Party's memory of the damage inflicted on the Truman administration by the Republican 'loss of China' propaganda and Kennedy's own long-standing antipathy to communist China, ensured that the KMT regime in Taiwan remained the only American-recognized Chinese government. Also influencing this policy was a strong suspicion that the Beijing regime was developing an atomic bomb. This was an alarming prospect for Kennedy and other members of his administration who were becoming concerned about Chinese ambitions to dominate Southeast Asia and were prepared to believe that the CCP would be willing to sacrifice millions of its own citizens in a nuclear war. So Kennedy's response was a new urgency in negotiations with the USSR for a nuclear test ban treaty, which had stalled under the Eisenhower administration. Initially, Krushchev did not respond favourably, being unsure about the emerging rift with China. But in 1963, after the Cuban missile crisis had generated mutual US–Soviet fears of nuclear war, Krushchev signed an agreement with the US to ban open air nuclear tests, which worsened relations between the USSR and China.[15]

Indonesia and Irian Jaya

In the Southwestern Pacific Basin there was also a contest for influence between the USSR and China in Indonesia, which had wider ramifications. After a dispute in 1959 between China and Indonesia about restrictions placed on Chinese people there, Beijing sought in 1960 an accommodation with Jakarta to counter growing Soviet influence in Indonesia. Moscow

---

14   Interview with Bundy in Charlton and Moncrieff, *Many Reasons Why*, 68–9. Chen Jian, 'China and the Vietnam Wars', in Peter Lowe (ed.), *The Vietnam War* (New York 1998), 162–3. Iya V. Gaiduk, 'The Soviet Union and Vietnam, 1945–75', in ibid., 138–42.

15   Gordon M. Chang, *Friends and Enemies: The United States, China and the Soviet Union, 1948–1972* (Stanford 1990), ch. 8. Michael R. Beschloss, *The Crisis Years: Kennedy and Krushchev 1960–1963* (New York 1991), chs 17–21. James Fetzer, 'Clinging to Containment: China Policy', in Paterson, *Kennedy's Quest for Victory*, ch. 7. Constantine Pleshakov, 'Nikita Krushchev and Sino-Soviet Relations', in Odd Arne Westad (ed.), *Brothers in Arms: The Rise and Fall of the Sino-Soviet Alliance, 1945–1963* (Stanford 1998), 238–9.

in turn provided increased credit to Sukarno's government, resulting in an Indonesian build-up of arms supplied by the Soviet Union and communist Eastern European countries. By 1961 Indonesia had received its first long-range bombers, submarines and other advanced military hardware. These arms gave Sukarno the confidence to force the Irian Jaya issue with strong support from the PKI and the army. So, army 'volunteers' were sent from the beginning of 1962 into Irian Jaya to start guerrilla action against Dutch rule.[16]

US concern about Soviet influence in Indonesia affected Washington's policy in the Irian Jaya conflict. A study of the Indonesia–Netherlands military balance in 1962 demonstrates that the Dutch forces in the region, especially aircraft, had the capacity to prevent a full-scale Indonesian invasion of Irian Jaya. The Australian government also supported diplomatically the Netherlands' insistence on retaining control of the territory in order to prepare its Melanesian people for self-determination. Australia preferred not to have an expansionist Indonesia camped on the western border of Papua New Guinea. But the US chose to support Indonesia. Roger Hilsman, the State Department's Director of Intelligence and Research, explained that the 'spectacle of the Soviet Union and the other communist countries supplying Indonesia with a billion dollars of military arms and equipment and the increasing communist influence that was the logical resultant of this aid' caused the US to abandon its 'policy of passive neutrality'. Therefore, the US pressed Holland to agree in September 1962 to transfer control of Irian Jaya to Indonesia on 1 May 1963, with provision for a UN-supervised expression of self-determination by the indigenous people in 1969. Also, the Netherlands was not well placed to fight single-handedly a lengthy guerrilla war in Irian Jaya. Australia was unwilling to join the Dutch in a war with Indonesia without US or British support. The British Cabinet had backed away from a previous promise to provide 'logistical support' for a Dutch defence of Irian Jaya.[17]

---

16 David Mozingo, *Chinese Policy Towards Indonesia 1949–1967* (Ithaca 1976), ch. 6.
    R.A. Longmire, *Soviet Relations with South-East Asia: An Historical Survey* (London 1989),
    60–8. Franklin B. Weinstein, *Indonesia's Foreign Policy and the Dilemma of Dependence:
    From Sukarno to Suharto* (Ithaca 1976), 306–14.
17 Ian MacFarling, 'Military Aspects of the West New Guinea Dispute, 1958–1962',
    Australian National University Strategic and Defence Studies Centre (ASDSC), Working
    paper, no. 212 (Canberra 1990), 21–47. Roger Hilsman, *To Move a Nation* (New York
    1967), 374–5. Gregory Pemberton, *All the Way: Australia's Road to Vietnam* (Sydney 1987),
    ch. 3. Amry Vandenbosch, 'Indonesia, the Netherlands and the New Guinea Issue',
    Journal of Southeast Asian Studies, 6, 1975, 109–15. Christopher J. McMullen, *Mediation
    of the West New Guinea Dispute, 1962: A Case Study* (Washington 1981). The Earl of Home,
    'Assistance to the Netherlands Government in the Event of an Indonesian Attack on West
    New Guinea', 29 Dec. 1961, CAB 129/107/222, Public Record Office (PRO), London.

Confrontation

Indonesia's success in gaining Iryan Jaya encouraged further conflict in the Southwestern Pacific Basin over the inauguration of the new state of Malaysia on 16 September 1963. The concept of Malaysia had been advocated in May 1961 by Malaya's Prime Minister, Tunku Abdul Rahman, to solve the problem of amalgamating Malaya and Singapore without a Chinese majority by adding Britain's territories in Borneo, Brunei, Sarawak and Brunei. However, the plan had earlier been advocated in London as a means of heading off a left-wing independence movement in Sarawak led by members of its commercially powerful Chinese community who were one third of the territory's population. Singapore's PAP government still envisioned in Malaysia a fruitful wider stage for its political activities. The island's economic interests also would be advanced in the promised Malaysian common market. However, the Sultan of Brunei was unhappy about sharing the oil riches of his small state with his Malay cousins and did not join the federation.[18]

Emboldened by its victory in Irian Jaya, Indonesia launched a similar military campaign against Malaysia, known as Confrontation. Sukarno condemned the Malaysian federation as a neo-colonialist plot by a declining empire to ensure continued British influence in the region. Such rhetoric was good propaganda. But probably it also reflected the anti-imperialist ideology that had informed the long struggle by Indonesian nationalists for liberation from Dutch influence, which had continued after the formation of Indonesia. Now there was a chance for Sukarno to arouse his people to eradicate the last remnants of British influence in Southeast Asia. Moreover, Anglophobia in Indonesia had been generated previously by the British handing back of power to the Netherlands in 1946 and by the support provided by Malaya and Singapore to the 1957–58 rebellions in Sumatra and Sulawesi. Those rebellions indicated the fragility of Indonesian unity, which could be subject to interference by a British-dominated Malaysia. Malaya and Singapore also were economically more prosperous than Indonesia. The new federation gave Malaysia potentially greater economic power in the region, in glaring contrast to Indonesia's economic problems. Furthermore, Confrontation could divert public attention from the economic troubles in Indonesia. The expulsion of Dutch enterprise, internal unrest and galloping inflation, fuelled by Sukarno's heavy expenditure on military

---

18   N.J. Ryan, *A History of Malaysia and Singapore* (Kuala Lumpar 1976), ch. 20. Greg Poulgrain, *The Genesis of Konfrontasi: Malaysia Brunei Indonesia 1945–196* (Bathurst 1998), 181–2. CM. Turnbull, *A History of Singapore 1819–1980* (Singapore 1989), 264–80.

hardware and on grandiose building projects, had seriously damaged Indonesia's economic health. One suggested motive for Confrontation, for which there is no good evidence, is that Indonesia had expansionist ambitions to incorporate some of Malaysia's territory.[19]

The occasion for launching the anti-Malaysia campaign was presented by the use of British troops in December 1962 to suppress a left-wing rebellion against the Sultan of Brunei. New evidence suggests that the revolt was a plot by the local British secret service in probable collusion with British oil interests in Brunei. Information was deliberately fed to the left-wing leaders to entice them to rebel so that they could be crushed by the British troops.[20]

The military thrust of Confrontation began in April 1963 with army 'volunteer' groups mounting raids across the Kalimantan border into Sarawak and Sabah. Their aim, in particular, was to stimulate popular opposition to Malaysia from groups such as Sarawak communists and the Brunei rebels. At this stage Sukarno seems to have been testing the water with a three-pronged strategy that included diplomatic efforts to prevent the formation of Malaysia and the propaganda campaign against British neocolonialism.[21]

Sukarno was unable to prevent the inauguration of Malaysia. But, having aroused Indonesian public opposition to the new nation, he was unwilling to suspend Confrontation. The campaign also was backed by his two major political support groups, the army and the PKI.[22]

So, after the formation of Malaysia, the Indonesian government stepped up its raids into Sabah and Sarawak. Commercial relations were severed in an attempt to drive Indonesian trade from Malaysian ports. Diplomatic links between the two countries were broken. The British embassy in Jakarta was burned to the ground by a rampaging mob on 17 September, and two days later all British property in Indonesia was seized. Also in December 1963 Indonesian regular troops severely mauled a Malay regiment in Sabah.

Malaysia did not have to face Confrontation alone. British troops based there were swung into action, and reinforcements were sent from Britain. Initially they were able to cope with the Indonesian raids. The British commander of Borneo operations, General Sir Walter Walker, explained that in 1963: 'the threat was from small, ill-trained and poorly armed

---

19   Ide Anak Agung Gde Agung, *Twenty Years of Indonesian Foreign Policy 1945–1965* (The Hague 1973), ch. 16. J.A.C. Mackie, *Konfrontasi: The Indonesia-Malaysia Dispute 1963–1966* (Kuala Lumpar 1974), 326–33. Anne Booth, *The Indonesian Economy in the Nineteenth and Twentieth Centuries* (London 1998), 69–70, 176–7.

20   Poulgrain, *The Genesis of Konfrontasi*, 280–1.

21   Mackie, *Konfrontasi*, chs 6–7.

22   Ibid., ch. 8. Agung, *Twenty Years*, 467–72.

gangs', which were met with 'tactics . . . similar to those of the Malayan emergency: platoons operating independently from company bases'. But the increasing frequency and strength of raids late in 1963 caused a request from Britain to Australia for military assistance. The Australian government did not wish to upset relations with Jakarta that previously had been strained by the Irian Jaya dispute. So, Canberra pleaded the unavailability of troops. Further pressure from the Malaysian and British governments for the release of the Australian battalion serving in Malaya succeeded after it was used to capture a small party of Indonesian guerrillas landed by sea on the Malacca coast. The Australian troops, along with British, Gurkha and Malay regiments, went into action in Sarawak against Indonesian army units, a development that caused considerable nervousness in Canberra about the possibility of Indonesian retaliation in New Guinea.[23]

However, the undeclared war was not widened. Britain rejected proposals to launch air and sea strikes against Indonesian military bases. Instead, with the availability of 50,000 overseas troops plus three Malay battalions, incursions were authorized into Indonesian territory for up to 10,000 yards (nine km) in order to ambush Indonesian supply parties. Consequently, Indonesian insurgents were placed on the defensive to protect supply lines, which limited their offensive capabilities. A 'hearts and minds' program, as in the Malayan Emergency, also was used to conciliate the local population and to limit support for the insurgency by the small number of communists in Sarawak and Sabah.[24]

Diplomatically, Indonesia received some support. The Philippines condemned the formation of Malaysia, because of a Philippine claim to Sabah, which was based on an eighth-century cession of that region by the Sultan of Brunei to the Filipino Sultan of Sulu. China, which was establishing closer relations with Indonesia, denounced Malaysia as an imperialist plot. The USSR used its veto to block any action by the UN Security Council and continued to ferry arms to Indonesia.[25]

The US did not support Indonesia in Confrontation. The Kennedy administration welcomed the formation of Malaysia as a nation that would anchor an anti-communist arc across the South China Sea to the Philippines and

23 Sir Walter Walker, 'How Borneo was Won, the Untold Story of an Asian Victory', *The Round Table*, 59, 1969, 17. Peter Edwards, *Crises and Commitments: The Politics and Diplomacy of Australia's Involvement in Southeast Asian Conflicts 1948–1965* (Sydney 1992), 285–92, 340–4. David Horner, 'The Australian Army and Indonesia's Confrontation with Malaysia', *Australian Outlook*, 43, 1989, 61–76. Peter Dennis and Jeffrey Grey, *Emergency and Confrontation: Australian Military Operations in Malaya and Borneo 1950–1966* (Sydney 1996), ch. 13.

24 Walker, 'How Borneo was Won', 17. Mackie, *Konfrontasi*, 258–64.

25 Mackie, *Konfrontasi*, 264–89.

Taiwan. Kennedy regarded Malaysia as 'the best hope of security for that very vital part of the world'.[26] It was not considered necessary to send any US aid, because the new nation was seen as a British responsibility, and the US was already carrying a major burden in supporting South Vietnam. Washington also tried to cushion the impact on Indonesia of American diplomatic support for Malaysia. A reduced flow of military and economic aid to Indonesia continued, much to the annoyance of Malaysia. This was an American balancing act attempting to stop Indonesia falling into the communist camp. However, increased Indonesian military pressure on Malaysia caused the US in 1964 to suspend all military assistance to Jakarta as well as a $400 million economic aid package. Also Tunku Rahman was invited that year to visit Washington, where he was promised military training for Malaysian troops in the US and was given a credit line for arms purchases.[27]

Sukarno defiantly rejected US attempts to use the threat of withdrawal of economic aid to pressure him to cease Confrontation. The US embassy was burned down in Jakarta and paratroopers were landed in Malaya, though they were quickly rounded up. There were, however, limits to the Indonesian military campaign. There were no attempts to assassinate Malaysian leaders, which could have caused much political instability in Malaysia. No more than 30,000 Indonesian troops were used at the height of Confrontation, which reflected Sukarno's need to station his army in other parts of Indonesia to prevent dissidents using the undeclared war as a cloak to cover local rebellions. Sukarno also refrained from provoking total war against superior British technology. Furthermore, there were attempts by the Indonesian army high command to limit the military extent of Confrontation in case it provoked more extensive British reaction.[28]

Confrontation ended because of violent political change in Indonesia. Growing communist influence there resulted in an attempted coup on 30 September 1965 against the army leadership; six generals were killed. One of the non-targeted generals, General Suharto, then seized power with the support of loyal troops. The PKI was blamed for the September coup, resulting in an anti-communist popular frenzy, encouraged by the army, which resulted in the slaughtering of as many as half a million known or suspected communists in late 1965 and early 1966. The more likely sponsors of the coup were younger officers acting, with support by some PKI elements, against generals accused of plotting a military coup. Sukarno also

---

26 Hilsman, *To Move a Nation*, 385.
27 Pamela Sodhy, 'Malaysian-American Relations during Indonesia's Confrontation against Malaysia, 1963–66', *Journal of Southeast Asian Studies*, 19, 1988, 111–36.
28 Mackie, *Konfrontasi*, 221–47. Dennis and Grey, *Emergency and Confrontation*, 228.

was accused of complicity in the coup planning, which was a major reason, as well as poor health, why he failed to reclaim power. His actual involvement in the putsch remains uncertain because of the unreliability of the evidence produced after his death in 1970 to implicate him.[29]

Suharto's 'new order' military regime in Indonesia sought an end to Confrontation. With Thailand acting as a mediator, an agreement was signed in Bangkok by the Indonesian and Malaysian foreign ministers to terminate all hostilities. Indonesia gave diplomatic recognition to Malaysia and suspended relations with China, which had already withdrawn its ambassador and cut economic and technical aid to Indonesia. The minimal US military aid to the Indonesian army and probable CIA support for Suharto after the PKI coup paid a rich dividend. Suharto's Indonesia was now secured as a supporter for the US-led anti-communist crusade in the Western Pacific Basin.[30]

Malaysia expels Singapore

Ironically, the end of Confrontation was accompanied by the separation of Singapore from Malaysia. Singapore's Chinese people, who were three quarters of the island's population of 1,700,000, were uncomfortable partners for Malays in Malaysia. There was irritation there from the start when Singapore unilaterally declared its independence from Britain fifteen days before the inauguration of the federation and held prompt elections in which Alliance Party-supported candidates were defeated. The PAP also campaigned on the mainland in the March 1964 federal election in an attempt to supplant the conservative Malay Chinese Association in the allegiance of the Chinese population of Malaya. This was a PAP tactical mistake, given the conservatism of communal politics in Malaya. There was in fact little in common between urban Singapore and predominantly rural Malaya, and the Tunku condemned Lee Kuan Yew for breaking a promise to refrain from entering national politics. Racial tensions exploded into

29   Nawaz B. Mody, *Indonesia under Suharto* (New York 1987), ch. 1. Oey Hong Lee, 'Sukarno and the Pseudo-Coup of 1965: Ten Years later', *Journal of Southeast Asian Studies*, 6, 1975, 119–35. Robert Cribb and Colin Brown, *Modern Indonesia: A History Since 1945* (London 1995), 97–102. Harold Crouch, *The Army and Politics in Indonesia* (revised edition, Ithaca 1988), chs 4–5.

30   Mackie, *Konfrontasi*, ch. 12. Brian May, *The Indonesian Tragedy* (London 1978), 125–8. Mozingo, *Chinese Policy Towards Indonesia*, ch. 8. William Blum, *The CIA: A Forgotten History* (London 1986), ch. 31. Robert Cribb (ed.), *The Indonesian Killings* (Clayton, Victoria 1990), 7–14.

communal riots in Singapore in July and September 1964, the latter said to be the work of Indonesian agents. But the PAP blamed Malay extremists for the violence, and Lee Kuan Yew and other PAP leaders started calling for a 'democratic Malaysian Malaysia' in which there was no place for special Malay privileges. In May 1965 the PAP succeeded in organizing a united opposition front, the Malaysian Solidarity Convention (MSC), to compete against the Malaysian National Alliance Party. Many Malays saw the MSC as a Chinese challenge to political leadership in Malaysia, which was achievable if the 42 per cent of the federation's population who were Chinese gained the support of other non-Malays. For many rural, conservative and Muslim Malays, Lee Kuan Yew personified aggressive and materialistic Chinese ambition. A fear of spreading racial violence was uppermost in the minds of the Tunku and his deputy Tun Abdul Razak, when they decided to expel Singapore from the federation, which was ratified by the Federal Parliament on 9 August, to the consternation of Lee Kuan Yew, who tried to stave it off. An alternative move to depose the Singapore government had been rejected because of likely opposition from Britain and Australia, which played major roles in Malaysia's defence.[31]

Consequently, Singapore was a small island state forced into independent existence. Lee Kuan Yew publicly wept at the collapse of his dream of the PAP ruling a multi-racial Malaysia. The separation agreement provided for economic, political and foreign policy cooperation between Malaysia and Singapore, and PAP leaders hoped the breach might soon be healed. But competition rather than cooperation was the order of the early days of the relationship as Malaysia erected tariff barriers to protect its industries and Singapore rejected a defence alliance. Immigration controls also vexed travellers daily crossing the causeway connecting Singapore and Malaya. The island state was forced to find new forms of economic wealth to compensate for the blighted vision of a Malaysian common market. Fortuitously a new source of prosperity was emerging across the Gulf of Thailand in the form of massively increasing US involvement in the conflict in Vietnam.[32]

The Johnson Administration and Vietnam

Lyndon Johnson, who stepped into the shoes of the assassinated Kennedy, was a Texas politician and masterful manipulator of Senate votes before he

---

31 Turnbull, *History of Singapore*, 279–85. Chan Heng Chee, *Singapore: The Politics of Survival, 1965–1967* (Singapore 1971), *passim*.
32 Turnbull, *History of Singapore*, 288–93.

was chosen as Kennedy's presidential running mate in the 1960 election campaign to give the Democratic ticket a Southern sectional balance. From the outset of his presidency, Johnson declared that the US was 'not going to lose Vietnam' and see 'Southeast Asia go the way China did'.[33] The Democratic Party's 'loss of China' memory influenced him as much as Kennedy. Johnson also had Kennedy's confidence in American wealth and know-how to defeat communist insurgencies. Nor did the big majority of his advisers, inherited from Kennedy, provide any convincing reasons to go against his political judgement.[34]

An alternative to the Vietnam conflict was being advocated by the ARVN junta which now controlled the RVN, headed by General Duong Van Minh, a French-trained officer who had become an opponent of Diem. The junta considered that the preceding regime's main problem was hostility aroused among the large non-Catholic majority in South Vietnam, which prompted many non-communists to support the NLF. Their solution was to conciliate Buddhists and the powerful Cao Dai and Hoa Hao sects, by freeing their leaders from the imprisonment that had been Diem's response to their opposition, and by supporting their religious activities. The junta moved to win rural support by starting to dismantle the mostly ineffective and hated strategic hamlets. The new leaders opposed any increase in the US military presence and advocated reducing the visibility of American troops in order to improve the government's nationalist credentials. The junta preferred to work towards a negotiated peace rather than to prosecute vigorously an unwinnable war. Indeed, there was a groundswell of public support in South Vietnam for an offer by President Charles de Gaulle of France to assist in negotiations for the neutralization of all the states of Indochina. This proposal had been initiated by the NLF and the DRV. They saw a neutral South Vietnam government an easy prey to communist influence, a means of achieving victory without further warfare.[35]

Such a prospect was particularly disturbing to the French-trained General Nguyen Khanh, supported by dissident ARVN officers who had been demoted by the junta or who had not received expected rewards. The result was another coup that toppled Minh's junta on 29 January 1964. Khanh gave prior warning of the coup to Lodge, who withheld the information from Minh. Neither Lodge nor his superiors in Washington had conspired in the coup, but Khanh had received encouragement from General Paul Harkins, the US area commander in South Vietnam. The stage had

---

33 *UGVW*, II, 209.
34 Ball, *Vietnam-on-the Potomac*, ch. 6. Schwab, *Defending the Free World*, 85–7.
35 Kahin, *Intervention*, 182–92. Robert K. Brigham, *Guerrilla Diplomacy: The NLF's Foreign Policy and the Vietnam War* (Ithaca 1999), ch. 2.

been set for a major escalation of the American effort to defeat the NLF insurgency.[36]

Johnson's decisions to escalate American involvement in Vietnam evolved gradually in a climate of indecision. Since late 1963 military chiefs had been urging a bombing campaign against the DRV in order to deter Hanoi's support for the insurgency in South Vietnam. But Johnson hesitated to take the bombing plunge, especially as in the latter half of 1964 he was campaigning as peacemaker in an election campaign against the Republican Party's hawkish Barry Goldwater. Johnson also tried a peace initiative via the Canadian representative on the virtually defunct Indochina Commission. But Hanoi rejected his proposal for a guarantee of the DRV borders and no American forces in the RVN. Also reports were arriving about Khanh's irresolute leadership, and the US's Military Assistance Command Vietnam (MACV) was urging the despatch of more American troops.[37]

A *casus belli* emerged on 3 August when three North Vietnamese torpedo boats attacked the US destroyer, *Maddox*, which was assisting South Vietnamese patrol boat attacks on DRV targets. An alleged second attack on an accompanying US destroyer, the *C. Turner Joy*, on the next night never occurred: its guns fired at ghost images caused by tricky radar. But that allegation triggered a retaliatory response from Johnson's administration in the shape of air strikes against DRV torpedo boat bases and oil storage installations. Congress also dutifully passed, with only two dissenting votes, the Southeast Asia (Gulf of Tonkin) resolution, which gave the President a free hand to take any measures to repel armed attack on American forces and to protect any state covered by SEATO, including all the nations of Indochina.[38]

Johnson did not use the Gulf of Tonkin incident to endorse a continuous bombing campaign in the DRV. His overnight rise in popularity from 42 to 72 per cent in the Harris opinion poll for his firm but restrained response to the alleged gulf attack, encouraged restraint. Thereby he was able to campaign as a lover of peace compared with the aggressive Goldwater, whom he trounced in the November 1964 election.[39]

However, conditions in Vietnam were deteriorating. Khanh, whose popularity had been sliding, used the Tonkin Gulf affair to assume near-dictatorial

---

36   Lodge to Department of State, 29 Jan. 1964, *FRUS, 1964–1968*, vol. I: Vietnam 1964 (Washington 1992), 37–9. Anthony O. Edmonds, *The War in Vietnam* (Westport 1998), 40. Blair, *Lodge in Vietnam*, 107–11.

37   Schulzinger, *A Time For War*, 136–50.

38   Ibid., 150–3. Edwin E. Mose, *The Tonkin Gulf and the Escalation of the Vietnam War* (Chapel Hill 1996), chs 6–9.

39   Herring, *America's Longest War*, 136–7.

powers and to clamp down on civil liberties in expectation of military reprisals against the RVN by the DRV, which did not materialize. He received support from Washington except for pressure to soften the most draconian elements of his proposed new constitution, such as no provisions for elections. But he miscalculated. Angry Buddhist mobs rose in mass protests, which had an anti-American flavour and were encouraged vigorously by the NLF. Though Khanh promised constitutional reforms, continuing popular demonstrations against him provoked American intervention to achieve a compromise. Minh and a Catholic leader, General Tran Thien, both Khanh's bitter rivals, were added to the leadership – a triumvirate that would serve until promised elections. The Gulf of Tonkin crisis had led to political instability in the RVN rather than generating any sense of national unity.[40]

Furthermore, PLAF aggression was increasing, especially a mortar attack on the Bien Hoa airfield on 1 November, which destroyed six US B-57 bombers and killed five American servicemen. Johnson responded to that attack by ordering an interdepartmental working group to prepare submissions about increasing pressure on the DRV. He then chose the softest option of continuing covert attacks on the North and implementing controlled reprisals to PLAF attacks rather than implementing fuller bombing 'squeezes' on North Vietnam.[41]

The DRV was expecting increasing American involvement in the Vietnam War. North Vietnam was being prepared to resist US air attacks and the NLF in the South was boosted by sending there in 1964, for the first time, regiments of the People's Army of Vietnam (PAVN). In fighting the world's greatest economic and military power, Hanoi perceived major American weaknesses. The VCP's chief, Le Duan, explained: 'South Vietnam is not a life-and-death issue for the United States.' Also 'the US has to face other issues in other places in the world . . . That is why the US cannot use all its forces to fight in Vietnam.' Moreover, 'the US is thousands of miles away from Vietnam'.[42]

Furthermore, the DRV was receiving greater outside support. From 1963 there was increasing aid from China, which was seeking to bolster its communist credentials in the contest with the USSR and to enhance its role as promoter of Third World revolutionary movements. This also reflected Mao Zedong's new domestic radicalization program, which was justified by

---

40 Kahin, *Intervention*, 227–35. Truong Nhu Tang, *A Vietcong Memoir* (San Diego 1985), 91–2.
41 Herring, *America's Longest War*, 137–41.
42 McNamara, Blight and Brigham, *Argument Without End*, 205. Nguyen Vu Tung, 'Coping with the United States: Hanoi's Search for an Effective Strategy', in Lowe (ed.), *The Vietnam War*, 46.

propaganda about threats from international capitalist imperialism. There had also been a change in USSR relations with the DRV, which had been cooling under the impact of Hanoi's pro-China stance. The Tonkin Gulf incidents were the catalyst. Moscow was now alarmed at the prospect of a growing conflict in Vietnam. So the USSR decided to boost its aid to the DRV so as to increase Soviet influence there.[43]

In the RVN during 1964 the NLF was increasing its influence. Decreased government control had been caused by political instability, by political rivalry among the ARVN's officers, by desertion of soldiers and by the continued reluctance of many units actually to fight the enemy. The best ARVN units were preserved to protect the shaky Saigon government. As well as employing violence against RVN officials, the NLF implemented land distribution, lower taxation, appointment of local people as village officials, and disbandment of the hated fortified villages. By the end of 1964 all the rural area of Long An province on the southern side of Saigon was under NLF control, leaving only the provincial capital and six district towns in government hands. The same was largely true of the other provinces surrounding Saigon except Bien Hoa on its eastern flank.[44]

The Johnson administration did not perceive how far the Saigon regime had lost control of its country. But in response to a PLAF attack on 7 February 1965 on Pleiku airfield in the Central Highlands, which killed nine Americans, Johnson decided on 13 February to implement the bombing plan, code-named 'Rolling Thunder'. However, the use of RVN airfields for this purpose raised the question of their protection. Hence, a marine regiment, the first ground troops as distinct from reinforcements for the MACV, arrived in Vietnam six days later to protect Danang air base on the northern coast of South Vietnam. They were welcomed by a government now firmly in the hands of the military after a further coup in February 1965 had installed another triumvirate: a French-trained air force general, Nguyen Cao Ky, the Buddhist First Army Corps commander, Nguyen Chanh Thi, and a US trained ARVN divisional commander, Nguyen Van Thieu. But RVN diplomat Bui Diem has pointed out that there had been no attempt to assess South Vietnamese opinion about the US decisions to send troops to the RVN and to bomb the DRV. 'Had the South Vietnamese been consulted early in 1965', he wrote, 'it is likely that they

---

43   Chen Jian, 'China and the Vietnam Wars', in Lowe (ed.), *The Vietnam War*, 163–5.
     Ilya V. Gaiduk, 'Turnabout: The Soviet Policy Dilemma in the Vietnamese Conflict',
     in Lloyd C. Gardiner and Ted Gittinger (eds), *Vietnam: The Early Decisions* (Austin 1997),
     209–19.
44   Race, *War Comes to Long An*, 167. Post, *Revolution, Socialism and Nationalism*, IV, 235.
     Bergerud, *Dynamics of Defeat*, 68–84.

would have preferred either no intervention or a limited effort to stabilize the military situation.'[45]

The decision to widen the war with Rolling Thunder was not taken lightly by Johnson. He had no blind faith that air-power would win the war. He knew that more troops would have to be sent to protect airfields and to counter the expected arrival of additional PAVN regiments. He realized that the necessary increased war expenditure could gravely threaten his first priority – his 'Great Society' social reform program for the US. But he said later that if he abandoned the war and 'let the Communists take over South Vietnam, then I would be seen as a coward and my nation would be seen as an appeaser, and we would both find it impossible to accomplish anything for anybody anywhere on the entire globe'.[46] It has been argued recently that Johnson had alternative freedom to pursue a negotiated peace in Vietnam, after his sweeping election win in November 1964. At that time he had high public popularity and there were major press and other public voices urging a peaceful solution to the crisis. But Johnson had made the issue his own personal crusade.[47] However, that argument does not give full credit to the historical and political forces influencing his decision. His problem was that Eisenhower and Kennedy had laid US prestige on the line in South Vietnam. They also had given that small nation a strategic importance accepted by Johnson without question. Furthermore, his decisions to implement Rolling Thunder and despatch US troops were approved by all members of his Cabinet and followed a series of conversations with congressmen and Democratic Party leaders.[48]

The American escalation of the war provoked a debate within the VCP in North Vietnam. A minority spoke out about the threat of the American bombing to the party's socialist objectives. Was the cost of supporting the rebellion in the South worth the price? The NLF in South Vietnam responded with a stern declaration about the need for continuing armed struggle against American aggression and hardened its support for no negotiations unless there was first a complete American withdrawal from

---

45   Interview with W. Bundy, Charlton and Moncrieff, *Many Reasons Why*, 20. Kahin, *Intervention*, 292–344. Bui Diem with David Chanoff, *In the Jaws of History* (Boston 1987), 338.

46   Doris Kearns, *Lyndon Johnson and the American Dream* (New York 1976), 252.

47   Frederick Logevall, *Choosing War: The Lost Chance for Peace and the Escalation of War in Vietnam* (Berkeley 1999), ch. 9. For another view that Johnson's personality was a major factor in the escalation decision see Blema S. Steinberg, *Shame and Humiliation: Presidential Decision Making on Vietnam* (Montreal 1996), ch. 3.

48   David M. Barrett, *Uncertain Warriors: Lyndon Johnson and his Vietnam Advisers* (Lawrence 1993), 13–23. Michael H. Hunt, *Lyndon Johnson's War: America's Cold War Crusade in Vietnam* (New York 1996), 95–107.

Vietnam. The Northern VCP refused to accept that prescription, but its four point negotiating platform, agreed to on 8 April 1965, contained a compromise point that final negotiations must be between the South Vietnamese people themselves on the basis of the NLF program. That became a major sticking point with the US. Also when Johnson tried to start peace talks by temporarily halting the bombing campaign on 12 May, Hanoi denounced it as a trick and did not respond to the American initiative until after the bombing recommenced on 20 May, a pattern repeated in the future. Luu Doan Huynh, a member of Vietnam's Foreign Ministry at the time, explained: 'Our objectives . . . [were] to fight in order to defeat the US air war, to exhaust the US troops in the South, and to weaken the determination to fight of both American politicians and soldiers.' Otherwise, the US would be negotiating from a position of strength.[49]

The end result was a major escalation of US forces in the RVN. In response to the request from the new commanding officer in South Vietnam, General William Westmoreland, for troops to counter a threatened PAVN offensive in the highlands, Johnson announced on 28 July another 50,000 soldiers to be sent to Vietnam. By the end of 1965 there were 155,000 US ground forces in the RVN, a larger number than French troops in the whole of Vietnam at any time during the First Indochina War. A year later the number of US troops in South Vietnam had almost doubled. They reached a peak of 441,000 at the end of 1968, when there were also 95,000 US airforce and naval personnel serving in the Vietnam War.[50]

However, American soldiers, with their heavy artillery, helicopter gun ships, napalm, and 'agent orange' to defoliate forests, were not the best means for combating the NLF insurgency. They undoubtedly saved the Saigon government from being overwhelmed by the PLAF. But the inrush of Americans encouraged the ARVN, with the exception of airborne battalions and the Saigon marines, to engage the PLAF in combat even less energetically than before. Vann, who had resigned from the army but was back in Vietnam as a US provincial pacification representative, wrote in December 1966: 'I consider the performance of the ARVN to be more disgraceful than ever.' He saw no significant progress in winning the war. The Pentagon's own analysis suggested otherwise. It measured an increase in the 'secure' Vietnamese population from 6.8 million in December 1964 to 11 million in June 1967, with a decrease of NLF controlled population

49   Brigham, *Guerrilla Diplomacy*, 41–6. McNamara, Blight and Brigham, *Argument Without End*, 220–32 (quotation 226–7).
50   R.B. Smith, *An International History of the Vietnam War*, vol. III *The Making of a Limited War, 1956–66* (Houndmills 1991), ch. 9. Thomas C. Thayer, *War Without Fronts: The American Experience in Vietnam* (Boulder 1985), 37.

from 3.3 million to 2.4 million, and also a decline from 6 million to 3.8 million people in 'contested' areas. However, most of the government's gains were caused by people moving into the secure areas, rather than from the small increase in the region under government control. Furthermore, even in so-called secure areas, especially at night-time, the PLAF had some presence. For example, in 1968 PLAF guerrillas enjoyed virtual free movement in My Thuy Phuong village near the central coast city of Hue, despite the presence nearby of an encampment of American marines.[51]

Indeed, the massively increased American military presence and the US army's 'search and destroy' strategy were not winning the war. American fire power that stemmed the Chinese onslaught in the Korean War was far less successful in combating elusive Vietnamese guerrillas. PAVN General Nguyen Xuan Hoang explained to an American interviewer: 'You seldom knew where we were, and you seldom had a clear goal.' Only about 5 per cent of ground assaults by PLAF/PAVN units from 1965 to 1967 were conducted at battalion or greater strength. Most PLAF action consisted of long distance fire, harassment and terrorist attacks. The American establishment of free fire zones for bombs and artillery also was, in Vann's view, counterproductive in terms of destruction of civilian life and property.[52]

Johnson's administration did pay some attention to the need for alternative pacification programs in South Vietnam. Initially it relied on the ARVN to carry them out. But, as McNamara acknowledged, the ARVN 'do not understand the importance (or respectability) of pacification nor the importance . . . of proper, disciplined conduct'. He also admitted 'bad management on the American' side. An improvement, which arrived in South Vietnam in May 1967, was the Civil Operations and Rural Development Support program; but it had major problems. It circulated propaganda composed without reference to Vietnamese customs or circumstances. Food and medicines for villagers often were misappropriated by corrupt officials. New rural schools and hospitals lacked trained staff. Paramilitary Vietnamese were trained to carry out guerrilla style tactics against NLF villages, but irregular troops were peasants who were often left without military support from upper class ARVN officers and so suffered high casualties.[53]

---

51   Sheehan, *Bright Shining Lie*, 628. Thayer, *War Without Fronts*,137–43. Wiesner, *Victims and Survivors*, ch. 4. Ken Post, *Revolution, Socialism and Nationalism in Viet Nam*, vol. IV (Aldershot 1989–90), 333–4. Trullinger, *Village at War*, 121–2.

52   Cecil B. Currey, *Victory at Any Cost: The Genius of Viet Nam's Gen. Vo Nguyen Giap* (Washington 1997), 258. Bergerud, *Dynamics of Defeat*, 109. Turley, *Second Indochina War*, ch. 4. Douglas Pike, *PAVN: People's Army of Vietnam* (Novata 1986), ch. 9.

53   *PP*, II, 596. James William Gibson, *The Perfect War: Technowar in Vietnam* (Boston 1986), ch. 8. Richard A. Hunt, *Pacification: The American Struggle for Vietnam's Hearts and Minds* (Boulder 1995), chs 6–8.

An improvement to counterinsurgency operations later in 1967 was the Phoenix program implemented by American-led Vietnamese paramilitary personnel and supported by the CIA. Phoenix failed to capture many known PLAF members because of poor intelligence and the low support for the RVN government in the countryside. Phoenix did achieve some damage to lower PLAF ranks, but not to any grave extent because of PLAF reinforcements from South and North Vietnam. Also Phoenix received adverse publicity because of its use, at times, of kidnappings, torture and assassinations. Furthermore, people were targeted on the basis of lists compiled by informers, who at times had other agendas to fulfil when naming alleged NLF supporters. Moreover, Phoenix was responsible for providing the misinformation that prompted some American soldiers to massacre nearly 500 civilians, including many women and children, in the village of My Lai on 16 March 1968. Many of the women were raped before they were shot.[54]

Nor did Rolling Thunder serve its purposes of seriously damaging the DRV's war effort and persuading its government to sue for peace. The political restraints imposed on the bombing were a reason. Fear of provoking China kept the bombs thirty miles from the Chinese border. Airfields were off limits to avoid killing Russian technicians. Haiphong and Hanoi were initially out of bounds to avoid any international outcry about murdering civilians. The earliest targets were military installations and lines of communications mainly south of the 20th latitudinal parallel. There was another month's pause from 27 December 1965 to allow for a Soviet peace initiative, which gave the DRV breathing space. When Hanoi again denounced the pause as a sham, the bombing was widened to include oil storage areas, industrial plant and electric power stations; but installations in civilian areas were exempt. The controls on the air campaign also were influenced by Johnson's concern to limit the impact of the war on his Great Society program.[55]

However, a major factor in the limitation of Rolling Thunder's impact was the Second World War basis of the airforce's strategic bombing doctrine, which emphasized attacks on economic infrastructure in order to destroy the DRV's war-making capacity. The manifestly smaller industrial capacity

---

54 Hunt, *Pacification*, ch. 15. Douglas Valentine, *The Phoenix Program* (New York 1990), 344–5 and *passim*. Michael Bilton and Kevin Sim, *Four Hours in My Lai* (New York, 1992), *passim*. Mark Moyer criticizes Valentine's charges about Phoenix and the My Lai massacre. But while he shows that Phoenix was not directly involved, he does not disprove that the attack on the village was in response to misinformation supplied by Phoenix. See Mark Moyar, *Phoenix and the Birds of Prey: The CIA's Secret Campaign to Destroy the Viet Cong* (Annapolis 1997), 218–20.

55 Mark Clodfelter, *The Limits of Air Power: The American Bombing of North Vietnam* (New York 1989), 73–134.

of North Vietnam made such attacks allegedly more important. But this approach ignored its ability to mobilize manpower to repair damaged communications quickly, to build by-pass roads and to disperse oil reserves. The thick vegetation over much of the country and the frequency of cloudy weather during the monsoon season aided hidden transportation and reconstruction. In the DRV by 1968 35 per cent of oil storage capacity, 41 per cent of power plants and 45 per cent of major bridges had survived the 643,000 tons of bombs dropped by US and RVN planes. The Vietnamese war effort, depending on low technology, was only marginally damaged. Even railway engines were powered by coal rather than by the targeted oil. For the North Vietnamese people, many of whom were evacuated from Hanoi and Haiphong, the bombing encouraged the same spirit of resistance as exhibited by the people of Britain during the Second World War.[56]

Furthermore, the bombing of North Vietnam generated increased imports from China and the USSR. To assist against the air attacks the USSR sent anti-aircraft artillery, surface-to-air missiles, war-planes, rockets and radar. It also dispatched communications and industrial equipment and armaments and brought thousands of North Vietnamese to Moscow for pilot and air defence training plus general military education. By 1968 the USSR was contributing aid worth US$582 million to the DRV, which was 50 per cent of all assistance from socialist countries, and which for the first time outstripped Chinese aid. Beijing also increased its assistance, sending engineering units, a railway corps and anti-aircraft batteries. There was a peak of 170,000 Chinese government personnel in the DRV in 1967.[57]

The limits to the effectiveness of Rolling Thunder were most dramatically demonstrated with the NLF Tet offensive, which began on 30 January 1968. Taking advantage of a truce called during the traditional Tet holiday time, over 80,000 PLAF troops and popular militia, who had smuggled themselves into most of South Vietnam's provincial and major cities, staged a well-coordinated series of attacks. They blew a hole in the wall of the American embassy in Saigon and engaged in all night battle with troops landed on the embassy roof by helicopter. The insurgents attacked Saigon's presidential palace and the ARVN general staff headquarters. They seized a large sector of Hue, where it has been claimed that 2,800 officials and other RVN supporters were massacred while the NLF flag flew above the citadel.[58]

---

56   Ibid., 134–46.
57   Ilya V. Gaiduk, *The Soviet Union and the Vietnam War* (Chicago 1996), 58–60. Chen Jian, 'China and the Vietnam Wars', in Lowe, *The Vietnam War*, 175–7.
58   Ronnie E. Ford, *Tet 1968: Understanding the Surprise* (London 1995), ch. 7. Larry Berman, 'The Tet Offensive', in Marc Jason Gilbert and William Head (eds), *The Tet Offensive* (Westport 1996), ch. 2. Valentine, *Phoenix Program*, 179–80.

The Tet offensive was a new VCP strategy. Though prepared for a long war, Hanoi was now seeking, in Le Duan's terms, 'a decisive victory'. The strategy, he told the VCP Central Committee in December 1967, was 'a general offensive and general uprisings in South Vietnam' at a time when 'the US war efforts in Vietnam have reached their highest peak' with attendant domestic 'political, social and economic' pressures.[59]

However, the decisive victory in the South was not achieved. PAVN had supported the offensive with attacks and threats in border areas, especially besieging a 6,000 strong garrison at Khe Sanh near the DRV border, which provoked Johnson in early mornings to pace White House floors fretting about a second Dien Bien Phu. However, compared with the French in that battle, the Americans at Khe Sanh had much more artillery and air power. Also, while much of the US army in Vietnam had been drawn to the frontiers, American and ARVN troops were still able to gain the upper hand over urban insurgents. But the efforts to blast the PLAF from the Cholon District in Saigon and from Hue caused many civilian deaths, and throughout the whole country more than half a million South Vietnamese lost their homes. Eleven hundred Americans were killed.[60]

The Tet offensive was a military failure for the DRV. While the US estimate of 40,000 PLAF and PAVN deaths probably was inflated, many died in second and third offensive waves against RVN cities in May and in August–September. Urban South Vietnamese people had not risen to support the insurgents. The Hue massacre, which NLF leader Huyen Tan Phat admitted was a PLAF mistake, also diminished public support for the NLF. Furthermore, the absence of so many warriors fighting in the towns and cities in the three offensives of 1968 left many NLF hamlets unprotected against attack by RVN and US forces. In Hau Nghia province, where the presence of an American division in the previous year had only freed main roads during day time between government-held provincial cities, the RVN was able to extend control over most of the province by 1969.[61]

The DRV's Defence Minister, General Giap said later: 'The Tet Offensive had been directed primarily at the people of South Vietnam, but as it turned out it affected the people of the United Sates more.'[62] Indeed, the

---

59 Nguyen Vu Tung, 'Coping with the United States', in Lowe (ed.), *The Vietnam War*, 46–8.

60 Peter Brush, 'The Battle of Khe Sanh, 1968', in Gilbert and Head (eds), *The Tet Offensive*, ch. 12. Larry Berman, *Lyndon Johnson's War: The Road to Stalemate in Vietnam* (New York 1989), ch. 9. Keith William Nolan, *The Battle of Hue: Tet, 1983* (Novata 1983). Turley, *Second Indochina War*, 97–108.

61 Tang, *Vietcong Memoir*, 154. Valentine, *Phoenix Program*, 179–92. Bergerud, *Dynamics of Defeat*, 205, 215–22.

62 Peter Macdonald, *Giap: The Victor in Vietnam* (New York 1993), 269.

Tet offensive was a watershed in American public attitudes to the Vietnam War. Dramatic television and newspaper pictures, such as the RVN police commissioner shooting a PLAF prisoner in the head in a Saigon street, were shattering illusions about a winnable war for the glorious cause of freedom. The grisly statistics of American deaths in the offensive reinforced rising resentment at the price that was being paid by the 30,347 Americans who had died in combat in Vietnam by the end of 1968. Already in 1967 there had been a huge demonstration in New York of over 200,000 people protesting against the war and big protest marches in other cities. Resistance by young people to being drafted for the war was spreading. There was growing disquiet caused by reports and photos of massacres of innocent people by indiscriminate bombing and napalm attacks on Vietnamese villages. The 10 per cent surtax in 1967 for an increasingly expensive war diminished public support for it. After the Tet offensive, a Gallup Poll result published on 10 March revealed that 49 per cent of Americans believed the US was wrong to have entered the Vietnam War, and only 33 per cent believed that America was making any progress in it. A majority of Johnson's closest advisers now opposed any expansion of the war and advocated more reliance on the ARVN, which had demonstrated surprising resilience and tenacity during the Tet offensive. Johnson then announced publicly his refusal to agree to Westmoreland's call for 206,000 more troops for an offensive strategy across the DRV border. But on 31 March the President told the nation that he would not stand for re-election. How far he was influenced by the anti-war movement, or by his apprehension of failure to win Democratic Party endorsement against a challenge by Robert Kennedy, or by a fear for his physical health is hard to determine. All these factors probably played a part. Johnson also announced a halt to bombing north of the 20th parallel in a search for a negotiated peace, though his government insisted on the preservation of an independent and non-communist RVN.[63]

The months of 1968 after the Tet offensive saw mounting opposition to the Vietnam War with large street demonstrations in American cities. In August the Democratic Party held its national convention in Chicago, while outside the convention hall street battles raged between police and anti-war demonstrators. The administration's search for peace talks did evoke a favourable response from Hanoi which, having failed to achieve a military

---

63 Herring, *America's Longest War*, 186–201, 209–28. Charles DeBenedetti and Charles Chatfield, *An American Ordeal: The Antiwar Movement of the Vietnam Era* (New York 1990), 203–15. Lloyd C. Gardiner, *Pay Any Price: Lyndon Johnson and the Wars for Vietnam* (Chicago 1995), ch. 19. Tom Wells, *The War Within: America's Battle over Vietnam* (Berkeley 1994), 261–2.

victory, was now ready to seek a diplomatic end to the war. So the DRV offered negotiations if the US ceased all bombing in North Vietnam. Johnson ordered that halt on 31 October. His announcement also was aimed at boosting the popularity of the Democratic Party candidate, Hubert Humphrey, who had been loyally supporting the president's Vietnam policy. But the Republican candidate, Nixon, who had publicly declared the Vietnam War above politics, used private Republican Party connections to support RVN President Thieu's refusal to attend any peace talks in Paris in order to stymie Johnson's peace initiative. The announcement of Thieu's intransigence deflated a surge of public euphoria about peace prospects before the 5 November election, which Nixon won narrowly, with a mere 0.7 per cent advantage in the popular vote. However, Thieu would have opposed the peace plan without the Republican Party pressure, since the whole rationale of his regime depended on US support.[64]

Other nations and the Vietnam War

Many other countries in the Pacific Basin became actively involved in or were strongly influenced by the Vietnam War. Though this time the US had entered a war without UN sanction, pressure was placed on allies of America to make it a 'free world' crusade against communism. By the end of 1968 there were 65,761 allied military personnel in Vietnam, nearly all from five other Pacific Basin nations: South Korea, Thailand, the Philippines, Australia and New Zealand.[65]

The Australian government in 1964 was eager to join the contest because of its belief in Chinese complicity in the war and the threat to Australia that would flow from expanding Chinese influence in Vietnam and the rest of Southeast Asia. Sending Australian troops to South Vietnam also was considered an insurance policy for future support from the US, especially if Confrontation developed into a war between Indonesia and Australia. By 1968 Australia had a task force in Phuoc Tuy province, plus an air squadron and a naval destroyer, totalling 7,661 men. Their previous counterinsurgency experience in Malaya and Borneo encouraged the three Australian battalions to operate more effectively at foot patrol level than did the Americans with

64   Schulzinger, *A Time for War*, 269–73. Gardiner, *Pay Any Price*, ch. 21. Nguyen Vu Tung, 'Coping with the United States', in Lowe (ed.), *The Vietnam War*, 50–1. Stephen E. Ambrose, *Nixon: The Triumph of a Politician 1962–1972* (New York 1989), 206–22.

65   Robert M. Blackburn, *Mercenaries and Lyndon Johnson's 'More Flags': The Hiring of Korean, Filipino and Thai Soldiers in the Vietnam War* (Jefferson, N.C. 1994), 158.

their abundant technological mobility. Australia also provided economic and technical aid worth over $10.5 million from 1966 through 1968.[66]

New Zealand's contribution of two infantry companies, an artillery battery plus army and airforce support, numbered 516 men by 1968. They supported the Australian task force but were little more than a token gesture in response to US pressure for more foreign flags in the RVN. The National Party New Zealand government had preferred united action by SEATO, which had not been able to come to any agreement about military intervention in South Vietnam. The strong opposition to the military commitment by the New Zealand Labour Party reflected the comparative isolation of the country from Southeast Asia.[67]

Among America's Asian allies, Thailand sent 6,005 men to the RVN by 1968 and was providing pilot training for its airforce plus two naval ships to patrol its waters, the cost being paid for by the US. More valuable were the US airfields in Thailand that made major contributions to Rolling Thunder and to American air strikes in South Vietnam. These commitments reflected a $50 million military aid package to Thailand provided by the Kennedy administration, which had also stationed US troops there. American bases in the Philippines were important repair stations and staging posts for American ships and planes serving in the war zone. A new president, Ferdinand Marcos, sent in February 1966, at American expense, a 2,061 strong engineering battalion to the RVN. By far the biggest manpower contribution, 50,000 troops, came from South Korea, as repayment for American support during the Korean War and for continued US military protection. Washington, however, rejected Chiang Kai-shek's enthusiastic offer of troops for South Vietnam because of fear of provoking Chinese intervention in the war. Nationalist China provided only some technical and medical assistance. Japan, which remained loyal to its US ally, supplied medical teams and over $50 million worth of economic assistance to South Vietnam. US bases in Japan and Okinawa were also valuable for prosecuting the war.[68]

However, protests against American involvement in Vietnam emerged in Japan after the start of Rolling Thunder. Liberals, socialists, neo-nationalists and politically uncommitted intellectuals joined in public statements and

---

66 Ian McNeill, 'The Australian Army and the Vietnam War', in Peter Pierce, Jeff Doyle and Jeffrey Grey (eds), *Vietnam Days: Australia and the Impact of Vietnam* (Melbourne 1991), 11–61. Pemberton, *All the Way*, ch. 9. Stanley Robert Larsen and James Lawton Collins, Jr, *Allied Participation in Vietnam* (Washington 1975), 88–101.

67 Larsen and Collins, *Allied Participation in Vietnam* 23, 104–10, 116–35. Mark Pearson, *Paper Tiger: New Zealand's Part in SEATO 1954–1977* (Wellington 1989), 95–100.

68 Blackburn, *Mercenaries*, chs 3–5. Larsen and Collins, *Allied Participation*, 26–42, 52–76, 161–2. Thomas R.H. Havens, *Fire Across the Sea: The Vietnam War and Japan 1965–1975* (Princeton 1987), 223.

street rallies which tapped widespread anti-war sentiment. The Japanese anti-Vietnam War campaign became violent in October 1967 when helmeted and stave-carrying students, who were protesting against a planned visit by Prime Minister Sat Eisaku to South Vietnam, battled with riot police. This confrontation caused the first death of a Japanese anti-Vietnam War demonstrator. Other riots followed, provoked by incidents such as the first visit of a nuclear-powered American warship to Japan in January 1968; and the tension exploded into widespread violence on a day of national protest on 21 October 1968. Opinion polls showed that a clear majority of Japanese people wanted the Americans to stop using Japanese facilities for the war and to withdraw from Vietnam. But Sat did not budge from supporting the US in recognition of the US defence treaty that allowed Japan to ignore heavy expenditure for self-defence.[69]

Even Canada, while maintaining official neutrality in the Vietnam War, provided significant support for South Vietnam and for the American war effort. Canadian economic assistance to the RVN increased by 250 per cent in 1965–66 to CAN$1,254,700, and rose again to CAN$2,694,000 in 1967–68. The Liberal Party Canadian government insisted that it was not shipping arms to South Vietnam. In literal terms this statement was true. Canadian arms merely found their way to Vietnam via the US with the full knowledge of government authorities in Ottawa, who actively encouraged their production and sale and even suggested ways around Canada's own arms-export control legislation. A possible reason for this government duplicity was the estimated 125,000 jobs in Canada that had some relationship to the arms sales. Also about 10,000 Canadian volunteers joined the US army in South Vietnam.[70]

On the other side of the Vietnam War, the Soviet Union, from 1965 was becoming a stronger supporter of the DRV. After deciding to increase its military aid, USSR leader, Andrei Kosygin visited Hanoi in February 1965 and signed a defence pact between the USSR and the DRV. The USSR also condemned the American bombing of North Vietnam as a violation of the rules of the Cold War and declared its duty to give full support to North Vietnam's defence capability. Washington, however, breathed a sigh of relief that the criticism was so relatively mild and correctly interpreted that there was no prospect of any Soviet military intervention in Vietnam. One motive for the increased Soviet aid to the DRV was to counter the stronger Chinese influence. Moscow was miffed by the way DRV leaders turned to

69   Havens, *Fire Across the Sea*, chs 2–6.
70   Victor Levant, *Quiet Complicity: Canadian Involvement in the Vietnam War* (Toronto 1986), 68–78, 210–11. chs 6, 11–12.

Beijing for advice and withheld information about their war plans from the USSR. Indeed, the leadership in Moscow did not support the DRV military victory policy because of the Soviet concern to prevent the conflict becoming a global war. From 1964 Moscow was searching for a peaceful end to the conflict with offers of mediation starting with one that prompted a US bombing pause in December 1965. Indeed, the USSR was instrumental in achieving the first preliminary peace talks between American and North Vietnamese representatives in Paris in May 1968.[71]

China was a stronger supporter of the DRV war effort in the South. On a visit by Ho Chi Minh to Beijing in May 1965 he explained that the DRV would undertake the burden of fighting the war, but he also sought Chinese material assistance. Mao readily agreed. There was a further DRV–China agreement in June 1965 that if the US used naval and air power to support a South Vietnamese invasion of the North, China would send air and naval forces to North Vietnam. If American soldiers invaded the DRV China would send its army there. These Chinese guarantees and material support allowed the DRV to commit more resources to the war in South Vietnam. China also strenuously opposed negotiations for an end to the Vietnam War because that would free American forces to oppose liberation movements elsewhere; it would increase Soviet influence in Vietnam; and continued American aggression in Vietnam was useful to justify the cultural revolution in China. But consequently China opposed Vietnam's political use of peace initiatives. Also the thousands of Chinese military and technical personnel entering North Vietnam from 1965 created inevitable friction between Chinese and North Vietnamese. Furthermore, Hanoi was annoyed at the presence of a Chinese support team in Laos. In turn Beijing was angered when the DRV pressured the Laos government to expel the team in 1968 and was irritated by the growing Soviet influence in the DRV. Consequently, by that year there were serious tensions between North Vietnam and China. These tensions were exacerbated that year by the DRV's willingness to start negotiations with the US. The Chinese reaction was to start withdrawing engineering and anti-aircraft troops from North Vietnam.[72]

A by-product of the Vietnam War was North Korea's capture in international waters on 23 January 1968 of the USS *Pueblo*, which was engaged in electronic intelligence gathering. North Korea had used the distraction of the Vietnam War for provocative acts against the ROK. The latest had

---

71 Gaiduk, 'The Soviet Union and Vietnam', in Lowe (ed.), *The Vietnam War*, 143–5. Gaiduk, *The Soviet Union and the Vietnam War*, chs 5–7.

72 Chen Jian, 'China and the Vietnam War', in Lowe (ed.), *The Vietnam War*, 167–70, 176–8. Qiang Zhai, 'Opposing Negotiations: China and the Vietnam Peace Talks', *Pacific Historical Review*, 68 (1999), 21–50.

been a thwarted attempt on 21 January by a DPRK commando squad to assassinate President Park Chung Hee. There was fear in Washington that this new provocation against the world's largest naval power was designed to suck the Americans into another war when there were nearly 500,000 US troops in South Vietnam. Bob Lisky, who worked in US Military Intelligence at the time, says there was discussion about employing a tactical nuclear air-burst over North Korea's harbour of Wonsan in order to deny North Korean access to the *Pueblo*. But the US administration rejected any hostile act against North Korea. Consequently, the *Pueblo*'s crew languished for eleven months in North Korean prisons knowing they were there because the USS *Enterprise* had failed to provide their ship with expected air protection.[73]

Japan was a major beneficiary from the Vietnam War. It provided a base for an estimated 40,000 American troops during the war and served a greater number of Americans on rest and recreation leave, all of whom contributed to the Japanese economy. Japan's exports to South Vietnam boomed from about $35 million per year before 1965 to $199 million in 1968. Some of the exports were American procurements, but South Vietnam's American-injected wealth attracted a host of Japanese consumer goods. Japan further benefited from the increased buying power of other Southeastern Asian states, which also were experiencing a Vietnam War-driven economic boom. The year 1965 was a turning point for the entry of Japanese capital into Southeast Asia, which by 1969 was worth $355 million. The Vietnam War assisted Japan's gross national product (GNP) to climb back to the levels of the 1950s from a low of 4 per cent per annum in 1965 to 14 per cent per annum in 1968. That year's GNP of $141.9 billion moved Japan past West Germany into second place behind the US, though the Japanese per capita GNP was only about half that of West Germany and one-third of the American level.[74]

The other East Asian non-communist economies started to experience accelerated growth rates under the influence of the trade boom generated by the Vietnam War. South Korea was well placed to take advantage of increased trading opportunities as a result of a military coup in 1961, which overthrew Rhee, who displayed little interest in economics and presided over a country still suffering from the ravages of war and dependency on US aid. The new president, Park, placed a priority on economic development,

---

73 Bob Lisky, 'Participated in decision regarding nuclear response to USS PUEBLO seizure as Ch, Intel Br, G-2, EUSA', world wide web accessed 10 November 1999 at www.koreanwar.org/htm/units/dmz_pueblo.htm.

74 Havens, *Fire Across the Sea*, 103–5. *The Far East and Australasia: A Survey and Directory of Asia and the Pacific* (London 1969–) (*FEA*), 1969, 709; 1970, 779.

inaugurating fiscal reform and emphasizing expansion of exports by freeing them from restrictive regulations. With the assistance of the Vietnam War trade boom, the ROK's exports of goods and services, at prices adjusted for inflation, rose from 57.06 billion won in 1964 to 235.03 billion in 1968. This era marked the beginnings of the South Korean 'economic miracle'. Taiwan also enjoyed an export-led economic boom that started earlier in the 1960s as a result of economic reforms centring on export incentives, but which received a fillip from the Vietnam War. Taiwan's exports rose from NT$17.998 billion in 1965 to NT$31.567 billion in 1968.[75]

The general growth of trade generated by the Vietnam War also was benefiting Hong Kong. The colony experienced a five-fold growth in the value of its manufacturing, which was diversifying from its textiles base into electronic and other goods and which contributed to 80 per cent of the colony's exports by 1969. Whereas in 1951 there were 2000 factories in Hong Kong supporting 95,000 workers, by 1966 there were 10,413 factories employing 635,000. But there had not been commensurate increases in personal wealth for many of Hong Kong's people, who had swollen in number to 3.7 million people in 1966. That year protests over increased ferry fares boiled over into two nights of ugly rioting. There was a much longer four month period of rioting in 1967 emerging from an industrial dispute that became a left-wing challenge, influenced by the cultural revolution in China, to the paternalistic British Hong Kong administration.[76]

In Southeast Asia a new cooperative arrangement was developing in the wake of the international turmoil in that region. On 8 August 1967 the Foreign Ministers of Indonesia, the Philippines, Singapore and Thailand and the Deputy Prime Minister of Malaysia signed in Bangkok an agreement to establish an Association of Southeast Asian Nations (ASEAN). The main objectives of ASEAN were to promote economic growth, to foster social and cultural relations and to preserve peace among its members. Provision was made for an annual meeting of foreign ministers and for a standing committee, but there was no permanent secretariat. Though accused by China of being an anti-communist league, ASEAN had no pretensions to be a defensive alliance or to project military power. However, Indonesia's Foreign Minister, Adam Malik, commented 'it was the fact that there was a

---

75 Paul W. Kuznet, *Economic Growth and Structure in the Republic of Korea* (New Haven 1977), 90–2, 220. Rong-I Wu, 'The Distinctive Features of Taiwan's Development', in Peter L. Berger and Hsin-Huang Michael Hsiao, *In Search of an East Asian Developmental Model* (New Brunswick 1990), 179–96. Samuel S. Ho, *Economic Development of Taiwan, 1860–1970* (New Haven 1978), 198, 392.

76 Theodore Geiger and Frances M. Geiger, *The Development Progress of Hong Kong and Singapore* (London 1975), 78–9. Felix Patrikeeff, *Mouldering Pearl: Hong Kong at the Crossroads* (London 1989), 43–51.

convergence in the political outlook of the five prospective member-nations
. . . which provided the main stimulus to join together in ASEAN'. Indeed,
the idea grew out of Thailand's facilitating of the agreement between
Malaysia and Indonesia to end Confrontation. In 1968 there was a suspension of ASEAN meetings when the Philippines reactivated claims to Sabah,
with a consequent disruption of diplomatic relations between Kuala Lumpur
and Manila. This dispute demonstrated the early fragility of ASEAN, but it
was to be resolved in 1969.[77]

Conclusions

The Western Pacific Basin in 1968 was therefore a mixture of international
conflict and cooperation. The US and its Asian and Australasian allies were
locked in a bitter conflict with the NLF in South Vietnam and with North
Vietnam supported by China and the USSR. The US take-over of the war
effort in 1965 was partially a repetition of the Korea experience with the
development of a similar military stalemate. However, a fundamental difference was that in Vietnam there was a mainly guerrilla conflict rather
than a conventional war, and there was a failure in Washington to understand
the strength of home-grown support for the NLF, resulting in inadequate
pacification programs.

The Vietnam War had other major Pacific Basin consequences, especially
in the Western Pacific Basin. The massively increased US war effort in
Vietnam was generating significant economic growth in Japan and in the
emerging East Asian economies of South Korea, Taiwan, Hong Kong and
Singapore. The war was also boosting Japanese economic expansion in
East and Southeast Asia. ASEAN was a new venture in Southeast Asian
cooperation after the failure of Sukarno's military confrontation of Malaysia.

---

77   Roger Irvine, 'The Formative Years of ASEAN: 1967–1975', in Alison Broinowski (ed.),
     Understanding ASEAN (London 1983), 8–20 (quotation 14).

CHAPTER FOUR

Détente, Disengagement and Invasion in East and Southeast Asia, 1969–1979

The main theme of this chapter is the way the new US administration sought to disengage from the Vietnam War and how the process included the beginnings of a new détente between the US and China plus improvements in US–Soviet relations that were to have a major influence on weakening the impact of the Cold War in the Pacific Basin. Another theme is how new conflicts in Indochina emerged after the US disengagement. An additional subject is the Indonesian invasion of East Timor and its aftermath. Economic growth in the Western Pacific Basin is further discussed, including the beginnings of trade friction between Japan and the US.

Searching for an end to the Vietnam War

The Vietnam War was a pressing concern facing Nixon when he became the US president in January 1969. He and his special advisor in national security affairs, Henry Kissinger, a German-born political science professor and government international affairs consultant, realized that no military victory was feasible, given the strength of the anti-war movement in the US. Determined to make their mark in history, they refused to contemplate a 'dishonorable' withdrawal, which could leave them open to the accusation of 'losing Vietnam' to communism. Nixon had been prominent in such attacks on the Truman administration's China policy. Furthermore, as new administrators of the awesome power of the US, Nixon and Kissinger believed they could pressure Hanoi into agreeing to a peace that would preserve the integrity of the RVN. However, they also saw the iridescent anti-Vietnam War writing on US political walls and were determined to commence a process of withdrawal of American troops from Vietnam. Hence the Nixon administration supported increasing the size and power of the ARVN, so that it could eventually defend a non-communist South Vietnam, a policy known as 'Vietnamization', which had commenced under the Johnson administration in 1968. Initially, however, Nixon did not publicly announce any plan to withdraw troops from Vietnam.[1]

On the diplomatic front, he proposed to Hanoi, through French intermediaries, a mutual US–DRV troop withdrawal from South Vietnam. Nixon and Kissinger also wished to project an image of American toughness by demonstrating their willingness to remove constraints imposed on the US war effort by Johnson. They ruled out resuming any bombing of North Vietnam to avoid inflaming the peace movement, which would encourage the DRV to believe that Americans wanted to abandon the war. Instead, Nixon and Kissinger implemented on 18 March 1969 Operation Menu, which extended the bombing campaign to Cambodia, but they also ensured its secrecy. The main military targets were PLAF sanctuaries and a reported NLF command structure, the Central Committee Directorate for South Vietnam (COSVN).[2]

Since achieving independence in 1954, Cambodia had been walking a neutral tightrope under its leader, Prince Norodom Sihanouk. Born in 1922 and ruler of his country since 1941, he was a flashy potentate but also an intelligent and shrewd politician, whose overriding aim was to preserve his country's independence. His refusal to join SEATO and his rejection of American pressure to suppress communists caused American expenditure of military and economic aid that was used to win support for the US among Cambodian army officers and the social elite. The prince, who considered that Hanoi would win the war in South Vietnam and who was outraged by South Vietnamese military raids across the Cambodian border, in 1964 rejected US aid and expelled American citizens. In the next year he broke diplomatic relations with the US after *Newsweek* accused his family of running brothels in the capital city, Phnom Penh. More fundamentally, he was protesting at the US bombing of North Vietnam and continued RVN cross-border attacks. The US army's 'search and destroy' strategy forced PLAF units to seek shelter in Cambodia, which Sihanouk tolerated. He also submitted to Chinese pressure in 1966 to use the port of Sihanoukville as a source of supply for the PLAF. His 6,557,000 subjects in 1968 lacked power to resist such pressures.[3]

---

1   Stephen E. Ambrose, *Nixon: The Triumph of a Politician* 2, 256–8.
2   William Shawcross, *Sideshow: Kissinger, Nixon and the Destruction of Cambodia* (New York 1981), ch. 1. Joan Hoff, *Nixon Reconsidered* (New York 1994), 227, 210–16.
3   Shawcross, *Sideshow*, ch. 3. *FEA*, 1971, 422–7.

Starved of military supplies and accusing China of supporting communist Khmer Rouge rebels in his country, Sihanouk turned back to the US in 1967. One result was a visit to Phnom Penh in January 1968 by the US ambassador in India, Chester Bowles. The Nixon administration later claimed that Sihanouk gave Bowles the green light for Operation Menu. This is very doubtful, given that the purpose of Bowles's Mission was to smooth relations between the two countries, including the easing of Cambodian fears about American 'hot pursuit' of NLF insurgents across the Cambodian border.[4]

Operation Menu, which in the next fifteen months dropped over 100,000 tons of bombs on Cambodia, did not achieve its aim of frightening the DRV into offering negotiating concessions. Hanoi had reacted to the debilitating failure of its Tet offensive by reducing large-scale military actions in South Vietnam. Battalion or greater size attacks on US/ARVN forces declined from 126 in 1968 to 34 in 1969, the lowest rate since 1964. However, small-scale attacks and other terrorist activities did not diminish in number, which represented the switching back to the 'swarm of gnats' strategy of destabilizing the enemy. There was recognition by the VCP Politburo in January 1969 of the country's 'limited material resources', its unwillingness to be 'dependent on any other country' and 'the worsening Sino-Soviet Relations'. Therefore, it would be impossible 'to defeat the US militarily, and force the US to withdraw'. So Hanoi had added a diplomatic dimension to its strategy. On the other hand, the Tet offensive had delivered the advantage of a larger American peace movement, which would eventually force an American withdrawal from Vietnam. Therefore, it was unnecessary to submit to American peace demands. Consequently, Nixon and Kissinger learned from Hanoi that the prerequisite for peace would be a total US withdrawal from South Vietnam and abandonment of Thieu's government.[5]

Hanoi's decision was also influenced by increased Soviet military materiel support. Moscow was acting to bolster its influence in the DRV at the expense of China. The USSR therefore rejected American moves to link the Vietnam War issue to other issues in Soviet–American relations such as peace in the Middle East and nuclear arms control. Moscow staunchly supported Hanoi's stance in negotiations with the US.[6]

---

4   Shawcross, *Sideshow*, ch. 4. Kenton J. Clymer, 'The Perils of Neutrality: The Break in US–Cambodian Relations, 1965', *Diplomatic History*, 23 (1999), 609–31.

5   Thomas C. Thayer, *War Without Fronts: The American Experience in Vietnam* (Boulder 1985), 44–5. Douglas Pike, *PAVN: People's Army of Vietnam* (Novala 1986), 226–8. Nguyen Vu Tung, 'Hanoi's Search for an Effective Strategy', in Peter Lowe (ed.), *The Vietnam War* (New York 1998), 52–6.

6   Ilya V. Gaiduk, 'The Soviet Union and Vietnam', in Lowe (ed.), *The Vietnam War*, 148–9. Ilya V. Gaiduk, *The Soviet Union and the Vietnam War* (Chicago 1996), ch. 10. Robert K. Brigham, *Guerrilla Diplomacy: The NLF's Foreign Policy and the Vietnam War* (Ithaca 1999), 87.

Nixon and Kissinger also realized the need to convince the American public that they genuinely sought peace. So on 29 April 1969 Nixon announced that during the next twelve months 150,000 men would be withdrawn from Vietnam in concert with improving the ARVN. In May he publicly revealed his peace initiatives to the DRV. In June, after a conference with Thieu on Midway Island in mid Pacific, Nixon announced the evacuation of the first 25,000 US troops from South Vietnam.[7]

Nevertheless, anti-war protesters were soon disillusioned by the absence of any announced progress in US–DRV negotiations. The planned troop withdrawal was condemned as much too slow. On 15 October tens of thousands marched and attended teach-ins in American cities in a 'Moratorium' day of protest. Nixon, already showing intolerance of dissent by authorizing FBI surveillance and legal harassment of left-wing organizations, went on a counter offensive with an organized pro-administration campaign. Especially effective was a nationally televised address on 3 November, in which he plucked his audience's patriotic heart strings, dismissed the anti-war movement as a noisy minority and appealed for the support of the 'great silent majority' of Americans. This speech regained for him the political initiative. A Gallup Poll soon declared that 77 per cent of American people were supporting the President's Vietnam policy.[8]

The Vietnamization policy had resulted by 1970 in a growth of the ARVN from 311,000 in 1967 to 429,000. Including air, naval irregular forces, the RVN had nearly a million men under arms. A huge stock of US arms also had been handed over, and many US troops were pulled out of large-scale offensive operations to join the ARVN in an accelerated pacification program.[9]

However, relations between US troops and Vietnamese people were bedevilled by racism and cultural arrogance. A feature of the closer contact was the often contemptuous American attitude towards the ARVN, which many US soldiers regarded as reluctant to fight and a threat to the safety of Americans. The US troops brought with them a 'civic action' program to South Vietnamese villages aimed at improving agricultural production, education and other facilities. But too many Americans regarded Vietnamese, especially peasants, as subhuman, calling them 'gooks', 'dinks' and other derogatory names. The consequent arrogant and at times brutal behaviour

---

7 George C. Herring, *America's Longest War: The United States and Vietnam 1950–1975* (3rd edition, New York 1996), 257–8.

8 Charles DeBenedetti and Charles Chatfield, *An American Ordeal: The Antiwar Movement of the Vietnam Era* (New York 1990), 238–61.

9 William S. Turley, *The Second Indochina War: A Short Political Military History, 1954–1975* (Boulder 1986), 128–30.

of the soldiers, who also were becoming disillusioned with withdrawal from active fighting and disaffected by the peace movement at home, was counter productive. In My Thuy Phuong village, which in 1968 experienced the establishment of the US 101st Air-borne Division 'Camp Eagle' on its boundary, villagers had few good words for the aid programs.[10]

Furthermore, there were still grave inadequacies in the quality of the ARVN and popular forces. Officers continued to be drawn mainly from the urban elite. Corruption was rife in promotions and even in the supply of basic services to poorly paid troops. The popular forces, on which village security mostly depended, were even less effective. A study of their operations in Hau Nghia province during 1970 concluded that a very large percentage of contacts with insurgents were made by a very small percentage of the province's thirty-three regional and seventy-seven popular force units. In My Thuy Phuong village few popular force soldiers could shoot straight; most preferred to stay in base and could not be trusted to stay awake on guard duty. A fundamental morale weakness was summed up by a villager's comment: 'How could the Regional Forces be good? None of the soldiers wanted to fight and die for Mr Thieu.'[11]

There were members of Thieu's administration who advocated reforms in order to create wider popular support, and also to counter a growing view in the US that the South Vietnam was a corrupt autocracy unworthy of the blood and treasure that the US had poured out to save it. The RVN ambassador to the US, Bui Diem, sent a stream of such advice in his regular correspondence with Saigon, reinforcing it on a home visit in July 1970. Thieu was prompted to redress some of the worst errors of previous regimes with a return to local election of village officials, and in 1970 he launched a 'land for the tillers' programme. But capable villagers were unwilling to stand for office. Nor did the new village councils have sufficient authority to break the power of corrupt provincial chiefs. Also in Hau Nghia province much of the government land distributed to landless peasants was soon abandoned because of continuing guerrilla warfare, and the government land reform paled into insignificance compared with previous NLF land redistribution. Furthermore, Thieu in 1971 destroyed much of his credibility by using CIA money, assassinations and voting instructions to provincial chiefs to convince political opponents that there was no point in standing against him in that year's presidential election. Bui Diem regarded

---

10 Eric M. Bergerud, *The Dynamics of Defeat: The Vietnam War in Hau Nghia Province* (Boulder 1991), 223–34. Louis A. Wiesner, *Victims and Survivors: Displaced Persons and Other War Victims in Viet-Nam, 1954–1975* (Westport 1988), 356. James Walker Trullinger, *Village at War: An Account of Revolution in Vietnam* (New York 1980), 138–9.
11 Trullinger, *Village at War*, 169–70. Bergerud, *Dynamics of Defeat*, 294–5.

the consequent one-man election as 'a point of no return, at which the search for a vivifying national purpose was finally discarded in favor of the chimerical strength of an autocrat'.[12]

The government of South Vietnam had benefited from a short breathing space in its struggle with the NLF, which now called itself the People's Revolutionary Government of South Vietnam (PRG). The failed offensive strategy in 1968 placed the insurgent cause on a back foot. In both Long An and Hau Nghia provinces on the southern and western sides of Saigon, government influence extended dramatically under the impact of US army action at village level. In Long An surrenders of PLAF members rose dramatically in March–April 1969 and remained high into 1970, when US intelligence calculated 427 surviving insurgents in the province. In Hau Nghia, PLAF units had retreated into jungle hideouts or into Cambodian sanctuaries. Local recruiting for the PLAF also had fallen off, forcing reinforcement by PAVN troops.[13]

However, communist influence in the RVN had not been eliminated. A major reason was the flexible small cell basis of PRG organization and the way many of its members blended into the community, including serving in government militia and police. In Hau Nghia intensive Phoenix hunting of PRG personnel was bedevilled by inadequacy of information, by police corruption and by PLAF retaliatory assassinations. Thus during 1970 in South Vietnam, while battalion sized attacks on US/ARVN forces dramatically declined to thirteen, smaller unit attacks merely fell to 3,526 from 3,578 the year before. Also the morale of the PRG had been boosted in 1969 by recognition by the USSR, which was followed in 1970 by many third world countries, including India.[14]

An American response to continuing insurgent aggression in South Vietnam was a joint US–ARVN invasion of the PRG's Cambodian sanctuaries in April 1970. A green light for this campaign was shone by a new regime in Cambodia which overthrew Sihanouk on 18 March. The coup was led by Lieutenant-General Lon Nol, a French educated former Minister for National Defence, who had been appointed as Sihanouk's prime minister in January 1970. Sihanouk, who was visiting Europe at the time of the coup, blamed the CIA for organizing it. Nixon and Kissinger claimed they were surprised to hear of the coup, but, if so, their administration had

12 Bergerud, *Dynamics of Defeat*, 268–72, 298–300. Bui Diem with David Chanoff, *In the Jaws of History* (Boston 1987), 277, 293.

13 Jeffrey Race, *War Comes to Long An: Revolutionary Conflict in a Vietnamese Province* (Berkeley 1973), 269. Bergerud, *Dynamics of Defeat*, 251–4.

14 Bergerud, *Dynamics of Defeat*, 255–61, 313–15. Thayer, *War Without Fronts*, 44. Brigham, *Guerrilla Diplomacy*, 87–8.

been ignoring intelligence reports. Furthermore, Nixon on the next day was issuing instructions 'for maximum assistance' to pro-American groups in Cambodia. There were good reasons for Washington to support a coup. Operation Menu had failed in its objectives. Sanctuaries for NLF forces were still being used, and COSVN had not been destroyed. Nor had Sihanouk, in Washington's opinion, done enough to expel the PLAF. A CIA agent in Saigon at the time, Frank Snepp, says that his agency and the MACV believed that Lon Nol 'would welcome the United States with open arms and we would accomplish everything'.[15]

The Cambodian invasion was a poisoned chalice for Cambodians and for Nixon. The much sought-after COSVN prize was never found. The invasion's main result was to drive PLAF forces deeper into Cambodia. When the US troops pulled out, the ARVN engaged in an orgy of indiscriminate violence and looting of the civilian population. In Beijing Sihanouk formed a government in exile containing members of the Khmer Rouge, who now were receiving support from Hanoi and China. The invasion of Cambodia thereby gave a major push to Cambodia's roller-coaster ride to the abyss of mass destruction. In the US, the Cambodian invasion served to re-ignite the anti-war movement, especially on university campuses, resulting in the killing on 4 May of four students at Kent State University in Ohio by national guardsmen. Even Cabinet members protested, resulting in the sacking of Warren Hickel, the Secretary for the Interior. The new wave of anti-war anger was feeding the growth of a siege mentality in the White House that was to lead to the destruction of Nixon's presidency.[16]

The Nixon administration, however, was continuing its phased evacuation of troops from South Vietnam. By the end of 1969 a withdrawal of 90,000 army, airforce and naval personnel had been authorized; further major reductions occurred in the next two years. By the end of 1971 American troops had shrunk to 120,600 plus 37,000 air and naval personnel. US combat deaths also had dropped dramatically from 14,592 in 1968 to 1,380 in 1971.[17]

The major reduction in US forces and casualties in Vietnam helped to quieten the American peace movement. There was a small bout of protests after the ARVN was sent on a disastrous incursion into Laos in February 1971. There was a major anti-war public campaign in late April–early May with an encampment in Washington of Vietnam Veterans Against the War

15 Henry Kissinger, *The White House Years* (London 1979), 465. Snepp quoted in Shawcross, *Sideshow*, 115.
16 Shawcross, *Sideshow*, ch. 10. Turley, *Second Indochina War*, 134–5. Young, *The Vietnam Wars*, 245–50.
17 Thayer, *War Without Fronts*, 37–8, 107.

and the arrival in that city of thousands of others to declare their opposition to the war. Military-style police action against these protesters after 1 May, including mass arrests, deterred future potential demonstrators. The violence of the college protests in 1971, which had included the torching of buildings, had created an anti-demonstration backlash among many students. The winding down of the hated draft, which finally ended in January 1972, also decreased much personal anger against the war. Nixon was spared from living out his apocalyptic vision of 'a thousand incoherent hippies urinating on the Oval Office rug'.[18]

Nixon, however, had further reasons to be aggrieved with opponents of the Vietnam War. In July 1971 the *New York Times* started publishing excerpts from 7,000 pages of a secret Defence Department dossier and supporting documents, the *Pentagon Papers*. These extracts revealed the duplicity of many public statements of the Kennedy and Johnson administrations about the escalation of US military involvement in Vietnam and exposed the US role in supporting the RVN's breaking of the 1954 Geneva Agreements. An enraged Nixon sought a Supreme Court order against their publication, but this failed. Obsessed with a perception that government leaks might become a deluge that would politically drown him, Nixon authorized the formation of a group of 'plumbers' to take preventive action, employing illegal phone taps, surveillance, infiltration of 'enemy' groups and even burglary. Nixon thereby primed a political time bomb that later blasted him from office. Furthermore, despite diminishing street protests, a majority of Americans had become demoralized about the war. An opinion poll in November recorded that 65 per cent of respondents considered the war was 'morally wrong'. Encouraging this view was a national controversy over the sentencing on 31 March 1971 of Lieutenant William Calley to life imprisonment for murdering at least twenty-two of the many more Vietnamese victims at My Lai in 1968, though Nixon moved him from prison to house arrest. Many Americans justifiably considered Calley was a scapegoat for a much wider disorder in the American army in Vietnam. A hundred disillusioned young Vietnam veterans publicly testified for three days at a Detroit motel about many rapes, tortures and murders of Vietnamese civilians by American soldiers that they had participated in or had witnessed.[19]

The Nixon administration, however, was still hoping to preserve a non-communist RVN. It was relying on the Vietnamization program with

---

18   Melvin Small, *Johnson, Nixon and the Doves* (New Brunswick 1988), ch. 7. Nixon quoted in Benjamin F. Schemmer, *The Raid* (London 1977), 164.
19   *The Pentagon Papers as Published by The New York Times* (New York 1971), ix–xi. DeBenedetti and Chatfield, *An American Ordeal*, 314–18. Herring, *America's Longest War*, 266–7.

continued US air support. Nixon and Kissinger also were working towards an international agreement to impose a Korea-style solution upon Vietnam.

US moves towards China and the USSR

A key to this diplomatic game was improving US relations with Beijing. Nixon confessed later that he had not appreciated the Sino-Soviet split until 1966, but then he publicly argued that the US should reassess its China policy, though maintaining 'a policy of firm restraint'. In his first news conference as President in 1969 he struck a new foreign policy note by expressing an interest in any changes in Chinese government attitudes. He also asked President De Gaulle of France to convey a message to Beijing that the US was 'going to withdraw from Vietnam come what may', which was a response to China's concern about the large US military presence in South Vietnam.[20]

China responded positively. There were good diplomatic reasons to seek an accommodation with the US. Beijing had condemned, more vehemently than Western nations, the Soviet invasion of Czechoslovakia in 1968. The proclamation by the Soviet Premier, Leonid Brezhnev, about the right of the USSR to intervene in the affairs of socialist countries was ominous for China. In March 1969 the first of a series of armed border clashes between USSR and Chinese forces reflected the freezing of relations between the two nations. However, Beijing's initial approach to Washington was pursued very cautiously because of disputes about such a radical step within the Chinese government. The US made the running in a gradual process that led to a secret visit by Kissinger to Beijing in July 1971. The dramatic break-through occurred in February 1972 with Nixon's triumphant visit to China, the first by an American president. In China, Kissinger and Nixon promised that the US would not support Taiwan's independence and that Washington would reveal to Beijing any understandings between the US and the USSR. But China refused the request to pressure North Vietnam into a peace agreement. Nevertheless, the discussions confirmed that China would not intervene in the Vietnam War, a fear that had been limiting US bombing in North Vietnam. Also it was clear that there was no Chinese

---

20 Richard M. Nixon, 'Asia After Viet Nam', *Foreign Affairs*, 46, 1967, 123. Richard Nixon, *In the Arena: A Memoir of Victory, Defeat, and Renewal* (New York 1990), 11–15. William Burr (ed.), *The Kissinger Transcripts: The Top Secret Talks with Beijing and Moscow* (New York 1998), 12.

threat elsewhere in Southeast Asia. The Vietnam domino bogy that had so motivated the policies of Nixon's predecessors was dead.[21]

Nixon and Kissinger were also able to exploit Sino-Soviet tensions in US/USSR relations. Initially, Moscow tried to drive wedges between the USA and China. A strong message was given to the US in October 1969 that it would be 'a very grave miscalculation' if Washington tried to profit from approaches to China 'at the Soviet Union's expense'. Soviet intelligence also warned Beijing of US plans to escalate American military activity in Vietnam. But the warming of US/China relations continued, culminating in Nixon's visit to China. So the Kremlin tried a different strategy by inviting Nixon to Moscow in May 1972. The Soviet ambassador to the US, Anatoly Dobrynin explained an important motive: 'it was essential to avert or neutralize any collusion between Washington and Beijing'. Nixon was delighted to be the first American president to visit the Soviet capital city, where he and Kissinger negotiated agreements to foster trade and scientific cooperation, a pledge of peaceful coexistence and a commitment to further talks on arms reduction. But significantly, on his return, Kissinger informed Han Xu, the head of the new Chinese liaison office in Washington, that the US had rejected Brezhnev's request at the Moscow meeting for joint Soviet–American action against China's nuclear power industry.[22]

Ending the Vietnam War

While the Nixon administration was breaking the ice of US relations with the two communist superpowers, Hanoi launched another major military attack on South Vietnam. During 1970–71 the DRV had been playing a waiting game. There were only two PLAF/PAVN attacks of battalion size or greater during 1971, during which time there was successful rebuilding of the rural insurgency infrastructure that had been heavily damaged after the offensives of 1968. While there were violent reactions to RVN pacification efforts, small-scale attacks declined by more than a third during 1971. However, in May 1971, boosted by the receipt of new Soviet heavy weapons,

---

21 Chang, *Friends and Enemies*, 281–90. James Mann, *About Face: A History of America's Curious Relationship with China, from Nixon to Clinton* (New York 1999), chs 1–2.

22 Gaiduk, *The Soviet Union and the Vietnam War*, 227–30. Chang, *Friends and Enemies*, 285–6. Ambrose, *Nixon*, 525–6, 544–8. Anatoly Dobrynin, *In Confidence: Moscow's Ambassador to America's Six Cold War Presidents (1962–1986)* (New York 1995), 193. Burr (ed.), *The Kissinger Transcripts*, 126, 131.

Hanoi decided to launch a major offensive in 1972. The failure of the American peace movement in the US to shift the Nixon administration's hard-line negotiating stand motivated Hanoi to force the US to negotiate from a position of weakness after a North Vietnamese military victory in South Vietnam. It also was calculated that, with the American troop withdrawal nearly complete and an election year looming in the US, its army would not rush back to assist the RVN.[23]

However, Nixon and Kissinger were still prepared to use air power to frustrate the DRV objective. Upon receiving reports of military stockpiling on the northern side of the demilitarized zone, Nixon used the excuse of an insurgent artillery attack on Saigon, which broke the terms of the 1968 bombing halt, to resume on 26 December 1971 bombing of North Vietnam south of the 20th parallel. US air units in the RVN also were strengthened. Washington was hoping to dissuade Hanoi from the invasion that his military advisors predicted for February 1972. Nevertheless, the DRV attack on the RVN commenced on 30 March, the day before Easter.[24]

This Easter offensive was more powerful than Washington anticipated. Three PAVN divisions, backed by 200 Soviet-supplied tanks and heavy artillery, smashed across the demilitarized zone to quickly overrun Quan Tri province. Another division attacked in the western highlands. On 2 April a third front was opened by three more PAVN divisions from across the Cambodian border to the north of Saigon. Within five days they were besieging the provincial city of An Loc. When the ARVN 21st division was rushed north from the Mekong Delta to defend that city, a fourth front was opened in that region by three PAVN regiments supported by PLAF guerrillas.[25]

Nixon was furious at the news of the offensive. The US response was massive air strikes against PAVN forces in South Vietnam and their supply routes plus the most comprehensive-ever bombing campaign against North Vietnam. On 8 May Nixon ordered the mining of Haiphong harbour, correctly calculating that the USSR would not intervene. Moscow launched verbal protests but did not allow the détente process to be upset by the American 'aggression' against the DRV. With this Soviet acquiescence, Nixon and Kissinger increased their pressure on North Vietnam by launching

---

23   Thayer, *War Without Fronts*, 44. Ngo Vinh Long, 'South Vietnam', in ibid., 85–6. Nguyen Vu Tung, 'Hanoi's Search for an Effective Strategy', in Lowe (ed.), *The Vietnam War*, 55–6. Brigham, *Guerrilla Diplomacy*, 100–1.
24   Mark Clodfelter, *The Limits of Air Power: The American Bombing of North Vietnam* (New York 1989), 151–2.
25   Turley, *Second Indochina War*, 140–1.

Operation Linebacker against targets in Hanoi and Haiphong, using new laser-guided 'smart' bombs. 'The bastards have never been bombed like they're going to be bombed this time', exulted Nixon to his White House aides.[26]

Initially the intense bombing of PAVN troops did not stop their continued advance into the RVN. Much of the central highlands region was overrun. Quang Tri city in the north fell on 1 May with some 8,000 berserk ARVN troops fleeing to Hue, which was swelling with thousands of civilian refugees. Unprotected hamlets in the Delta were rapidly falling to PAVN/PLAF attacks. But the PAVN offensive, suffering the most intense bombing of the whole war, ran out of steam by mid June. An Loc was saved and, under a new more efficient commander, the ARVN inched forward to recapture Quang Tri city on 16 September, a major victory. Nevertheless, the PAVN retained control of northern Quang Tri province, much of the central highlands and over a million additional people in the Delta. It was only a partial ARVN victory, helped greatly by US air power.[27]

The battlefield stalemate in Vietnam encouraged both the US and the DRV to search for peace. Nixon faced a renewal of the anti-war movement. It was more muted than previously, with less massively attended public rallies. But it had a new institutionalized focus, with important Congressmen, such as Democratic Party Senators, Edward Kennedy and John Tunney, taking a public stand with peace demonstrators alongside a host of media and other national celebrities. Most ominously, there were threats in Congress to cut off funds for military action in Vietnam. Nixon had been able to keep ahead of his anti-war opponents by publicly announcing before the DRV offensive his peace terms, in which he offered to trade a complete American withdrawal for guarantees for the preservation of a non-communist South Vietnam and the return of US prisoners of war from North Vietnam. He was able to represent the PAVN attacks on the RVN as a breach of faith by Hanoi, and he justified the bombing as a means to achieve peace on honourable terms. He demonstrated his peace credentials with continued withdrawal of US military personnel from Vietnam to a level of only 39,000 by September 1972. His foreign policy prestige also was boosted by his trips to Beijing and Moscow.

Furthermore, the anti-war movement succeeded in derailing the Democratic Party. Peace activists succeeded in nominating Senator George

---

26 Clodfelter, *Limits of Air Power*, 147–63. Nixon quoted in DeBenedetti and Chatfield, *An American Ordeal*, 333.

27 Turley, *Second Indochina War*, 142–4. G.H. Turley, *The Easter Offensive: Vietnam 1972* (Novato 1985).

McGovern as presidential candidate on a platform of unilateral withdrawal from Vietnam. But he was weakened by dissension within his party, by an early image of indecisiveness and by vulnerability to charges of lack of patriotism. His campaign was damaged further by much more lavish Republican spending and by covert destabilizing activities. Nevertheless, Kissinger was enamoured with the prospect of adding peace in Vietnam to the administration's China and USSR foreign policy triumphs before the presidential election.[28]

Hanoi was also being pressured to find a peaceful solution to the war. Its offensive in the South had stalled and had not been approved by the USSR or China. Beijing did respond to the renewed US attacks on the DRV with additional military aid in a desire to win back some of the lost Chinese credibility in Hanoi, which had been further damaged by the Sino/American rapprochement. But the USSR was now pressing the DRV to resume negotiations with the US, and Hanoi appreciated the strategic advantages of freeing its territory from heavy bombardment and the economic burden of constant warfare. At resumed talks between Kissinger and the French-educated DRV negotiator, Le Duc Tho, in Paris, Hanoi retreated from its demands for Thieu's removal and for a coalition government in South Vietnam. Confident that the American withdrawal of ground troops had become irreversible, Hanoi was now prepared to accept a standstill cease-fire in the whole of Indochina, arrangements for consultations between political groups in the RVN about future elections and a promise to free US prisoners. The major condition was a US withdrawal of all forces from Vietnam within sixty days. Though such an agreement provided a much less-secure guarantee for a non-communist state, especially the retention of the PAVN's substantial gains from the Easter offensive, Kissinger was prepared to make a deal based on Tho's revised terms on 8 October 1972.[29]

However, Thieu strongly opposed this deal. The demand that he consult with the PRG would sanction the communist cause after the many years of trying to eradicate it, and the continued presence of PAVN troops within the RVN was too threatening for his political survival. He knew the shaky basis of his own public support. Nixon also backed away from the agreement, in order to prevent any questioning of his motives prior to his landslide electoral victory over McGovern on 7 November and used Thieu's objections as justification. After the election Kissinger, now the Secretary of

28 DeBenedetti and Chatfield, *An American Ordeal*, 323–40.
29 Chen Jian, 'China and the Vietnam War', in Lowe (ed.), *The Vietnam War*, 179–80. Nguyen Vu Tung, 'Hanoi's Search for an Effective Stategy', in ibid., 56–7. Gaiduk, *The Soviet Union and the Vietnam War*, 28–41. Brigham, *Guerrilla Diplomacy*, 104–5.

State, presented to Tho some of Thieu's many demands for changes to the draft agreement.[30]

Nixon made one more military attempt to extract further concessions from Hanoi. In eleven days from 18 December, with the exception of Christmas Day, over 20,000 tons of bombs were dropped on communications and storage facilities in Hanoi and Haiphong with many of the 'smart' bombs missing their targets, such as landing on Hanoi's largest hospital. The DRV had braced itself for the onslaught. Over half of the city's population had been evacuated, and the destruction was minor compared with Second World War bombing of European and Japanese cities. But 2,196 North Vietnamese civilians died in the raids. The US also lost fifteen B-52 bombers and ninety-two airmen.[31]

It was a high cost for the one major concession wrung from Hanoi, which was the deletion of the requirement for political negotiations in South Vietnam. US air chiefs claimed an extra week of bombing would have won much more. That was very doubtful. Hanoi was willing to renew negotiations, not because of the bombing, but because another force was propelling Nixon's administration to reach a settlement. Re-elected Democratic majorities in both Houses of Congress were threatening to choke the money supply for all US forces in Vietnam. Thieu remained opposed to the retention of PAVN troops in the RVN. But Nixon used the stick of threatening to cancel all economic and military aid and the carrot of an absolute commitment to come swiftly to the RVN's aid if the agreement was ever violated by the DRV. On 23 January, Tho and Kissinger signed the agreement which concluded US involvement in the second Indochinese War, for a cost of over 58,000 US deaths.[32]

But the war in Vietnam had not ended. While the VCP decided to respect the Paris agreement, it did not do so with the same naiveté as after the 1954 Geneva Agreements. This time the VCP was determined to offer military resistance to any government encroachments on its areas of control, and prior to the signing of the agreement it maximized military efforts to win more territory. Even then, by the party's own admission, fewer than four million of South Vietnam's 19.5 million people were under its control, a smaller number than on the eve of the 1968 Tet offensive. Also the RVN was still receiving substantial US military and economic aid and possessed

---

30 Robert D. Schulzinger, *A Time for War: The United States and Vietnam, 1941–1945* (New York 1986), 299–300. Nguyen Tien Hung and Jerrold L. Schecter, *The Palace File* (New York 1986), 124.

31 Turley, *Second Indochina War*, 147–9. Clodfelter, *Limits of Air Power*, 179–95.

32 Clodfelter, *Limits of Air Power*, 196–202. Nguyen and Schecter, *The Palace File*, ch. 9. Thayer, *War Without Fronts*, 105. Brigham, *Guerrilla Diplomacy*, 111.

the world's fifth largest army replete with military hardware and supplies left behind by the departing US troops. Furthermore, Thieu's government had the assurance that the US would bail it out if North Vietnam launched another invasion. So the ARVN sought actively to increase its area of control. There had been a sharp debate between the NLF and Hanoi about appropriate tactics. Already chagrined by Hanoi's disregard of Southern concerns in the final peace negotiations, the NLF was pushing for a more active response to the ARVN offensives. In response, in October 1973, the Central Committee in Hanoi authorized more specific attacks on RVN forces. The RVN reaction was to declare the peace agreement dead and proclaim the 'Third Indochina War'.[33]

But strategically, Thieu overstretched his forces in a futile attempt to control the whole of South Vietnam. He also ran an increasingly authoritarian state, with a rapidly deteriorating economy suffering from the withdrawal of the previous $400 million annual US expenditure in the RVN, combined with sharp rises in world oil prices and decreasing US aid. Inflation in South Vietnam in 1974 was 100 per cent, while ARVN wages rose by only 25 per cent. Thieu faced a rising tumult of public criticism and the emergence of non-communist anti-government movements.[34]

Furthermore, the guarantee of US support for the RVN was fast dissipating. The post-election bombing campaign increased the resolve of many members of the majority Democratic Party not only to stop any further funds for military action in Vietnam but also to curb the president's war-making power. This movement was boosted by the revelation in March 1973 of continued US bombing in Cambodia, where the Paris agreement had not halted a Khmer Rouge offensive against Lon Nol's pro-American government. Bolstered by American opinion polls reporting a two to one public opposition to the bombing in Cambodia, the Senate voted to restrict money for that campaign. Nixon found this challenge to his foreign policy much harder to shrug off than before, even though he vowed to find money for the Cambodia air campaign elsewhere. His authority was being crippled by growing allegations of an administration cover up of the pre-election burglarizing by the 'plumbers' of the Democratic Party national office in the Watergate building in Washington. In June Congress voted to stop all money for the bombing which, after Nixon exercised his veto power, became a compromise resolution to curtail it by 15 August. But the revelations in Senate hearings in July of the secret US bombing of neutral Cambodia ever since March 1969, and the falsifying of relevant records,

---

33 Ngo Vinh Long, 'South Vietnam', in Lowe (ed.), *The Vietnam War*, 87. Brigham, *Guerrilla Diplomacy*, 113–21.
34 Brigham, *Guerrilla Diplomacy*, 122–3. Turley, *Second Indochina War*, 157–69.

provoked Congress in November 1973 to pass, over Nixon's veto, the War Powers Act. It required the President to inform Congress within forty-eight hours of the deployment of any US forces abroad and obligated their withdrawal if, within sixty days, there were no congressional endorsement. While that act still gave the US President short-term freedom to use military force, the spirit behind it ensured no more American military action in Indochina. Congress also in 1974, misconceiving that nothing serious was wrong in the RVN, slashed the administration's request for $1.5 billion in military aid to South Vietnam to $700 million. That was a crippling blow, on top of the rampant inflation that year, to the ARVN's fighting capacity and morale. Moreover, Nixon resigned on 9 August 1974 to escape becoming the second president in US history to face impeachment by Congress.[35]

Hanoi in January 1975 considered the time was ripe to launch an invasion of South Vietnam. DRV leaders safely predicted that the US Congress would not allow the new Republican administration, headed by the former party leader in the House of Representatives and Vice President, Gerald Ford, to honour Nixon's promises to speedily come to South Vietnam's aid. Military clashes in late 1974 clearly revealed the sagging morale of the ARVN, which was becoming disaffected by the mounting opposition to Thieu's regime. Indeed, the ARVN collapsed like a house of cards when on 9 March 1975 the PAVN launched concentrated offensives against its outstretched defensive positions. On the last day of the next month PAVN tanks rolled unopposed into Saigon after frantic helicopter evacuations of Americans. Many of their former Vietnamese supporters were left behind to face the bloody revenge of the victors of twenty-one years of warfare.[36]

The long war had a brutal impact on many people in South Vietnam. It has been estimated that 171,331 ARVN soldiers died in the war and that the death toll of their communist opponents, including PAVN units fighting in the RVN, could have been as high as 850,000. While numbers of civilians who died or were wounded because of the war are unknown, an estimate of South Vietnamese civilian casualties, based on hospital admissions and other statistical data, from 1965 through 1972, is 1,025,000, including some 250,000 deaths. From 1954 to 1975 over half the South Vietnamese people fled from their homes, some more than once. The majority of them moved because of the effects of the war rather than because of political commitment. While US aid prevented starvation or epidemics among refugees, many became permanent camp dwellers dependent on handouts, though there were job opportunities near US, Korean and ARVN bases, including

---

35   Arnold R. Isaacs, *Without Honor: Defeat in Vietnam and Cambodia* (Baltimore 1983), 303–21. Herring, *America's Longest War*, 292–3.

36   Isaacs, *Without Honor*, 321–487. Brigham, *Guerrilla Diplomacy*, 123–4.

prostitution. There was also some movement back to villages during the pacification programs of 1969–71. But the refugee problem contributed to the collapse in support for the government. The people who felt compelled to flee from ancestral lands and homes, blamed mostly the government and the US for the shells and bombs that were the most powerful reasons why they became refugees.[37]

There has been a major American debate about whether the US could have won the Vietnam War. American officers who fought in the war, such as Westmoreland and Colonel Harry G. Summers, have argued that they were crippled by Johnson's restraints. If they had been given more troops to attack across the DRV border and into Cambodia and Laos after the 1968 Tet offensive, along with more intensified bombing of the DRV, its government would have capitulated.[38]

But how US forces would have maintained control of regions in Cambodia, Laos and in the DRV against concerted guerrilla opposition is a question unanswered by the military theorists. A PAVN colonel explained in 1984: 'Look what happened in 1970. Americans and ARVN forces did cross the border into Cambodia, but it was easier for us to fight in Cambodia than in South Vietnam.' He pointed out how any American invasion of the DRV would have encountered a population 'well-prepared to wage people's war'.[39] Also China probably would then have intervened in the war.

Other scholars of the Vietnam War have emphasized that it was unwinnable for Americans because of Vietnamese realities. A micro-study of Hau Nghia Province by Eric Bergerud demonstrates that the war there against the NLF was lost by the Diem regime and that no amount of US firepower or counterinsurgency pressure, both applied to a great extent in that province, could eradicate the NLF. A permanent US occupation may have preserved a degree of government control, but such a commitment was never an American aim. When the occupying US division left the province, the NLF quickly reasserted its dominance. This conclusion is supported by the studies by Jeffrey Race of Long Tan province and by James Trullinger of My Thuy Phuong village. These local analyses clearly demonstrate that the NLF won the 'hearts and minds' battle against corrupt

---

37   Thayer, *War Without Fronts*, chs 10, 12, 18. Wiesner, *Victims and Survivors*, ch. 16.
38   William Child Westmoreland, *A Soldier Reports* (New York 1976), 410. Harry G. Summers, *On Strategy: A Critical Analysis of the Vietnam War* (Novato 1982). See also, especially, Shelby L. Stanton, *The Rise and Fall of an American Army: US Ground Forces in Vietnam, 1965–1973* (Novata 1985); and Philip Davidson, *Vietnam at War: The History* (Novata 1988) and *Secrets of the Vietnam War* (Novata 1990).
39   Quoted in Turley, *Second Indochina War*, 190–1. See also Lawrence E. Grinter and Peter M. Dunn, *The American War in Vietnam: Lessons, Legacies, and Implications for Future Conflicts* (Westport 1987), 95–109.

RVN governments that were incapable of introducing meaningful land and other social reforms because they were beholden to the country's ruling classes. This view was confirmed at a series of discussions in the late 1990s by a group of American and Vietnamese historians and participants in the war. Colonel Herbert Y. Schandler summed up their conclusion: 'American forces could win individual battles', but like the French before them, 'military might could not overcome the ardor for unity and independence that burned in the hearts of old nationalists of both North and South Vietnam'.[40]

Indonesia's invasion of East Timor

A new war commenced on the edge of the Southwestern Pacific Basin when in December 1975 Indonesian forces invaded the former Portuguese colony of East Timor. In 1974 that territory was a colonial backwater with most of its 659,102 people, who were of a Malay-Melanesian stock, engaged in subsistence agriculture; 93 per cent of them were illiterate. A small educated Timorese elite was working for the Portuguese colonial administration, which maintained authoritarian control.[41]

A military coup, which overthrew the fascist government in Portugal in April 1974, provided the catalyst for dramatic change in East Timor. A sudden lifting of restrictions on free speech, and comments by radical members of the Portuguese junta in favour of independence for Portugal's African and Asian colonies, inspired the founding on 12 September 1974 of an independence movement in East Timor called Fretilin (*Frente Revolucionara do Timor Leste Independente*). It was led by young members of the educated Timor elite in the colony's capital city, Dili, some of who had been influenced by Roman Catholic Jesuit teachers who encouraged criticism of the Portuguese colonial state. Fretilin aimed to work for independence and economic development, concentrating on land reforms, agricultural cooperatives and promotion of literacy. Revolutionary brigades were formed to carry out these programs at village level, influenced by a Marxist minority within the Fretilin

---

40 Bergerud, *Dynamics of Defeat*, 1–7, 323–35. Race, *War Comes to Long An*, ch. 5. Trullinger, *Village at War*, chs 11–12. For a good survey of the debate see Grinter and Dunn, *The American War in Vietnam*, Robert S. McNamara, James G. Blight and Robert K. Brigham, *Argument Without End: In Search of Answers to the Vietnam Tragedy* (New York 1999), 369. See also Gary R. Hess, *Vietnam and the United States: Origins and Legacy of War* (revised edition, New York 1998), 157–67.

41 James Dunn, *Timor: A People Betrayed* (2nd edition, Sydney 1996), chs 1–2. John G. Taylor, *Indonesia's Forgotten War: The Hidden History of East Timor* (London 1991), ch. 1.

leadership. A more conservative party seeking autonomy within the Portuguese empire, the Timorese Democratic Movement (UDT), also had been formed in 1974 by more established members of the educated Timorese elite. A third political movement, called *Apodeti* (the Timorese Popular Democratic Association), had been organized by members of the colony's small Muslim community in favour of joining Indonesia and was being supported by *Bakin* (the Indonesian Army's Intelligence Coordinating Agency).[42]

Bakin was committed to work for the integration of East Timor into the Indonesian republic with the support of its military masters in Jakarta. The inherent political instability of the Indonesian archipelago, with previous major separatist revolts, induced great concern within the Indonesian government about a small independent nation on the southeastern flank, which could be subject to communist influence. The initial strategy was to achieve annexation of East Timor by political means. However, it soon became apparent that *Apodeti* commanded little public support in the colony, compared with UDT and Fretilin, which joined together in January 1975 in a coalition to support independence. Indonesian agents therefore worked to convince UDT leaders that communists were in charge of Fretilin and were seeking to import arms from China to launch a coup. In August 1975 UDT launched a counter coup, with the support of most Timorese members of the colonial police force. But more than 2,000 Timorese soldiers of the colonial defence force joined Fretilin along with additional arms from the Dili arsenal, which clearly tipped the military balance. The speedy success of Fretilin fighters forced a rethink by *Bakin*. It had been hoping that the civil war would be protracted enough to warrant Indonesian intervention to stop the bloodshed. So a Confrontation-style low-level military campaign was launched with incursions by Indonesian troops across the West Timor border to rescue UDT leaders and to destabilize the Fretilin government. One Indonesian attack on the border town of Balibo resulted in the murdering by Indonesian soldiers of one New Zealand, two Australian and two British journalists working for two Australian television networks.[43]

The Indonesian border crossings met with stiff resistance from Fretilin forces. Fretilin also rapidly formed a government, which had the clear majority support of the Timorese people. The Portuguese governor, deprived of his police and army, had left the island. The reform government in Portugal, embroiled in pulling out of Africa, had washed its hands of East Timor. Consequently, Fretilin, on 28 November 1975, declared East Timor's independence.

---

42 Taylor, *Indonesia's Forgotten War*, chs 2–3. Dunn, *Timor*, ch. 4.
43 Dunn, *Timor*, chs 8–9. Taylor, *Indonesia's Forgotten War*, 30–2, 38–62.

However, East Timor had no international support. Its nearest non-Indonesian neighbour, Australia, already had given the green light to Indonesia to annex the territory. In September 1974, on a visit to Jakarta, the Labor Party Australian Prime Minister, Gough Whitlam, told Suharto that: 'An independent East Timor would be an unviable state, and a potential threat to the area.' Whitlam's government was concerned not to allow the aspirations of East Timorese people to upset the good relations with Indonesia that had emerged since Confrontation. This was demonstrated in a cable from Richard Woolcott, the Australian Ambassador in Jakarta, in August 1975. He wrote: 'We should show as much understanding as we can of Indonesia's position and . . . there is no inherent reason why integration with Indonesia would in the long run be any less in the interests of the Timorese inhabitants than a highly unstable independence.' Washington supported Australia's appeasement, not wishing to upset the cosy relationship established with the anti-communist Suharto regime in Indonesia. Fretilin also had been successfully damned by Indonesian propaganda as 'communist', though few of its members were Marxists.[44]

With such international support, on 7 December 1975 Indonesia launched an invasion of East Timor. The delay after Fretilin's declaration of independence was influenced by an official visit by US President Ford, which ended on 6 December. The air and sea attack on Dili was ruthless. Some 2,000 people, including most men of the city were slaughtered, according to eyewitness reports. At one of the main killing areas, the harbour, one resident of Dili later reported: 'We were told to tie the bodies to iron poles, attach bricks and throw the bodies into the sea.' On the first day of the attack, women and children were herded out of the town while troops ransacked their homes. Cars, radios, items of furniture, cutlery and even windows were taken to ships in the harbour. Then Indonesian troops 'demanded women and girls to help them celebrate their victory'.[45]

One reason for the Indonesian ferocity was the strength of the Fretilin resistance, bolstered by some 2,500 regular soldiers, 7,000 part-time militia plus more reservists, all armed with Portuguese weapons. In preparation for the invasion, bases had been established in the interior to which many people retreated. The Indonesian forces, which increased to 25,000 by the

---

44 Taylor, *Indonesia's Forgotten War*, 32. Woolcott to Department of Foreign Affairs, 24 August 1975, in G.J. Munster and J.R. Walsh, *Documents on Australian Defence and Foreign Policy 1968–1975* (Sydney 1980), 217. Nancy Viviani, 'Australians and the East Timor Issue: The Policy of the Whitlam Government', in James Cotton (ed.), *East Timor and Australia* (Canberra 1999), 81–6.

45 Taylor, *Indonesia's Forgotten War*, 68–9. Amnesty International, *East Timor: Violations of Human Rights: Extrajudicial Executions, 'Disappearances', Torture and Political Imprisonment, 1975–1984* (London 1985), 26.

end of December, found themselves involved in a bitter guerrilla war in a mountainous environment, which favoured the insurgents. The use of paratroops in the interior failed because Fretilin units defeated them before coastal based Indonesian forces could reinforce them; and captured Indonesian arms added to Fretilin's fire power. The burning of villages and massacring of their inhabitants by Indonesian troops further fuelled the anger of Fretilin fighters. However, by March 1979 Jakarta was confident enough to proclaim the end to their military campaign. A strategy of encirclement of areas of Fretilin resistance, saturation bombing, chemical spraying to poison crops and herding of the population into concentration camps, where many died of starvation, had assisted the Indonesians to gain an upper hand. In the process the population of East Timor had been reduced by 130,778 since 1974, when under normal conditions it would have increased. Furthermore, despite this awful human cost, Fretilin had not been eradicated and would continue to trouble the Indonesians.[46]

The Indonesian invasion of Timor did receive some, but ineffective international condemnation. On 22 December 1975 the UN Security Council called for Indonesia to withdraw its forces from East Timor and for a genuine act of self-determination by the indigenous people. But the motion had no enforcement provision. The US reaction to the invasion was indicated when Ford was interviewed about it in Hawaii on the day after he left Indonesia. He said: 'We'll talk about that later.' Australia protested against the invasion. Whitlam's successor, Malcolm Fraser, kept up a moral protest, including an Australian vote for a successful UN Assembly resolution deploring the invasion and calling for withdrawal of Indonesian troops, thereby joining communist, African and Latin American countries, whereas the US and Western European countries abstained. But the US was trying to persuade other members of the UN to come to an accommodation with Indonesia and firmly told Australia not to upset the 'good will' of Suharto's government. Canberra was reminded of the strategic importance of Indonesian waters for the access of American ships and nuclear submarines from the Pacific to the Indian Ocean. There was also Australian government concern to repair damage to Australia's relations with Indonesia caused by its protest and voting in the UN. Consequently, Fraser visited Indonesia in October 1976 and tacitly recognized the Indonesian occupation of East Timor; formal *de jure* recognition was given in January 1978. Oil interests in the Timor Gap were also facilitated by this move. Significantly, in the first UN Assembly vote all the ASEAN states supported Indonesia, except Singapore which abstained. General Assembly motions in the remaining years of the 1970s

---

46   Taylor, *Indonesia's Forgotten War*, chs 6–8.

continued to condemn Indonesia, but support for them was dwindling, with countries such as Australia shifting to abstention. However, the UN never officially recognized the Indonesian annexation of East Timor.[47]

ASEAN, Cambodia, Vietnam and China

ASEAN's general support for the Indonesian invasion of Timor, reflected the growth of cooperation between its member states by the mid 1970s. The fifth ministerial meeting in 1972 declared that 'the important changes that had taken place in the relations among the major powers' necessitated ASEAN members 'cooperating even more closely' in the future. However, there was no move towards a European Economic Community (EEC) model. A UN report tabled at that meeting pointed out that only 6 per cent of the annual trade of ASEAN nations was between them, excluding Singapore's entrepôt trade. But the report praised the growth rate of the member countries, which had reached 6 per cent per annum in the second half of the 1960s. The 1972 meeting expanded the number of permanent committees to cover economic issues, and more economic cooperation flowed from a summit meeting of heads of state in Bali in 1976. Subsequent meetings of economic ministers resulted in the first set of preferential trading arrangements in 1977 and an agreement in 1978 on cooperative industrial projects. Also in 1978 a Japan–ASEAN Economic Council was established to coordinate Japanese investment in ASEAN countries. These developments were small beginnings of ASEAN economic cooperation reflected in an increase in the proportion of intra-ASEAN trade to 9 per cent in 1979.[48]

There was a greater sense of insecurity within ASEAN in the 1970s leading to the beginnings of diplomatic cooperation. In July 1969, as part of his decision to commence withdrawing US troops from Vietnam, Nixon had declared on the North Pacific island of Guam that in future, except for a threat from a nuclear power, the US was 'going to encourage and has a right to expect' Asian nations to 'increasingly' take responsibility for their own defence. This statement became known as the 'Guam' or 'Nixon'

47 Ibid., 64. Dunn, *Timor*, chs 11–12. Nancy Viviani, 'Australians and the East Timor Issue – the Policy of the Fraser Government', in Cotton (ed.), *East Timor and Australia*, 111–36. George J. Aditjondro, *Is Oil Thicker than Blood? A Study of Oil Companies' Interests and Western Complicity in Indonesia's Annexation of East Timor* (New York 1999), 24–5.

48 Ronald D. Palmer and Thomas J. Reckford, *Building ASEAN: 20 Years of Southeast Asian Cooperation* (New York 1987), 40, ch. 5. Broinowski, *Understanding ASEAN*, 37–65, 70–88. United Nations, *Yearbook of International Trade Statistics* (*YITS*), 1980 (New York 1981), vol. I, 477, 617, 770, 856, 928.

Doctrine. It was taken seriously by ASEAN nations in the context of the decreasing US involvement in the Vietnam War. Malaysia and Singapore also were perturbed when Britain withdrew its commitment to their defence in 1971. ASEAN foreign ministers responded to such developments by calling in November 1971 for a 'Zone of Peace, Freedom and Neutrality' in Southeast Asia, which was being promoted by Malaysia. But Singapore, conscious of its vulnerable small island status, had more faith in the Five Power Commonwealth Defence Agreement, which it had signed with Malaysia, Britain, Australia and New Zealand to cover its defence needs. Thailand and the Philippines were unwilling to give up their hosting of US military bases, though they agreed in 1973 to abandon the military component of SEATO. This was in response to US acceptance of pressure for this downgrading of that virtually moribund alliance from the Labor government of Australia and the Labour government of New Zealand. Indonesia was sceptical about foreign powers guaranteeing the neutrality of Southeast Asia and opposed Singapore's idea of allowing the naval forces of all the major naval powers to patrol the region's waters. A dispute also arose when Indonesia and Malaysia tried to declare the Straits of Malacca a non-international waterway, which Singapore strongly and successfully resisted with the assistance of the major maritime powers, including the US and the USSR. Such disagreements were barriers to early diplomatic cooperation in ASEAN.[49]

However, more concern was aroused in ASEAN with radical political changes in Indochina in 1975. In Cambodia, the Chinese-supported Khmer Rouge won a rapid victory over Lon Nol's government when the DRV overran South Vietnam. After achieving victory in an internal party struggle, from October 1976 to 1978 the Khmer Rouge chief, Pol Pot, and party cadres killed possibly as many as two million Cambodians. The Khmer Rouge, who had won their recruits among illiterate peasants rather than in urban areas, slaughtered in particular the educated elite, other urban dwellers and perceived enemies of the revolution. The slaughter was part of an over zealous and frantic effort to socialize the nation in the style of the Chinese cultural revolution. The death of Mao Zedong in September 1976 and uncertainty whether Chinese support for the Khmer Rouge would continue probably influenced the sense of urgency. A military coup in Thailand in October 1976 also introduced a more anti-communist regime

---

49 *Public Papers of the Presidents of the United States, Richard M. Nixon, 1969* (Washington 1971), 549. K.K. Nair, *Words and Bayonets: ASEAN and Indochina* (Selangor 1986), ch. 1. Michael Leifer, *ASEAN and the Security of South-East Asia* (London 1989), 52–62. C.M. Turnbull, *History of Singapore 1819–1980* (Singapore 1989), 298, 316. Leszek Buszynski, *SEATO: The Failure of an Alliance Strategy* (Singapore 1983), ch. 6.

there, removing a previous parliamentary government which had been pre-pared to cooperate with democratic Kampuchea, as the country was now named. Furthermore, there were frequent border clashes with the DRV over their French-drawn boundary. Many Khmers who were killed by Pol Pot's regime were condemned as friends of Vietnam. In Kampuchea there was a sense of embattled isolation, like revolutionary France in 1793, as expressed in a December 1976 party manifesto: 'Enemies without continue to approach; enemies within our frontiers have not been eliminated.'[50]

However, Kampuchea soon faced a full-scale invasion of Cambodia by 120,000 Vietnamese troops, beginning on 25 December 1978. There is a debate about Vietnam's motives. Most of its neighbours and other contem-porary commentators claimed that Vietnam seized an opportunity created by the chaos of Pol Pot's regime to dominate the whole of Indochina, a linguistically and culturally diverse region brought together only by French colonialism. An alternative explanation centres on border provocation by Kampuchea against Vietnam. The latest interpretation, with the benefit Soviet archival records, points out another factor: Vietnam's alignment on foreign policy issues with the Soviet Union after 1968. A result was growing Chinese hostility towards Vietnam, which in turn viewed Kampuchea as a Chinese client state, even though after the death of Mao Zedong in 1976 there was less fervent support for Kampuchea by China's more pragmatic communist regime led by Deng Xiaoping. Vietnam did not perceive this change. But Vietnam also had traditional territorial claims over its neigh-bouring Indo China states. Hanoi had installed a puppet regime in Laos in 1976 and now had ambition to control Cambodia. The border conflict with Kampuchea was the excuse.[51]

Khmers greeted the invading Vietnamese as 'liberators', reported the British journalist William Shawcross, who visited Cambodia in 1980. Ill-equipped to fight one of Asia's most powerful armies, the Khmer Rouge

---

50 'Report of Activities of the Party Center According to the General Political Tasks of 1976', 20 December 1976, in David P. Chandler, Ben Kiernan and Canthou Bova (eds), *Pol Pot Plans the Future: Confidential Documents from Democratic Kampuchea, 1976–1977* (New Haven 1988), 190. Grant Evans and Kelvin Rowley, *Red Brotherhood at War: Vietnam, Cambodia and Laos since 1975* (revised edition, London 1990), 81–92. Elizabeth Becker, *When the War was Over: Cambodia's Revolution and the Voices of its People* (New York 1986), chs 5–8. Craig Etcheson, *The Rise and Demise of Democratic Kampuchea* (Boulder 1984), ch. 7. For eye-witness accounts of the Khmer Rouge era see Martin Stuart-Fox, *The Murderous Revolution: Life and Death in Pol Pot's Kampuchea* (Chippendale, New South Wales 1985); and James Fenton (ed.), *Cambodian Witness: The Autobiography of Someth May* (New York 1986).
51 Becker, *When the War*, 337–43. Evans and Rowley, *Red Brotherhood*, 102–11. Stephen J. Morris, *Why Vietnam Invaded Cambodia: Political Culture and the Causes of War* (Stanford 1999), 23–46, 88–115, 143–218, 229–34.

retreated to the jungles and mountains of southwestern Cambodia near the Thai border, where they were able to regroup to fight again.[52]

The country the Khmer Rouge left behind them had been desolated. Shawcross was taken to mass graves of the thousands killed in the last days of the Khmer Rouge regime, full of blindfolded skulls. The terror of starvation stalked the land during 1979 because of economic dislocation and non-planting of rice. That year an estimated 188,000 Cambodians fled across the Thai border, joining over 100,000 others, who were refugees from Pol Pot's regime. A demographic estimate is that the population had declined to 6,100,000 in 1980 whereas, without the oppression of Pol Pot's regime, famine and emigration, it should have been over nine million.[53]

China was alarmed about the Vietnamese invasion of Kampuchea. Since the DRV conquest of South Vietnam, Beijing had been publicly condemning Hanoi's alleged imperialistic ambitions in Indochina. There were also border disputes involving ambiguities in the French demarcated land boundary between China and Vietnam. More contentiously, there were counter claims between China and Vietnam to the Paracel and Spratly Islands in the South China Sea. Those islands were mostly barren islets, reefs and sandbanks, but they possessed strategic command of the South China Sea, and from the late 1960s their region was known to have rich undersea oil deposits. In 1974 China took military control of the Paracels, which was promptly followed by Vietnamese occupation of six of the Spratly Islands, and another five islands were taken over by the Philippines. Relations between China and the DRV were further poisoned in 1978 by a mass exodus of many of Vietnam's more than one million, largely urbanized, Chinese residents. Most fled overland to China, but many took to the high seas in assorted boats which were prey to pirates, storms and the hostility of inhabitants of the ASEAN states where they landed. Increasing armed border clashes marked the rapid deterioration in China–DRV relations. China also assumed that the USSR had urged Vietnam to invade Cambodia, but in this case Moscow learned of it only after the event. That invasion was the breaking point for Beijing. On 17 February 1979 China launched an invasion of North Vietnam.[54]

---

52 Shawcross, *Sideshow*, 404.
53 Ibid.; Nair, *Words and Bayonets*, 95. William Shawcross, *The Quality of Mercy: Cambodia, Holocaust and Modern Conscience* (New York 1984), *passim*. Meng-Try Ea, 'Recent Population Trends in Kampuchea', in David A. Ablin and Marlowe Hood (eds), *The Cambodian Agony* (Armonck 1987), 3–15.
54 Pao-Min Chang, *The Sino-Vietnamese Territorial Dispute* (New York 1986), 11–53. King C. Chen, *China's War with Vietnam, 1979* (Stanford 1987), chs 2–4. Morris, *Why Vietnam Invaded Cambodia*, 215–18.

According to Deng Xiaoping, the invasion was a response to Vietnamese border provocations. Like the Sino-Indian border war of 1962, the Chinese attack involved only ground troops, not air or sea forces, though they were on standby. The official aim was to teach Hanoi a sharp lesson. Hence it was called the 'Punitive War'. But more important objectives were almost certainly to weaken Vietnamese pressure on Kampuchea by causing a withdrawal of Vietnamese troops to protect the border zone with China and to demonstrate that China was a major power to which Vietnam should defer.[55]

The Chinese force, which had been collected for the invasion, consisted of 330,000 soldiers, of whom about 200,000 were used in the fighting plus 1,200 tanks. The 600,000 strong PAVN had a third of its force occupying Cambodia and another third stationed in South Vietnam and in Laos. But the numerically superior Chinese army was hampered by the absence of any significant modernization since the Korean War. Attacking on three fronts, the troops were greatly hindered by their lack of modern logistical equipment, forcing them to rely on old trucks, donkeys and human labour in the mountainous terrain, which also compelled them to break down divisions to companies and even platoons. The Vietnamese defenders, who were mainly local militia and border guards, were able to exploit a defensive system of tunnels, trenches, land mines and other booby traps. A concerted series of Chinese attacks enabled the capture of the city of Lang Son 16 kms inside the border, situated on the edge of an open plain and only 136 kms from Hanoi. But on 5 March, the day Hanoi ordered mass mobilization for war, Beijing ordered a withdrawal. The attack had destroyed six Vietnamese missile sites and many bridges, roads, railways and buildings, systematically levelled by the retreating Chinese. But the invasion did not succeed in destroying any PAVN division; indeed, only one extra division was actually deployed to reinforce the border guards and militia at Lang Son. The war did not affect the Vietnamese conquest of Cambodia; nor did it diminish the campaign against Chinese residents in Vietnam. The PLA had faced unexpected Vietnamese resistance bolstered by the more modern PAVN artillery. Such was the ferocity of the fighting in the sixteen-day war, that China admitted 20,000 casualties, and its losses were probably considerably higher. Beijing realized, and admitted in the more open post-Mao environment, that the PLA needed much modernization before it ventured on any similar military expedition.[56]

There was a significant international reaction to the Sino-Vietnamese War. The USSR, which had a naval squadron in the South China Sea

---

55 Chen, *China's War with Vietnam*, 94–5. Evans and Rowley, *Red Brotherhood*, 117–19.
56 Evans and Rowley, *Red Brotherhood*, 115–19. Chen, *China's War with Vietnam*, ch. 5.

based at the former US naval base of Cam Ranh Bay in South Vietnam, sent an additional cruiser and destroyer to the region. Soviet arms were airlifted to Hanoi. Moscow warned Beijing about playing with fire, though Soviet officials admitted there was no thought of any Soviet military intervention. The USSR also was concerned about possible American collusion with China because, said Dobrynin, 'the Chinese aggression came hard on the heels of Deng Xaioping's visit to the United States' in the previous month. However, the US President, Jimmy Carter, assured Brezhnev in a hot line conversation that, while Washington considered the Chinese invasion a response to Vietnamese aggression in Cambodia, the US had not been informed in advance by Beijing and sought a speedy Chinese withdrawal from Vietnam. Indeed, the US publicly called for this withdrawal and supported an ASEAN resolution at the UN for the evacuation of all foreign troops in Indochina, including Vietnamese troops in Cambodia. But the USSR vetoed any Security Council action.[57]

For the ASEAN states, Vietnam's invasion of Cambodia was a challenge to the principle of respect for the rights of nation states and raised a fear of an expansionist Vietnam. The latter concern was greatest in Thailand. A new threatening superpower had loomed on Thailand's eastern border, with a further threat of Vietnamese support for communist subversion in Thailand. The Thai disquiet extended to the opening of secret negotiations with China for mutual support for a Khmer Rouge insurgency against Vietnam's occupation. The Thai premier also visited Washington in February 1979 and received a public reiteration of the US guarantee of Thailand's security.[58]

Fellow ASEAN members gave support to Thailand on the Cambodia issue. However, there were underlying differences of opinion. Indonesia was more interested in coming to an accommodation with Vietnam, because China was viewed as the main threat to Indonesia's security. Malaysia also was mostly concerned about China, being influenced like Indonesia by Chinese involvement in internal communist threats in the past. Singapore, however, was alarmed at Soviet support for Vietnam. Its leaders, especially Lee Kuan Yew, who perceived that superpower competition was the best guarantee for world peace, viewed the US withdrawal from Vietnam as creating a power vacuum in Southeast Asia, which the USSR was now moving to fill. The Philippines was in dispute with Vietnam and China over the Spratly Islands and opposed the invasion of Cambodia on legalistic grounds and its concern for ASEAN consensus. However, at an emergency

---

57   *Rod Brotherhood*, Chen, *China's War with Vietnam*, 109–12. Dobrynin, *In Confidence*, 418.
58   Nair, *Words and Bayonets*, chs 2–5.

meeting in Bangkok in January 1979 the ASEAN foreign ministers deplored the armed intervention in Cambodia and called for an immediate withdrawal of foreign troops from its soil. A follow-up statement urged Vietnam to stop the increasing flow of the mostly ethnically Chinese 'boat people' from Vietnam who were landing on ASEAN shores. Despite the doubts of some of its members, ASEAN was throwing its diplomatic weight on the China-Kampuchea side of the Indochina conflict.[59]

Consequently, the Vietnamese-supported People's Republic of Kampuchea (PRK), headed by Heng Samrin, the commander of a Cambodian anti-Pol Pot force, faced strong diplomatic opposition. China, the US and ASEAN supported a call by Pol Pot's deposed Democratic Kampuchea government, which had retreated to the Thai border region, for condemnation of Vietnam. In September 1979 this coalition gained seventy-one votes to thirty-five in the UN General Assembly with no Western nation in opposition, although some European nations abstained. But a vote in the Security Council calling for a withdrawal of Vietnamese troops ran into a Soviet veto. The US had been slow to supply aid to the victims of the massive famine in Cambodia. But by mid 1979 television pictures and news reports of the devastation were stirring public humanitarian concern and more government action. However, about half of over US$600 million of relief went to the Thai border region resulting, according to Shawcross, in an average of $1,124 per head for refugees in Thailand compared with $439 to those living under PRK control. This was another reason for the stream of Cambodians crossing into Thailand during 1979.[60]

The US and East Asia

Presiding over the US Cambodian policy was Jimmy Carter, the Democratic Party President of the US since 1977. He emphasized a new style of foreign policy that would take into account human rights and downplay past Cold War attitudes. Within his administration there was early concern about the killings in Cambodia. However, after Vietnam's invasion of Cambodia, that concern conflicted with a persistent view that Vietnam was

---

59 Ibid. Leifer, *ASEAN and Security*, ch. 4. Chen, *China's War with Vietnam*, 135–8. Lau Teik Soon, 'Singapore in South-East Asia', in C.T. Chew and Edwin Lee (eds), *A History of Singapore* (Singapore 1991), 378–9.

60 William Shawcross, *The Quality of Mercy: Cambodia, Holocaust and Modern Conscience* (London 1984), 391–3. Evans and Rowley, *Red Brotherhood*, 155–60.

a Soviet puppet and a consequent unwillingness to move against Chinese supported Kampuchea.[61]

This policy reflected new realities in the US policies towards Cold War détente with the USSR and China. Though openly critical of human rights abuses in the Soviet Union, Carter was willing to pursue arms reduction negotiations. A result was the Second Strategic Arms Limitation Treaty (SALT-2) between the US and the USSR in 1979. But that treaty was withdrawn by Carter's administration from ratification proceedings in the US Senate after the Soviet invasion of Afghanistan in December 1979. The collapse of that détente process also reflected a continued fear of Soviet expansionism within Carter's administration and a re-emerging American public hostility towards the USSR.[62]

Détente was becoming more a feature of US relations with China. While the US Seventh Fleet still patrolled the Taiwan Straits, China's shore based guns were silent in acknowledgement that the US fleet would prevent any nationalist invasion attempt. The KMT still clung to Jinmen and Mazu, in the now forlorn hope of returning to the mainland. Indeed, nationalist China also had suffered the ignominy in 1971 of being replaced by communist China, with US blessing, in the UN. After the new US–China relationship was marked with a visit by Deng Xiaoping to Washington in 1978, the US in 1979 withdrew its recognition of Taiwan as the Republic of China, to impotent KMT consternation. However, under continuing American military protection and the close economic relationship with the US, Taiwan's economy was booming. After a hiccup caused by the sharp oil price rise in 1973 and the post-Vietnam War recession, during the 1970s the average annual growth rate of GNP was 9.75 per cent, just above the high level of the 1960s. The island's 17.1 million people in 1978 were enjoying a GNP per capita six times higher than the citizens of China.[63]

South Korea also enjoyed good economic growth under continued US defence protection. However, in 1979 the export driven economy was suffering from a lack of new markets, another big rise in oil prices, and an overinvestment in heavy and defence industries. This economic distortion was influenced by the Park government's concern to improve the country's

---

61 Carl Lieberman, 'The Reaction of the Carter Administration to Human Rights Violations in Cambodia', in Herbert D. Rosenbaum and Alexej Ugrinsky, *Jimmy Carter: Foreign Policy and Post-Presidential Years* (Westport 1994), 269–84.

62 John Dumbrell, *American Foreign Policy: Clinton to Carter* (New York 1997), 40–5. Jerel A. Rosati, 'The Rise and Fall of America's First Post-Cold War Foreign Policy', in Rosenbaum and Ugrinsky (eds), *Jimmy Carter*, 44–7.

63 Stephen P. Gibert and William M. Carpenter (eds), *America and Island China: A Documentary History* (Latham 1988), 54. Nancy Bernkopf Tucker, *Taiwan, Hong Kong and the United States, 1945–1992* (New York 1994), 125–38.

war-making strength in the light of the Nixon doctrine. It was reinforced by the withdrawal of one of the two US divisions from the ROK in 1970. Carter in 1977 decided to implement a phased withdrawal of the other division over five years. However, pressure from the ROK via the US Congress and evidence of North Korean military growth stopped that process after only 3,600 troops were evacuated.[64]

North Korea's military expansion in the 1970s was a sign that Kim Il Sung's regime had not given up hope of conquering the South. But it faced a much more powerful ROK than in 1950 – militarily and economically. The presence of US troops, including tactical nuclear weapons, was also a deterrent, as was the ready availability of US air-power from bases in Japan. The USSR in fact declined to provide North Korea with modern arms to counter those being acquired by the ROK. Moscow was not interested in encouraging the union of a highly industrialized nation of 60 million people on its doorstep. The prevailing rapprochement between the US and China suggested that a united Korea might well be drawn into an anti-USSR camp. So North Korea made no move to attack the ROK even with the political uncertainty in the South after the assassination of the increasingly authoritarian Park in October 1979.[65]

Japan remained a firm anchor in the American alliance, but there was growing friction. A new security treaty between the US and Japan was signed in 1970 amidst greater public protests than in 1959. The US invasion of Cambodia provided political ammunition for communists, socialists and other peace activists. The police estimated that 774,000 Japanese protested against the treaty on 23 June 1970; the organizers claimed two million. There were further, often violent, protests until the treaty was passed by the Diet by a big majority on 19 October.[66]

Trade friction between the US and Japan also was emerging from Japan's huge economic expansion. The average annual Japanese GNP growth rate of 10 per cent since 1965 fell sharply in 1973 with the big oil price rise and the effects of the wind-down in the Vietnam War. The average annual GNP growth rate for the rest of the decade was 4.7 per cent. But the gap between Japan's exports to and imports from the US was widening because of the good quality of the cars, electrical goods, textiles and other Japanese

---

64   *FEA*, 1981–2, 646. Ralph N. Clough, *Embattled Korea: The Rivalry for International Support* (Boulder 1987), chs 3, 7. Don Oberdorfer, *The Two Koreas: A Contemporary History* (London 1997), ch. 4. Anne Hessing Cahn, *Killing Detente: The Right Attacks the CIA* (University Park 1998), *passim*.

65   Clough, *Embattled Korea*, 108–9, 243. Oberdorfer, *The Two Koreas*, 96–101.

66   John Welfield, *An Empire in Eclipse: Japan in the Postwar American Alliance System* (London 1988), 280–2.

goods and because the raw materials and foodstuffs that the US had traditionally supplied to Japan were coming from cheaper sources, such as Australia and Canada. The influx of Japanese textiles especially was alarming to US textile manufacturers, and Washington responded to this and complaints about other imports from Japan with tariff rises and pressure for voluntary restrictions. Nevertheless, the trade imbalance grew from US$1.7 billion in 1974 to US$10.4 billion in 1979. There was an increasing American perception that Japan was a dangerous economic competitor and even a potential military threat. The Japanese government, however, observing a growth in the size of the USSR's Pacific fleet, wanted no reduction in the US defence commitment, which allowed Japan to concentrate on economic growth with only a minor diversion of funds to its Self Defence Force (SDF). The US also remained Japan's most important market throughout the 1970s.[67]

One new opening for Japanese trade and investment was occurring in China. Progress, however, was slow during the 1970s because of political turbulence there. But by 1979 China had become Japan's sixth most valuable market; and Japan contributed 17 per cent of China's imports. That year Japan joined the US in extending diplomatic recognition to China and disavowing the Republic of China in Taiwan. Also the establishment of diplomatic relations with China in 1972 developed into a Peace and Friendship Treaty between these two former bitter enemies.[68]

A by-product of China's greater openness was a boom in the late 1970s in its major gateway to the outside world, Hong Kong. Following a post-Vietnam War recession there, domestic exports from Hong Kong leapt by 43 per cent in 1976 and continued to grow strongly for the rest of the decade. There was a significant growth of manufacturing in Hong Kong centring on textiles, plastics and electronics. This British colony also was emerging as a major financial sector, with the number of licensed banks increasing from seventy-four in 1977 to 105 in 1979. In this new prosperous environment there was no repetition of the riots of the previous two decades.[69]

The oil shock of 1973 with concomitant price rises for other raw materials also encouraged Japan to control sources of raw materials in Asia, being dependent on overseas sources for over 90 per cent of energy needs and other supplies. Already there had been capital investment in Asian countries

---

67 Ibid., 325–34. Akira Iriye and Warren I. Cohen (eds), *The United States and Japan in the Postwar World* (Lexington, Ky 1989), ch. 8. Michael Schaller, *Altered States: The United States and Japan since the Occupation* (New York 1997), 231–51.

68 Kurt Werner Radtke, *China's Relations with Japan, 1945–83: The Role of Chengzhi* (Manchester 1990), ch. 5. *FEA*, 1981–2, 364, 585.

69 Felix Patrikeeff, *Mouldering Pearl: Hong Kong at the Crossroads* (London 1989), 76–8.

to exploit cheaper labour costs because of the rising price of Japanese labour engendered by growing prosperity. By 1974 Japanese accumulated direct foreign investment in manufacturing in Asia was worth US$1.2 billion and was 38 per cent of all Japanese overseas manufacturing investment, a third of which was in Latin America. Textiles and electrical machinery were the principal Asian products, and the main countries for such investment were Japan's former colonies: Taiwan and South Korea. While this development continued after 1974, particularly in Southeast Asia, there was a deliberate emphasis on moving offshore into Asian primary processing stages of basic materials industries, such as steel, petrochemicals and paper. Furthermore, large Japanese corporations were moving into Asian and wider world investments, such as Mitsui Company, which by 1979 had fifty-nine subsidiaries in twenty-nine nations covering a large range of basic materials industries, like iron ore in Australia, petrochemicals in South Korea and rubber, timber and cement in Indonesia. The largest proportion of the investment was in mining to secure the raw materials needed by Japanese industry, such as oil and natural gas in Indonesia, Brunei and Malaysia, copper in Malaysia and the Philippines and iron ore in Australia. Japan's increasing economic interest in Southeast Asia was marked by a visit there by Prime Minister Fukuda Hideko in 1976, where he promised to cooperate as an 'equal partner' with ASEAN's members in building 'peace and prosperity'. Unspoken was his concern to promote further Japanese economic penetration in the region.[70]

Japanese investment was assisting the creation of an economic dynamism in the Western Pacific Basin. In particular the economies of Singapore, Hong Kong, Taiwan and South Korea were among the fastest growing in the world and had earned for them the title of new industrializing countries (NIC) or 'Tigers'. Along with the continued remarkable economic growth in Japan, they were in the process of making the Pacific Basin more economically important than the Atlantic Basin, which had been dominant in the world for the previous half millennium. During the 1970s most economies of the East Asian region had been achieving annual growth rates of 6 to 8 per cent, compared with between 3 and 4 per cent in Western Europe. By 1979 US trade with non-Soviet Asia was $23.9 billion greater than US trade with non-Soviet Europe.[71]

70 Rob Steven, *Japan's New Imperialism* (London 1990), 64–85. Bernard Eccleston, *State and Society in Post-War Japan* (Cambridge 1989), 242–51. William W. Haddad, 'Japan, the Fukuda Doctrine and ASEAN', *Contemporary Southeast Asia*, 2, 1980, 10–29.
71 Bernard K. Gordon, 'Pacific Futures for the USA', in Lau Teik Soon and Leo Suryadinata (eds), *Moving into the Pacific Century: The Changing Regional Order in the Asia-Pacific* (Singapore 1988), 11. *YTTS*, 1981, 1028.

Conclusions

Major changes had taken place in the Western Pacific Basin between 1969 and 1979. Prominent was the US withdrawal from Vietnam and the subsequent ending of the long war there. That war's impact on the US resulted in no American effort to save South Vietnam. But the DRV faced new enemies in the region with China's failed attempt to teach it a military lesson and the decision by the ASEAN nations to oppose its invasion of Cambodia.

The US retreat from Vietnam included the Nixon doctrine's signal of a wider American withdrawal from Asia. However, despite emerging détente with China, in 1979 the US still maintained army and naval forces to protect Taiwan and South Korea, and the US was still responsible for the defence of Japan, though a noisy minority of Japanese wished otherwise. Also tensions were emerging over Japan's continued economic expansion and the US growing deficit in bilateral trade. Japan's economic expansion was further influencing economic growth in the Asian Tiger nations of South Korea, Taiwan, Hong Kong and Singapore, which was increasing the economic importance of the Western Pacific Basin.

Though the Cold War was diminishing in significance in the Western Pacific Basin, in 1979 conflicts were still simmering in Southeast Asia. In Cambodia, Vietnam was facing a foreign power-backed insurgency. In the Philippines the dictatorial and corrupt government of Ferdinand Marcos was combating a rebellion by the Marxist New People's Army. Fretilin's insurgency in East Timor had not been completely suppressed. Indonesia was fighting another guerrilla conflict in Irian Jaya against a Melanesian independence movement, which will be discussed in the next chapter.

CHAPTER FIVE

Independence for some Pacific Islands, 1945–1980

The Pacific Islands are defined as the island groups whose indigenous people belong to the Melanesian, Polynesian and Micronesian ethnic groups. Micronesia incorporates the relatively small islands of the North Pacific, many of which are coral atolls. Melanesians, who generally have darker skins and more negroid features, inhabit the island chain extending from New Guinea southeastwards to Vanuatu and New Caledonia, which includes the biggest of the Pacific Islands. Melanesia is also the region of greatest linguistic and cultural diversity, with a general absence of hereditary authority. Polynesians are natives of the South Pacific Islands to the east of that island chain, with the exception of Fiji, where the indigenous people are mostly Melanesian, but which has a Polynesian culture, such as a strong chiefly system.

Many of the islands of the Pacific experienced during the Second World War the traumas of Japanese invasion and US counter attacks, leaving much physical devastation. After the war there were isolated islander protests against the return of colonial administrations. But there were not the same concerted movements for independence as in Southeast Asia. This chapter deals with the later processes and struggles for independence by Pacific Islanders to 1980 plus inter-relationships of the independent island states and with their former colonial masters.

Postwar reconstruction and islander aspirations to 1949

The one postwar political change in the Pacific Islands occurred in the North Pacific, where Japan's League of Nations mandated islands became an American mandate under UN trusteeship. The JCS wanted outright annexation, the Pacific War having made the Pentagon conscious of the region's strategic importance to the US. But the State Department continued Roosevelt's ideal of international control, though changing it to a UN mandate with special provisions enabling the US to draft its own terms for administering the islands. This allowed the US to keep out foreign powers, which accorded with the JCS strategic argument. Truman endorsed this approach because he opposed outright annexation and wished to support the UN. In these American considerations no thought was given to asking the opinion of the islanders. However, their experience of oppressive Japanese rule, the trauma of wartime destruction, the exhibition of US military power in expelling the Japanese and the generosity of many of the occupying American troops made most Micronesians happy about US rule, though some dissented.[1]

Elsewhere in the Pacific war zone, returning colonial powers easily re-established control. However, there were some challenges from islanders, the most serious being the Maasina Rule movement in the British Solomon Islands, centred on the island of Malaita. Many Malaitans had experienced for generations the wider Pacific world as contract labourers, and Maasina (brotherhood) Rule reflected the contrast islanders had drawn between the fleeing British administration in 1942 and the Americans, who treated them more like equals. Maasina Rule opposed the British return by setting up its own administration, by levying taxes and by demanding higher wages. The British administration responded by banning Maasina Rule, and after it spread to other islands, 2,000 of its supporters were arrested in 1949, which helped deflate the movement. It was further discredited in 1950 when a predicted arrival of American planes to drive out the British failed to materialise.[2]

In other Melanesian islands there were some millenarian movements making prophecies about the arrival of planes, tanks and machine guns to liberate the coloured people from their white masters. Major examples were Skin Guria on the Huon Peninsula in the Australian mandated territory of New Guinea and the John Frum movement on the island of Tanna in the Anglo-French administered New Hebrides Islands (Vanuatu). But a feature of such movements, called 'cargo cults' by Europeans, was their localized influence in the Melanesian region with its many languages and

---

1   Lester J. Foltos, 'The New Pacific Barrier: America's Search for Security in the Pacific, 1945–47', *Diplomatic History* 13, 1989, 316–36. Francis X. Hezel, SJ, *Strangers in Their Own Land: A Century of Colonial Rule in the Caroline and Marshall Islands* (Honolulu 1995), 244–57. Geoffrey M. White and Lamont Linstrom (eds), *The Pacific Theater: Island Representations of World War II* (Honolulu 1989), chs 3–6, 12. David Hanlon, *Remaking Micronesia: Discourses over Development in a Pacific Territory 1944–1982* (Honolulu 1998), 21–6.

2   Judith Bennett, *Wealth of the Solomons: A History of a Pacific Archipelago* (Honolulu 1987), ch. 13.

great cultural diversity. Consequently, none of the returning colonial administrations – British, Australian or French – had any major difficulty with widespread protest movements.[3]

The main task of those administrations was reconstruction after massive war damage. For this purpose, the Australian government increased its financial subsidy to its territories of Papua and New Guinea, which was only AUS£45,000 per annum in the 1930s, to AUS£4.5 million in 1949. This massive increase reflected the new Australian appreciation of the territories' defence value and a sense of responsibility in Australia to the many Papua New Guineans who had assisted the Australian war effort. The previously separated territories of Papua and New Guinea were combined under the one administration under UN mandate, even though Papua had been a colony.[4]

In the French colony of New Caledonia the postwar French Socialist government gave Kanaks citizenship rights and freedom from the pre-war restrictions that had confined them to small reservations. However, the colony also became an integral part of France. Another barrier to Kanak aspirations was the existence of a community of Europeans, known as Caldoche, with nineteenth-century roots and numbering 18,500 in 1946 compared with 31,000 Kanaks. Furthermore, Europeans controlled the best land and the colony's wealthy nickel production.[5]

Only in one Pacific Islands group was there a strong indigenous independence movement: New Zealand's mandated territory of Western Samoa. Samoans, who were largely self-sufficient in their mostly subsistence economy, had expressed violent dissent from New Zealand rule in the Mau movement of the 1920s and early 1930s. Heavy New Zealand military action and the granting to Samoans of village-level autonomy had worked to suppress this movement. However, during the Second World War, the presence of 2,000 American troops in Western Samoa, who treated Samoans better than did New Zealanders, prompted some islanders by 1944 to call for an end to New Zealand rule. But they were mollified by the visit to Samoa of the New Zealand Prime Minister, Peter Fraser, followed by the appointment of more sympathetic administrators and a firm promise to work towards independence.[6]

---

3 Peter Hempenstall and Noel Rutherford, *Protest and Dissent in the Colonial Pacific* (Suva 1984), ch. 5. Michael Allen (ed.), *Vanuatu: Politics, Economics and Ritual in Island Melanesia* (Sydney 1981), ch. 14.
4 Ian Downs, *The Australian Trusteeship, Papua New Guinea 1945–75* (Canberra 1980), chs 2–3.
5 John Connell, *New Caledonia or Kanaky? The Political History of a French Colony* (Canberra 1987), 97, 241–3.
6 Malama Meleisea, *The Making of Modern Samoa: Traditional Authority and Colonial Administration in the Modern History of Western Samoa* (Suva 1987), ch. 6. J.W. Davidson, *Samoa Mo Samoa: The Emergence of the Independent State of Western Samoa* (Melbourne 1967), chs 5–6.

In Fiji, the 117,488 Fijians in 1946 were outnumbered by 120,063 Indians. They had been brought into the colony in the nineteenth and early twentieth centuries to work in the predominant export crop, sugar, and now dominated, as well, the middle sections of an economy, which was controlled by Australian companies and by the 4,594 European and part-European residents. Like Malayans, Fijians had been shielded by the British administration from European economic influences, though they had widely embraced Christianity. In the face of pre-war Indian demands for equal rights, Fijian chiefs, who commanded strong Fijian loyalty, supported the continuation of a European-dominated legislative council. Further alienation between Fijians and Indians occurred during the Second World War when many of the former volunteered for military service and most of the latter stayed home. More tension arose when in 1944 Indian sugar farmers went on strike against the Australian Colonial Sugar Refining Company (CSR), which had monopoly control over the milling of cane and was able to sit out the strike until it collapsed.[7]

Slow Polynesian roads to independence

Independence was a slow process in the postwar Pacific even in Polynesia with its more culturally united societies than in Melanesia. Independence for Western Samoans was delayed by their strong attachment to traditional culture. Modern anthropological research suggests that Samoan social conservatism was related to the widespread 'matai' system of chiefs, who were heads of extended families, elected by their kindred, giving Samoans great faith in their own social and political organisations.[8] Their attachment to traditional culture created a prejudice in the minds of New Zealand officials about the readiness of Samoans for independence. Furthermore, the insistence of most islanders, except some Western-educated Samoans, on enfranchising only the matai for elections to a self-governing assembly offended New Zealand notions of democracy. Nevertheless, the New Zealand government was committed to bring the islands to independence and eventually agreed to graft the matai electorate on to a Westminster system

---

7 Timothy J. Macnaught, *The Fijian Colonial Experience* (Canberra 1982), chs 8–10.
   K.L. Gillion, *The Fiji Indians: Challenge to European Dominance 1920–1946* (Canberra 1977), chs 7 9. Michael Moynagh, *Brown or White? A History of the Fiji Sugar Industry, 1873–1973* (Canberra 1981), ch. 7.
8 Lowell D. Holmes, 'Factors Contributing to the Cultural Stability of Samoa', *Anthropological Quarterly*, 53, 1980, 188–96.

of government. On the voting register for the first Samoan legislature in 1957 there were only 5,030 matai voters in a Samoan population of 94,665. In a resultant plebiscite in 1961 70 per cent of the Samoan voters supported independence, though the minority against it might have been larger without matai pressure to support a constitution that cemented their power. Western Samoa thus became in 1962 the first tropical Pacific Islands group to be granted independence.[9]

The next territory to become independent was the small equatorial island of Nauru. It was a 'treasure island' for Australian and New Zealand farmers, who benefited from Nauru's phosphate production supplied to them at half world prices, a saving in 1939 of 32 shillings per ton. By contrast Nauruans then received only eight pence per ton in royalties, and their island was being transformed by the mining into a moonscape-like desert. After the Second World War, during which the occupying Japanese deported many Nauruans to other islands, some Nauruans were looking forward to more self-rule rather than a continuation of heavily paternalistic Australian control and for higher wages and phosphate royalties. But Australia was reluctant to grant them any real self-governing power because of its phosphate interests, but did grant a rise in the phosphate royalty to Nauruans to 2 shillings and 7 pence a ton by 1958.[10]

However, the Nauruan Head Chief from 1956, Hammer DeRoburt, who had received secondary school education in Australia and had led a strike in 1952 for wage increases, was pushing in 1959 for full Nauruan ownership of the phosphate mining. In the early 1960s Nauru's leaders envisaged that they would achieve self-rule on another island, perhaps one offshore from Australia, to compensate for the destruction of much of their island. The shifting of the Banaban people from phosphate mining-ruined Ocean Island to Rabi Island in Fiji had created a precedent. However, negotiations for an Australian offshore island foundered on the Nauruan demands for sovereign independence, though willing to concede to Australia control of defence and foreign affairs. The response in 1964 to this impasse was a demand by the Nauruan chiefs for independence in 1967. The Australian government was prepared to concede only a Nauruan legislative council with self-governing powers, but its laws could still be disallowed by Australia. When Nauruans reacted by demanding independence in 1968, the Australian government only talked about 'further political

---

9 Davidson, *Samoa Mo Samoa*, chs. 10–12. *Pacific Islands Year Book (PIYB)* (8th edition, Sydney 1959), 79. Ben Liuaana, 'Who Made Western Samoa Independent', in Donald Denoon (ed.), *Emerging from Empire? Decolonisation in the Pacific* (Canberra 1997), 40–6.
10 Roger C. Thompson, *Australia and the Pacific Islands in the Twentieth Century* (Melbourne 1998), 87, 120–4, 140–3.

progress' that year. But Australia was under pressure from its phosphate partner New Zealand to follow its example in giving independence to Samoa, though the other partner in the phosphate management, Britain, was unwilling to set a precedent of granting independence to such a small island. Also the UN was pressing for independence for Nauru. The decisive pressure came from the US. In 1968 Nauru became the world's smallest independent state. Its twenty-one square kilometres supported only 3,000 people.[11]

Fijians were much less keen than Samoans or Nauruans about independence. In the 1950s Fijian chiefs were happy to rely upon their alliance with the local European community and the maintenance of colonial rule in order to preserve their Christianized Polynesian social order from any challenge by the more numerous Indians. Any more democratic political change, said one of the leading chiefs in 1959, would be against 'the protection of fundamental Fijian interests'.[12] Nor in that decade, with high sugar prices and rising returns to Indian cane farmers, were there major pressures from the Indian community for political change.

However, in the 1960s Indian cane farmers in Fiji became more restive. A cane growers' strike in 1960 reflected dissatisfaction caused by an expansion of the sugar industry into marginal lands and its inability to keep up with a growing Indian population. A more immediate cause was falling world sugar prices influencing the monopolistic CSR to cut the price paid to growers and impose on farmers extra costs. The strike, however, failed because of previous CSR stockpiling of sugar.[13]

But the strike stimulated Indian leaders in the early 1960s to agitate for equal political rights for Indians. Such a move would give dominance in Fiji to the Indian population, which by 1970 comprised 51 per cent of the total population, compared with 43 per cent Fijians, 3 per cent Europeans and part-Europeans and 1 per cent Chinese. In the postwar years until the 1960s there was no change to the legislative council arrangement of 1936, which had sixteen official members and five each from the European, Fijian and Indian communities. Significantly, the Fijian members were nominated by the Council of Chiefs. The chiefs did not agree to universal suffrage for Fijians until 1960, and only then to prevent erosion of their authority by having such a change enforced upon them. The 1963 council elections saw another new phenomenon, the beginnings of an Indian political party, the Federation Party, led by the leader of the cane farmers' strike, A.D. Patel.

---

11   Ibid., 191–6.
12   Brij V. Lal, 'The Decolonisation of Fiji: Debate on Political Change, 1943–1963', in Denoon (ed.), *Emerging from Empire?*, 34.
13   Moynagh, *Brown or White?*, ch. 8.

This party demanded security for Indian cane farmers, the release of more Fijian-owned land for their use and equal voting rights for Indians. However, the party urged its supporters not to offend Fijians and tried to woo them, with some success in Western Viti Levu, where there was opposition to the power of the dominant chiefs of the Eastern region of Fiji. An alliance with a small Fijian party in that region created the National Federation Party (NFP).[14]

Britain responded to the Indian pressure. The new Labour government was keen to hand over the responsibility of governing Fiji to the local people. Fijian chiefs, who had formed their own political party to meet the Indian challenge, tried to resist the process, and they were able to achieve parity with Indians in a new legislative council, which emerged from a constitutional conference in London in 1965 attended by leaders of Fiji's communities. In this arrangement 'general electors', who were members of the European community and other races, would hold the balance of legislative power. The NFP accepted this imbalance as a first step towards achieving more political power for Indians with future electoral change. After more political discussions, Fijian chiefs agreed to independence in 1970 on the understanding that with their European allies they would still maintain political control. The fifty-two seat House of Representatives had twelve seats for each of the Fijian and Indian communities and three for the general electors, with ten Fijians, ten Indians and five general electors to be elected in national seats.[15]

In 1970 the British protectorate of Tonga also became an independent nation. Tonga was the one Pacific Islands group that had retained significant self-government under British colonial control, and where Europeans were denied land ownership in a nation of mostly small farmers. This freedom had been won by the Wesleyan mission-supported King George Tupou I, who in the 1860s established a British-style parliamentary government dominated by the king and the Tongan nobility. After the declaration of the British protectorate in 1901 a partnership developed between the royal Tongan government and British authority represented by the consul and British heads of government departments. The process was assisted significantly by Tonga's Queen Slote Tupou III, a politically gifted and gracious ruler, who reigned from 1918 to her death in 1965. By then, British involvement in the kingdom had diminished as overseas-educated

---

14   *Fiji Annual Report*, 1970, 12. Robert Norton, *Race and Politics in Fiji* (2nd edition, St Lucia 1990), 77–9, 89–104. Brij V. Lal, *A Vision: AD Patel and the politics of Fiji* (Canberra 1997), ch. 8.
15   Brij V. Lal, *Broken Waves: A History of the Fiji Islands in the Twentieth Century* (Honolulu 1992), 186–213.

Tongans assumed senior public service positions. With the British keenness to leave the Pacific, there was an easy transition to independence in 1970, the only real change being the independence celebrations.[16]

The British government had more difficulty in shedding its governing responsibilities in the Gilbert and Ellice Islands colony: a widespread collection of small low-lying atolls, except for phosphate-rich but largely worked-out Ocean Island. In this colony there were no demands for independence from the islanders. It was a quiet backwater of minimal government spending, and its subjects were relatively undisturbed by the challenges of secondary or tertiary education. As late as 1970 there were only 622 islanders enrolled in two secondary schools compared with 12,164 in primary schools. Furthermore, stretching across 1,600 kilometres of the Pacific Ocean, their small islands had few connections with each other, so that there was no sense of national unity. The relative poverty of the islanders made inter-island travel too expensive. Nevertheless, with orders from London, the colony's administration in 1967 transformed a nominated advisory council, established in the early 1960s, into an elected but still advisory House of Representatives. Seven years later, this legislature gained full self-governing power. This rapid political transformation gave few islanders any real interest or understanding of the changes. The only political party, the Gilbertese National Party, was started in 1965 by civil servants from the Gilbert Islands, who were determined to protect their culture and interests from better-educated Ellice Islanders. This concern diminished in the 1970s with the realization, after the first parliamentary elections, that Gilbertese would easily control the colony after independence. They had nineteen seats in the twenty-three member House, reflecting the fact that in 1968 they numbered 44,897 to 7,465 Ellice Islanders.[17]

This demographic reality encouraged Ellice Islanders to seek secession, although they spoke of it as separation. In one sense this demand was a reflection of history and geography. The two island archipelagos had been arbitrarily joined together in 1916, when two protectorates became one colony for economic and administrative convenience. But the Ellice Islanders were Polynesians and the Gilbertese Micronesians, a difference observable in their physical appearances and different languages and social systems. Also, with much more keenness for Western education, Ellice Islanders

16 Noel Rutherford (ed.), *Friendly Islands: A History of Tonga* (Melbourne 1977), chs 9–11.
    I.C. Campbell, *Island Kingdom: Tonga Ancient and Modern* (Christchurch 1992), 79–193.
    Elizabeth Wood Ellem, 'Queen Slote and the British Dual Mandate Policy', in Denoon (ed.), *Emerging from Empire?*, 22–5.
17 *Gilbert and Ellice Islands Annual Report*, 1970, 38–9, 6. Barrie Macdonald, *Cinderallas of the Empire: Towards a History of Kiribati and Tuvalu* (Canberra 1982), ch. 13.

considered themselves superior to Gilbertese. Indeed, Ellice Islanders gained a majority of overseas educational scholarships and senior civil service positions during the 1960s despite being only one-seventh of the population, a dominance that provoked the creation of the Gilbertese National Party. That party in turn encouraged Ellice Islanders to fear they would be discriminated against by the Gilbertese in a united independent country.[18]

The British government was caught unawares by this Ellice Islander outcry for separation. Having done nothing to foster any sense of national unity in the islands in the past, London was prepared to accept partition of the colony, remembering the violence that had occurred on the Caribbean island of Anguilla in 1969, when it was arbitrarily included in a federation in the West Indies. In a referendum observed by the UN in 1974, 92 per cent of Ellice Islanders voted for separation. By 1976 arrangements for partition of the colony were complete, and in October 1978 the Ellice Islands became the independent state of Tuvalu, which with 7,357 people living on twenty-six square kilometres of land was the world's second smallest state. In July 1979 the Gilbert Islands plus Ocean Island became the independent state of Kiribati. Though much more populous than Tuvalu, its 726 square kilometres of low lying atoll land also rendered its economic future dependent on outside aid.[19]

Pushing independence for Papua New Guinea

In the much bigger islands of Melanesia, greater cultural diversity and less educational and economic development than in Polynesia were major impediments to independence. So too were the prevailing views of colonial authorities that 'primitive' Melanesians would be incapable of governing themselves for many more decades. When he became the Australian Minister for Territories in 1951, Paul Hasluck considered that self-government could be fifty years away. Hence, he concentrated on extending primary school education with an aim of universal literacy as a basis for future political development. However, a rapidly expanding population and the discovery of more people in previously unopened areas of the vast highlands region of the country helped defeat this idealistic goal. In 1960 only 10 per cent of the known 1,815,391 Papua New Guineans were attending schools, compared with 31 per cent of Gilbert and Ellice Islanders. Attempts

---

18   Macdonald, *Cinderallas of the Empire*, 244–53.
19   Ibid., 253–75. *PIYB* (14th edition, Sydney 1981), 468.

to promote indigenous economic development were also limited. In 1960 Papua New Guineans produced only 38 per cent of the territory's coffee production, the largest proportion for any crop except rice. Agricultural production was dominated by Europeans who, with the opening of the climatically attractive highlands to settlement in the 1950s, had increased in numbers during that decade from 10,854 to 18,978. The one success story in indigenous development had been Hasluck's policy of establishing local government councils, though by 1960 they only covered about 15 per cent of the population.[20]

A major step forward in the movement in Papua New Guinea (PNG) towards independence was a visit in 1962 by a mission from the UN Trusteeship Council led by Sir Hugh Foot, a former British governor, who had presided over the introduction of self-government into northern Nigeria and Jamaica. He was astounded to hear from Australian officials that they would still be ruling the territory in the next century. His report firmly recommended a nationally elected parliament by 1964, concerted efforts to promote national unity, and an end to discriminatory practices, especially the repeal of laws banning the sale of alcoholic drinks to indigenous people. This report challenged the Australian government at a time when it was realizing that the slow pace of preparation of the territory for independence should be quickened. So Foot's report assisted the implementation of reforms already in the pipeline, such as lifting the alcohol ban and planning for a new legislature. An elected House of Assembly with majority indigenous representation was introduced in 1964 after a mammoth administrative program to inform people about how to vote and to deliver waterproof ballot boxes, mainly by aircraft, to 2,919 polling places.[21]

However, there was no demand for independence among Papua New Guineans in the early 1960s. There were some protest movements. The most serious at this time was a tax strike on the island of Buka by a millenarian cult, the Hahalis Welfare Society, which also upset local Catholic missionaries by encouraging teenage girls to offer sexual services to any takers. The consequent children were communally raised in a baby farm. This protest was suppressed by police action without bloodshed. But the Hahalis movement was a sign of future dissent in a region culturally distinct from the rest of PNG. The people of Buka and neighbouring Bougainville are mostly black rather than the shades of brown of other Papua New Guineans. Buka-Bougainvillians are culturally allied to the Western Solomon

---

20   Thompson, *Australia and the Pacific Islands*, 129–38. Robert Porter, *Paul Hasluck: A Political Biography* (Netherlands 1993), chs 5–6.
21   Thompson, *Australia and the Pacific Islands*, 157–9. Downs, *The Australian Trusteeship*, 239–51, 305–9.

islands, from whom they had been arbitrarily separated by colonial boundaries drawn principally because German and Australian administrations in New Guinea had valued the work of Bougainvillians as plantation labourers.[22]

A more concerted protest movement developed in the late 1960s in one of PNG's most economically developed regions, the Gazelle Peninsula on the island of New Britain. The Tolai people of that region had experienced the longest contact of any Papua New Guineans with Europeans, going back to the 1870s. Since then, 40 per cent of Tolai land had been alienated to European planters. With postwar population growth, land shortages were becoming a Tolai grievance by the 1960s. The catalyst for protest was the transformation in 1968 of the Tolai local government council into a multiracial one that included the town of Rabaul. This move was part of an Australian government plan to make local government councils more efficient. But the change was seized upon by Oscar Tammur, a Roman Catholic-educated Tolai, who had received army training in Australia, and who was campaigning in 1968 for a House of Assembly seat. Tammur linked the council issue with land grievances as denial of Tolai rights. After his electoral success, Tammur became convenor of the Mataungan Association, which campaigned against the new council, for Tolai land rights and for Tolai self-management. The movement also called for Tolais to stop paying taxes. The administration's reaction was to fly in riot police in September 1969 after Mataungan supporters seized the local government council building in Rabaul. Two Mataungan leaders were arrested. The association responded in November with a large protest march in Rabaul and a Sunday morning of violence as truck loads of club-wielding men descended on the houses of pro-administration Tolais, who received beatings, some very severe. Subsequent mass arrests of Mataungan leaders quietened the movement, but it did not die out. A huge 10,000-strong crowd greeted the Australian Labor Party leader, Gough Whitlam, on a visit to Rabaul in January 1970, who expressed support for Tolai land rights and for local self-government. Six months later a similarly large crowd in Rabaul confronted the Australian Prime Minister, John Gorton, raising fists and brandishing banners, with slogans such as: 'Gorton go to hell.' More violence between Mataungan supporters and police followed. But the movement lost ground after the local Australian District Commissioner, Jack Emmanuel, was murdered in August 1971, which shocked the largely church-attending Tolai people.[23]

---

22 Downs, *The Australian Trusteeship*, 159–60. Hugh Laracy, *Marists and Melanesians: A History of Catholic Missions in the Solomon Islands* (Canberra 1976), 135–42.
23 Thompson, *Australia and the Pacific Islands*, 176–8, 180–2.

Though the Mataungan Association was agitating for local rights, its militancy gave a significant push to the independence process for PNG. After 1963, preparations for independence had slowed down under Charles Barnes, a more conservative Australian Minister for Territories than Hasluck. Barnes stressed economic development to give PNG a secure financial base for independence before any move to self-government. This policy included welcoming European capital and settlers, who raised the non-indigenous population of the territory to 48,960 in 1970. However, this was not a troublesome expatriate community as in Kenya or in New Caledonia since, unlike those colonies, most of the settlers arrived after the Second World War, when ultimate independence for PNG was settled government policy and when new expatriate owned properties were restricted to lease-hold. But the Mataungan demonstrations convinced Gorton's government to start seriously to prepare for independence lest indigenous people become more troublesome. This process speeded up when Whitlam became Australian Prime Minister in December 1972. Full self-government was implemented in 1973 with a commitment to independence in two years' time.[24]

The independence preparations were a crash programme. Though education of Papua New Guineans had improved, including the founding of a university in 1966, there were in 1970 only 19,947 secondary school students in an indigenous population of 2,466,986. There was, consequently, a great shortage of skilled people to run an administration created on Australian lines. The time to train ministers and public servants for independence was less than two years. Furthermore, the nation had been given a Westminster system of government without much consideration of the wide linguistic and cultural diversity in the country, a recipe for political instability. Indeed, the first administration under self-government, led by Michael Somare, the head of the Pangu Parti, the only political party agitating for imminent independence, held only twenty-five of the 108 House of Assembly seats and had to govern with the support of smaller parties and independents. The largest party, the United Party, with thirty-seven House seats, opposed independence. It was based on the populous highlands region of the main island, where people feared domination by better-educated and more politically experienced coastal people and islanders.[25]

The cultural and geographic diversity of PNG also produced separatist movements. In Papua, outnumbered nearly three to one by New Guineans, some politicians were calling for separation. Few Papuans spoke pidgin, the

24 Ibid., 178–80, 182–7. *Papua New Guinea Annual Report*, 1970–71, 238.
25 *Papua New Guinea Annual Report*, 1970–71, 200, 238. Thompson, *Australia and the Pacific Islands*, 172–6, 178–80, 184. J.A. Ballard (ed.), *Policy Making in a New State: Papua New Guinea 1972–77* (St Lucia 1981), 19–74.

lingua franca in most of New Guinea. Papuans also had been more sheltered than New Guineans from economic development. However, cultural diversity within Papua and the cosmopolitan nature of its capital city, Port Moresby, limited the separatist appeal. More ominous was a movement in Bougainville for separation based on the distinct cultural and racial differences there – black Bougainvillians called other Papua New Guineas 'redskins'. The giant Australian-managed Panguna copper mine on the island, which since 1967 had been pumping money into the national treasury, was a particular grievance. However, at this stage a nationalist-minded Bougainvillian parliamentarian, Paul Lapun, had satisfied the owners of the land occupied by the mine by sponsoring legislation granting them 5 per cent of the central government's copper royalties. Somare's government also skilfully manoeuvred Bougainville and the other regions into the new nation by establishing provincial governments, which controlled significant powers. However, Bougainville was to become a major problem in the new nation, which celebrated its independence in September 1975.[26]

Independence for the Solomon Islands and Vanuatu

There were contrasting styles of progress towards independence in two other Melanesian island groups, the Solomon Islands and Vanuatu. The Solomons were one of the developmental backwaters of the British Empire. In 1960 there was one boys' secondary school in the protectorate, and primary education was in the hands of the Christian missions, with varying standards of quality. There were few all-weather roads, transport being mostly confined to sea and air. Revenue was based heavily on a single product, copra, which in the two years 1959–60 earned 98 per cent of domestic export revenue. During the 1960s the British government injected more funds to provide a wider economic base for an independent state. Education was improved, and an advisory council in 1960 was transformed into a nationally elected legislature by 1970. Nevertheless, that year there was a smaller proportion of the 156,066 Solomon Islanders attending secondary schools (0.6 per cent) than of the much more numerous Papua New Guineans (0.8 per cent). The reliance on copra had declined to 54 per cent of domestic export revenue in 1969–70 because of a big increase in less renewable and greater land-destructive timber exports (42 per cent). There had been a

---

26 Thompson, *Australia and the Pacific Islands*, 182–7.

major fall in copra prices because of wider world competition from synthetic substitutes; in 1970 copra earned 25 per cent less than in 1960.[27]

In the 1970s, with Britain's keenness to abandon remaining colonies growing under the impact of balance of payment problems at home, independence was strongly pushed in the Solomon Islands. However, a crash program to equip Solomon Islanders to run their own government ran into problems. There was no islander demand for independence, apart from a few graduates from overseas universities. A committee system of government after 1970 based on British experience in other small colonies, and said to be suited to the major role of consensus in Melanesian culture, displeased aspiring islander politicians because they were deprived of publicity platforms. The slowness of decision making also discredited the system. Therefore, the government was reorganized in 1974 on Westminster lines, under which limited self-government was introduced in 1976.[28]

A more serious problem was a threat of secession by the Western Islands of New Georgia, Choisel and nearby smaller islands. That sector contains the blackest of the Solomon Islanders, who were better educated than the rest because of long-standing Methodist mission schooling. The Western Islands' lighter population density gave their people larger average landholdings than in other islands, supplemented by good fishing resources. Western Islanders were proud of their status as independent producers who were not reliant on migratory labour, and they looked down upon other islanders, especially those from much more densely populated Malaita, which supplied the bulk of the protectorate's labour force. Fearing being swamped by uncouth Malaitans, one of whom, Peter Kenilora, became chief minister in 1977, some Western leaders were calling for secession from the coming independent nation. However, the sentiment was more fear for the future than a concerted independence movement and attracted only a minority of the people in the region. The central government headed off the separatist movement by giving the Western Islanders more autonomy and increased financial resources. Independence arrived in the Solomons on 7 July 1978 with no significant dissension.[29]

By contrast, there was an active independence movement in Vanuatu. Its main cause was the Anglo-French division of the administration of

27 *British Solomon Islands Annual Report*, 1959–60, 21, 35, 54–5; 1970, 10, 15, 142. Bennett, *Wealth of the Solomons*, 312–13.
28 Bennett, *Wealth of the Solomons*, 318–22.
29 Ibid., 327–9. Ian Fraser, 'Decentralisation and the Postcolonial State in Solomon Islands', in Brij V. Lal and Hank Nelson (eds), *Lines Across the Sea: Colonial Inheritance in the Post Colonial Pacific* (Brisbane 1995), 100–1.

those islands. The bizarre New Hebrides Condominium, locally known as 'Pandemonium', had created separate health, education, police and other administrative systems for French and British nationals, leaving the islanders as stateless people. French citizens were more numerous because of the geographic propinquity of New Caledonia with its large European population. In 1967 there were 2,835 French nationals in Vanuatu, compared with 621 British in a population of 77,982. But the Australasian-based Presbyterian mission had a predominant influence over the islanders, with the Anglican Melanesian Mission covering most of the rest. By contrast, French Roman Catholic missionaries had gained only a small foothold in the islands. The French administration woke up to this mission legacy too late. Though by 1960 a new French school-building programme had commenced, the emerging islander leaders were almost entirely educated by the Anglo-Protestant missions.[30]

In 1971 the New Hebrides National Party (NHNP) was formed in Vila, the capital of the Condominium. The party's leader was Walter Lini, an Anglican priest. Its main policies were the promotion of islander culture (*kastom*) and land rights, which tapped emerging islander grievances about the 36 per cent of the territory's land alienated to Europeans – 32 per cent to French citizens. The French administration tried to head off the dissent by releasing much of the French-owned properties for islander use, but the choicest 6 per cent of the archipelago's land remained in European hands. In response, the NHNP agitated for independence. But this campaign ran into a brick wall of French opposition, whereas the British government was eager to facilitate a quick preparation for independence.[31]

However, having granted all its other colonists universal suffrage, France could not object to the British proposal for an elected national assembly. In the elections in 1976 the NHNP won 59 per cent of the vote, gaining seventeen of twenty-nine elected seats. But other seats were reserved for community groups, including the French dominated Chamber of Commerce, producing a deadlock in the assembly. The NHNP responded by boycotting the assembly, depriving it of a quorum. Consequent public demonstrations organized by the party and by its opponents during 1977 included the wielding of sharpened sticks and stones and police teargas responses. By the end of the year the NHNP, now re-named the Vanua'aku (Our Land)

---

30 Norma McArthur and J.F. Yaxley, *Condominium of the New Hebrides: A Report of the First Census of the Population, 1967* (Sydney 1978). Howard Van Trease, *The Politics of Land in Vanuatu: From Colony to Independence* (Suva 1987), chs 3–4. R. Hodgson to A. Tange, 22 September 1960, A1838/T53, 338/1 Pt. 1, Australian Archives, Canberra.
31 Van Trease, *Politics of Land*, 206–24.

Party, declared the independence of the islands and the establishment of a People's Provisional Government. It controlled large sections of the territory.[32]

Paris could not respond, as desired, by sending troops to crush the provisional government without the agreement of the British government, which was embarrassed by public criticism of the use of teargas against pro-independence demonstrators. A pragmatic French Minister for Overseas Territories, Paul Dijoud, travelled to Vanuatu and negotiated a compromise agreement for a constitution for an independent state that would respect French language and culture and allow some regional autonomy. Land would be returned to customary owners and future expatriate land ownership would be banned. Under the terms of this Dijoud Plan elections were held under UN supervision on 14 November 1979 for a new representative assembly. Despite intensive campaigning by the French local administration in favour of two francophone parties, the Vanua'aku Party won with 62 per cent of the vote and a two-thirds majority of the thirty-nine assembly seats. Self-government had been achieved with Lini as Prime Minister, with the required majority to make constitutional changes.[33]

This degree of supremacy for an anglophone party was too much for some French settlers and for francophone ni-Vanuatu, as the islanders were calling themselves. A prominent dissident was Jimmy Stephens, a part European, who had been leading an indigenous francophone movement named Nagriemal. On 28 May 1980, with the backing of French colons, Stephens launched a rebellion on the island of Santo against Lini's government. There were attacks on British and Vanua'aku Party property with smashing of buildings and looting of possessions, forcing that party's supporters to flee into the bush or retreat from the island along with the British police. There was no attack on any French property or any attempt by the French police to stop the violence. Lini declared a blockade of Santo, but his government had no military force. Clear evidence emerged afterwards that the French administration in Vanuatu supported the insurrection. Whether Paris sanctioned such complicity is unknown, but the highly centralized French state normally kept a tight control of its colonial administrations.[34]

Lini's government responded with a declaration of independence on 30 June 1980 under the terms of the Dijoud Plan. The rebels on Santo

---

32 Ibid., 224–31. Christopher Plant, 'New Hebrides 1977: Year of Crisis', *Journal of Pacific History*, 13, 1978, 194–204.

33 Van Trease, *Politics of Land*, 231–46. Stephen Henningham, *France and the South Pacific: A Contemporary History* (Sydney 1992), 38–9.

34 Henningham, *France and the South Pacific*, 28–31, 38–43. John Beasant, *The Santo Rebellion: An Imperial Reckoning* (Honolulu 1984), chs 5–6. Matthew Gubb, *Vanuatu's 1980 Santo Rebellion: International Responses to a Microstate Security Crisis* (Canberra 1994), 19–32.

greeted the news with more violence against non-French property. But Lini played a totally unexpected trump card. On 19 August 1980 a contingent of PNG troops, accompanied by police from Vila, were landed on Santo by Australian military aircraft. This Australian logistic support for Australian trained Melanesian troops was decisive. The insurrection quickly collapsed with the arrest of Stephens and many of his supporters. All of Vanuatu was now fully independent.[35]

Opposition to independence in the French Pacific

The attempt to retain a French presence in Vanuatu was part of the maintenance of France's status as a *puissance mondiale moyenne* (middle-sized world power). A Pacific centrepiece to this 'grand design' was the *Centre d'Expérimentation du Pacifique* (CEP), the euphemistically named nuclear testing facilities on Moruroa Atoll, which lies on the southern edge of the Tuamotu Archipelago in French Polynesia, about 110 kilometres southeast of that territory's main island of Tahiti. This remote sector of the Pacific Basin assumed a new importance in France's efforts to maintain world power status after being expelled in 1962 from Algeria, the previous centre for atomic testing. Open air nuclear testing began at Moruroa in 1966.[36]

An early postwar independence movement had emerged in the widely scattered island groups of French Polynesia where, in 1956, 87 per cent of the 73,202 people were Polynesians (Maohi), 9 per cent were Chinese and 3 per cent were French. More than half of the Maohi were Protestant in religion, a legacy of the London Missionary Society, which reached the islands before French occupation and which reinforced anti-French popular attitudes.[37]

A Maohi advocate for independence was a First World War veteran, Pouvanaa a Oopa, an eloquent Tahitian orator, who was apt to use biblical comparisons of his people under French rule with the captive Hebrews in ancient Egypt. From 1949 he was the territory's elected member in the French parliament, and his political party, the *Rassemblement Démocratique Peuples Tahitiennes* (RDPT), achieved majorities in the territory's legislative assembly in 1953 and 1957. But the assembly had limited powers.

---

35 Beasant, *The Santo Rebellion*, ch. 7. Van Trease, *Politics of Land*, 257–8.
36 Jean Chesneaux, 'The Function of the Pacific in the French Fifth Republic's "Grand Design": Theory and Practice of the "Puissance Mondiale Moyenne"', *Journal of Pacific History*, 26, 1991, 256–72.
37 *PIYB*, 8th edition, 139.

Nevertheless, French settlers felt threatened by the RDPT, especially after it used its legislative majority in April 1958 to pass resolutions in favour of independence and to impose an income tax that hit richer French members of the population. A shopkeepers' strike in Papeete, the capital of Tahiti, against the tax and a large protest march forced a back down by the RDPT. Pouvanaa campaigned strongly for a 'no' vote in the referendum on the continuation of French rule in September 1958, which President de Gaulle arranged for all France's colonies. But a split in the RDPT reduced Pouvanaa's ability to deliver a majority vote for independence; 76 per cent of the voters in the territory favoured continuing French rule. Pouvanaa's opponents achieved their revenge when in October 1959 he was tried and convicted to eight years' imprisonment and sixteen years' exile for conspiring to burn down the legislature building in alleged bitterness at the defeat of the referendum, though in defence Pouvanaa said his threats were no more than a metaphorical use of biblical analogies.[38]

Maohi parties subsequently played down the independence issue after the RDPT was banned in 1964 for circulating petitions opposing the stationing of French troops in the territory. The fragmented Maohi parties now argued for autonomy as a first step to independence. The conservative majority in the legislature after Pouvanaa's imprisonment rescinded the independence motion and handed back some powers to the governor.[39]

Furthermore, a major economic transformation was taking place in French Polynesia. The CEP brought new prosperity. The proportion of French financial transfers to the territory's GNP expanded from 16 per cent in 1960–63 to 59 per cent in 1964–69. The attraction of Tahiti as the economic and administrative centre increased, with its share of the territory's population growing from 49 per cent in 1951 to 70 per cent in 1977. By that year new French settlers to French Polynesia had trebled the proportion of the European population since 1956 to 9 per cent. Also 7 per cent of the population were part-Europeans, though labelled 'Polynesians'.[40]

The CEP was opposed by a coalition of pro-autonomy parties, called the *Front Uni*, which achieved a majority of seats in the two assembly elections of 1967 and 1972. The French government strongly resisted the autonomy aim because it was seen as a step towards independence, which could

---

38 Henningham, *France and the South Pacific*, 117–26. Robert Langdon, *Tahiti: Island of Love* (5th edition, Sydney 1979), ch. 22.

39 Henningham, *France and the South Pacific*, 132–3. Robert Aldrich, *France and the South Pacific since 1940* (London 1993), 171–80.

40 Aldrich, *France and the South Pacific*, 127–9. Barry Shineberg, 'The Image of France: Recent Developments in French Polynesia', *Journal of Pacific History*, 21, 1986, 153–7. *PIYB*, 14th edition, 131.

threaten the CEP's future. However, in 1974 the nuclear testing went under-ground, partially in response to the *Front Uni*, but more as a concession to wider world opposition to open air testing. The elected legislature was given more responsibility, and the governor became High Commissioner, with the legislature appointing a council of government with local administrative responsibility, but still under overall French control. Nevertheless, in return for the concessions, the *Front Uni*'s leaders, Francis Sanford and John Teariki, stopped campaigning against the nuclear tests or for more autonomy, recognizing a new economic dependency created by the CEP. That was indicated by a growth in food imports, which by 1980 had more than doubled from 37 per cent of food consumption in 1960. Indeed, the French government increased its expenditure in the territory in the late 1970s in order to strengthen the economic chains binding its people to France. Only two small parties, *Ia Mana Te Nunua* and the Polynesian Liberation Front, were keeping the pro-independence light burning.[41]

Struggle for independence in New Caledonia

A reverse independence process was occurring in New Caledonia. In 1951, Kanak franchise was increased close to adult suffrage, a spin-off from reforms in France's wider colonial empire. Also an educated Kanak elite had been formed through educational programs run by the Roman Catholic and Protestant Churches in New Caledonia. At first Kanak leaders mostly gave their support to a new multiracial political party, the *Union Calédonienne* (UC), led by Maurice Lenormand, a French-born pharmacist, who had a Kanak wife and who was willing to support Kanak social and economic advance-ment. Though such policies placed him at odds with many Europeans, the UC's liberal policies, such as redistributing land and more territorial control over the dominant nickel mining company, *Société le Nickel* (SLN), attracted votes from the economically depressed white small farmer community and from the urban working class in a society dominated by a landholding and mining investment elite. In 1953 the UC won fifteen of the twenty-three seats in New Caledonia's legislature. Two years earlier Lenormand had been elected as New Caledonia's sole representative in the French parliament because of divisions among conservative opponents. Outraged European conservatives could not agree on any united opposition to the UC.[42]

---

41 Henningham, *France in the South Pacific*, 127–40. Shineberg, 'Image of France', 162–3.
42 Myriam Dornoy, *Politics in New Caledonia* (Sydney 1984), 154–64. Connell, *New Caledonia or Kanaky*, 241–5.

Entrenched in power for the rest of the 1950s, the UC introduced a minimum wage for all people in the territory, family allowances and holiday pay and increased opportunities for Kanak education. Lenormand's emphasis was on integrating Kanaks into the community, and he strongly affirmed the link with France. The UC's campaign for a 'yes' vote in the 1958 referendum on retention of French rule produced a 95 per cent affirmative majority in New Caledonia. However, the UC found the land reform problem too hard to solve because of competing demands from its Caldoche and Kanak supporters and because of the entrenched nature of the existing pattern of land holdings in white society. Nevertheless, the party was bolstered by the election in 1956 of a socialist government in France, which introduced universal suffrage in all France's overseas territories, and ensured that the New Caledonian territorial assembly would have much local power.[43]

However, from 1957 the UC's power started to wane. Conservative political propaganda about defending European society against upstart Kanaks was draining Caldoche support from the party. The advent of the conservative de Gaulle to power in France in 1958 inspired conservatives to demonstrate in Noumea for the resignation of Lenormand and his government. A threat of Kanak counter demonstrations caused Europeans in Noumea to dig trenches and raise barricades. But the governor defused the situation by banning the carrying of arms, and the agitation temporarily collapsed. De Gaulle's government also started stripping powers from the legislature in a calculated bid to oust Lenormand. De Gaulle had visited New Caledonia in 1957 and had made contacts with conservatives there. A downturn in the price of nickel, the mainstay of the colony's economy was exacerbating tension in the colony. In 1962, two days after the UC government rejected a request from the SLN for export tax exemption, a bomb exploded in the legislative assembly. More violence followed including a bomb blast at UC headquarters. Of three suspects two were members of the UC but recent immigrants with suspected French secret service connections. They confessed that Lenormand had consented to the planting of the bomb in order to discredit conservatives, but later retracted that accusation. Despite obvious weaknesses in the prosecution evidence, Lenormand was convicted for allowing a crime to occur and was awarded a year's suspended jail sentence. Crucially, for his political power, his civil liberties were suspended for five years. Conservatives had achieved their revenge for his desertion of racial ranks.[44]

---

43 Ibid., 194–7, 245–8. Dornoy, *Politics*, 60, 164–8. Henningham, *France in the South Pacific*, 54–6.
44 Henningham, *France in the South Pacific*, 56–60. Connell, *New Caledonia or Kanaky*, 248–51.

The UC remained in existence under Lenormand's Kanak deputy Roch Pidjot. However, the assembly had lost much of its autonomous power. The importance of the territory in French government eyes was growing, in contrast to diminishing British interest in Pacific colonies. One reason for the difference was the CEP and the feeling in French government circles that independence for New Caledonia could inspire the independence movement in French Polynesia. The CEP also enhanced the importance of all French Pacific territories in supporting France's world power aspirations. Under de Gaulle's Fifth Republic, the traditional French attitude of regarding French dependencies as extensions of metropolitan France was reinforced. The people of New Caledonia were all encouraged to think of themselves as French, even though Kanaks suffered from socio-economic discrimination at the hands of local Europeans. Furthermore, New Caledonia's nickel exports were increasing, making the colony the world's second largest nickel producer. New laws increased French government control of the economy including all aspects of the mining industry. Electoral changes, such as increasing seats in Noumea, weakened the UC, though it still won enough European working-class votes to remain in power throughout the 1960s.[45]

However, demographic changes were eroding the position of Kanaks in their own country. European immigration was growing, boosted by a Vietnam War-driven boom in nickel prices and by deliberate French government policy. The French Prime Minister, Pierre Messmer, told his Secretary of State for Overseas Departments and Territories in 1972: 'It is necessary to seize this last chance to create another Francophone country so that the French presence . . . [is not] threatened . . . by nationalist claims from the indigenous people.'[46] Many of the new settlers were former French colonists expelled from independent Algeria, who were strongly racist in their views. The influx of Europeans decreased the Kanak proportion of the colony's population from 51 per cent in 1956 to 46 per cent in 1969. During those years the proportion of Europeans rose from 37 per cent to 41 per cent; and 9 per cent of the 100,579 people in New Caledonia in 1969 were from other Pacific islands, especially the French Wallis and Futuna Islands. The conservative strongly Roman Catholic Polynesian inhabitants of those islands had voted overwhelmingly in 1958 to convert their French protectorate into an integrated French overseas territory. Many of these islanders were using their French citizenship to escape to New Caledonia from the subsistence economy and high population growth of their islands.[47]

---

45   Connell, *New Caledonia or Kanaky*, 251–6. Henningham, *France in the South Pacific*, 47–8.
46   Quoted in Connell, *New Caledonia or Kanaky*, 218.
47   Ibid., 211. Henningham, *France in the South Pacific*, 179–80, 183–4.

Kanaks in New Caledonia also were suffering from the greatest land inequity in the Pacific Islands. While there was some transfer of land to Kanak reservations, which grew from 126,000 hectares in 1945 to 161,932 hectares in 1969, Europeans still owned 370,000 hectares, much of it of better quality than Kanak land. The economy was dominated by the nickel industry, shared by the SLN in which the French government had direct vested interests, and by ten Caldoche families, inappropriately called 'small miners'. The European dominance was increasing with the nickel boom and was widening the gap between wealthy urban Europeans and Kanaks. Many Kanaks were still living on marginal rural land, and few Kanaks in urban areas had better than unskilled employment.[48]

This contrast helped spawn a new Kanak radicalism in the late 1960s. This development also was influenced by the return to New Caledonia of a small number of the first Kanak university students from France, where they had been influenced by radical French students and teachers who encouraged them to reflect on colonial oppression in their home islands. Another important cause of radicalism was dissatisfaction among politically aware Kanaks with the failure of the UC to introduce major reforms, especially land reform. Riotous protest meetings and arrests and imprisonment of Kanak leaders began in 1969. The arrests stoked the fires of Kanak anger. Slogans like 'Calédonie libre' were being daubed on Noumea walls, and Kanak rebellions during the colonial past were being commemorated in song and story.[49]

Kanak protests grew in the early 1970s and inevitably provoked a right-wing back lash. In December 1975 communal violence produced its first death when a young Kanak, Richard Kamouda, acting out a mock boxing match with a friend in a Noumea street, was shot at point blank range while resisting arrest by a French policeman, who escaped with a suspended sentence. Kamouda's death was to most Kanaks an assassination; to most Europeans it was justified homicide. The two communities were moving further apart.[50]

Kanak frustration with French intransigence about self-government also had a radical political fallout. In 1970 some of them launched the *Union Multiraciale de Nouvelle Calédonie*, led by Yann Celene Uregei. Despite its name, it was the first wholly Kanak political party, the beginning of the break up of the political alliance of the previous two decades between left-wing Europeans and Kanaks. In 1975 Uregei shocked Europeans with a

48 Henningham, *France in the South Pacific*, 63–6. Alan W. Ward, *Land and Politics in New Caledonia* (Canberra 1982), 10. Connell, *New Caledonia or Kanaky*, 125–7.
49 Ibid., 248–50.
50 Dornoy, *Politics in New Caledonia*, 207–8.

speech in the Assembly calling for independence for New Caledonia. Disagreements, however, about the extent of radical social policies and rivalries among Kanak leaders caused further divisions.[51]

A Kanak cultural festival in 1975, called Melanesia 2000, reflected growing Kanak cultural and political consciousness. It was a massive festival attended by Kanaks from all over the territory to celebrate their Melanesian culture. A central organizer was Jean-Marie Tjibaou, a former Kanak Catholic priest and UC leader on the East Coast of New Caledonia. The festival had obvious political overtones and boosted Kanak nationalist fervour. Symptomatic was the formation of a new radical and socialist Kanak party, the *Parti de Libération Kanak* (PALIKA).[52]

The UC also was losing most of its remaining European supporters. In 1967 some radical working-class leaders left to start a socialist party. More seriously a group of moderate European supporters broke away in 1971 and formed the *Mouvement Libéral Calédonien*. However, with continued political fragmentation among conservatives, the UC, with Lenormand back as its leader from 1971, remained the majority party in the territorial legislature until 1977, with support from the more radical Kanak parties. But this coalition had much less freedom to introduce reform policies with French economic control of the territory. Indeed, in response to the tightened French control, the UC was moving towards the more radical Kanak viewpoint in favour of independence from France, further eroding its European support.[53]

Consequently, the 1977 election produced the first clear political polarization in the territory. This was the European-dominated Noumea and the West Coast against the Kanak-controlled East Coast and Loyalty Islands. Also supporting the European side were Polynesian immigrants, who feared for their future under a Kanak-dominated independent state. The moderate and conservative parties also picked up a minority of Kanak voters, who saw their economic future dependant on the French presence or who feared the radicalism of the majority Kanak opinion. After this election the centre and right parties gained a majority in the legislature and the governing council.[54]

By the late 1970s all the Kanak political parties had declared their support for independence. In 1979 they formed a coalition, the *Front Indépendantiste* (FI), in order to outmanoeuvre an electoral law that sought

51 Ibid., 178–82, 185–7. Connell, *New Caledonia or Kanaky*, 262–3.
52 Connell, *New Caledonia or Kanaky*, 265–6. Dornoy, *Politics in New Caledonia*, 209–12. Henningham, *France in the South Pacific*, 67–8.
53 Dornoy, *Politics in New Caledonia*, 170–8, 187–90.
54 Ibid., ch. 7.

to diminish their representation by imposing a 7.5 per cent minimum of votes cast for a party to gain a seat. The FI won fourteen of the thirty-six seats. A new conservative coalition, the *Calédonie dans la République* (RPCR), formed in 1978, won fifteen seats, which formed a majority with the seven elected members of the centrist *Fédération pour une Nouvelle Société Calédonienne* (FNSC). A big minority of Kanaks had deserted the FI, and it attracted very few non-Kanak voters. Ominously for the future, by 1979 violence was breaking out again as radical Kanaks took their protest against French hegemony to the streets with militant conservatives spearheading counter demonstrations.[55]

The French government, however, was starting to realize the dangers of racial confrontation in New Caledonia. In 1979 Dijoud advanced a plan for social and economic reforms to correct the previous discrimination against Kanaks if they abandoned their calls for independence. However, the FI refused angrily to be seduced from the independence struggle. Violence escalated in 1980 when two Kanaks were shot by two Europeans, who escaped with limited prison sentences rather than being charged with murder. The territory was facing a stormy future.[56]

Pacific outposts of the American Empire

In the three decades after 1950 strategic and economic bonds were tying Pacific islands to the American empire nearly as tightly as in the French empire. The economic benefits of American rule in East Samoa, established in 1900 to utilize the magnificent harbour of Pago Pago as a naval base, were sufficient to prevent most islanders there from wishing to join their cousins in independent Western Samoa. In 1980 East Samoa's population of about 31,000 Samoans in a total of 32,395 were all American citizens, with their own song 'Amerika Samoa' and a territorial flag, which included the American eagle. More than twice as many of their kindred were living overseas, mostly in Hawaii and on the American west coast. With significant government employment, a prosperous fishing industry and emerging tourism, the median household annual income in 1980 was US$9,241, much higher than in Western Samoa.[57]

---

55   Connell, *New Caledonia or Kanaky*, 266–80.
56   Ibid., 276–7, 281–2.
57   *PIYB* (16th edition, Sydney 1989), 1–24. Gordon R. Lewthwaite, Chistiane Mainzer and Patrick J. Holland, 'From Polynesia to California: Samoan Migration and its Sequel', *Journal of Pacific History*, 8, 1973, 133–57.

Plate 1. LAST CUSTODIANS OF COLONIALISM IN VIETNAM: French soldiers at Dien Bien Phu, 24 March 1954, Popperfoto.

Plate 2. MUSHROOM CLOUD OVER THE MARSHALL ISLANDS: American nuclear bomb testing at the island of Elugelab, 31 March 1954, Popperfoto.

Plate 3. DINNER DIPLOMACY IN CHINA: Richard Nixon and Chou-Enlai
at a banquet in Nixon's honour, Beijing, 27 February 1972, Popperfoto.

Plate 4. HONG KONG'S COMMERCIAL HUB: The modernized cargo-
handling complex, 24 April 1975, Hulton Getty.

Plate 5. NATION BUILDING IN PAPUA NEW GUINEA: Traditional dance and modern sound system, National Day, Port Moresby, 15 August 1984, Roger C. Thompson.

Plate 6. SANDINISTA STRIKE-BACK IN NICARAGUA: Firing a Soviet-made rocket at US-backed Contras, 17 November 1987, Popperfoto.

Plate 7. CULTIVATING PACIFIC BASIN COOPERATION: APEC
Economic Leaders' Meeting, Seattle, USA, 20 November 1993, reproduced with
permission from the APEC Secretariat, Singapore. For more information please
visit www.apecsec.org.sg

Plate 8. AFTERMATH OF TERROR IN EAST TIMOR: A Timorese
survivor consults a list of missing people after the massacre on 7 September 1999
at Suai, with the courtesy of Lieutenant-Colonel Charles Reynolds.

Some North Pacific Islanders became less content with US rule because of nuclear testing. The worst case occurred on 1 March 1954, when at Bikini Atoll in the northwestern corner of the Marshall Islands the US exploded the world's first hydrogen bomb in an operation code-named *Bravo*. An unexpectedly huge explosion deposited a cloud of radioactive dust for a distance of over 360 kilometres to the east, not into the vacant ocean to the north as weather forecasters had predicted. The US blamed this horrendous accident on an unexpected wind shift. However, the eighty-two islanders on the closest inhabited atoll, Rongalep, who soon experienced itching, nausea, burns to exposed limbs and hair falling out, became convinced they were guinea pigs for American experimentation. In support of this condemnation, meteorologists involved in *Bravo* knew that the wind started blowing from the west before the detonation, but their superiors had ignored them. There was also a delay of two days to evacuate the Rongalep people, whereas a US destroyer spent the day of the test at the entrance of the island's lagoon, with its men sheltered from radiation and measuring its extent, and then sailed away. There was a further day's delay to evacuate the 157 islanders on more distant Utirik Atoll, who were also adversely affected by the fallout from *Bravo*. A counter argument is that American ships were in the fallout area and that twenty-eight American servicemen involved in meteorological and radiological testing on Rongalep were forced to shelter in an aluminium building when they saw the level of radiation suddenly soar. But these men and other US servicemen in the area had radiation-proof protection. There was no protection for islanders, nor any warning given to them. There is still no proof that indigenous people were deliberately exposed; at best it was a case of Americans looking after their own people before they considered the needs of islanders after an unexpectedly huge nuclear explosion.[58]

There was some diplomatic fallout for the US from *Bravo*. A Japanese fishing vessel was near Bikini at the time and sailed home with its crew obviously suffering from effects of nuclear radiation, that many Japanese knew only too well from their 1945 experiences at Hiroshima and Nagasaki. One of those fishermen later died from the exposure. The Eisenhower administration felt compelled to pay compensation to the dead man's family after a Japanese government protest. Marshall Islanders also petitioned the UN about the harmful effects of the radiation and called for an immediate end to nuclear testing in their islands. However, the US was able to contain the damage by keeping secret much of the evidence and assuring the world there would be no lasting ill effects to the Marshallese people. The US still

---

58   Stewart Firth, *Nuclear Playground* (Sydney 1987), 14–20.

used the Marshall Islands for nuclear testing until the long-negotiated open-air test ban was concluded with the USSR in 1963. However, by 1961 concern about adverse UN opinion was prompting a US request to use British atomic testing facilities on Christmas Island, far to the east of the Marshall Islands.[59]

In the North Pacific Trust Territory the US honoured the UN commitment to develop the people towards self-government. In the island group of Palau in 1955 an elected congress was given limited self-government, with a commitment to eventual self-rule. On other islands in the 1950s there were developments of islander controlled local governments. There was little self-assertion among Micronesians who had been cowed by increasingly oppressive Japanese rule in the pre-war and Second World War years and who had not previously been provided with opportunities to express their views. The Marshallese nuclear test protest in 1955 was couched in very polite terms and was regarded in Washington as an aberration. However, in 1959 islander university students in Hawaii formed a Micronesia Club. When its members returned to the islands, they started pressing for faster progress towards a US withdrawal from their homelands. This small agitation contributed to the establishment of a territory-wide Congress of Micronesia in 1965, which was also influenced by the more critical attitude towards trust territories in the UN in the 1960s and by some pressure from within the US administration. The congress had an upper house with two members from each island group and a lower house elected on a population basis; but the US High Commissioner still controlled administration. For many educated Micronesians the progress towards self-government was too slow. Indeed, in 1963 a secret report of an investigating commission, headed by Harvard University Professor Anthony Solomon, had advocated a permanent association of the islands with the US because of their strategic importance and recommended economic development to entice Micronesians to affirmatively vote for that destiny in a future plebiscite.[60]

Nor did the hasty development of the Congress of Micronesia engender a strong sense of national unity among the scattered island groups. The Chamorro and Carolinian people of the Northern Mariana Islands were aware of their distinctive Spanish colonial heritage and their status as the Micronesian area of greatest US strategic interest, being the islands closest to Asia. They also looked forward to joining their ethnic cousins on the island

---

59 Ibid., 21–6. Cabinet Minutes, 14 November 1961, CAB 128/35, PRO.
60 Harold F. Nufer, *Micronesia Under American Rule: An Evaluation of the Strategic Trusteeship (1947–77)* (Hicksville 1978), 49–68. Hezel, *Strangers in Their Own Land*, 276–303. Hanlon, *Remaking Micronesia*, 91–4.

of Guam, a separate American possession, gained as a naval-base prize in the War of 1898 against Spain. Also the Northern Marianas were the wealthiest of the island groups at that stage, assisted by US military expenditure, by the presence on Saipan of the Trust Territory administration, and by developing tourism. So there were objections by these islanders to sharing financial resources with poorer Micronesians. Therefore in 1972 the Northern Marianas sought separate talks with the US, and in a plebiscite in June 1975, 79 per cent of voters opted to withdraw from the Trust Territory and to negotiate Commonwealth status with the US. Washington was happy to oblige, since the Commonwealth agreement, which was implemented in January 1978, gave to the US control of defence and foreign affairs and the right to station armed forces in the now self-governing North Mariana Islands.[61]

The granting of separate political status to the Northern Marianas became a precedent for a rash of separatist movements in the Trust Territory. Palauans were concerned about their limited voice in the lower house of the Micronesian Congress because of their smaller population (14,800 in 1980) compared with the bigger island groups of Phonpei (23,140), Truk (38,650) and the Marshall Islands (29,670). Palauans also were determined to preserve their own culture, though many valued American education. Furthermore, there was a divisive community debate in the mid 1970s in Palau about the introduction of a super-port for a Japanese–American oil storage and petrochemical scheme. Its aim was to utilize·the archipelago's good harbours and its strategic position to the east flank of Japan's main oil supertanker route from the Middle East. The argument between supporters of this scheme and its opponents, who were concerned about threats to the environment and Palauan culture and were supported by American environmentalists, came to physical blows. Supporters of economic development favoured separation from the rest of the Trust Territory in order to give Palau freedom to make its own arrangements with outside developers, even though the super-port proposal was blocked in the US Congress by Democrats concerned about its environmental impact. Consequently, in a plebiscite in 1978 to establish a Micronesian Federation, 55 per cent of Palauan voters approved separation from it. However, American pressure to remove a clause in their new constitution preventing the usage, testing, storage or disposal of any nuclear weapons in Palau failed to stop 78 per cent of Palauan voters approving its inclusion. Their memories of the devastation to their territory caused by the Second World War and a fear of

61   Agnes McPhetres, 'Northern Mariana Islands: US Commonwealth', in Ron Crocombe and Ahmed Ali (eds), *Politics in Micronesia* (Suva 1983), 148–60.

loss of land to US military institutions were the probable major reasons for this vote.[62]

Also in 1978, 62 per cent of Marshall Islanders voted to leave the Federation of Micronesia. This vote was influenced by disagreements over the Congress of Micronesia's taxation policy, fear of domination by the more numerous Truk Islanders, opposition to provisions in the draft constitution for a continued US base on Kwajaleen and personality-based factionalism. In 1980 Marshall Islanders were still negotiating about a compact of free association with the US. It was dangling the bait of economic aid to capture the use of Kwajaleen Lagoon as a missile landing zone, after already spending $20 million to clean up Enewetak Atoll from nuclear contamination and more money on a still unsuccessful effort to make Bikini habitable. Therefore the Federated States of Micronesia (FSM) consisted only of Truk, Phonpei and the lesser populated islands of Yap and Kosrae, which in 1980 had respectively 9,320 and 2,940 people. In 1980 the FSM was still negotiating a compact agreement with the US.[63]

Full-scale independence for Micronesians had been compromised by their economic dependence on the US and by the strategic value of their islands. The long memory of the Second World War made US administrations as reluctant to relinquish the right to establish military forces in Micronesia as was the Soviet Union in Eastern Europe. The North Pacific's value for nuclear testing and missile landing enhanced its military worth. The greatest defence impact was on the island of Guam. There in 1978 only about 62 per cent of the 109,000 people were of indigenous Chamorro ancestry, and there was a major naval base and widespread American educational services. Consequently, most islanders on Guam believed their destiny was with the US. Their struggle was to become an American state, as did Hawaii, with a small indigenous minority, in 1959.[64]

Melanesians under Indonesian rule

In 1969 Indonesia organized the take-over of the Melanesian territory of Irian Jaya, called West Papua by indigenous nationalists. When Indonesia

---

62 Arnold H. Leibowitz, *Embattled Island: Palau's Struggle for Independence* (Westport 1996), ch. 4. Ellen Wood, 'Prelude to an Anti-War Constitution', *Journal of Pacific History*, 28, 1993, 53–67.
63 Daniel Smith, 'Marshall Islands: Tradition and Dependence', in Crocombe and Ali, *Politics in Micronesia*, 55–78. David Hanlon and William Eperiam, 'Federated Micronesia: Unifying the Remnants', in ibid., 79–99.
64 Robert F. Rogers, *Destiny's Landfall: A History of Guam* (Honolulu 1995), 204–38.

took control of the territory on 1 May 1963 to prepare it for a UN supervised self-determination plebiscite in 1969, as set out in the agreement with the Netherlands, every effort was made to obliterate Papuan nationalism and culture. The process started on 2 May with a huge bonfire of symbols of Papuan life, school textbooks and West Papuan flags in the central square of the principal city of Jayapura, which was located on the north coast close to the PNG border. The next day a Papuan council elected under Dutch rule was replaced by an appointed Regional People's Assembly to operate on Guided Democracy principles. The first governor was a Papuan, Eliezer Bornay, who later said, after he was removed from office in 1964, that he first thought there would be a genuine free choice for his people in 1969. But such hopes were snuffed out by 'numerous brutalities, thefts, torture, maltreatment, many things that had not happened before'.[65] The result was the emergence in 1965 of Papuan armed resistance led by Arfak tribesmen, some of whom had been trained by the Dutch Papuan Volunteer corps. They used weapons surviving from the Second World War as well as traditional bows and arrows and called themselves *Organisasi Papua Merdeka* (OPM) (Free Papua Movement). Indonesian responses to the rebellion included airforce strafing and army burning of Papuan villages and mass executions. The act of 'free choice' was carried out in 1969 by 1,025 Papuan 'representatives'. They were carefully trained to vote unanimously on behalf of 800,000 Papuans to 'remain with Indonesia' in front of UN representatives and foreign diplomats, who duly declared that the farce was a legitimate expression of the will of the Papuan people.[66]

The OPM did not give up its struggle, even though it suffered from disunity, a paucity of firearms and mass reprisals by the Indonesian army assisted by US-supplied helicopter gun ships. The OPM had neither the cohesiveness, the degree of military training nor the many modern weapons possessed by Fretilin in East Timor. However, the OPM was assisted by a much vaster mountainous and jungle clad terrain. The Indonesian government soon realized that large force action was counter productive, since villagers were driven further into the mountains, where they were much harder to control and where the guerrillas had plenty of hiding places. So from 1973 a strategy was introduced to use security agencies in the style of dictatorial Latin American governments to detain or kill educated Papuans suspected of OPM leanings and thus deprive the organization of its leadership.

---

65 C. Budiardjo and L.S. Liong, *West Papua: The Obliteration of a People* (revised edition, London 1984), 25.
66 Ibid., ch. 2. Nonie Sharp, *The Rule of Sword: The Story of West Irian* (Malmesbury 1977), 15–23. Robin Osborne, *Indonesia's Secret War: The Guerilla Struggle in Irian Jaya* (Sydney 1985), ch. 1.

Such tactics increased villagers' hostility to the brutal administration. Concerted attempts to impose Indonesian culture on Papuans were also bedevilled by cultural insensitivity. For example traditional tribesmen who wore nothing but penis sheaths were ordered to wear trousers that caused itching and sores. The sentiments of many Papuans became obvious in 1977 when Suharto chanced his popularity with a national election which included Papuans, who were all considered Indonesian citizens. There were OPM influenced mass uprisings all over the territory trying to catch wider world attention and to urge fellow Papuans to boycott the election, much of which was suspended by the authorities. The uprisings did attract wider publicity. Also insurrection in the region bordering PNG, where OPM activity was strongest, caused many people to flee across border after the inevitable Indonesian reprisals. But the OPM lived on to continue the struggle during the 1980s.[67]

There was no international support for the OPM. The PNG government did not have the means to stop 'border crossers'; so its army was not ordered to hunt down OPM personnel. At the same time, fearful of Indonesian hot pursuit across the border, Michael Somare's government gave the OPM no official support; and Somare made a state visit to Indonesia in 1977 to express his desire for mutual friendship between the two countries. The Australian government, which showed its willingness to appease Indonesia over the invasion of Timor in 1975, also gave no support to the OPM. Nor did the US abandon its staunch anti-communist ally, Suharto.[68]

Independent Pacific Island states

Political instability was a problem for some of the newly independent island states. In PNG, Somare's Pangu Parti improved its performance in the 1977 election but still won only 40 of the 106 seats. To govern, it needed to form a coalition with the People's Progress Party led by Julius Chan. This coalition soon split in 1978 when Somare pushed for a strong anti-corruption leadership code, which would have forced Chan to divest himself of his many business interests. Somare continued to govern with the

---

67 Ibid., 50–76. Jan Pouwer, 'The Colonisation, Decolonisation and Recolonisation of West New Guinea', *Journal of Pacific History*, 34, 1999, 177–8.

68 Osborne, *Indonesia's Secret War*, 59–63, 153–60. R.J. May, 'East of the Border: Irian Jaya and the Border in Papua New Guinea's Domestic and Foreign Policies', in R.J. May (ed.), *Between Two Nations: The Indonesia–Papua New Guinea Border and West Papua Nationalism* (Bathurst, NSW 1986), 85–100.

support of his old political foes, the United Party. But Somare's government was weakened by the resignation of half of the supreme court judges when he released from jail his justice minister who had been committed for contempt of court. In March 1980 a no-confidence motion, which set a pattern for future PNG politics, overthrew the government and installed Chan as the Prime Minister. But he headed a more diverse coalition, which did not augur well for future political stability.[69]

There was a portent of more serious future trouble in Fiji in the first general election in 1977. After achieving independence, the Alliance Party, led by a prominent chief, Ratu Mara, had held power with the support of general electors and some Indians, especially from the Moslem minority in the Indian community. But in 1977 the Alliance won only twenty-four seats to twenty-six for the NFP. There was one independent and one member from the new Fiji National Party. That party was the principal reason for the Alliance defeat. It captured 25 per cent of the Fijian vote by campaigning on the racist themes that Fijians should have more political power and that Indians should be repatriated to India. However, since the death of Patel in 1969, the NFP was affected by divisions which, after the election, resulted in a leadership struggle. There was a consequent delay in forming a cabinet, which allowed the Fijian Governor General to call instead on Ratu Mara to form a minority government. This government did not survive long. However, in new elections in 1977 the NFP factionalism boiled over into an open split, which reduced the party's parliamentary representation to only fifteen seats. The Alliance was able to appeal sufficiently to Fijians to reduce the National Party's support to 17 per cent of the Fijian vote, resulting in thirty-six seats to the Alliance. Fijians felt safe again.[70]

The other independent states were blessed with more political stability. However, Tonga's royal and noble dominated government invited future challenges from Tongan commoners. The Samoan matai system was also potentially a weak base for government and, along with divisions among the matai, was soon to produce a constitutional crisis. Nauru's political stability depended on the dominance of DeRoburt, who briefly lost political power for eighteen months in 1977-78.

Few of the newly independent island groups in the 1970s had economic self-sufficiency. Nauru stood out because of continued phosphate mining, now managed by a national corporation. Its people also were benefiting from

69   Ralph R. Premdas, 'Papua New Guinea: The First General Elections After Independence', *Journal of Pacific History*, 13, 1978, 77–89. Sean Dorney, *Papua New Guinea: People Politics and History since 1975* (Sydney 1990), 62–6.

70   Ahmed Ali, 'The Fiji General Election of 1977', *Journal of Pacific History*, 12, 1977, 189–201. Lal, *Broken Waves*, 235–42.

accumulating overseas investments. In 1979–80 the Phosphate Royalties Trust reported a 22 per cent profit rate on its AUS$292 million investments. They included fifty-two-storey Nauru House which, from its completion in 1977, dominated the top end of the most fashionable street in the heart of Melbourne, Australia's leading financial centre. The per capita income of the 4,600 Nauruans was among the highest in the world. Much of it was locked up in investments, but available income was sufficient to provide one or two modern motor cars for most Nauruan families, compared with the predominance of bicycles in the pre-war era.[71]

The other independent Pacific Islands states depended to some extent on overseas aid or assistance. Of those, the most self-reliant state, Tonga, relied on remittances from its many people who had migrated to Australasia and the US. PNG was depending in 1980 on Australia to finance 30 per cent of its budget. There was also a growing reliance in PNG on revenue from the Panguna copper mine on Bougainville, which by 1980 was providing 45 per cent of export earnings. More dependent on a single commodity was Fiji. In the three years 1977–79 sugar was worth 54 per cent of Fiji's exports. However, Fiji's total exports were sufficient to pay for only 56 per cent of the nation's imports in the same period, with a consequent need for assistance to Fiji from the International Monetary Fund. The most vulnerable state was Tuvalu, which in 1980 depended on aid from Britain for nearly a third of its small budget and upon Australia, New Zealand and international agencies for development aid.[72]

Australian aid to Pacific Islands was influenced by fear of growing USSR interest in the South Pacific during the 1970s. A particular shock wave was news in 1976 of a Soviet Union offer of economic assistance to the King of Tonga; and there was increasing activity in the South Pacific, by Soviet fishing trawlers, which were suspected of intelligence gathering. There were also signs of an emerging Chinese interest in the South Pacific with Beijing's opening of embassies in Fiji and Western Samoa, though the Sino-Soviet split and Australian and New Zealand establishment of diplomatic relations with China, made that country less of a potential threat than the USSR. Concern about these new outside great power influences in the South Pacific contributed to an increase in Australian development assistance aid to South Pacific states, other than PNG, from AUS$15 million in the three financial years 1973–76 to AUS$60 million for 1977–79. Australia also had

71 Ron Crocombe and Christian Giese, 'Nauru, the Politics of Phosphate', in Crocombe and Ali (eds), *Politics in Melanesia*, 39–42. Macdonald, *In Pursuit of Sacred Trust*, 61–2. *PIYB*, 14th edition, 275.

72 *FEA*, 1981–82, 941–89.

economic reasons for assisting the newly independent nations of the South Pacific, which, including PNG, were the location of 27 per cent of Australia's overseas capital investments in 1975–76, though the source of only 3 per cent of Australia's overseas trade.[73]

New Zealand played a significant aid role in the South Pacific. In 1980 NZ$58 million was spent on economic assistance to South Pacific islands, but a third went to New Zealand's continued dependencies: the Cook Islands, Niue and Tokelau in Polynesia. The 18,128 people in the Cook Islands (1976 census) and the 3,578 in Niue (1979 census) enjoyed self-government but had opted for free association with New Zealand, which looked after their defence and foreign affairs and provided economic aid. This arrangement allowed free access for the islanders to New Zealand, where more lived in 1980 than in their home islands. The economic aid in 1977–78 contributed to 55 per cent of the budget of Niue and 27 per cent of Cook Islands government revenue. The 1,615 people on Tokelau were still ruled directly by New Zealand. With weakening ties with her traditional trading partner and patron, Britain, as a result of its entry into the EEC, New Zealand was pursuing a more independent foreign policy in the South Pacific. Consequently, economic aid to South Pacific Islands was linked to a concern, announced in the 1978 New Zealand Defence White Paper, that New Zealand should assist to 'preserve peace and security in our own part of the world'.[74]

New Zealand's greatest foreign policy concern was to maintain close relations with her big neighbour, Australia. No two independent countries in the world are more alike in culture, social composition and political institutions. Apart from geographic and economic differences between a continent and islands, the only other major difference was the much larger indigenous and immigrant Pacific Islander population in New Zealand. But the majority of its people, like Australians, were white Anglo-Saxons. Though experiencing past trade friction and rivalry in the South Pacific, the two nations enjoyed past and present close defence cooperation extending to the training of New Zealand's senior army officers in Australia's premier military college. In the 1970s a process of freeing trade relations between

---

73 Greg Fry, '"Constructive Commitment" with the South Pacific: Monroe Doctrine or New "Partnership"?', in Greg Fry (ed.), *Australia's Regional Security* (Sydney 1991), 126–8. Parliament of the Commonwealth of Australia, *Australia and the South Pacific: Report from the Senate Standing Committee on Foreign Affairs and Defence* (Canberra 1978), 19, 30–2, 39, 47.

74 *FEA*, 1981–82, 857, 892, 918. *PIYB*, 14th edition, 68, 404. K. Janaki. 'International Regimes, New Zealand and the Pacific', in Roderic Alley (ed.), *New Zealand and the Pacific* (Boulder 1984), 303.

the two nations commenced. In policies towards Pacific Islands there was a growing cooperation between Australia and New Zealand in the 1970s. There were joint protests against French nuclear testing, Australian naval support for New Zealand naval monitoring of the tests and cooperative support for Fiji's initiative for the establishment in 1971 of a Pacific Forum of Heads of Governments of Independent Pacific Nations. That move was a response to France's banning of the discussion of political issues in the South Pacific Commission, a club of colonial powers in the Pacific, established in 1947 to foster development in the islands, into which independent island states were admitted.[75]

Wider cooperation between Australia, New Zealand and the Pacific Islands states was emerging with the establishment of the South Pacific Forum. The most dramatic example of this was a meeting during the July 1980 Forum meeting in Tuvalu between PNG's Prime Minister, Julius Chan, Malcolm Fraser of Australia and Walter Lini of Vanuatu. Chan and Fraser agreed to help in suppressing the rebellion in Santo. The consequence was the Australian-supported despatch of PNG troops to Santo. Such cooperation revealed a new style of military intervention different from the 'gunboat diplomacy' in the inter-World War years employed by Australia and New Zealand to suppress striking Indians in Fiji, militant tribesmen in the Solomons and protesting Samoans.[76]

Relations between South Pacific Forum members were not always amicable. Nauru's development of an independent airline was at odds with a push for a regional air consortium. There were differences of opinion about French colonialism, with PNG and the Solomons calling for strong diplomatic protest on behalf of their Melanesian brothers in New Caledonia and Vanuatu, and Australia and New Zealand fearing a French backlash against their important trade links with the EEC. The upshot was a typical Forum compromise at the 1979 meeting in Honiara with an expression of concern about islanders still under colonial rule, but without explicitly naming France. There was also a cleavage developing between Melanesian and Polynesian members of the Forum because of the greater size of the Melanesian states and Polynesian fears of Melanesian assertiveness.[77]

75 Mary Boyd, 'Australian New Zealand Relations', in William S. Livingston and Wm. Roger Louis (eds), *Australia, New Zealand and the Pacific Islands since the First World War* (Canberra 1979), 47–61. J.D.B. Miller, 'Australasia and the World Outside: Foreign Policies Since World War II', in Keith Sinclair (ed.), *Tasman Relations: New Zealand and Australia, 1788–1988* (Auckland 1987), 183–201. Graeme Thompson, 'New Zealand and the Wider Pacific', in Alley (ed.), *New Zealand and the Pacific*, 232–5.
76 Van Trease, *Politics of Land*, 257. Thompson, *Australia and the Pacific Islands*, 76–7, 92–3, 207–8.
77 R.A. Herr, 'South Pacific Regionalism', in Alley (ed.), *New Zealand and the Pacific*, 165–76.

Conclusions

The Pacific Islands were by 1980 a potentially more unstable region in the Pacific Basin than before. Restive islanders were contesting French control, especially in New Caledonia. The continued strategic demands of the US in Micronesia were creating dissent despite the economic dependency of the islanders on the US. Papuans were proving difficult for Indonesia to control. The newly independent states were also potential sources for instability. The cultural diversity of PNG was a recipe for political instability, and secessionist feelings among Bougainvillians were soon to re-emerge. The racial divide between Fijians and Indians was a threat to future political stability. Undemocratic political systems in Tonga and Western Samoa were open to future challenge. Most of the island states were dependent on outside economic aid. Furthermore, there were threats of disunity between the Melanesian and Polynesian regions, though the South Pacific Forum was a medium for potential cooperation between the disparate island states.

CHAPTER SIX

Arresting Communism in Latin America, 1945–1979

Along the long eastern rim of the Pacific Basin after the Second World War the Latin American republics were relatively peaceful under their mixture of democratic, single party and military governments. But American economic interests, exploitation by ruling elites and widening gaps between rich and poor were storing troubles for the future. The determination of the US to prevent radical movements, which were readily condemned as communist led, is a major theme of this chapter, which was a mirror along the Eastern Pacific Rim to the Cold War struggle in the Western Pacific Basin. The effects of the US support for right-wing regimes and political movements in the Pacific Basin's Latin American countries are examined, because it contributed to a continuation of revolutionary wars and US intervention into the 1980s, compared with the relative peace in the Western Pacific Basin by then. Relations between the Pacific Basin's Latin American countries, especially attempts for free trade agreements and the disputes that hindered them, are also discussed. The chapter concludes with an analysis of increasing Japanese economic links with Latin America that were breaking down the previous isolation of Latin America from the Western Pacific Basin.

The CIA and Guatemala

In 1954 the Eisenhower administration demonstrated its commitment to fight the Cold War in Latin America, especially in the Central American region that was strategically close to the US, by supporting the overthrow of the government of Guatemala. In 1951 Jacobo Arbenz Guzmán had been elected as the Guatemalan president, promising a radical reform program. Included was a move in 1953 for widespread expropriation of large-scale landholdings, including 225,000 acres of mostly unused land owned by the American United Fruit Company (UFC), which dominated the Guatemalan economy. The company was offered a compensation payment of $627,000, which was its valuation for taxation purposes, but which the UFC now claimed was worth $16 million. This radical agrarian reform program suggested communist influence. In fact Arbenz was not a communist; nor were there any communists in his Cabinet; and the UFC land was to be handed over to small farmer private ownership. There was a small local Communist Party, which strongly supported Arbenz, and some communists held sub-Cabinet posts. But their influence was exaggerated by Arbenz's opponents. They included, as well as the UFC, other members of the 2 per cent of landowners who controlled 72 per cent of the nation's agricultural land, the conservative Catholic Church, members of the armed forces and other Guatemalans upset by radical policies. The right-wing dictators of Honduras, El Salvador, Nicaragua and Venezuela also opposed the Arbenz regime. There is a debate among historians about the extent of popular opposition in Guatemala to Arbenz's government, which depends on the use of primary sources that were heavily influenced by propaganda. However, it is now clear that with US government approval the CIA supported a rebel invasion of Guatemala from neighbouring Honduras on 18 June 1954 led by Colonel Carlos Castillo Armas.[1]

One allegation is that the Eisenhower administration's willingness to back a revolution against the Arbenz government was influenced by the UFC. There is circumstantial evidence for this viewpoint. For example, Dulles had been a legal counsel for the UFC and had drafted the contract in 1936 that gave it exceptional privileges in Guatemala.[2]

However, in 1951 during the Truman administration the State Department had been alarmed by the Arbenz government's attack on the UFC as being communist influenced. There was indecision then about authorizing any covert action to overthrow Arbenz. This concern became a sufficient cause for Eisenhower's administration actively to oppose the Arbenz government, given its determination to prevent communist expansion anywhere

---

1 Frederick W. Marks III, 'The CIA and Castillo Armas in Guatemala, 1954: New Clues to an Old Puzzle' and Stephen G. Rabe, 'The Clues Didn't Check Out: Commentary on "The CIA and Castillo Armas" ', *Diplomatic History*, 14, 1990, 67–95. Nick Cullather, *Secret History: The CIA's Classified Account of its Operations in Guatemala* (Stanford 1999), chs 2–3.
2 Stephen Schlesinger and Stephen Kinzer, *Bitter Fruit: The Untold Story of the American Coup in Guatemala* (London 1982), chs 6–7. Richard H. Immerman, *The CIA in Guatemala: The Foreign Policy of Intervention* (Austin 1982), 125–32.

in the Pacific Basin, especially in its own region. Consequently, Castillo's rebel force of some 200 troops received training from the CIA and was bristling with American arms to distribute to supporters in Guatemala. In fact the operation faltered against determined resistance by Guatemalan police units and hastily armed workers. However, the army, which feared the growth of communism and emerging peasant and rural worker activism, deserted Arbenz. He was forced to resign only nine days after the start of the invasion. The important American involvement in the rebellion was covered up. It clearly breached the principles of the Good Neighbor policy established by Roosevelt in the 1930s and the Eisenhower administration's own public renunciation of the use of force in the internal affairs of Latin American nations. The Guatemala coup added one more right-wing dictatorship – Castillo soon disfranchised most Guatemalans – to the many other dictatorial governments in Latin America at that time.[3]

The intervention in Guatemala was part of a consistent policy pursued by Eisenhower's administration in Latin America. It was seeking to ensure continued Latin American support for the US in the Cold War and to preserve free trade and investment, which benefited American economic interests and supported the capitalist alternative to communism. It also was argued that US economic influence would increase standards of living, which would help preserve the region from communist influence. But there were no significant improvements in overall living standards of Latin American people, given the elitist nature of economic power in most of the republics and falling prices for the region's agricultural exports. Vice-President Nixon discovered consequent popular resentment against 'Yanqui' influence in hostile demonstrations against him on his Latin American tour in May 1958.[4]

The Alliance for Progress era

President Kennedy sought to implement a new set of American policies towards Latin America under the title of Alliance for Progress. The program's aim was to eliminate illiteracy, hunger and poverty-based disease in Latin America by the end of the decade, in the same way as the Marshall

---

3   Immerman, *The CIA in Guatemala*, ch. 7. Richard H. Immerman, *John Foster Dulles: Piety, Pragmatism and Power in US Foreign Policy* (Washington 1999), 108–15. Cullather, *Secret History*,14–31, 74–92, 95–104. Bryce Wood, *The Dismantling of the Good Neighbor Policy* (Austin 1985), 152–90.
4   See Stephen G. Rabe, *Eisenhower and Latin America: The Foreign Policy of Anticommunism* (Chapel Hill 1988), chs 2–6.

Plan had revived war-torn Europe. His kick-start of $500 million plus $100 million for reconstruction after a severe earthquake in Chile, expanded to a total of $18 billion in public and private American aid during the 1960s, including over $10 billion from US government agencies. But results fell far short of aims. Literacy programs barely kept pace with population growth, and the number of unemployed people grew from eighteen million in 1960 to twenty-five million by 1969. The average annual economic growth rate for Latin American countries in the decade was 1.5 per cent, whereas the annual population increase was 2.9 per cent.[5]

Furthermore, the main aim of the Alliance for Progress was to remove conditions for the breeding of communist subversion, which could be fed by the communist regime established in 1959 by Fidel Castro in Cuba. That communist penetration of Latin America was interpreted as a major Soviet Cold War victory, to the extent that at the beginning of his presidency Kennedy launched against Cuba a Guatemala-style intervention which was a miserable failure. Kennedy was determined that there should be no more communist successes in Latin America. So, while Kennedy extolled the virtues of democracy, his administration supported military regimes with good anti-communist credentials, and assistance was provided to political opponents of left-wing groups. Among the Eastern Pacific Basin countries a prominent example was Chile. There, former CIA director William Colby admitted, the CIA 'had been clandestinely funneling a wide variety of support to the center democratic parties and political forces in Chile since 1963, in an effort to ward off a Castro-supported Communist takeover'. This included providing $3 million to support the Christian Democratic Party's (CDP) Eduardo Frei Montalva in the presidential election campaign to stop his main opponent, the Marxist leader of the Socialist Party, Salvador Allende Gossens. With this assistance, which concentrated on a scare campaign linking Allende with atheistic communism to frighten especially women voters, the CIA gave itself the credit for Frei's victory in 1964 with 56 per cent of the vote, the first absolute majority in a Chilean presidential election since 1938. However, that was an inflated claim, since Frei was a moderate reformer supported by conservatives and liberals.[6]

---

5   Stephen G. Rabe, 'Controlling Revolution: Latin America, the Alliance for Progress, and Cold War Anti-Communism', in Thomas G. Paterson, *Kennedy's Quest for Victory: American Foreign Policy, 1961–1963* (New York 1989), 105–10. Stephen G. Rabe, *The Most Dangerous Area in the World: John F. Kennedy Confronts Communist Revolution in Latin America* (Chapel Hill 1999), ch. 7.

6   Rabe, 'Controlling Revolution', 109–22. William Colby and Peter Forbath, *Honourable Men: My Life in the CIA* (London 1978), 302. Paul E. Sigmund, *The United States and Democracy in Chile* (Baltimore 1993), 22–5. James R. Whelan, *Out of the Ashes: Life, Death and Transfiguration of Democracy in Chile, 1833–1988* (Washington 1989), 130–42.

The Kennedy administration also acted to protect other Pacific Basin Latin American countries from the threat of radicalism. In 1963 the government of Carlos Julio Arosemena in Ecuador was overthrown by a military coup because it was 'soft on Communism'. Philip Agee, a CIA officer serving at that time in the capital city, Quito, later explained the CIA's aims in Latin America: 'we were fighting to arrest the influence of the Cuban Revolution which had an enormous impact throughout Latin America' and to 'buy time' for 'friends' of the US against its 'enemies', who ranged 'from left social democrats . . . to armed revolutionaries'. In Guatemala after a military coup in 1963 to stop the election of a radical government, Johnson's administration lived comfortably with the subsequent anti-communist military regime. When the progressive government of President Ramón Villeda Morelles in Honduras, who had been strongly anti-communist, was overturned by a coup in 1963, Kennedy suspended aid to and recognition of the military administration, but both were restored in the next year. Kennedy also viewed with distaste the Somoza family, who treated Nicaragua as its personal fiefdom. But Anastasio Somoza Debayle supplied the base for the CIA's abortive attempt to invade Cuba in 1961 and continued to be a staunch ally of the US in quarantining communist Cuba. So Washington continued to support him.[7]

Nor were Alliance for Progress programs under Kennedy and Johnson allowed to upset the huge American economic interests in Latin America, which in 1960 absorbed 25 per cent of US overseas investments and 20 per cent of American exports. For example, in Honduras, Villeda was successfully pressed by Washington in 1962 to modify agrarian reform legislation after complaints by the UFC. Moreover, a significant amount of financial aid was devoted to equipping Latin American military and police personnel to strengthen their ability to resist communist subversion. But such assistance gave them greater abilities to establish and maintain authoritarian rule. Military and economic aid also was fraudulently directed to line the pockets of military leaders.[8]

In Central America the Kennedy administration financially supported moves towards a common market. Road building, including the completion

---

7   Philip Agee, *Inside the Company: CIA Diary* (London 1975), 295. Philip Agee, *On the Run* (Secaucus 1987), 15, 89. George Philip, *The Military in South American Politics* (London 1985), 338. Lester D. Langley, *The United States and the Caribbean in the Twentieth Century* (revised edition, Athens Ga. 1985), 237–9. Bernard Diederich, *Somoza and the Legacy of US Involvement in Central America* (New York 1981), ch. 5.

8   Rabe, 'Controlling Revolution', 108, 121. Daro A. Euraque, *Reinterpreting the Region and State in Banana Republic Honduras, 1870–1972* (Chapel Hill 1996), 113.

of the Inter-American Highway to Panama in 1964, and other economic aid facilitated industrial growth. But the new industries tended to be capital rather than labour intensive. Also the common market was not fully developed, especially because of the fears of the most-developed republic, Costa Rica, of competition from cheaper labour elsewhere in Central America. Costa Rica was also distrustful of Nicaragua. There had been an armed confrontation between the two nations in 1954 over alleged Costa Rican support for a plot to assassinate Anastasio Somoza García and retaliatory Nicaraguan support for Costa Rican rebels.[9]

In Panama in the 1960s there was a growing nationalist opposition to US ownership of the Panama Canal Zone that divided the country into two halves. The seizure of the Suez Canal by Egypt in 1956, prompted Panamanian pressure on the US to concede Panama's sovereignty over the sixteen kilometre-wide Canal Zone, that had been ceded 'in perpetuity' to the US by newly independent Panama in 1903. Eisenhower's administration had insisted that solely the US under the terms of a bilateral treaty had constructed the Panama Canal. Panamanian students responded with a march into the Canal Zone to plant Panamanian flags there. After sending his brother to investigate, Eisenhower was inclined to allow a symbolic flying of the Panamanian flag in the Canal Zone, but he ran into strong Congressional opposition, where there was dark talk of communist agitators inciting the Panamanians. This opposition only served to provoke anger in Panama with another flag-planting attempt in the Canal Zone in 1959, which caused an outbreak of rioting and an inrush of US troops to restore law and order. Eisenhower responded with an agreement for a symbolic flag in one area of the Canal Zone, while maintaining that it in no way impugned US sovereignty. Kennedy encouraged negotiations with Panama's President, Roberto Chiari, about economic aid to Panama and wider flying of Panamanian flags, but Chiari pressed for renegotiating the Canal treaty. Johnson soon faced in January 1964 another foray by Panamanian students to plant flags that degenerated into four days of armed conflict, which left four US soldiers and twenty-four Panamanians dead and led to Panama's severing of diplomatic relations with the US. Johnson defused the crisis with a promise to negotiate a new treaty, which proposed revoking the US perpetual right to the Canal Zone in favour of American occupation expiring in 1999. But the US claim for continued unfettered military presence plus nationalist sentiment for an immediate end to American occupation aroused enough popular

---

9 Ralph Lee Woodward, Jr., *Central America: A Nation Divided* (2nd edition, New York 1985), 270–5.

opposition to the treaty to cause the Panamanian government to refuse to ratify it.[10]

Panama and the Central American republics, except democratic Costa Rica, were characterized by oligarchic or dictatorial rule, with small percentages of the population holding enormous economic power. Five per cent of Panamanians earned more than a third of the national income. In El Salvador 2 per cent of the populace owned 60 per cent of the land, and the thirty-six largest landlords controlled two thirds of the capital of the 1,429 largest companies. US policies did little to lessen the yawning gaps between rich and poor in Central American republics, and even less to prevent dictatorial political control. The results were growing rebellions that were to prove major headaches to later American administrations. A prominent sign was the Cuban supported Marxist-led guerrilla movement in Nicaragua, the Frente Sandinista de Liberación Nacional, which drew its name from a Nicaraguan rebel hero, Augusto Sandino, who was assassinated in 1934 by Somoza's US-supported National Guard. This movement, whose members were called Sandinistas, was founded in Honduras in July 1961. In the 1960s the Nicaraguan National Guard, well equipped by the US, had little difficulty in containing the Sandinistas.[11]

During the 1960s, there were guerrilla movements feeding on political and economic oppression in other Pacific Basin Latin American republics, which were significant consumers of American military aid. In Peru two insurgencies, with Marxist and anti-American biases and drawing their inspiration from Cuba, required 5,000 American-equipped soldiers and police to suppress them in 1965. In the mid 1960s an active Cuba revolution-inspired guerrilla movement in Guatemala was attracting significant US assistance for military counter-insurgency operations. In 1968 the US was confronting Marxist insurgencies on both sides of the Pacific Basin, which were major foreign policy problems for the next American administration.[12]

---

10 Langley, *United States and the Caribbean*, 241–51. Michael Hogan, *The Panama Canal in American Politics: Domestic Advocacy and the Evolution of Policy* (Carbondale 1986), 71–80. Michael L. Conniff, *Panama and the United States: The Forced Alliance* (Athens, Ga. 1992), 111–26.

11 Walter La Feber, *The Panama Canal: The Crisis in Historical Perspective* (Oxford 1979), 150. Thomas P. Anderson, *The War of the Dispossessed: Honduras and El Salvador, 1969* (Lincoln 1981), 33. James Dunkerley, *Power in the Isthmus: A Political History of Modern Central America* (London 1988), 342–50. Langley, *United States and the Caribbean*, 121–5. Saul Landau, *The Guerrilla Wars of Central America: Nicaragua, El Salvador and Guatemala* (London 1993), 22–4.

12 George D.E. Philip, *The Rise and Fall of the Peruvian Military Radicals 1968–1976* (London 1978), ch. 1. Richard F. Nyrop (ed.), *Peru: A Country Study* (Washington 1981), 36–70. Lawrence A. Clayton, *Peru and the United States: The Condor and the Eagle* (Athens, Ga. 1999), 178–81. Thomas E. Leonard, *Central America and the United States* (Athens 1991), 155–8. Dunkerley, *Power in the Isthmus*, 425–58.

Crushing Marxism in Chile

Though in the Western Pacific Basin the Republican administrations of Nixon and Ford abandoned South Vietnam to communist rule and worked for a détente with China, they were more concerned about threats of communist expansion in the Eastern Pacific Basin. Therefore, the CIA tried to stop the Marxist Allende winning the 1970 presidential election in Chile. As in 1964, the agency channelled money to opposing parties and funded propaganda with themes such as: 'An Allende victory means violence and Stalinist repression.'[13] However, Allende headed the poll, even though his 36.2 per cent of the national vote was 2.4 per cent less than he received in 1964. This time the CDP was internally divided, and Chile's constitution prevented Frei from running for a second term. Its candidate received only 18.7 per cent of the vote compared with 34.1 per cent for a former conservative president, Jorge Assendri Rodriguez. Colby acknowledged a CIA mistake in concentrating on a 'spoiling campaign' and not in directing funds to one of Allende's two opponents, putting pressure on the other one to withdraw.[14]

'Nixon was furious', said Colby. 'He was convinced that Allende's victory meant the spread of Castro's anti-American revolution to Chile, and from there throughout Latin America.' Nixon insisted, wrote Kissinger, 'on doing something, *anything*, that would reverse the previous neglect', which threw 'all agencies . . . into a frenzied reassessment'. Richard Helms, the CIA director, was called to an Oval Office meeting with Nixon, Kissinger and the Attorney General. Helms was ordered to implement a program of covert action. He was to exploit the Chilean constitutional requirement for congress to elect the president when there was no absolute majority in the popular vote. The CIA was to arrange to bribe CDP congressmen to vote for Alessandri or, if that failed, to turn 'to the Chilean military for help'.[15]

The CDP was determined to respect the political convention that the candidate with the most votes should become president. So the military coup option was pursued. However, the army's commander, General René Schneider, declared that the military should not interfere with the constitutional process. 'In desperation', wrote Colby, 'an attempt was made to kidnap him.' When the kidnappers in four cars pushed Schneider's car off

13 William Blum, *The CIA: A Forgotten History: US Global Interventions since World War 2* (London 1986), 235. Sigmund, *The United States and Democracy in Chile*, 39–41.
14 Colby and Forbath, *Honourable Men*, 303.
15 Ibid., 303–4. Henry Kissinger, *The White House Years* (London 1979), 670.

the road, he drew his revolver in self-defence but was shot and died in hospital three days later. This first major political assassination in Chile since 1837 backfired, because the leaders of the army, navy and airforce reacted by reinforcing their constitutional loyalty. Also an attempt to create economic chaos so as to invite a military coup failed. The CIA and the International Telephone and Telegraph Company, one of the largest US private investors in Chile, which contributed $350,000 to Alessandri's election campaign, initiated this move. However, other US companies and banks refused to cooperate.[16]

A major problem with the abortive schemes to stop Allende, was their last-minute nature. In the years prior to the election, the CIA had concentrated on funding non-Marxist political parties, which recognized a fundamental feature of the Chilean polity. Chileans had great pride in their constitutional system of government, which had survived since the mid nineteenth century, despite a period of military rule from 1924 to 1932. The military forces, after chaos created by military factionalism in 1931–32, accepted the principle that they should support a democratic constitution. There were officers who distrusted constitutional government, some of whom supported the CIA's coup option, but they were a minority. Furthermore, most members of the CDP, which held the congressional balance of power, did not have the fears of Allende that haunted Nixon's administration. Communists in the 1930s and 1940s had participated in popular front governments in Chile, and Allende's commitment to democracy was respected.[17]

Allende's 'Popular Unity' government, a coalition of the Marxist Socialist and Communist parties, the Radical Party and a leftist breakaway group from the CDP, still faced strong US hostility during its three years of existence. In a speech to the UN General Assembly on 4 December 1972, Allende complained that Chile was the victim of a US 'financial-economic blockade'; 'not an open aggression . . . but an attack at once oblique, subterranean, but no less lethal to Chile', which aimed to 'strangle our economy'.[18]

Certainly, the Inter-American Development Bank and the World Bank granted no new loans to Chile. This was in line with a NSC memorandum of November 1970, which stated that: 'The US would use its predominant position in international financial institutions to dry up the flow of new multilateral credit and other financial assistance' to Chile. That memorandum also

---

16   Colby and Forbath, *Honourable Men*, 303. Frederick M. Nunn, *The Military in Chilean History: Essays on Civil-Military Relations, 1810–1973* (Albuquerque 1976), 266–8. Mark Falcoff, *Modern Chile 1970 1989: A Critical History* (New Brunswick 1989), 207–17. Sigmund, *The United States and Democracy in Chile*, 48–56.

17   Falcoff, *Modern Chile*, ch. 4. Nunn, *Military in Chilean History*, chs 5–11.

18   Quoted in Falcoff, *Modern Chile*, 218.

called for the withdrawal of US government 'financial assistance or guarantees' to American companies investing in Chile and to ensure that 'US
businesses would be made aware of the government's concern and its restrictive policies'.[19] Accordingly, private US bank lending to Chile declined
sharply during Allende's regime. However, it can be argued that his government's expropriation of the American copper mining companies in July
1971 and other nationalization of business enterprises would have influenced investor reluctance, especially as Chile decided that the excess profits
of the copper companies did not justify any financial compensation. US
public aid programs to Chile were drastically reduced, though this reflected
a high level of aid to Frei's government and the Nixon administration's
abandonment of much of the Alliance for Progress. Military aid to Chile
actually increased during Allende's regime, part of a US policy to maintain
its influence in Chile's armed forces. Though the US also attempted to stop
the supply of industrial spare parts to Chile, there was no implementation
of such a program. The shortages that occurred were caused by a decline in
the country's short-term financing capacity after 1971. Furthermore, the
drying up of US capital was compensated for by credit supplied by Western
European and communist countries.[20]

Indeed, the major economic problems plaguing the Allende government in
its second and third years were caused much more by wider world conditions,
by the weaknesses of the Chilean economy and by the government's own
policies than by US economic pressure. Chile's economy depended heavily on
mining exports, which produced 85 per cent of export earnings in 1969, and
which had caused a neglect of agriculture, resulting in the need to import
food. Copper mining revenue was the principal source for industrial development and even for the food imports for a population in 1970 of 9,340,200
that was the most literate (90 per cent) in Latin America and one of the most
highly urbanized (75 per cent). But the dominance of mining in Chile's economic history had created high dependency on world prices. A fall in the world
copper price from 64 cents per pound in 1970 to 49 cents in 1971, caused by
the wind-down of American involvement in the Vietnam War, burst the
bubble of the previously war-inflated copper boom. There were also increases
in world food prices by 8 per cent in 1971 and by 41 per cent in 1972.[21]

Allende government policies compounded the resultant economic squeeze
on Chile. There was a boom in consumer spending in 1971 influenced by

---

19 United States Congress, *Hearings before the Select Committee to Study Governmental Operations with
Respect to Intelligence Activities of the United States Senate, Ninety-Fourth Congress, First Session*,
vol. VII, *Covert Action in Chile 1963–1973* (Washington 1973), Appendix A, 180.
20 Falcoff, *Modern Chile*, 217–30.
21 Ibid., ch. 6.

redistribution of income policies, higher wages for workers, expansion of production assisted by government take-overs of industries, a more than doubling of the money supply and strict price controls. But in the next year the expansion was overtaken by an inflation rate of 163 per cent, inducing much black marketing and hoarding to escape the government's retention of price controls. The euphoria of 1971 became black despair for many Chileans in 1972–73.[22]

The Chilean democracy's other major problem was sharp political diversity. The mining-dominated economy had created a wide gap between the rich and the poor in Chile's community. The latter were a minority of the population living mainly in depressed agricultural regions and in the three big cities, Santiago, Valparaíso and Concepción, which contained 45 per cent of the population. The urban and rural poor provided a breeding ground for the communists and the uniquely Marxian Chilean socialists. But this was not a big enough base for those parties to enjoy a political majority, since the larger middle classes of the big cities mainly supported the CDP or more conservative parties. The result was that the Allende government pursued radical socio-economic reforms, which did not have majority popular support. When the bottom fell out of the economy in 1972 many members of the middle-class majority started to protest vehemently against the government, including strike action and violence. Especially effective were protests by women banging pots and pans. The CDP also veered to the right. Extremist Popular Unity supporters responded with heightened militancy, fuelling increasing social conflict. By August 1973 the country was polarized between bitter protagonists for and against the government, a struggle bordering on civil war.[23]

This social conflict was a major cause of the violent military coup in Chile on 11 September 1973 carried out by military officers. They perceived a clear anti-government majority, reinforced by the 'popular' women's protests and by the congressional elections of March 1973, in which Popular Unity made only a small gain and remained a minority with 44 per cent of the vote. Allende also had compromised the separation of military and civil power by bringing officers into his government as a means of countering anti-government activities. But by April 1973, having supervised the congressional election, all officers had stepped down from the Cabinet, opening the way for a coup. Allende's chief military supporter, the army commander, General Carlos Prats Gonzales, remained loyal. However, he was pressured

22   Ibid., ch. 3. Simon Collier and William F. Slater, *A History of Chile, 1808–1994* (Cambridge 1996), ch. 12.
23   Edy Kaufman, *Crisis in Allende's Chile: New Perspectives* (New York 1988), chs 10, 11. Lois Hecht Oppenheim, *Politics in Chile: Democracy, Authoritarianism, and the Search for Development* (2nd edition, Boulder 1999), 53–73.

by most of his generals to resign on 23 August, freeing his successor General Augusto Pinochet Ugarte to organize the coup, which ousted the elected government and resulted in the president committing suicide. Moreover, despite Allende's policy of conciliating the military, many officers were alienated by pressure from militant government supporters to form an armed popular militia. This was a response to a violent right-wing group, the Partria y Libertad.[24]

Nixon's administration has been blamed for complicity in the Chilean coup. Certainly, the CIA had remained active during the Allende regime by providing funds to opposing political parties and newspapers and by maintaining links with the military. In the American Senate hearings on the subject, which were controlled by the majority Democratic Party, Helms insisted that the CIA deliberately distanced itself in 1973 from the military in order to avoid any hint of involvement in a coup. Disbelieving Democrats on the investigating committee could find no firm evidence of US involvement in the coup. But CIA funds that supported Allende's opponents, including probable financial support for two long and economically damaging strikes by private truck drivers, certainly increased the Allende government's difficulties. Also Prats, who went into exile in Argentina after the coup, remarked that the government had not appreciated 'how profound the North American influence is in our armed forces, and especially on the mentality of the Chilean military man'. He accused his former military colleagues of not liberating their country from 'the enemy within' but of rendering it dependent on 'the enemy without', namely the US. He was assassinated for such opinions by agents of Chile's military strongman, Pinochet, in Argentina in 1974, while many other Chilean supporters of Popular Unity were subjected to imprisonment, torture and execution.[25]

The Nixon/Ford administrations, Peru and Central America

North of Chile, Peru also was 'heading in directions that have been difficult to deal with', wrote Kissinger in 1970. The left-wing Peruvian military junta, headed by General Juan Velasco Alvarado, had expropriated the

---

24 Oppenheim, *Politics in Chile*, 73–83. Nunn, *Military in Chilean History*, 276–308. The cause of Allende's death became controversial, but there is clear evidence that it was suicide. See Mary Helen Spooner, *Soldiers in a Narrow Land: The Pinochet Regime in Chile* (Berkeley 1994), 41–4.

25 Falcoff, *Modern Chile*, 230–40. Sigmund, *The United States and Democracy*, ch. 3. Salvatore Bizzarro, *Historical Dictionary of Chile* (Metuchen 1987), 411.

oilfields controlled by the American International Petroleum Company. In the junta's view, the company had been illegally granted in 1922 ownership of all the oil reserves under its fields, which offended Peruvian nationalist sensibilities. No financial compensation was offered to the company on the grounds that it owed Peru US$690 million in foregone revenue because of the 1922 agreement. This refusal caused a crisis in US–Peruvian relations, given the existence of the Hickenlooper Amendment to the Foreign Assistance and Sugar Acts passed by the US Congress in 1961, which required the president to suspend all aid and also sugar import quotas for any country expropriating an American company's assets without adequate compensation. Not wanting to push the Velasco regime further down a pro-Cuban path, Kissinger wrote that the US sought to 'reach an equitable settlement', which was achieved with a compromise compensation agreement. However, the Peruvian junta remained a nuisance to Washington by enforcing a 200-mile sea zone and seizing US fishing boats. Consequently, there was a cessation of US military aid to Peru. So the military regime turned to the USSR for arms which cost $1.6 billion in the twelve years after 1973. The junta pursued a conspicuously neutralist foreign policy. It was also an enthusiast for the 1969 Andean Pact, which included Venezuela, Colombia, Ecuador, Bolivia and Chile, though Chile withdrew in 1976 because of the pact's code restricting foreign investment.[26]

In Central America the Nixon–Ford administrations maintained a hard line against left-wing insurgencies. From 1970 the Sandinistas became more active in Nicaragua. Assisting their rising popularity was a weakening of Somoza's authority, particularly after he pocketed aid money sent to Nicaragua after a devastating earthquake in 1972 that destroyed part of the capital city, Managua, and killed nearly 10,000 people. Somoza received US military aid to launch in 1975 a major campaign against Sandinista insurgents.[27]

Central American unity was shattered in 1969 by the 'Fútbol' War between El Salvador and Honduras. Their never properly defined mutual border was a simmering dispute. This tension was exacerbated by population pressures in small El Salvador, and by its land-owning elite, which concentrated on coffee exports at the expense of food production. There was a consequent increase of migration of Salvadorians to Honduras in the 1960s,

26 Kissinger, *White House Years*, 657, 673. Philip, *Rise and Fall*, ch. 2. Daniel M. Masterson, *Militarism and Politics in Latin America: Peru from Sánchez Cerro to Sendero Luminoso* (Westport 1991), chs 9–10. Clayton, *Peru and the United States*, 254–64. Virginia Gamba-Stonehouse, *Strategy in the Southern Oceans: A South American View* (New York 1989), 35.
27 Langley, *United States and the Caribbean*, 282–3. Dunkerley, *Power in the Isthmus*, ch. 6. Dennis Gilbert, *Sandinistas: The Party and the Revolution* (New York 1988), 3–8.

which caused a growing Honduran clamour to expel them from land they occupied, which was carried out in 1968. Subsequently, there was a wave of violence against Salvadorians in Honduras after attacks on Hondurans attending the 1969 World Cup soccer match in San Salvador. The arrival in El Salvador of Salvadorian refugees from the violence triggered the invasion that started the war. The superior Salvadorian army was soon well on its way towards the Honduran capital, Tegucigalpa. But four days after the commencement of the war a cease-fire was arranged by the Organization of American States (OAS). As many as 2,000 people were killed, and over 100,000 Salvadorian refugees fled back into El Salvador. Dissension between El Salvador and Honduras continued through the 1970s and wrecked the Central American Common Market ideal of the previous decade. El Salvador was the long-term loser of the contest. Its previous valuable trade with Honduras was lost, refugees contributed to rampant unemployment and there was further concentration of land into the hands of the 116 families of the land-owning oligarchy, which in 1979 received 60 per cent of the country's commercial income.[28]

The US and Mexico

Mexico was causing a different kind of concern for the US in the mid 1970s. After the Second World War relations between the two countries had improved since the pre-war tension over Mexican nationalization of American oil companies. In the postwar era Mexico was still ruled by the Partido Revolucionario Institucional, but it had lost much of its revolutionary zeal and was concerned to build up industrial development in order to improve the country's agricultural–mining economic base. This economic policy involved protectionism to foster import replacement industries, which incurred displeasure from the US government, which was emphasizing free markets for US exports. Mexico also maintained a non-interventionist foreign policy, which resulted in disapproval of the US intervention in Guatemala in 1954 and, more seriously, a refusal to agree to isolate Castro's Cuba. From 1964 to 1970 Mexico was the only Latin American country to maintain diplomatic relations with Cuba. Mexico also pursued a policy of reducing its economic dependence on the US. However, Mexico was careful not to ruffle the feathers of the dominant American eagle excessively, such as by courting

---

28 Woodward, *Central America*, 274–6. Anderson, *War of the Dispossessed, passim*. Dunkerley, *Power in the Isthmus*, 345.

the USSR. Consequently, the American administrations of the 1960s were prepared to allow Mexico a measure of diplomatic independence.[29]

However, in 1976 there was a sharp deterioration in US–Mexico relations. A background factor was an economic crisis, caused principally by deteriorating prices for mineral exports in the post-Vietnam War recession and the populist policies of President Luis Echeverría Alvarez. A consequent 60 per cent devaluation of the Mexican peso alarmed American investors, who controlled 62 per cent of the country's burgeoning foreign debt. Of more serious concern in US right-wing circles was Echeverría's widespread effort to reduce Mexican economic and diplomatic dependency on the US, including growing warmth in Mexico's relations with Cuba and support for Allende's Chile. After the coup there, Mexico severed diplomatic relations with Chile and harboured many Chilean refugees. A concern that Mexico was drifting into the communist camp caused some US congressmen to warn President Ford of leftist trends in Echeverría's government. However, the Mexican government accepted a dose of financial austerity imposed by the International Monetary Fund, to the consternation of left-wing groups in Mexico who accused the government of selling out to the US. Mexico's relations with the US were restored temporarily to an even keel, though Echeverría's successor, José López Portillo, continued an independent stance by breaking diplomatic relations with Somoza's Nicaragua in 1978 and by welcoming that year a visit to Mexico by Cuba's Castro. But in the next year US–Mexican relations slumped again with Mexico's active support for the Sandinistas in Nicaragua and, in particular, because López broke a pledge to give sanctuary to the fleeing Shah of Iran, which drove President Carter into a fury.[30]

The Carter Administration and Latin America

President Carter's human rights policies in Latin America were stronger than elsewhere but still were erratic. Though cutting economic and military aid to the Somoza regime for its abuses of human rights in Nicaragua, the Carter administration did not support the demand of moderates in Nicaragua for American pressure on Somoza to resign. There were divisions within the administration about abandoning an old American ally. Instead Washington sought an accommodation between Somoza and his critics,

29 Josefina Zoraida Vázquez and Lorenzo Meyer, *The United States and Mexico* (Chicago 1985), ch. 9.
30 Ibid., 183–90. Lester D. Langley, *Mexico and the United States: The Fragile Relationship* (Boston 1991), 75–87. W. Dirk Raat, *Mexico and the United States: Ambivalent Vistas* (Athens, Ga. 1992), 157–60.

which was too late. Moderates were now switching support to the Sandinistas, whom the US had accused of being communist, but who now won a bloody war and swept to power in 1979, with Somoza and his cronies fleeing to Miami in the US. The Carter administration, however, did show a new face to the advent of a radical regime in Central America by offering recognition to the new government and economic aid.[31]

Carter's administration also was concerned about human rights abuses in El Salvador. There a Marxist guerrilla movement was exploiting the growing economic power of the oligarchy, including bomb attacks in urban areas. The government responded with campaigns against any forms of radicalism, such as murdering suspected leftist activists. US congressional criticism was aroused in 1977 about attacks on church workers who were influenced by Latin American liberation theology and who were supporting and organizing peasant movements. Carter threatened to cut off economic aid to El Salvador. A new government under General Carlos Humberto Romero, who gained office in a fraudulent national election, promised to respect human rights. However, after the threat of US aid suspension was removed, his government renewed state terrorism to stifle political opposition and to maintain the power of the oligarchy. So the US did not oppose, indeed some US officials supported, a coup in October 1979 against Romero by army officers concerned to introduce a reform government which would address the social conditions that were assisting active Marxist guerrillas.[32]

Another Central American republic, Guatemala, earned the Carter administration's ire. Rural unrest, exacerbated by commercialized agriculture, which was swallowing up peasant land, resulted in repressive government policies. The most notorious case was the mass slaughter in May 1978 of over 100 protesting Mayan Indian peasants who had been called by the army to a meeting in the town of Panzós to discuss their grievances. Troops were waiting for them around the town square to machine-gun them down and then bury them in a previously prepared mass grave. But already in 1977 Carter had banned military aid and sales of arms to Guatemala, a decision that the Panzós massacre reinforced.[33]

Carter's administration solved the problem of simmering dissent in Panama by negotiating a new treaty guaranteeing a US withdrawal from

---

31 John Dumbrell, *The Carter Administration: A Re-Evaluation* (Manchester 1995), 150–61.
   Gilbert, *Sandinistas*, 8–13. William LeoGrande, *Our Own Backyard: The United States in Central America, 1977–1992* (Chapel Hill 1998), 19–32.
32 LeoGrande, *Our Own Backyard*, 38–43. Tommie Sue Mongomery, *Revolution in El Salvador: From Civil Strife to Civil Peace* (2nd edition Boulder 1995), 63–111.
33 Dunkerley, *Power in the Isthmus*, 434, 437–84. Michael McClintock, *The American Connection*, vol. II (London 1985), 140–1.

the Panama Canal in 1999. The treaty allowed four Panamanians to join five Americans in a commission to administer the canal, and a formal disbandment of the Canal Zone, though the US retained responsibility to defend the canal. There was a long tussle to achieve the necessary two-thirds majority in the Senate for the treaty's ratification. Die-hard nationalists were defending American perpetual ownership of the canal. But the JCS supported the treaty on the grounds that a 'friendly Panama' was important for the defence of a canal that was less significant in the nuclear age. This opinion assisted the final passage of the treaty through the Senate by one vote.[34]

A Pacific Basin South American country especially targeted by Carter for human rights condemnation was Pinochet's Chile. It had become a pariah of the international scene for killing hundreds of its citizens and causing many others to flee into exile. Carter even put pressure on the Philippines to suspend an invitation for Pinochet to visit that country in March 1980. The American Congress also imposed an arms embargo on Chile after Allende's overthrow, and US economic aid to Pinochet's government was confined to surplus food and other humanitarian assistance. The arms embargo was a worry to Chile in 1974 when the possibility of war loomed with Soviet-armed Peru. Appreciating its military disadvantage, Chile sought a diplomatic solution, which was assisted by a coup in Peru, which replaced the physically ailing Velasco with the more moderate General Francisco Morales Bermúdez Cerrutti. Washington probably supported this coup, which removed from South America the only remaining radical Soviet-supported regime. But there was a renewed threat of war between Chile and Peru approaching the centennial in 1979 of the War in the Pacific when Peru had lost territory to Chile. Contentious issues were Chile's support for land-locked Bolivia's push for access to the Pacific Ocean and expulsion of Chilean diplomats from Peru for alleged spying activities in 1978. But the tension eased after the Pacific War anniversary passed, and as a result of intense pressure on Peru from the Carter administration.[35]

Latin America and the wider Pacific Basin

After the end of the age of Spanish trade across the Pacific, Latin American states became isolated from the Western Pacific Basin. This isolation was

---

34 Conniff, *Panama and the United States*, 127–39. Mark Flacoff, *Panama's Canal: What Happens When the United Nations Gives a Small State What it Wants* (Washington 1998), ch. 2.

35 Whelan, *Out of the Ashes*, 672–711, 780–8. Falcoff, *Modern Chile*, ch. 9. James D. Rudolph, *Peru: The Evolution of a Crisis* (Westport 1992), 69–70. Clayton, *Peru and the United States*, 255–6.

influenced by competing agricultural and mineral exports with many other Pacific Basin countries, by tariff-protected economies, by poor communications with the Western Pacific, and by traditional Latin American dependence on the US and Europe for trade and investment. However, in the 1960s the isolation was weakening. The major influence was the spreading of Japan's growing economic empire across the Pacific. During the 1960s Japanese trade with Latin America was increasing at an average annual rate of 15 per cent per annum and rose to an average of 20 per cent per annum in the 1970s. Feeding this growth was Japan's increasing need for raw materials, which along with rising commodity prices raised the value of Latin America's exports to Japan from $1.3 billion in 1970 to $4.3 billion in 1979. In turn there were increasing Latin American demands for Japanese manufactured goods, including machine tools for industrial development. Japan's favourable trade balance with Latin America was demonstrated by her $6.3 billion exports to the region in 1979. Though this was only 6 per cent of Japan's total export trade, Japan had become the second most important source of Latin American imports behind the US. Latin America also was attracting Japanese capital, which had risen to $1.2 billion directly invested in 1979. Brazil was the main location for this capital; the second most important country was Peru. Mexico, with its emphasis on import substitution development was not yet a major Japanese investment target. Throughout the whole of Latin America, Japan was still well behind the United States and Western Europe as a source of capital, and the main emphasis of Japanese investment in Pacific Basin Latin America was on mining operations.[36]

However, Japan's emerging interest in Latin America was stimulating a greater interest in Pacific Basin affairs in Latin American countries. Mexican presidents visited Japan in 1962, 1972 and 1978 and there were return trips to Mexico by Japanese prime ministers plus exchange visits by foreign ministers and other high-level officials. A Joint Mexico–Japan Economic Commission was established in 1967, and in 1969 the two countries granted each other most-favoured trading nation status. In the late 1970s Pinochet's Chile looked to Japan as a means to break the country's diplomatic isolation, arranging a visit there by the Chilean Chancellor in 1979. Pinochet also was eyeing Southeast Asia in a new diplomatic strategy, called the

---

36 Claudio Veliz, 'Latin America's Opening to the Pacific', in Joseph Grinwald (ed.), *Latin America and the World Economy: A Changing International Order* (London 1978), 212–32. Susan Kaufman Purcell and Robert M. Immerman (eds), *Japan and Latin America in the New Global Order* (Boulder 1992), 9–10, 18–21, 72–4. Yale H. Ferguson and Sang-June Shim, 'Mexico's North American and Pacific Relations', in Gavin Boyd (ed.), *Region Building in the Pacific* (New York 1982), 216–19. *YITS*, 1981, 537.

'Pacific drive'. But the campaign had a shaky start when a trip to the Philippines by Pinochet in 1980 was prevented by Marcos's submission to Carter's pressure against it. Pinochet only travelled as far as Fiji, which he saw as having access to Australasia, but where he encountered hostile public demonstrations.[37]

Conclusions

By the end of the 1970s the Cold War, which was declining in intensity in the Western Pacific, was very much alive in the Eastern Pacific Basin because of the US determination to oppose allegedly pro-communist political movements spawned by the same kind of concentration of wealth in the hands of oligarchic rulers and repression of peasant masses as had occurred in China and Vietnam. The coup in Guatemala in the early 1950s was matched by US support for coups in Latin America into the 1970s against perceived communist threats to US dominance in the region. Even the Alliance for Progress of the 1960s can be viewed as mostly an attempt to prevent communist subversion, which was not allowed to upset American economic hegemony. The link between US political and economic control was demonstrated by the close relationship between the government and US companies in pressure on Chile, though US businesses were not united in this action; and there were fundamental Chilean reasons for Allende's overthrow. In Peru's case there was a US attempt at compromise in the interests of keeping the radical military junta away from an embrace with Cuba. But US patience wore out when American fishing boats were seized. The unwillingness of even the Carter administration to pressure the unpopular Somoza in Nicaragua to resign demonstrated the continuity of American fear of Latin American radicalism during the whole of the 1945–1979 era. Carter made a small progress in accepting the Sandinista regime and keeping bans on aid to Chile, but even this degree of respect for the wishes of Latin Americans was to disappear after his electoral defeat in 1980. The US also supported many military governments in Latin America in 1979. Attempts at economic cooperation between Latin American republics were limited by conflicts between countries, which produced threats of war, and the short one between El Salvador and Honduras.

---

37   Boyd, *Region Building*, 206. Gamba-Stonehouse, *Strategy in Southern Oceans*, 38–9.

Japan's emerging trade and investment in Latin America was a small challenge to the US economic empire there. It reflected the bigger growth elsewhere in the Pacific Basin of Japan's new economic order, which was causing American trading headaches. In turn Japan's growing economic contact was stimulating Latin American interest in the Western Pacific Basin.

CHAPTER SEVEN

Asian Economic Expansion and Strategic Change, 1980–1990

The first major theme of this chapter is the growth and nature of Japanese economic dominance in the Pacific Basin and its implications for Japan's relations with the US and other Pacific Basin countries. The effect of Japanese investment on the economic development of East and Southeast Asian countries is also examined. The second major theme is an analysis of changes in the strategic balance in the Western Pacific Basin resulting from growing rapprochement between the US, China and the USSR and its implications for the US–Japanese defence relationships. Relations between the two Koreas and the Cambodian conflict are sub-themes including developments among the ASEAN states.

Japan's new economic order in the Pacific Basin

In 1980 Japan was achieving, by trade and capital investment, the economic order in Asia and the wider Pacific that it had failed to establish by military means before 1945. Japanese accumulated direct investment in Asia increased from US$2.359 billion in 1974 to US$8.643 billion in 1980, which was 27 per cent of Japanese world-wide direct investments, compared with 26 per cent in North America and 18 per cent in Latin America. A total of 404,682 Asians were working for Japanese affiliated companies, 57 per cent of such overseas workers. This was influenced by Asian wages, which in 1980 averaged only 20 per cent of Japan's. Most of Japan's Asian investment continued to be in manufacturing, with textiles still the major sector, though their proportion had fallen from 40 per cent in 1974 to 23 per cent in 1980. There were big rises in metals and chemicals, reflecting new Japanese investment trends in the late 1970s. Also the mining component of the Asian investments had soared from US$605 million in 1974 to US$2.815 billion in 1980. Asian countries generally were willing to accept such new capital despite the environmental degradation that mining can produce. Other overseas Japanese industries had damaging effects, such as illness and death caused by iron dust among Filipino workers at Kawasaki Steel's sintering plant in Nabacaan village on the Philippines island of Mindanao. Anti-pollution agitation in Japan was influencing such offshore industrial relocation.[1]

Japanese overseas relocation of industries was linked to trade expansion. In 1980 Japan was the most important trading partner of ASEAN countries, accounting for 27 per cent of their exports and 22 per cent of their imports. Exceptions were Japan's smaller role in the exports of Singapore, with its lack of raw materials; and the US was ahead of Japan in the commerce of the former American colony, the Philippines. Indonesia was the ASEAN nation most closely tied to Japan, the source of 32 per cent of Indonesia's imports and 49 per cent of its exports.[2]

Japan's competitiveness in world markets grew during the 1980s. After the oil price shock of 1973 there had been an emphasis on the introduction of new technologies and rationalism into Japanese home industry, which improved industrial competitiveness. The second oil price shock in 1979 convinced Japanese captains of industry that they were correct in re-establishing resource-hungry industries overseas. The Japanese business emphasis was now to concentrate on high technology products for export. The result was a turnaround of a Japanese current account trade deficit in 1979–80, influenced by the oil price rises, to surpluses, which grew from US$8.74 billion in 1981 to US$82.743 billion in 1986. There was an accompanying rise in the value of the Japanese currency, which made Japanese investment in the US increasingly profitable. It was also influenced by a growing US trade deficit with Japan from $18.1 billion in 1981 to $59.825 billion in 1986.[3]

By the late 1980s there was significant tension in US–Japanese relations caused by the declining terms of America's trade with Japan. Initially, the growing trade deficit was cushioned by the large surplus in the American international capital account and by explanations that the problem was a

---

1 Rob Steven, *Japan's New Imperialism* (London 1990), ch. 3. William R. Nester, *Japan's Growing Power over East Asia and the World Economy* (London 1990), ch. 4.

2 Narongchai Akrasanee (ed.), *ASEAN-Japan Relations: Trade and Development* (Singapore 1983), 1–35. *YITS*, 1981, 483, 623, 787, 879, 952.

3 Steven, *Japan's New Imperialism*, 18–30. Bela Balassa and Marcus Noland, *Japan in the World Economy* (Washington 1988), 23–7.

temporary one caused by the second oil shock. Furthermore, the administration of the new President in 1981, Ronald Reagan, a conservative
Republican and a former Governor of California, was wedded to free-trade
ideology. So, rather than any US protectionist measures, Reagan concentrated on negotiations with Japan for freer access to US exports with
only minor successes. In 1986 there was a significant agreement, the Plaza
Accord, which resulted in a dramatic upward re-evaluation of the yen from
254 yen per dollar in mid 1985 to 127 yen per dollar two years later. This
was aimed to assist American exports to Japan. But there was also mounting
American business and Congressional anger centred on Japanese import
restrictions and unfair trade practices, especially the dumping of goods at
low prices, though higher US labour costs were a major reason for the
trade imbalance. In 1987 a punitive 100 per cent tariff on Japanese semi-
conductors was one response to dumping accusations. Then, after a hysterical
reaction in the US to the Japanese Toshiba company's sale of computer
software and silent motor technology to the USSR, Congress passed by huge
majorities the 1988 Omnibus and Competitiveness Trade Act. It authorized penalties against countries committing unfair trade practices. Japan was
named as one of those nations in 1989.[4]

However, by the late 1980s, Japan's imports of manufactured goods were
increasing. Japanese tariff rates on manufactured products had been lowered
to an average rate of 2.6 per cent in 1986, the lowest among major industrial
countries. A changing trend was evident in a rise of imported manufactured goods into Japan from US$28.8 billion in 1984 to US$ 84.4 billion
in 1988. The benefit to the US was smaller. But America's unfavourable
trade balance with Japan did fall to US$44.9 billion in 1989, a 25 per cent
decline from the peak deficit in 1986, and more if inflation is taken into
account. This Japanese trend was notable, given the entrenched anti-import
prejudice in Japan, which was hard to change. This was because of the
strength of group behaviour in Japanese society, reinforced by barriers to
outside economic interests presented by the cooperation between Japanese
firms against foreign take-over bids and by linkages between Japanese manufacturers and retailers. There were other anti-importation factors. There
was a large home market created by Japan's 122 million people, so that the
proportion of manufactured goods in Japan's exports was less than the
average level of industrial countries.

---

4   Chris C. Carvounis, *The United States Trade Deficit in the 1980s: Origins, Meanings and Policy
    Responses* (Westport 1987), chs 1–2. Edward J. Lincoln, *Japan's Unequal Trade* (Washington
    1990), 1–11, 142–55. Jongryn Mo, 'Strategic Alliances as a Corporate Response to
    Protectionism: The Case of the Japanese Semiconductor Industry in the Late 1980s',
    The Pacific Review, 12, 1999, 557–80.

In September 1989 Reagan's successor, his Vice-President George Bush persuaded Japanese leaders to enter into negotiations for a 'Structural Impediments Initiative' (SDI) to loosen the internal Japanese restrictions on foreign imports, which were seen by US officials as a last resort to balance US–Japanese trade. The negotiations ended in June 1990 with both sides agreeing to make changes to encourage freer trade. Bush praised Japan's Prime Minister Toshiki Kaifu for his cooperativeness. However, US business and congressional antipathy towards Japan remained.[5]

The nature of Japanese overseas investment also was changing during the 1980s. The rising value of the yen inspired Japanese capitalists to seek foreign partners or outright purchase of businesses in the advanced industrial countries. US real estate was a major area. However, there was also a search for involvement in productive industries, such as the Sony Company's buying of CBS Records for $2 billion in 1987 and of Columbia Pictures in late 1989 for $5 billion. At the end of 1989 the number of Japanese factories in the US topped 1,000. Such investment contributed to American bitterness about Japan's economic dominance, with accusations after the Columbia Pictures sale that Japan was even trying to take over American culture as well as the US economy.[6]

On the other hand mergers with US companies created an alliance between Japanese and American capitalists. Indeed, Japanese money was being used to prop up failing American enterprises, such as providing an emergency loan to the Bank of America. In 1990 seven US states applied to the Japanese Export–Import Bank for low-interest loans that were normally extended to Third World nations, and the US government asked Japan for $2.6 billion to assist in the construction of a giant superconducting supercollider. A special area of Japanese involvement in American production was the selling of motor car parts for assembly in the US by joint Japanese–US firms, such as production by Toyota and General Motors in California of the Nova and Corolla makes, and wholly owned Japanese firms, such as the Honda plant in Ohio. Electronics was the other major joint US–Japan venture area, whereby Japan supplied cheap components for assembly in factories in the US. To avoid tariff restrictions over the

---

5   *FEA*, 1991, 502–3. *Japan: Country Report*, 1991: 1, 4. Organisation for Economic
    Co-operation and Development (OECD), *OECD Economic Surveys 1988/89: Japan* (Paris
    1989), 83–102. *OECD Economic Surveys 1989/90: Japan* (Paris 1990), 133. Kent E. Calder,
    'Japan in 1990: Limits to Change', *Asian Survey*, 31, 1991, 21–35. Mayumi Itoh, *Globalization
    of Japan: Japanese Sakoku Mentality and US Efforts to Open Japan* (New York 1998), 26–8.
    Research Institute for Peace and Security, *Asian Security 1990–91* (London 1990),
    23–32, 114–16.
6   *Asian Security 1990–1991*, 11, 43. Calder, 'Japan in 1990', 21–2. Steven, *Japan's New
    Imperialism*, ch. 4.

imports of electronic equipment, which were creating the most trade friction, there was a new drive in the late 1980s for Japanese companies involved in electrical goods production in the US to increase the use of locally produced parts, not only for American sales but also, with the high value of the yen, for re-export to Japan. A similar process was occurring in other countries, which was another reason for the increase of foreign manufactured imports into Japan in the late 1980s. Imports into Japan of electrical equipment rose from US$4.5 billion in 1986 to US$9.3 billion in 1988.[7]

In the changed patterns of Japanese investment in the 1980s Asian nations took on a new role. The Asian Tigers – South Korea, Taiwan, Singapore and Hong Kong – became the major Asian centre for Japanese investment in new forms of manufacturing, particularly electronics and automobile components. Japan was taking advantage of cheaper wages, which in South Korea, Taiwan and Singapore in 1987 ranged from one-fifth to a quarter of the Japanese wage level.[8]

South Korea also was being used by Japan as an offshore production site for the export of manufactured goods to other countries. By 1988 cumulative Japanese direct investments in the ROK were worth US$3.3 billion, a tenth of the total Japanese direct investment in Asia. Koreans easily adapted to Japanese technology, which was easy to obtain from a geographically close country with which Koreans had a long familiarity. Consequently, South Korea's imports of electrical and other equipment for industrial production, principally from Japan, nearly doubled from the 1986 level to a value of US$6 billion in 1988; while in the same years the ROK's exports of electrical machinery and transportation products nearly doubled to US$12.9 billion. A notable item in this export rise was motor cars. In 1983 only 8 per cent of automobiles made in South Korea were exported; by 1988 70 per cent of Korean cars were being sold overseas. The major automobile exporter, Hyundai Motor Company, received 50 per cent of its capital equipment from Japan, and 15 per cent of its capital was owned by the Japanese Mitsubishi corporation. In another major export growth area, electronics, which increased from 7 per cent to 25 per cent of the ROK's exports between 1983 and 1988, the technology employed by the Korean companies came from Japan. There were resultant licensing fees of as much as 10 per cent of export revenue being paid to Japanese corporations. However, a growing balance-of-payments surplus, and a rise in the value of

---

7   Jeffrey E. Garten, *A Cold Peace: America, Japan, Germany and the Struggle for Supremacy* (New York 1992), 202. *FEA*, 1991, 502. Masataka Kosaka (ed.), *Japan's Choices: New Globalism and Cultural Orientations in an Industrial States* (London 1989), ch. 2.
8   Steven, *Japan's New Imperialism*, 150.

the Korean won, were encouraging South Korean direct investments abroad, which grew from US$633 million in 1986 to US$1.2 billion in 1988, principally in North America, Southeast Asia and the Middle East.[9]

There was a similar story of Japanese involvement in Taiwan's industrialization, though in 1988 the island had absorbed only 6 per cent of Japan's Asian direct investment. The emphasis of the Japanese investment there in the 1980s was in electrical goods production and in other manufacturing. Consequently, Taiwan's exports of calculating machines and television and radio receivers increased during the period 1980–89 from 5.5 to 9.1 per cent of total exports. The contribution of manufacturing to Taiwan's GNP grew from 26 to 36 per cent in those years, compared with 31 per cent in 1989 in South Korea. Assisted by the high value of the yen and the movement of Japanese industry into high technology areas, Japan was becoming a market for mid-technology electronics exports from Taiwan and from the other Tigers. For example, their exports of coloured television sets to Japan boomed from 25,000 in 1986 to 370,000 a year later.[10]

Such exports, however, did not weaken the dependency of Taiwan and South Korea upon Japan for imports to fuel their industrialization. In 1989, 31 per cent of Taiwan's and 28 per cent of the ROK's imports came from Japan, proportions that were slightly higher than in 1980, with the value of the imports inflated by the rising value of the yen. Both countries still had unfavourable trade balances with Japan, with deficits of US$6 billion for Taiwan and US$4 billion for the ROK. However, for both Tigers the US remained their leading export market. They contributed to the US trade deficit in 1989, to the extent of a US$12 billion profit to Taiwan and US$4.7 billion to South Korea, though its trade surplus had almost halved since 1987. Pressure was placed by the US on Taiwan and South Korea to raise the value of their currency. The ROK, especially, in 1985–86 drew US protests for unfair trading practices and maintenance of high protectionism, leading to a major trade confrontation between those two closely allied nations. The falling imbalance of trade for the US in the late 1980s reflected a significant relaxation of restrictions in South Korea on

---

9 Ibid., 146–68. Alice H. Amsden, *Asia's Next Giant: South Korea and Late Industrialization* (New York 1989), 175–6. *FEA*, 1991, 570. Robert Castley, *Korea's Economic Miracle: The Crucial Role of Japan* (London 1997), ch. 4. Bon-Ho Koo, 'The Korean Economy: Structural Adjustment for Future Growth', in Chong-Sik Lee (ed.), *Korea Briefing, 1990* (Boulder 1991), 55–73. Walden Bello and Stephanie Rosenfeld, *Dragons in Distress: Asia's Miracle Economies in Crisis* (San Francisco 1990), 113–15. James Riedel, 'Intra-Asian Trade and Foreign Direct Investment', *Asian Development Review*, 9, 1991, 140.

10 Riedel, 'Intra-Asian Trade', 140. *FEA*, 1981–82, 386; 1991, 342, 569. Steven, *Japan's New Imperialism*, 132. Bill Emmott, *The Sun Also Sets: The Limits to Japan's Economic Power* (New York 1989), 192.

American exports, which almost doubled in value from 1987 to 1989 to only US$1.5 billion less than Japan's exports to the ROK in 1989. This was a by-product of South Korea's continued dependence on the US for defence assistance, and it indicated a limitation placed by US military hegemony upon Japanese economic dominance in South Korea.[11]

In Singapore in 1986, for the first time, Japanese investment in manufacturing exceeded the US input. Japan increased its proportional share of Singapore's overseas investments from 16 per cent in 1980 to 42 per cent in 1986, and by that year this Asian Tiger had received 12 per cent of Japan's direct investment in Asia, second only to Hong Kong. Utilizing Singapore's well-educated population, the primary Japanese investment was in electronics, firms that were either wholly Japanese owned or with the Singapore government as a partner. In no other part of Asia was Japanese money more welcomed, since it was seen as promoting the development of Singapore's role as the leading commercial and industrial centre in Southeast Asia. Consequently, electronics increased from 12 to 20 per cent of Singapore's exports from 1980 to 1989.[12]

The policies of a stable and interventionist government were major reasons for Singapore's economic success. Enforcing a puritanical discipline on its population based on traditional Chinese culture, Lee Kuan Yew's PAP government utilized the crisis of independence to impose curbs on trade unions as part of a strategy to open the republic to foreign investment. Its Economic Development Board was a major instrument in providing the financial catalyst for rapid industrialization. Government policies ensured the island was well equipped to take advantage of the trade boom generated by the Vietnam War and the growth of international trade in the late 1970s after a short recession induced by the 1973 oil shock. Along with political stability created by PAP electoral dominance, the island rapidly became Asia's leading financial centre. By 1975 its port had become the third busiest in the world, behind New York and Rotterdam – although later overtaken by Hong Kong – and its industries by the end of the 1970s were moving out of the labour-intensive stage of development assisted by a

11   *FEA*, 1991, 343, 570. Jiann-Jong Guo and Raymond Chung, 'Taiwan's Economic
     Relations with the United States of America', in Gary Klintworth (ed.), *Modern Taiwan in
     the 1990s* (Canberra 1991), 106–21. Paul W. Kuznets, 'Trade Policy, and Korea–US
     Relations', in John P. Hardt and Young C. Kim (eds), *Economic Cooperation in the Asia-Pacific
     Region* (Boulder 1990), 69–81. Peter A. Petri, 'Korea's Export Niche: Origins and
     Prospects', and P.F. Alleigeier, 'Korean Trade Policy in the Next Decade: Dealing
     with Reciprocity', in Danny M. Leipziger (ed.), *Korea: Transition to Maturity*
     (New York 1988), 47–63, 85–97.
12   *FEA*, 1980, 1052; 1991, 978. Riedel, 'Intra-Asian Trade', 140. Steven, *Japan's New
     Imperialism*, 133–45.

government 'Second Industrial Revolution' strategy. There was an economic downturn in 1985 caused by wages outstripping productivity, but the
strength of Singapore's economy was demonstrated in the way it bounced
back in 1987 with the assistance in reductions of government charges for
businesses. In 1990, when Lee Kuan Yew finally stepped down in favour of
his Deputy Prime Minister, Goh Chok Tong, the economy had been growing at an average rate of 10 per cent the preceding three years, fuelled by a
continuing regional economic boom.[13]

Hong Kong's 5,761,400 people in 1989 had been experiencing strong
export-driven industrial growth. Exports of goods and non-factor services,
including re-exports, contributed to 95 per cent of its GNP in 1983, giving
Hong Kong's citizens a per capita income nearly as high as Singapore's.
This economic growth resulted much less from government interventionist
policies than in Singapore, Taiwan and South Korea. British government
assistance was confined to the provision of economic infrastructure and
educational and training resources, though there were less formal contacts
between the government bureaucracy and the colony's business world. The
educational and training resources were helpful in the growth of Hong
Kong's industrial development and in the adaptability of the manufacturing
labour force, but overall Hong Kong was an example of free market capitalism. American investment was still predominant in provision of overseas
capital for the colony, though it was Japan's most prominent field of Asian
investment. Hong Kong's role as a major trading door to the outside world
for China was another source of the colony's prosperity. In the years 1987
to 1989 China contributed 25 per cent of Hong Kong's imports compared
with 18 per cent from Japan. Much of the foreign investment and technological transfer traffic to China was routed through Hong Kong.[14]

However, there were problems facing the Tiger economies by the end of
the 1980s. Rising wage rates were destroying the textile industries that were
the original basis for export-oriented industrial expansion. The average cost
in 1989 per operator hour in the NIC textile industry ranged from US$2.44

---

13 C.M. Turnbull, *A History of Singapore 1819–1980* (Singapore 1989), ch. 9. Cheng Siok Hwa,
    'Economic Change and Industrialization', in C.T. Chew and Edwin Lee (eds), *A History of
    Singapore* (Singapore 1991), 190–216. Chong Li Choy, 'Business in the Development of
    Singapore: The Creation of an Environment', in Chong Li Choy, Tan Chwee Huat,
    Wong Kwei Cheong and Caroline Yeoh (eds), *Business, Society and Development in Singapore*
    (Singapore 1990), 2–11. *Asian Security 1990–91*, 173–4. Gavin Peebles and Peter Wilson,
    The Singapore Economy (Cheltenham, UK 1996), ch. 2.

14 Organisation for Economic Co-operation And Development, *The Newly Industrialising
    Countries: Challenge and Opportunity for OECD Industries* (Paris 1988), 47–52. Felix Patrikeeff,
    Mouldering Pearl: Hong Kong at the Crossroads (London 1989), chs 5–6. *FEA*, 1990, 365–8.
    T.K. Ghose, *The Banking System of China and the China–Hong Kong Nexus* (Perth 1990), 39.

in Hong Kong to US$3.58 in Taiwan. The average cost in China was US$0.40 and in the Philippines US$0.64, with lower costs in Indonesia and Sri Lanka. Higher technology exports were the preferred new NIC option. But success in this area faced the strong reluctance of Japanese corporations, and also US companies, to part with their technology, using the Tigers for lower technology operations. South Korea and Taiwan have discovered this reality in attempts to establish their own fully controlled automobile industries. That was exemplified by the collapse of the Big Auto Plant project in Taiwan and by a comment by a Mitsubishi Motors representative that his company in the ROK 'does all the critical design work while Hyundai constructs the pieces and puts them together'. The same situation was facing the NICs in their attempts to break into high electronics technology beyond the level of the computer clones that Taiwanese companies became so adept in assembling.[15]

Elsewhere in the ASEAN states in the 1980s Japan was still mainly concentrating on resource development, exploiting the region's rich raw materials. These ASEAN nations were known as newly exporting countries to distinguish them from the NICs. Partial exceptions were Thailand and Malaysia, which by the late 1980s were experiencing significant industrial development; in both countries in 1988 manufacturing contributed to 24 per cent of GNP. Japan had become the dominant investor in Thailand, and in Malaysia Japanese investments were greater than those of Japan's two main competitors, Singapore and Britain. Much of the Japanese investment in Thailand was in joint ventures with Thai firms, such as the Siam Toyota Manufacturing Company, established in partnership with Siam Cement, Thailand's largest manufacturing firm. It contributed to an increase in the country's production of motor vehicles from 74,200 in 1986 to 157,600 in 1989. In Malaysia there was a significant linkage of Japanese investors with local Chinese capitalists and with the Malaysian elite. The largest Japanese ventures in Malaysia were still exploiting the country's rich natural resources, such as Malaysia LNG, a joint venture between Mitsubishi, the Dutch Shell company and the Malaysian state petroleum company. However, by the late 1980s Thailand and Malaysia were becoming major sources for relocation of Japanese industries, utilizing the cheap labour there. Consequently, in 1988 exports of machinery and transport equipment by Thailand and Malaysia, as a proportion of total exports, were respectively 18 and 28 per cent, compared with 8 per cent by the Philippines and 0.7 per cent by Indonesia. Malaysia and Thailand also by the late 1980s were becoming fields for Japanese electronics production, which was

---

15 Bello and Rosenfeld, *Dragons in Distress*, 135 (quotation), chs 6, 15.

extending into the Philippines. There was a sharp jump in Japanese direct investment in Indonesia, from $US631 million in 1989 to $US1.1 billion in 1990, which was stimulating new industrial growth there. Indonesia's exports of manufactured goods, as a proportion of total exports, increased from 18 to 35 per cent from 1986 to 1990. However, raw materials, especially oil, rubber and metals, were still the top ASEAN exports to Japan.[16]

A new region for Japanese economic expansion in Asia was China. By the 1980s Japan had become China's leading supplier of high technology and manufactured consumer goods. The Japanese proportional contribution to China's imports increased from an average of 13 per cent in the three years 1977–79 to 20 per cent in 1987–89, though in 1988–89, Japanese imports were overtaken by goods from Hong Kong. Japanese government and business circles, however, were ambivalent about China. While they were seeking to promote prosperity there for increased reception of Japanese goods, there were Japanese predictions of future political and social instability after the architect of China's modernisation, Deng Xiaoping, who was eighty-five years of age in 1989, died or stepped down. The Tigers were seen as more stable and profitable areas for Japanese investment in East Asia.[17]

The Pacific Islands were another region for increasing Japanese economic attention in the late 1980s. In December 1990 the skyline of Tuamon Bay in the US territory of Guam was punctured by cranes erecting Japanese hotels to add to those already dominating the shoreline. Local Chamorro people called their island 'Japan's Disneyland', where groups of young Japanese experience jungle river tours, have their photographs taken alongside blonde Americans, and spend their money in glittering Japanese-owned department stores. The US was still dominant in the trade of Guam and of other North Pacific islands; and Australia was the leading supplier of imports by the South Pacific's independent states. But Japan was either the second or third largest source of their imports. Japan was also the most important purchaser of the agricultural and mineral production of Papua New Guinea and of the Solomon Islands. Furthermore, there was a notable increase in Japan's financial aid to Pacific States, from US$53.9 million in 1982 to US$251

16   Ibid., ch. 6, 250–4. *FEA*, 1990, 462–3, 631–2, 946, 1041–2. Richard Stubbs, 'US–Japanese Trade Relations: The ASEAN Dimension', *The Pacific Review*, 5, 1992, 63. J. Thomas Lindblad, *Foreign Investment in Southeast Asia in the Twentieth Century* (London 1998), 142–7. Robert J. Muscat, *The Fifth Tiger: A Study of Thai Development Policy* (New York 1994), 223–30. Hal Hill, *Indonesia's Industrial Transformation* (Sydney 1998), 41.
17   *FEA*, 1981–82, 363–4; 1991, 322. Gary Klintworth, *China's Modernisation: The Strategic Implications for the Asia-Pacific Region* (Canberra 1989), 92–3. Yoichi Yokoi, 'Plant and Technology Contracts and the Changing Pattern of Economic Interdependence Between China and Japan', in Christopher Howe (ed.), *China and Japan: History, Trends and Prospects* (Oxford 1996), 127–46.

million in 1988. This was part of a Japanese response to US pressure to spend some of the trade surplus on aid to poorer regions of the world that had strategic importance. The new areas of aid provision were Polynesian and Micronesian islands. By far the biggest amount in 1988, US$114 million, went to Japan's former mandated islands in Micronesia, the Pacific Islands region of greatest Japanese economic activity and highest US strategic interest.[18]

Another Pacific Basin region of growing Japanese investment was Australia, a continent rich in mineral resources and agricultural and pastoral production. In the years 1983–88 Japanese capital inflows totalled A$16,861, which was 17 per cent of all incoming foreign capital in Australia, second only to Australia's traditional financial source, Britain (20 per cent) and outstripping the US (15 per cent). Only 22 per cent of the Japanese capital was direct investment, but this was just 1 per cent less than the direct investment proportion of Japanese worldwide capital outflow in 1989. In the 1970s the Japanese investment in Australia had concentrated on raw materials, especially mining, and on automobile manufacturing. In the 1980s, with liberalization of Australian capital markets, there was significant Japanese investment in the financial sector. There was also major investment in properties and tourism. In the year 1987–88 Japan was Australia's best customer, receiving 26 per cent of Australia's total exports, principally mining, agricultural and pastoral products. That year Japanese exports to Australia were 19 per cent of the total, 2 per cent less than imports from the US.[19]

While Japanese investment was welcomed by Pacific Basin governments, there was popular apprehension about the new Japanese economic order. In Australia Japanese-financed land developments were arousing local community hostility in a country where bitter memories of Japanese mistreatment of Australian prisoners of war had not completely died out. An Australian trade unionist, Abe David, received strong support from groups of Australian unionists when addressing them about the threat of Japanese capitalism, which he expounded in the book he co-authored in 1989, *The Third Wave*. An opinion poll commissioned by the Australian Department of Foreign Affairs and Trade in 1989 discovered that only 49 per cent of respondents supported the existing or any increased levels of Japanese investment. However, anti-Japanese rhetoric was not part of politics in Australia, which has traditionally relied on overseas sources of capital.[20]

---

18 Personal observations. *FEA*, 1991, 760–872. OECD, *Geographical Distribution of Financial Flows to Development Countries* (Paris 1989).

19 Ross Garnaut, *Australia and the Northeast Asian Ascendancy* (Canberra 1989), 94–6. *FEA* 1991, 191.

20 Personal information. Abe David and Ted Wheelwright, *The Third Wave: Australia and Asian Capitalism* (Sydney 1989). Garnaut, *Australia and the Northeast*, 96–7.

In Guam, where there were some Chamorro memories of Japanese wartime brutality, there was broad acceptance, though also cynicism about the prominent Japanese economic presence. However, one American resident businessman aroused significant popular support in November 1990 when, under a Japanese nom de plume, Kenji Matsumoto, he wrote 'tongue in cheek' to a local newspaper. He thanked 'a passive but greedy administration' for permission 'to dispense with the formality of even using local businesses', so that 'our forays into operations, such as merchandising, autosales, charter boat operators, etc., allow us to send a much larger percentage of the local dollar back to Japan'.[21]

The Japanese inroads into the American economy had aroused widespread public antipathy in the US towards Japan. The racism of the pre-Second World War era, which denigrated all things Japanese, had been transformed into a new fear of Japan provoked by apprehensions of a decline in US power. When in 1987 the British resident academic Paul Kennedy addressed that theme in his book, *The Rise and Fall of the Great Powers*, it became a best seller as Americans avidly sought to discover why their country was in the process of decline compared with the rise of Japan. This combination of racism and fear had bred an American xenophobia about Japanese activities and intentions. Japanese scholar Kan Ito responded in 1990 that the Americans, who were nominating in opinion polls that 'the Japanese threat' was more dangerous to the US than the 'Soviet threat', should reflect that, while the Soviets had the capacity to kill most Americans, 'no Japanese put guns to Americans' heads to make them buy Toyotas or Sonys'.[22]

In Asia there was significant hostility in the 1980s towards the Japanese for past military expansionism and new financial dominance, as expressed in a Singapore cartoon that juxtaposed a Second World War Japanese soldier with a modern cigar-smoking Japanese capitalist. While the governments of the Tigers and ASEAN states have welcomed Japanese investment, many of their citizens resent Japanese economic dominance and fear a revived Japanese militarism. Koreans, who remember bitterly their four decades under Japanese rule, were the most hostile towards the Japanese. This antipathy was nourished by an outcry in the ROK at the LDP

---

21 Personal information. *Pacific Daily News*, 27 Nov. 1990, 27; 29 Nov. 1990, 3.
22 Paul Kennedy, *The Rise and Fall of the Great Powers: Economic Change and Military Conflict from 1500 to 2000* (London 1987), ch. 8. David McLean, 'Symposium: the Decline of America? Paul Kennedy and his Critics', *Australian Journal of International Affairs*, 45 (1991), 60–9. D. Eleanor Westney, 'US Industrial Culture and the Japanese Competitive Challenge', in Alan D. Romberg and Tadashi Yamamoto (eds), *Same Bed, Different Dreams: America and Japan – Societies in Transition* (New York 1990), 67–82. Kan Ito, 'Trans-Pacific Anger', *Foreign Policy*, 78, 1990, 132.

government's move in 1982 to rewrite Japanese school textbooks, gloss-
ing over pre-war oppression on the Asian mainland, by substituting, for
example, the word 'advance' for 'aggression'. Government protests from
South Korea and China about the textbook changes were supported by
Taiwan, by Southeast Asian countries and by North Korea. Only the fear
that anti-Japanese agitation in South Korea could cause a breakdown in
recently improved Japan–ROK relations caused the stubborn Japanese
government finally to offer to withdraw the offending books in two years'
time, which did not mollify many Koreans. The textbook controversy served
to reinforce Japan's negative image in Southeast Asia. When in 1987 people
in ASEAN countries were asked in an opinion poll whether they believed
that Japan might once more become a dangerous military power, affirmative answers were given by 53 per cent of Thais and by 47 per cent of
Filipinos. There were smaller affirmations in the other ASEAN states –
34 per cent of Malaysians, 29 per cent of Singaporeans and 21 per cent of
Indonesians, a reflection of increasing geographic distances from Japan.
While such opinion polls have limited value, the degree of fear revealed in
them was expressed at a time when Japan was keeping low defence and
foreign policy profiles.[23]

Japan and the American defence network

Despite some American fears of future Japanese militarism, US administrations started pressing Japan in 1980 to increase its defence expenditure,
which that year was only 0.9 per cent of GNP, compared with 5.3 per cent
in the US. Though the Japanese total expenditure of US$10 billion was
eighth in the world, during the first half of the 1980s there were growing complaints in Washington that Japan was sheltering under American
defence protection while profiting from the increasing American trade deficits. However, there was growing integration of the US and Japanese defence
forces and industries, especially the exchange of electronics technology with
military applications. Japan also accepted responsibility for defence of a
1,000 nautical mile zone around its shores. Furthermore, Japan remained a
vital base for the US navy and airforce for their watching brief over communist Asian powers.[24]

---

23 Chong-Sik Lee, *Japan and Korea: The Political Dimension* (Stanford 1985), ch. 6. Emmott, *Sun also Sets*, 205.
24 Malcolm McIntosh, *Japan Re-armed* (London 1986), 38–60.

Guiding such US–Japan defence cooperation was Japan's Prime Minister from 1982 to 1987, Yasuhiro Nakasone, who promised Reagan in 1983 that Japan was 'an unsinkable aircraft carrier' in the 'alliance' between Japan and the US. He had served in the Japanese navy during the Second World War and in 1950 had joined the national Territory Defense Research Association, an anti-communist group formed to promote national security. As Prime Minister, Nakasone sought a military strength commensurate with his nation's economic power so that Japan could take an appropriate place among the great powers of the world and free itself from dependency on the US to become an equal partner in the Japan–US alliance. However, his LDP never had the two-thirds parliamentary majority necessary for amendments to the anti-war provisions of the Japanese constitution. Indeed, there were vocal critics in opposition political parties in Japan. They argued that the existence of a 'self-defence' force of 272,000 soldiers, sailors and airmen in 1986 already breached the constitution, and there were accusations that the Supreme Court was biased in constantly upholding the legality of these forces. The Japanese Socialist Party was advocating instead unarmed neutrality. Nakasone's government did breach in 1987 a previously established convention of 1 per cent of GNP as the ceiling on defence expenditure. In 1988 defence spending rose to 1.01 per cent of GNP, which pleased Washington. Japan also agreed in 1987 to pay some of the expenses of the US forces stationed there. However, the US was unable to achieve any fundamental change in the level of Japanese defence expenditure. Under the less hawkish Prime Minister Kaifu, the 1990 Japanese defence budget had drooped to 0.99 of estimated GNP, though this was the sixth largest defence expenditure in the world.[25]

Prior to 1990 the US was unable to persuade Japan to use its military power any wider than in Japanese waters. In 1987 when the war between Iraq and Iran was causing missile attacks on oil tankers in the Persian Gulf, through which 55 per cent of Japan's oil was shipped, the Japanese government rejected a call to share the cost of and provide naval assistance for the protective US naval action because of the anti-war provisions of the Japanese constitution. Nakasone could not persuade his Cabinet to support such a precedent. When in 1990 the US sent troops to Saudi Arabia after Iraq invaded Kuwait, there was renewed pressure on Japan to join other allies of

---

25   Nester, *Japan's Growing Power*, 78. 'Nakasone's Neo-Nationalism', *Far Eastern Economic Review*, 19 Feb. 1987, 82–9. Kenneth B. Pyle, 'In Pursuit of a Grand Design: Nakasone Betwixt the Past and the Future', *Journal of Japanese Studies*, 13, 1987, 243–70. Merion and Sue Harries, *Sheathing the Sword: The Demilitarisation of Japan* (New York 1987), ch. 25. Janet E. Hunter, *The Emergence of Modern Japan: An Introductory History Since 1853* (London 1989), 284–6. Defense Agency, *Defense of Japan 1990* (Tokyo 1990), 163.

the US in military and naval support. Because the Japanese constitution clearly forbade sending troops to the Gulf, the government considered providing naval ships, but public opinion clearly opposed Japan sending SDF troops or ships to the Persian Gulf. Under strong US pressure Japan did agree to provide $4 billion to help pay for the military and naval forces protecting much of Japan's oil supply. Conversely, the US was not willing to concede major economic power to Japan. Washington opposed Japanese requests in 1984 and 1987 for increased voting power in the World Bank and the Asia Development Bank.[26]

Furthermore, at the end of the 1980s there was a controversy over development of a fighter support experimental (FS-X) aircraft to replace the F-1 used by the Japanese SDF. Initially, the Japanese Defence Agency was led to understand that Japan could produce the aircraft. But the US companies General Dynamics and McDonnell Douglas pushed for joint US–Japanese development of improvements to their F-16 or F-18 aircraft with support from Congress, where the issue was linked to other dissatisfactions about Japan's trade tactics. An agreement was reached with Japan in November 1988 that allocated 40 per cent of FS-X's development work to US firms, but with full Japanese production. However, many members of the US Congress opposed the deal as giving away aircraft technology to Japan. Despite the government's negotiation with Japan to restrict the transfer of such information, a final compromise allowed the agreement to go ahead on the basis of 40 per cent US participation in development and production. But the controversy damaged the faith of many Japanese in the efficacy of joint ventures with the US.[27]

Within Japan there has been significant public debate about the nation's acceptance of US military leadership, which was heightened by the FS-X affair. A leading advocate for change was the publicist and LDP politician, Ishihara Shintar, who argued that Japan's toadying to the US was encouraging a national moral malaise that portended social disintegration. Therefore it was imperative to restore Japan's military power and her national independence in a new form of partnership with the US. A book he co-authored in 1989 with the chairman of Sony Corporation, Morita Akio, entitled '*No*' *to ieru Nihon* (A Japan that can say No) caused a big controversy in Japan, as well as hostile American reactions, over statements such as how the 'global

26   Defense Agency, *Defense of Japan*, 238. Courtney Purrington, 'Tokyo's Policy Responses During the Gulf Crisis', *Asian Survey*, 31, 1991, 307–23. Emmott, *Sun Also Sets*, 231.
27   Michael J. Green, *Arming Japan: Defense Production, Alliance Politics and the Postwar Search for Autonomy* (New York 1995), ch. 5. Mark Lorell, *Troubled Partnership: A History of US–Japan Collaboration on the FS-X Fighter* (New Brunswick 1996), chs 4–10.

military balance' could be overturned if 'Japan decided to sell its computer chips to the Soviet Union instead of the United States'. One of Shintar's Japanese critics, university professor, Nakanishi Terumasa, pointed out in 1990 that Japan had often said no to the US, such as to the 1987 Persian Gulf plea. He pointed out that the Japan–US alliance was still important in a potentially turbulent East Asia with continuing hostility between North and South Korea and with China's uneasy relationship with Taiwan.[28]

The US, the USSR and the East Asian strategic balance

During the 1980s a major change was taking place in the strategic balance in the East Asian sector of the Pacific Basin with a growing rapprochement between the US and China, which began in the 1970s. The establishment of four special economic zones in China for foreign capitalists, to help promote the economic modernization sought by Deng Xiaoping, was utilized by American capitalists. China also sought technical assistance from the US, including American university places for students and the hiring of technical experts to go to China. One of them, E.E. Bauer, who arrived in 1980 to assist the Civil Aviation Administration to establish a modern airline, considered that Chinese assimilation of Western technology 'would take a full century' given the absence of technically trained people and other major impediments, such as poor transport and communication facilities. But by the time he left in 1984, he considered that an industrial 'take-off' had occurred. By 1985 China was producing 16,676,600 television receivers, compared with 517 in 1978, and there were similar huge increases in other low to middle technology manufacturing. The development was still controlled by the state, and import controls were used in 1984 to stop a surge in the country's trade deficit. Nevertheless, the benefit of the economic development for US exports to China rose from US$906 million in 1978 to US$7.9 billion in 1989, and the American contribution to China's imports had increased from 5 per cent to 13 per cent – in third place behind Hong Kong and Japan. By 1987 the US also had

---

28   Ishihara Shintar, 'A Nation Without Morality', *The Silent Power: Japan's Identity and World Role* (Selected essays from *The Japan Interpreter* Tokyo 1976), 76–95. Ishihara Shintar, 'Learning to Say No to America' and Nakanishi Terumasa, 'Saying Yes to the Japan–US Partnership', *Japan Echo*, 17, 1990, 29–42.

direct investments in China worth US$3.5 billion, the largest of any of the nations taking advantage of China's search for foreign capital.[29]

The increasing warmth of the US–China relationship was marked by Washington's willingness to allow the sale of arms and military-related equipment to Beijing. A major example was the sale in 1983, for US$11 million, of a ground satellite-tracking station, which gave China the capacity to launch a communications satellite that would assist missile-targeting capabilities. The main American motive for such sales was to increase China's military power to counterbalance the USSR in East Asia. There was a wide range of US military assistance for improving the technological capacity of the Chinese army, airforce and navy, such as anti-submarine sonars, fighter aircraft avionics and anti-tank missiles. US sales of military equipment reached a value of $106.2 million by 1989. However, this American defence support did not develop into a military alliance between China and the US. Beijing sought to maintain an independent foreign policy, and in the late 1980s was willing to respond positively to Soviet overtures. China also sold arms freely to Third World countries, much to US displeasure.[30]

New developments in USSR–China relations in the late 1980s were especially the work of Mikhail Gorbachev, who assumed the top position in the Kremlin in 1985. His concentration on economic development and reform in the USSR encouraged him to remove Sino-Soviet border tensions. In a major speech in the strategically vital Soviet Far Eastern port, Vladivostok, he said the 'USSR is prepared to discuss any measure aimed at creating an atmosphere of good neighbourliness in a most serious way'. He subsequently offered a readjustment of boundary disputes in China's favour and withdrew Soviet forces from Mongolia and from Afghanistan. Full normalization of relations between the two nations was sealed at a summit meeting in Beijing between Gorbachev and Deng from 15 to 18 May 1989. A consequence of the improved relationship and economic reform in the USSR, which gave considerable freedom of trade to border regions, was an increase in Soviet Union exports to China from a mere

---

29   E.E. Bauer, *China Takes Off: Technology Transfer and Modernization* (Seattle 1986), chs 1, 21 (quotation, 25). *FEA*, 1982–3, 362–4; 1990, 323. *YTTS*, 1988, 172. Gary Klintworth, *China's Modernisation: The Strategic Implications for the Asia-Pacific Region* (Canberra 1989), 11–28, 89. Richard Conroy, 'Technology and Economic Development', in Robert Benewick and Paul Wingrove (eds), *Reforming the Revolution: China in Transition* (Chicago 1988), ch. 9. See also Robert Kleinberg, *China's 'Opening' to the Outside World: The Experiment with Foreign Capitalism* (Boulder 1990). Harry Harding, *A Fragile Relationship: The United States and China since 1972* (Washington 1992), 33–47, 94–100, 145–54.

30   Harding, *A Fragile Relationship*, 87–94, 162–9, 371. Klintworth, *China's Modernisation*, 87–91. A. James Gregor, *Arming the Dragon: US Security Ties with the People's Republic of China* (Lanham 1987), ch. 5. James Mann, *About Face: A History of America's Curious Relationship with China, from Nixon to Clinton* (New York 1999), ch. 7.

1 per cent of China's imports in 1979 to 4 per cent in 1989. China's exports to the USSR recorded the same increase.[31]

Gorbachev's USSR had a much harder task in establishing good relations with Japan as part of his *perestroika* doctrine of improving relations with the outside world. Soviet requirements were for foreign capital and technology to resuscitate a moribund economy; therefore capital rich, but resource poor Japan was a vital target. The major stumbling block was the Soviet occupation of the four islands at the southern end of the Kurile archipelago, which stretches between Japan and the Soviet Kamchatka Peninsula. These islands had been ceded to Japan in 1855 and 1875 by Czarist Russia in return for the cession to Russia of Japanese interests on Sakhalin, north of the Japanese archipelago. The four southern Kurile Islands had a land area of 4,996 square kilometres and a population of only about 17,000 when the USSR annexed them on 20 September 1945 in accordance with the Yalta Agreements. However, the islands were of major strategic importance. The only free Soviet naval access to the Pacific was through the Kuriles, since the other outlet, the Korea Strait, was dominated by Japan and by South Korea. While the Soviet navy used a route through the central Kurile Islands, it could easily be blocked in war time with Japanese control of the bigger southern Kurile Islands. Japan also made the southern islands into a symbol of Japanese national aspirations, concentrating on them rather than on the other Soviet occupied territory of southern Sakhalin, which Japan had seized in the Russo-Japanese War of 1904–05, and which had been reoccupied by the USSR in 1945. The Kurile Islands were also important to Japan for the rich fishing region around them.[32]

The southern Kurile Islands were known as the 'Northern Territories', and in January 1981 the Japanese government decided to proclaim 7 February as 'The Day' of the Northern Territories, to start a week of official and unofficial protest meetings. The USSR reacted sharply, informing Japan's ambassador in Moscow that the protests bordered 'on enmity toward the Soviet Union' and declaring the islands non-negotiable. There the issue remained with consequent strained relations between Japan and the USSR, which encouraged the continuance of the Japan–US alliance and closer relations between Japan and China. Consequently, despite growing rapprochement between the USSR and the US, Kaifu firmly announced in July 1990 at a summit meeting of world leaders that there would be no

31 Klintworth, *China's Modernisation*, 85–6. See also Ramesh Thakur and Carl Thayer (eds), *The Soviet Union as an Asian Power* (Boulder 1987).
32 David Rees, *The Soviet Seizure of the Kuriles* (New York 1985), ix–xix (quotation xii), chs 6–8. For more detail on this dispute see Tsuyoshi Hasegawa, *The Northern Territories Dispute and Russo-Japanese Relations*, 2 vols (Berkeley 1998).

Japanese aid for the ailing Soviet economy until the southern Kurile Islands were returned to Japan.[33]

A problem for the USSR was that Siberia was not seen as a major area for Japanese investment. By 1990, when many Soviet restrictions on foreign investment had been lifted, Japan's post-industrial economy had little need for the raw materials of the Soviet Far East. Of the 1,274 joint foreign-Soviet business ventures at the end of 1989, only twenty-one involved Japanese firms and all had a capital of less than US$1 million. The angry US reaction to Toshiba's venture into the Soviet market in 1987 also had deterred Japanese capitalists from contact with the USSR. Those who did venture into Siberia found the Soviet bureaucracy a great hindrance to adequate profits; and in 1990, with the lifting of many Soviet restrictions, a surviving barrier was the non-convertibility of the rouble.[34]

Gorbachev had an easier task in establishing closer relations with South Korea. Increasing contacts between the USSR and South Korea in the early 1980s suddenly halted when, on the night of 31 August 1983, Soviet fighters shot down KAL 007, a ROK airliner, which had strayed into USSR air space, with the loss of 269 lives. President Chun Doo Hwan declared it 'an utterly inhuman act', but the USSR refused to apologize. Foreign Minister Gromyko was convinced that 'the violation of Soviet airspace was carried out for purposes of [US] military intelligence', and one American scholar mounted a strong case for that hypothesis, though it could not be proved.[35]

However, the ROK soon resumed a search for better relations with the USSR, though it had to await the advent of Gorbachev. On the eve of the Olympic Games in Seoul in 1988, he declared publicly that conditions on the Korean peninsula had greatly changed since the 1950s and suggested improving economic relations between the two countries. The reform-minded USSR government was looking to this booming Asian Tiger for economic advice and capital investment. While there was initial caution by South Korean capitalists because of the absence of diplomatic relations to protect their investments, the value of trade between the two nations increased from only US$36 million in 1980 to almost US$600 million in 1989. In April 1989 the ROK and the USSR agreed to establish trade offices, which

---

33 Rees, *The Soviet Seizure*, chs 9–10. *FEA*, 1991, 1076–7. Hoshira Kimura, 'Recent Japan–Soviet Relations: Gorbachev's Dilemma and his Choices', in Peter Drysdale (ed.), *The Soviets and the Pacific Challenge* (Sydney 1991), ch. 6.

34 Evgenii Kovrigin, 'Problems and Prospects for Japanese Investment in the Soviet Far East', in Drysdale (ed.), *The Soviets*, ch. 7.

35 Ralph N. Clough, *Embattled Korea: The Rivalry for International Support* (Boulder 1987), 334–5 (quotation 334). Andrei Gromyko, *Memoirs* (London 1989), 297. R.W. Johnson, *Shootdown: The Verdict on KAL 007* (London 1986), ch. 12.

eight months later became consulates. Further negotiations produced full diplomatic relations between the two nations on 30 September 1990. A sign of new Korean investor confidence was the investment in 1990 by Hyundai Construction Company of $1 million in a joint logging venture, and an announcement by the company of plans to participate in the development of natural gas in East Siberia. Unlike Japan, South Korea's economic development was at a stage where it could benefit from Siberian natural resources.[36]

The Soviet diplomatic recognition of South Korea occurred with the blessing of the US. When he came to power in 1981, Reagan damned the USSR as an 'evil empire' in a deepening of Cold War confrontations between the two superpowers in the early 1980s. But Reagan was stronger in rhetoric than in practice. Before Gorbachev came to power, the US was searching for nuclear arms limitation and other agreements with the USSR. A major stumbling block in the Asian sphere was the massive Soviet military action in Afghanistan. But Gorbachev made positive movements to improve relations with the US, driven by the huge strain that the war in Afghanistan and other defence expenditure was placing on his nation's faltering economy. Therefore he started withdrawing Soviet forces from Afghanistan in April 1988 and completed the withdrawal in February 1989. He announced in January 1989 that he would reduce by 200,000 the 597,600 Soviet armed forces personnel stationed east of the Ural Mountains that divide European Russia from Asia. In December 1989 he started winding down the Soviet naval base at Cam Ranh Bay in Vietnam. Such positive actions helped significantly to smooth relations with Reagan's successor, the less ideologically conservative President Bush, who also was impelled by the need to reduce the US military expenditure that had contributed to a large budget deficit. There were constant exchanges of diplomatic and even, from 1988, military visits between the two nations. In 1990, with the Berlin Wall tumbling down in Germany, the emergence of non-communist states throughout Eastern Europe, and mutually observed Soviet and US destruction of weapons systems, the Cold War effectively was over, a reality symbolized in East Asia by the Soviet recognition of the ROK.[37]

North Korea reacted angrily to Soviet diplomatic recognition of South Korea. Kim Il Sung, the longest surviving national leader in Asia, condemned

---

36   Yu-Nam Kim, 'The Soviet Reforms and Relations with the Koreas', in Drysdale (ed.), *The Soviets and the Pacific*, 98–101. Byung-Joon Ahn, 'Foreign Relations: An Expanded Diplomatic Agenda', in Lee (ed.), *Korea Briefing*, 35–8.

37   *Asian Security 1989–90*, 50, 65–6, 72–6.

it, with some accuracy, as 'diplomatic relations bargained for dollars'. There had been signs of improvement in relations between the North and South in 1980 with discussion between representatives of both countries, in which each side referred to the other for the first time by their DPRK and ROK titles. But this was still a long way from mutual diplomatic recognition. In September 1984 South Korea accepted food and other material aid from North Korea for flood victims, which prompted official talks between the two sides. A result in September 1984 was the reunion of fifty families separated by the Korean War. However, from 1985 to 1987 relations deteriorated with the North condemning joint ROK–US military exercises. A nadir for the decade was reached with the blowing up of a South Korean airliner in November 1987 by a DPRK agent, killing 115 people. Nevertheless, in 1988 Kim Il Sung took a major step by accepting the principle of coexistence. An ailing North Korean economy and the opening of trade and other relations between South Korea with China and the USSR were probable motives for this major DRPK policy change. Top-level negotiations from 1989 led in September 1990 to a visit to Seoul by the North Korean premier, Yon Hyong-Muk, a landmark occasion. His South Korean counterpart, Kang Young-Hoon, went to Pyongyang in the next month.[38]

Nor was South Korea willing to abandon its alliance with the US. In 1980, despite the Carter administration's concern for human rights, Washington was silent when ROK troops brutally crushed a popular uprising in the southwestern city of Kwangju, which killed at least 193 people. This insurrection developed from student demonstrations for more freedom during a time of unstable civilian government, exacerbated by a military coup, in which General Chun Doo Hwan seized the presidency. The failure of Washington to condemn the Kwangju massacre, and especially a Korean belief that ROK troops could not have been used without the permission of the US commander of the Combined Forces in the ROK, aroused significant public hostility towards the US. The US, however, exerted pressure on the South Korean army in 1986–87 not to intervene in a growing political crisis in the ROK. Inspired by the popular overthrow of President Marcos in the Philippines, Korean students were attempting, with some middle-class support, to depose Chun with widespread violent demonstrations. Though distancing themselves from the radical students, opposition parties pressed for major political reforms, which produced a stand-off with the

---

38   Rhee Sang-Woo, 'North Korea in 1990: Lonesome Struggle to Keep Chuch'e', *Asian Survey*, 31, 1991, 75. Chong-Sik Lee, 'North and South Korea: From Confrontation to Negotiation', in Lee (ed.), *Korea Briefing*, 39–53.

ruling Democratic Justice Party. Chun's nominee as president, Roh Tae Woo, solved the impasse dramatically in June 1987 by accepting virtually all the opposition demands, with reforms including liberation of political prisoners, freedom of the press and a promise of direct popular election for the presidency before February 1988. The South Korean opposition and the US government welcomed the reforms, and a grateful ROK public elected Roh as president in December 1987. However, there was continued student unrest against the Roh government, and in May 1990 students burnt down the US Information Center building in Seoul. Yet public opinion polls in South Korea revealed continued majorities favouring the maintenance of a military alliance with the US.[39]

In 1990 with the disappearance of former communist friends in Europe and growing liberalization in the USSR, North Korea's foreign relations were changing. To assist an economy which was growing at less than 3 per cent per annum in the late 1980s, and which provided a GNP per person only one-fifth of the size of South Korea's GNP, Kim Il Sung turned to his old enemy, Japan, for capital investment. He also moved to restore relations with China, which had cooled during the period of economic liberalization there.[40]

China was seeking better foreign relations in 1990 because of the international reverberations of the massacre of Chinese students and other citizens in Tiananmen Square in Beijing that started in the early morning hours of 4 June 1989. Over 1,000 people died as PLA tanks and soldiers moved into the square to arrest and disperse students camped there in a mass call for democratic reforms. The protests had started in April, centred on rising inflation and spreading corruption that had flowed from economic reforms. Exploiting the visit in May of the world's media to cover the summit between Gorbachev and Deng, the students had increased their demands to advocate the introduction of democracy. The newly free and often sympathetic Chinese media reported these calls, prompting widespread protests in other cities. The government was initially hamstrung

---

39   Donald Stone Macdonald, *The Koreans: Contemporary Politics and Society* (Boulder 1988), 56–60, 233–8. Tae-Hwan Kwak and Wayne Patterson, 'The Security Relationship between Korea and the United States, 1960–1984', in Yur-Bok Lee and Wayne Patterson (eds), *One Hundred Years of Korean–American relations, 1882–1982* (University, Alabama 1986), 119–26. James Cotton, 'Conflict and Accommodation in the Two Koreas', in Stuart Harris and James Cotton (eds), *The End of the Cold War in Northeast Asia* (Melbourne 1991), 164–70. *Asian Security 1987–88* (London 1988), 13–17, 85–8. *Asian Security 1988–89* (London 1989), 3–4, 77–80. *Asian Security 1989–90*, 131–40. *Asian Security 1990–91*, 7–9, 132–5. See also Donald N. Clark (ed.), *The Kwangju Uprising: Shadows over the Regime in South Korea* (Boulder 1988).

40   Cotton, 'Conflict and Accommodation', 74–5.

in its approach to the dissent because of differences of opinion between reformers and conservatives. However, by late May conservatives, including Deng and his premier Li Peng, gained the upper hand and ordered the military crackdown. Beside the deaths in Tiananmen Square, during the next twelve months there were some 1,100 executions and tens of thousands of arrests across the country. The aged Beijing leadership succeeded in crushing what it saw as a serious rebellion against its authority that had arisen from the economic reform it had been promoting.[41]

A major diplomatic problem for China was that a recent opening of the country to Western media produced dramatic TV pictures and eyewitness reports of the massacre for the outside world. There was immediate and widespread condemnation. Only China's few remaining communist allies accepted Beijing's propaganda that the massacre was a repression of a 'counterrevolutionary revolt'. Concerned to maintain improved relations with China, the Soviet Congress of Peoples' Deputies on 7 June described the massacre merely as 'clashes' between troops and 'participants in mass youth protests'. The US suspended all military and most economic aid to China and called successfully on international agencies to postpone new loans. EEC nations had already taken such a lead, and Japan suspended aid projects worth US$10 billion. Investors postponed new investments; some withdrew from China. A tourist industry worth US$2.2 billion in 1988 was under serious threat. Such economic punishment came in a year when Beijing already had predicted a US$2 billion budget deficit.[42]

The conservative leadership of China was reluctant to bow to the international pressure until it succeeded in placing the lid of repression on all dissidence and in purging reformers from the administration. Not until the end of June 1990 was a conciliatory gesture made to the Western World. This allowed Fang Lizhi, an eminent physicist and strong supporter of a Westernized China, who had been sheltering in the US embassy in Beijing, to go into exile to Britain. A few other dissidents were released from prison with the lifting of martial law. However, these small concessions were enough for Western nations, with Japan in the lead, to begin the restoration of economic relations after Bush gave a green light at the meeting of the

41 Lowell Dittmer, 'China in 1989: The Crisis of Incomplete Reform', *Asian Survey*, 30, 1990, 250–34. David Sambaugh, 'China in 1990: The Year of Damage Control', *Asian Survey*, 31, 1991, 41–2. Yan Sun, 'The Chinese Protests of 1989: The Issue of Corruption', *Asian Survey*, 31, 762–82. Harrison E. Salisbury, *Tiananmen Diary: Thirteen Days in June* (London 1989). *Asian Security 1989–90*, 5–6.
42 Dittmer, 'China in 1989', 34, 37–8. Alexander Lukin, 'The Initial Soviet Reaction to the Events in China in 1989 and the Prospects for Sino-Soviet Relations', *The China Quarterly*, 125, 1991, 121. Harding, *Fragile Relationship*, chs 7–8.

Group of Seven leading industrial powers of the world in Houston, Texas, in July 1990. Japan soon opened new lines of credit for China up to ¥810 billion for five years from 1990. Bush encountered stiff opposition in Congress to any relaxation of his government's hard line. However, China succeeded in restoring significant US economic assistance by cooperating in UN sanctions against Iraq. China also sent to the US in October 1990 a high-level trade mission, which offered to purchase $700 million of US products, though this would be only a small reduction of the US trade deficit with China, which was $3.5 billion in 1989. China also was able to improve relations with Asian countries by the end of 1990. Progress towards re-establishing diplomatic relations with Indonesia, for the first time for twenty-four years, was suspended after the Tiananmen massacre but was revived and consummated in August 1990. Singapore, which was waiting for Indonesia, quickly followed suit. By the end of 1990 China had recovered much of the diplomatic ground lost at Tiananmen Square in June 1989.[43]

China's relations with Taiwan showed major improvements in the late 1980s. Representatives of the two estranged territories engaged in their first-ever negotiations in May 1986 when they met in Hong Kong to discuss the return of a China Airlines plane and crew members to Taiwan after their captain had flown it to China. Trade between the two territories was increasing. In 1990 Taiwan capitalists, exploiting labour costs as low as one-twentieth of those in their home island, had invested US$1.3 billion in China. Over 450,000 Taiwanese visited China between January and October 1989, using Hong Kong as the gateway, which was a 35 per cent rise on the same time period in the previous year, despite anger in Taiwan over the Tiananmen Square massacre. However that incident destroyed, at least in the short term, any hope of talks between China and Taiwan about reunification of their territories. Nevertheless, in 1990 the KMT government allowed the first visits by mainlanders to Taiwan. The new relations between communist China and Taiwan were being demonstrated in the way Xiamen and Jinmen islands had become popular tourist spots rather than targets for Red Chinese artillery.[44]

The Tiananmen massacre made many people in Hong Kong fearful for their future after 1997. That was the year of the expiration of the

---

43   *Asian Security 1990–91*, 91–4, 90–1. Sambaugh, 'China in 1990', 36–49. Patrick Tyler, *A Great Wall: Six Presidents and China. An Investigative History* (New York 1999), 371–9.
44   Bello and Rosenfeld, *Dragons in Distress*, 279–80. Martin L. Lasater, *Policy in Evolution: The US Role in China's Reunification* (Boulder 1989), 141–3. Gary Klintworth, 'Taiwan: Evolution and Response', in Harris and Cotton (eds), *End of the Cold War*, 115–18. *Asian Security 1990–1991*, 96–102.

ninety-nine-year lease on the New Territories, which were vital for Hong Kong's existence. Britain, keen to divest itself of colonial remnants no longer of economic or strategic value, agreed with Beijing in 1984 to hand over on 1 July 1897 Hong Kong island as well as the New Territories. China agreed to allow the existence of a 'Hong Kong Special Administrative Region' which would 'enjoy a high degree of autonomy, except in foreign and defence affairs'. China promised that 'the current social and economic systems in Hong Kong will remain unchanged and so will their life style'. Freedom of speech, of assembly, of travel, the right to strike and the protection of private property would be preserved by law. The independence of the Hong Kong dollar, freedom from any Chinese taxation or tariffs and permission for 'Hong Kong China' to develop its own 'economic relations' with 'other countries' would be preserved. These Chinese promises reflected the value placed by the reform-minded government of Deng Xiaoping on the thriving economic performance of Hong Kong and its role as a capitalist doorway to the Western World. However, the deaths in Tiananmen and the subsequent violent purges of dissidents throughout China made many citizens of Hong Kong, who had been publicly and vociferously protesting their opposition to the crushing of the Chinese pro-democracy movement, deeply suspicious of China's willingness to honour the commitments of 1984. This pessimism encouraged emigration from the colony of almost 50,000 people in 1988–89. Many of these were skilled people, whose departure had ominous implications for the future of the colony's economy. A growth rate in GDP of 7 per cent in 1988 dipped to an estimated 2.5 per cent in 1989, though a contraction in China's trade that year because of the Tiananmen massacre was a major reason for the decline.[45]

There was also significant public dissatisfaction in Hong Kong about Britain's role in the future transfer of power. Though approximately 3.2 million Hong Kong people carried British passports, a revised British nationality law in 1982 had limited their rights to move to Britain. Concern about the hostility in Hong Kong leading to economic and administrative collapse, induced Britain in April 1990 to promise British nationality to 50,000 key civil servants and professionals in the private sector plus their families in order to keep them in the colony until 1997. That move aroused displeasure in Beijing. Also in reaction to the strong criticism of the Tiananmen incident in Hong Kong, China sharply restricted the democratic content in the Basic Law, which provided a 'mini-constitution' for

---

45 *Asian Security 1990–1991*, 103–6. Y.C. Jao, Leung Chi-Keung, Peter Wesley-Smith and Won Siu-Lun (eds), *Hong Kong and 1997: Strategies for the Future* (Hong Kong 1985), 551–3, 1990–1. *FEA*, 367. Richard Y.C. Wong and Joseph Y.S. Cheng (eds), *The Other Hong Kong Report 1990* (Hong Kong 1990), ch. 11.

Hong Kong China. Whereas democrats in Hong Kong were pressing for sixty legislature seats, half of which would be filled by popular election by 1995 and all of them by 2003, Beijing allowed only twenty elective seats in 1995, twenty-four in 1999 and thirty in 2003, with a chief executive first appointed by China. London agreed to this arrangement in February 1990. Britain was under criticism from human rights activists for refusing most people in Hong Kong citizenship and political rights.[46]

There was also wider world humanitarian criticism of the British decision in December 1989 to forcibly return fifty-one of the many people who had fled by boat from Vietnam to Hong Kong. There were 54,341 of them in the colony in June 1990, of whom less than one fifth had been classified as genuine refugees awaiting overseas resettlement. However, the forcible repatriation was a single event designed to send a signal to Vietnam, which seemed to work, there being an 87 per cent reduction in the number of boat people arriving in the first six months of 1990 compared with the first half of the previous year. Nor was there any international criticism of the return of 320,740 illegal immigrants from China since 1979 who had been caught by Gurkha soldiers and guard dogs who patrolled Hong Kong's land border.[47]

By 1990 the strategic balance in East Asia had dramatically altered. Gorbachev's concern to concentrate on economic reform at home had encouraged an end to the long hostility between China and the USSR since the late 1980s. The growing warmth of relations between Moscow and Washington created a climate by 1990 for reductions in US defence expenditure, which had grown by 35 per cent in real terms during the 1980s. In 1990 US defence expenditure was reduced by 2.7 per cent in real terms. East Asia was an obvious target area for reduced military expenditure with the retreat of the Soviet threat and China's search for international good will. In July 1989 the US and South Korea agreed about increased ROK financial contributions to the US defence umbrella and the handing over of full command of the ROKA to a South Korean general. Washington's objective was to increase ROKA capacity so that the US could start reducing its remaining forces. In January 1990 the US announced the beginnings of a phased withdrawal from South Korea, commencing with the evacuation that year of 2,000 of the 45,000 US troops stationed there. Developments in the USSR also in 1990–91 were reducing North Korea's ability to rely on the Soviet military assistance that had been maintaining what, by 1990, was probably only parity in military strength with South Korean

---

46 Wong and Cheng (eds), *The Other Hong Kong*, ix–xv, ch. 2. *Asian Security 1990–1991*, 104–5.
47 Wong and Cheng (eds), *The Other Hong Kong Report*, ch. 8.

forces. The one potential threat from North Korea was its suspected development of atomic weapons.[48]

The improved US–Soviet relations had implications in 1990 for the Japan–US alliance. That year the Japanese Minister of State and Director General of the Defense Agency, Yozo Ishikawa, considered the Third World still vulnerable to conflict, as evidenced by the Iraqi invasion of Kuwait. Though there were also now greater possibilities of UN action to resolve such conflicts, his Defense Agency pointed to Japan's own region with the potentialities of conflict in Korea as well as the Japan–USSR Northern territories issue. This analysis presented the case for an actual increase of Japanese defence expenditure in 1990 of 6.1 per cent, despite the reduction in its proportion of GNP, and the ministry argued for a further 'modest' defence build-up.[49]

There were also portents of potential future economic conflict between the US and resource-starved Japan. That nation's surplus trade balance, on which its wealth depended, was declining. The percentage of imports in Japan's total trade increased from 37 per cent in 1986 to 44 per cent in 1990. If the upward trend continued there would be a potential increase in efforts by Japan to push its products in overseas markets, of which the US was still by far the most important, receiving 31 per cent of Japan's exports in 1990 compared with 38 per cent in 1986. US exports to Japan in 1990 were only 37 per cent of the total Japan–US trade.[50]

The Cambodian conflict

By 1990 one conflict which had been poisoning diplomatic relations in Southeast Asia was heading towards a resolution. Since 1980, backed by from 150,000 to 200,000 Vietnam troops, the PRK in Cambodia had been fighting an intermittent insurgency. In 1980 the Khmer Rouge had regrouped in the Thailand border region with some 25,000 to 30,000 soldiers. It was supported by Chinese military aid channelled through Thailand, which had concluded a secret agreement with Beijing in January 1979 for this purpose. Away from the Thai border the Khmer Rouge only had the capacity to operate in small groups, employing guerrilla tactics, such as ambushes, night raids and planting of mines. Though hailed in the West as the beginning

---

48 *Asian Security 1990–1991*, 149–50. William W. Kaufmann, *Glasnost, Perestroika, and US Defense Spending* (Washington 1990), 1–4. *Defense of Japan*, 21.
49 Kaufmann, *Glasnost*, v, 4, 167, 173.
50 *FEA*, 1990, 497 *Japan: Country Report* 1991: 2, 40.

of 'Vietnam's Vietnam', this insurrection was very different from the NLF in South Vietnam because the murderous brutality of Pol Pot's regime had aroused much Cambodian hostility to the Khmer Rouge. Therefore, its army could operate openly only in a belt of territory some twenty-five kilometres wide along the Thai border.[51]

The Chinese-supported Khmer Rouge was an embarrassing force for the ASEAN nations who were determined to prevent the Vietnamese-backed PRK from claiming to be the legitimate government of Cambodia. So the ASEAN states supported the Khmer People's National Liberation Front (KPNLF), formed in Paris in March 1979 and led by Son Sann, a former Cambodian businessman and politician. This non-communist front was employing ex-officers of Lon Nol's army to organize refugees along the Thai border into an army and engaged in a violent struggle with other right-wing groups to emerge as the dominant one by 1981. With about 8,000 troops in 1983, the KPNLF failed to win Cambodian peasant support. A third force on the Thai frontier was led by Sihanouk, who also was supported by ASEAN.[52]

Sihanouk was willing to join with the KPNLF and the Khmer Rouge in the Coalition Government of Democratic Kampuchea (CDGK), which was formed in Kuala Lumpur in June 1982. This disparate coalition of monarchists, republicans and communists was a marriage of convenience, the Khmer Rouge seeking diplomatic respectability and the weaker non-communist groups welcoming Khmer Rouge military strength. CDGK forces operated only at guerrilla level, but with increasing boldness with the flow of Chinese and Western arms. The insurgent border camps also were protected by Thai artillery fire against Vietnamese attacks, which from 1980 included forays across the Thai border in hot pursuit of insurgents. Hanoi concentrated on a military defeat of the coalition, claiming that once this was achieved, and if the PRK were internationally recognized as the government of Cambodia, then Vietnamese troops would be withdrawn. In a big dry season offensive in 1984–85 the Vietnamese army succeeded in smashing the border camps. However, in a reverse situation from its experience in South Vietnam, the PAVN's opponents retreated across the border, where they could regroup and refit in safety. The Khmer Rouge response was to avoid fighting and to infiltrate men and Chinese military supplies

51   Grant Evans and Kelvin Rowley, *Red Brotherhood at War: Vietnam, Cambodia and Laos since 1975* (revised edition, London 1990), 201–4. Leifer, *ASEAN and Security*, 91. Timothy Carney, 'The Heng Samrin Forces and the Military Balance in Cambodia', in David Ablin and Marlowe Hood (eds) *The Cambodian Agony* (Armonk 1987), 180–207.
52   Evans and Rowley, *Red Brotherhood at War*, 205–8. K.K. Nair, *Words and Bayonets: ASEAN and Indochina* (Selangor 1986), 125–6, 141–50. Leifer, *ASEAN and Security*, 110–13.

back into Cambodia for an uprising after the Vietnamese troops left the country. The KPNLF, however, was crippled by faction fights, with some of its men indulging in robbing and raping refugees. Sihanouk concentrated on a diplomatic offensive much more than a military one.[53]

The diplomatic arena was the area of greatest success for the CDGK and its international supporters. Under Reagan's anti-Soviet crusade, USSR-supported Vietnam became a prime target. Washington swung its diplomatic and financial support of about $5 million per annum behind the two non-communist groups in Cambodia; the financial aid was doubled in 1986. The administration was also accused in the US Congress of secretly channelling funds to the Khmer Rouge, but the charge has not been proved. China was regarded as an ally in the struggle, which included an ASEAN-supported US economic blockade of Vietnam.[54]

However, Beijing's moves to end Sino-Soviet hostility after 1985 bore the most diplomatic fruit. A price asked of the USSR for rapprochement was not only withdrawal of troops from Afghanistan, Mongolia and the Chinese border but also an unconditional Vietnamese withdrawal from Cambodia. Gorbachev initially was unwilling to sacrifice Vietnam, but Beijing was able to make the evacuation of Vietnamese troops from Cambodia a precondition for the summit meeting between Gorbachev and Deng in May 1989. In January that year Hanoi announced that Vietnamese troops would be withdrawn by September. Soviet Foreign Minister Shevardnadze later commented about USSR negotiations with China: 'The key problem was Cambodia . . . From the beginning of our talks with Deng Xiaoping on ways to normalise Soviet-Chinese relations, we invariably stumbled over this issue.'[55]

The USSR, in fact, did not need to place great pressure on Vietnam to withdraw from Cambodia. Confident of its success in gaining control of all the country, apart from the Thai border region, Vietnam had offered in 1985 to pull its troops out of Cambodia by 1990 under a plan of 'national reconciliation'. The CDGK put forward its own reconciliation scheme for a coalition government in Cambodia, but major complications were the proposed relegation of the PRK to a minority of one among four equal partners and, especially, the inclusion of the Khmer Rouge. Khieu Kanhraith, editor of the *Kampuchea Weekly* and a member of the PRK parliament explained that if the Khmer Rouge was given a place in an interim government it 'might then use its position to take up armed struggle to eliminate the other factions'. After the failure of conversations between Sihanouk and the

---

53   Nair, *Words and Bayonets*, 181–5. Evans and Rowley, *Red Brotherhood at War*, 209–23.
54   Evans and Rowley, *Red Brotherhood at War*, 231–3.
55   Ibid., 233–42. Eduard Shevardnadze, *The Future Belongs to Freedom* (New York 1991), 159.

PRK Prime Minister, Hun Sen, in Paris in December 1987 and January 1988, there was a round of low-key shuttle diplomacy between Phnom Penh and ASEAN capitals by the Soviet Union's Igor Rogachev. The result was an agreement by Hanoi in May 1988 to withdraw half of its troops by the end of the year. However, a meeting between all Cambodian parties in Jakarta in July 1988 about terms for an interim government ended in failure. Hanoi, nevertheless, agreed in January 1989 to withdraw all troops, the agreement that set the wheels in motion for the USSR–China summit. Having lost 55,000 soldiers in Cambodia since 1979 and suffering diplomatic and economic isolation, Vietnam was keen for a settlement, but not one that would include Pol Pot's Khmer Rouge. An international conference in Paris in July–August 1989, chaired by Indonesia's Foreign Minister, Ali Alatas, and attended by the four Cambodian parties, Vietnam, the ASEAN countries, the US, the USSR, China and other UN members, failed to reach a settlement. With Vietnamese troops gone, the Khmer Rouge went on the offensive, having pressed refugees into military service. Civil war again broke out in Cambodia, with the Khmer Rouge succoured by a flow of Chinese arms and Vietnam supporting the PRK.[56]

However, in 1990 a diplomatic solution to the Cambodian imbroglio was emerging. Australia, a nation with clean hands in the recent Indochina past, but also bearing a sense of responsibility for its role in the Vietnam War, led the way for a UN-sponsored settlement. The plan was for an interim Cambodian council of twelve representatives without full government powers and containing only two Khmer Rouge members. UN peace-keeping troops would monitor a cease-fire, and there would be national elections employing a secret ballot and on a proportional representative basis. Negotiations in the UN and at a conference in Jakarta in September 1990 produced a peace plan based on the Australian proposal. The US swung its weight behind this move in a belated realization that the PRK was vital to prevent a Khmer Rouge take-over in Cambodia, and the US Congress passed in October $20 million in aid to the Hun Sen government. However, from November 1990 objections from the PRK, supported by Hanoi, about demobilization and other procedures were delaying a settlement of the conflict.[57]

---

56 Evans and Rowley, *Red Brotherhood at War*, 278–98. Khieu Kanhraith, 'What Future for Cambodia?', in Gary Klintworth (ed.), *Vietnam's Withdrawal from Cambodia: Regional Issues and Realignments* (Canberra 1990), 95. Gary Klintworth, *Vietnam's Strategic Outlook* (Canberra 1990), 1–12.

57 Gareth Evans and Bruce Grant, *Australia's Foreign Relations in the World of the 1990s* (2nd edition, Melbourne 1995), 221–34. Justus M. van der Kroef, 'Cambodia in 1990', *Asian Survey*, 31, 1991, 94–102.

The ASEAN states

The Cambodian conflict was a major test for the cohesion of ASEAN and a proving ground for its diplomatic strength. The organization achieved a coup on the world stage by successfully lobbying for and running a UN-sponsored international conference on Cambodia in New York in July 1981. Attended by ninety-two nations, but not by Vietnam, which objected to UN acceptance of Democratic Kampuchea as the representative of Cambodia, the conference called for a cease-fire and UN-organized elections in Cambodia. This resolution provided the imprimatur for ASEAN's opposition to Vietnam's occupation of Cambodia and for its support of the CDGK. ASEAN also kept up a continued dialogue with Vietnam, which elicited no positive response until after the successful Vietnamese offensive in 1984–85.[58]

In its approach to the Cambodian conflict, ASEAN retained a united front even though the interests of its members continued to diverge. Thailand remained the country most concerned about the Vietnamese occupation because of the potential threat to its security, though there is no evidence that Vietnam harboured any expansionist designs on its territory. Singapore, as a small vulnerable state, took a lead in maintaining a hard line against Vietnam because of the view that the war was a proxy one between the USSR and China, and that the Soviet Union was the greater threat with air and naval bases in Vietnam and Vietnamese troops dominating the whole of Indochina. Malaysia preferred a strong Vietnam as a buffer between China and the rest of Southeast Asia but regarded the invasion of Kampuchea as a violation of the principle of territorial sovereignty. The Philippines, facing a communist insurgency in its own backyard, saw a Soviet-backed Vietnam as the major threat to the region. Indonesia continued to be the ASEAN nation most ambivalent about the issue, given its desire to see a strong Vietnam as a bulwark to China. However, Jakarta supported ASEAN initiatives for the sake of regional unity. The leadership Indonesia displayed in seeking a negotiated peace demonstrated its concern to resolve the conflict and encourage the international rehabilitation of Vietnam.[59]

58 Carlyle A. Thayer, 'ASEAN and Indochina: The Dialogue', in Alison Broinowski (ed.), *ASEAN into the 1990s* (New York 1990), 138–61. Leifer, *ASEAN and Security*, chs 4–5. Nair, *Words and Bayonets*, chs 5–6.
59 Nair, *Words and Bayonets*, ch. 8. Clark D. Neher, 'The Foreign Policy of Thailand', in David Wurfel and Bruce Burton (eds), *The Political Economy of Foreign Policy in Southeast Asia* (London 1990), 194–6. Richard Stubbs, 'The Foreign Policy of Malaysia', in ibid., 111–14. Juwono Sudarsno, 'Global Political Trends: An Overview', *Indonesian Quarterly*, 13, 1985, 169–75.

Another of ASEAN's achievements was the maintenance of peaceful relations between its members. Their membership of ASEAN had encouraged cooperation between Malaysia and Thailand in managing border problems, such as a rebel Thai Muslim movement and remnants of the Malaysian Communist Party. At the ASEAN summit meeting in 1976 Marcos formally buried the claim of the Philippines to Sabah, despite some attempts by Filipino congressmen in 1986 to revive it. Disputes between Malaysia and Singapore were not allowed to get out of hand. The Muslim ASEAN nations also supported the Philippines government in its suppression of the Muslim insurgency by the Moro National Liberation Front on the island of Mindanao, which aroused the hostility of Islamic states in the Arab world. Indonesia also had its own reasons to refuse to encourage any Muslim separatist movement in neighbouring countries.[60]

The security of ASEAN was assisted by the military hegemony of the US. The closest US link with an ASEAN state was with the Philippines. When Marcos declared a state of emergency in September 1972, blaming communists for bomb blasts organized by his own henchmen, the US ambassador gave his support. Nixon and Kissinger were diverted by the problems of Vietnam, but Marcos's seizure of dictatorial power was sanctioned by Washington's silence. Marcos's firm anti-communist stance earned him continued US support, though there was haggling over the financial compensation and other details in the late 1970s for continued US leasing of the Clark Air Base and the Subic Naval base in the Philippines. These bases had become more important to the US after North Vietnam's conquest of South Vietnam. Carter was concerned about abuses of human rights in the Philippines but applied little pressure on Marcos lest he be accused of abandoning a staunch ally. Reagan particularly warmed to Marcos, praising him on a state visit to Washington in September 1982 as 'a respected voice of reason and moderation'. This was at a time when underpaid and ill-trained troops were engaging in murder and plunder in the Philippines countryside, which daily added recruits to the communist New People's Army. Reagan's support for Marcos was not even disturbed by the assassination of opposition leader Benigno Aquino, on a return from exile in the US, at Manila airport on 21 August 1983 while under military 'protection'. Reagan even resisted, for a time, information flooding to the US about ballot rigging and fraud in an election that Marcos called in February 1986 to paper over his rapidly diminishing popularity in the Philippines. But, when on 25 February popular support for Benigno Aquino's widow, Corazon (Cory), aided by the desertion

---

60   Stubbs, 'The Foreign Policy of Malaysia', 106–8. David Wurfel, 'Philippine Foreign Policy', in Wurfel and Burton (eds), *Political Economy of Foreign Policy*, 166. David Wurfel, *Filipino Politics: Development and Decay* (Ithaca 1988), 155–65.

of Marcos by his Minister for Defence, Juan Enrile and elements of the military, became irresistible, Washington recognized reality and offered Marcos and Imelda asylum in Hawaii. The Aquino movement had received some assistance from US officials in the Philippines, but many Filipinos were galled to hear Americans claim that the overthrow of Marcos was 'a triumph of Reagan's foreign policy'. A significant background to the Aquino uprising was an economic crisis created by a flight of capital from the country after the assassination of Cory's husband. Other causes were a loss of confidence in the Marcos regime by the World Bank, by the International Monetary Fund (IMF) and foreign investors, plus a world trade slump.[61]

The other ASEAN states retained good relations with the US through the 1980s. Thailand valued continued US economic and military support. The Reagan administration increased financial aid to Thailand from $63 million in 1980 to $133 million in 1983. US military equipment also flowed into Thailand to counter Vietnamese attacks on insurgent border camps in Cambodia. Singapore was prepared to throw out a US diplomat in 1988, who was accused of consorting with opposition members, which followed American criticisms of violations of press freedom in Singapore. However, the expulsion probably had more to do with the government's wish to discredit the political opposition. The incident was a ripple on the surface of basically good relations between a nation which valued American investment and overall military protection and the US, which saw the island state as a valuable anti-communist hub of the Southeast Asian region. Malaysia's relations with the US were closer in the 1980s than previously. With the cutting of defence ties with Britain, Malaysia was buying military supplies from the US and engaged in joint exercises with US forces. Suharto's Indonesia remained firmly allied to the US, with Washington providing military aid in the late 1980s of between $35 million and $50 million a year. The US also turned a blind eye to human rights abuses in Indonesia including continued brutal oppression of irrepressible rebels in East Timor and their Timorese supporters.[62]

---

61 Wurfel, *Filipino Politics*, ch. 10. Stanley Karnow, *In Our Image: America's Empire in the Philippines* (New York 1989), 356–60, 388, 397–400. William E. Berry, Jr, *US Bases in the Philippines: The Evolution of a Special Relationship* (Boulder 1989), chs 4–5. Raymond Bonner, *Waltzing with a Dictator: The Marcoses and the Making of American Foreign Policy* (New York 1987), *passim*. Albert F. Celoza, *Ferdinand Marcos and the Philippines: The Political Economy of Authoritarianism* (Westport 1997), chs 4–6. For the New People's Army see Richard J. Kessler, *Rebellion and Repression in the Philippines* (New Haven 1989).

62 R. Sean Randolph, *The United States and Thailand: Alliance Dynamics, 1950–1985* (Berkeley 1986), 223–31. Linda Y.C. Lim, 'The Foreign Policy of Singapore', in Wurfel and Burton (eds), *The Political Economy of Foreign Policy*, 140. Stubbs, 'The Foreign Policy of Malaysia', 110. Dwight King, 'Indonesia's Foreign Policy', in ibid., 88. John G. Taylor, *Indonesia's Forgotten War: The Hidden History of East Timor* (London 1991), ch. 12. Prof Dr Mubyarto *et al.*, *East Timor: The Impact of Integration: An Indonesian Socio-Anthropological Study* (Northcote, Australia 1991), *passim*.

ASEAN's greater unity in foreign policy in the 1980s was not matched by economic union. Using tariff rates, ranging on average from 25 per cent in Malaysia to 33 per cent in Indonesia, for their own developing economies, the ASEAN states reduced tariffs only in the least threatening areas. Except for Singapore, which was an entrepôt for regional commerce, the complementary nature of the ASEAN economies provided little incentive for freer trade. Even with Singapore's imports that were re-exported, outside the regions, such as refined oil products from Indonesian crude oil, inter-ASEAN trade from 1984 to 1990 hovered around 20 per cent of all ASEAN exports. The end result, however, probably was to the advantage of the economic development of countries which were being called 'Tigercubs'. Despite falling prices for their agricultural and mineral exports, the yearly growth rates in GDP from 1980 to 1990 averaged 7.9 per cent in Thailand, 6.3 per cent Indonesia and 5.9 per cent in Malaysia, but only 1.6 per cent in the Philippines. One prosperous new member also joined ASEAN in February 1984: oil rich Brunei, where in 1985 one in three people owned a motor car, though about 40 per cent of the 249,000 people were less than twenty years of age.[63]

Conclusions

Along the Asian rim of the Pacific Basin there was great strategic change after 1980. By 1990 the Cold War between the US and the USSR was ending; China had restored good relations with the Soviet Union; even the two Koreas were beginning to negotiate with each other. Chinese relations with the US had shown continued improvement and, after the hiatus created by the Tiananmen massacre, were being restored. The Cambodian conflict was on its way to achieving diplomatic resolution because of the new spirit of cooperation between the three superpowers and especially because of Vietnam's desire to break out of economic and diplomatic isolation, though the Khmer Rouge was still a potential threat to a lasting peace in Cambodia. In Southeast Asia ASEAN had emerged as a new diplomatic force and a harbinger of international peace in its region.

The 1980s also saw the continuing spread of the tentacles of Japanese economic supremacy throughout Eastern and Southeastern Asia and into

---

63 Riedel, 'Intra-Asian Trade', 122–36. *FEA*, 1991, 263. Amina Tyabji, 'The Six ASEAN Economies: 1980–88', in Broinowski (ed.), *ASEAN into the 1990s*, 32–57. Srikanta Chatterjee, 'ASEAN Economic Co-operation in the 1980s and 1990s', in ibid., 58–82. Gerald Segal, *Rethinking the Pacific* (Oxford 1990), 357–60. Shinchi Ichimura, *Political Economy of Japanese and Asian Development* (Tokyo 1998), 27.

the wider Pacific Basin. Feeding off increasing flows of Japanese invest-ment, the economies of the four Tigers were booming. However, changes in the Japanese trade balance and the degree of Japanese control over technological transfers portended future trade problems for Japan and for the Tigers. The 1980s also had seen greater trade conflict between the US and Japan as well as American impatience with protectionism in the Tigers. The growth of the other ASEAN economies, with the exception of the Philippines, was creating potential new Tigers, though much of the develop-ment depended on Japanese investment and trade.

CHAPTER EIGHT

Conflicts and Coups in the Islands, 1980–1990

The Pacific Islands, which had been relatively peaceful since 1945, experienced much more internal conflict and international confrontation in the 1980s, which is the main theme of this chapter. It ranges from violent independence movements in New Caledonia, Irian Jaya and Bougainville, violence in Palau and in New Zealand associated with opposition to nuclear weapons and testing, and military coups in Fiji. The chapter also considers the involvement in the islands of the greater Pacific rim powers, including Australia and New Zealand, and reactions by Pacific Islands states.

The coups in Fiji and their consequences

Despite the decline in support for the Fiji National Party in the second 1977 election, racist attitudes among Fijians simmered below the political surface. During the 1982 election campaign the Great Council of Chiefs called for a new constitution that would reserve two-thirds of House of Representatives seats and the offices of Prime Minister and Governor-General for ethnic Fijians. In a racially charged campaign the Alliance Party won a four-seat victory. But its hold on the Fiji government was to disappear in the next election in 1987.[1]

A backdrop to the political change was economic decline in Fiji in the 1980s. Its economy suffered from falls in world commodity prices. The price

---

1 Brij V. Lal, 'The Fiji General Election of 1982', *Journal of Pacific History*, 18, 1983, 134–57. Brij V. Lal, *Boken Waves: A History of the Fiji Islands in the Twentieth Century* (Honolulu 1992), 245–50.

received for Fiji's sugar, which in 1985 earned 65 per cent of export income, fell from F$35.19 per ton in 1980 to F$23.6 in 1985. Consequently, the balance of trade had worsened significantly, with imports worth F$507.993 million compared with a F$271.427 million export income; and the growth rate of gross domestic product had slipped into reverse, to minus 1.5 per cent.[2]

This depressed economic climate encouraged the emergence of the Fiji Labour Party in July 1985 with the backing of trade unions. It was a multi-racial party combining Fijian and Indian workers, some radical Indian intellectuals and young well-educated Fijians. It also attracted Fijian support from the Western region of Viti Levu. In particular the party objected to a wage freeze imposed by the Alliance government in the previous year to cope with the economic problems.[3]

Just before the election in March 1987 the Labour Party formed a coalition with the Indian NFP, a marriage of convenience that succeeded in defeating the government. The Alliance Party suffered from a record low Fijian voter participation of 71 per cent, a reflection of the disillusionment with Ratu Mara's government of many Fijians, who had no wish to vote for an Indian-dominated coalition. The Coalition also increased its Fijian vote from the NFP's 0.8 per cent of Fijian voters in 1982 to 9.6 per cent in 1987. This swing was not dramatic, but was sufficient to provide a twenty-eight to twenty-four seat majority to the Coalition, whose members were nineteen Indians, seven Fijians and two general electors. However, they received 46.2 per cent of the vote compared with Alliance's 48.6 per cent because the Coalition won some seats by small margins, especially in Suva, compared with big Alliance majorities in Fijian rural areas.[4]

Some Fijians started protesting against a government with an Indian majority, despite the fact that the Prime Minister was a Fijian medical doctor, Timoci Bavadra. The Taukei movement, a militant Fijian pressure group, which had emerged in the last week of the election campaign to protest against the prospect of an Indian dominated government, organized mass marches to protest against threats to Fijian rights. Land rights were a major concern of the demonstrators, despite ironclad constitutional protection for Fijian land. Some Taukei leaders openly called for the deportation of all Indians.[5]

---

2   *PIYB*, 16th edition, 91–118.
3   Robert Norton, *Race and Politics in Fiji* (2nd edition, St Lucia 1990), 128–32. Lal, *Fiji Coups*, ch. 12.
4   Lal, *Fiji Coups*, 131–6. Brij V. Lal, *Power and Prejudice: The Making of the Fiji Crisis* (Honolulu 1988), ch. 3.
5   Lal, *Power and Prejudice*, 70–6. Robert T. Robertson and Akosita Tamanisau, *Fiji Shattered Coups* (Sydney 1988), 64–8. Deryck Scarr, *Fiji Politics of Illusion: The Military Coups in Fiji* (Sydney 1988), ch. 11.

Then, on 14 May, a group of armed and masked soldiers marched into the Fiji parliament, announcing, 'This is a take-over'. Their leader, Lieutenant-Colonel Sitiveni Rabuka, the third ranking officer in the Fijian army, ordered Bavadra and all members of his party to leave the chamber, where more soldiers were waiting to pile them into trucks which transported them to temporary detention. The Governor-General, Ratu Sir Penaia Ganilau, refused to sanction the coup. However, Rabuka organized an interim government containing Mara and most other members of the Alliance Cabinet.[6]

The idea of the coup was first discussed at a meeting on 15 April at Epworth House, the headquarters of the Methodist Church in Fiji, between Rabuka and three civilian colleagues from his own province, including Ratu Inoke Kubuabola, an Alliance Party backbencher and a Taukei movement leader. All were alarmed at the result of the election that had been announced on 12 April. They regarded the new Prime Minister, Bavadra, a tool for the Indo-Fijian majority in his party. For the first time, Fiji would be ruled non-Christian Indians. They were worried about the dominance of Indo-Fijians in their community, who not only outnumbered Fijians but also dominated the professions and non-European-owned commerce. Indians had stolen the birthrights of Fijians. Rabuka then started training a hand-picked group of soldiers whose discipline had been sharpened by peacekeeping experience in Lebanon. Their plan covered every conceivable option including the fact that the soldiers entering the parliament were wearing gas masks in case the police, led by an Indo-Fijian, responded with tear gas. Rebuka also shared his plans at a meeting on 20 April, which included Ratu Mara's eldest son and two former Alliance Party ministers. On 10 May Rabuka told Mara about his plan for a military coup, and Rabuka left that meeting with the conviction that he had Mara's support, a final seal of approval. The timing of the coup was also influenced by the absence in Australia of the army commander, Brigadier Epeli Nailatikau, who had declared the army's loyalty to the new government, was absent in Australia.[7]

After the coup, the Taukei movement started a chain of violence on Suva's streets when, on 20 May, its bully-boys punched and kicked Indians at a protest prayer vigil. The intense phase of violence was short-lived, but it instilled widespread fear in the Indian community, as the author discovered when speaking five weeks later with a number of Indians, ranging from a senior public servant to a hotel cook. Furthermore, the almost

---

6   Ibid., chs 17–20. Robertson and Tamanisau, *Fiji: Shattered Coups*, ch. 4. John Sharpham, *Rabuka of Fiji: The Authorized Biography of Major-General Sitiveni Rabuka* (Rockhampton, Qld 2000), 89–92.

7   Sharpham, *Rabuka of Fiji*, 93–109.

entirely ethnically Fijian army began exerting its new found power with a series of arbitrary arrests of political opponents, foreign journalists and anybody else deemed to be acting suspiciously. The only person killed, however, was an Indian whose car was blown up by a bomb he was conveying.[8]

The coup had devastating economic effects. Australian and New Zealand unions placed black bans on ships travelling to Fiji, and numerous Indians with professional and other skilled qualifications fled the country. New foreign investment dried up. Tourism, one of the mainstays of Fiji's economy, collapsed. The author had the unique experience of being the only visitor on the last Saturday morning in June to Coral Gardens, a major tourist attraction, which was closed down when he travelled back to Suva with the Fijian manager, who spoke of his opposition to the coup.[9]

The Indian community also tried to use economic pressure against the military regime. Indian sugar cane farmers maintained a two month long harvest strike. But economic realities and army coercion, including threats of sequestration of property, drove them back to work.[10]

The military regime was not concerned about the economic consequences of the coup. The army became a *de facto* unemployment relief agency for Fijians as it grew from about 2,500 troops to close to 5,000. Other unemployed youths became useful street thugs for the Taukei movement. Some Taukei leaders even welcomed publicly the prospect of economic collapse as a means to revive traditional village life, reflecting a reactionary communalism which motivated many Taukei supporters.[11]

Governor General Ganilau worked hard for a compromise solution, and church leaders were prominent in trying to restore constitutional government. Indeed, Ganilau reached an agreement by September 1987 between the members of the Coalition and the Alliance Party, for a united caretaker government until new elections could be held.[12]

Such a solution was not what Rabuka or his Taukei supporters were seeking. On Friday 25 September soldiers stormed into radio and newspaper officers and seized public buildings in a well-organized second coup. When Ganilau protested, Rabuka declared Fiji a republic.[13]

The second coup showed lines of division among Fiji's chiefs. Some, such as Mara and Ganilau, were prepared to compromise with the Coalition,

---

8   Robertson and Tamanisau, *Fiji: Shattered Coups*, 123–5.
9   Ibid., 172–9.
10 Scarr, *Politics of Illusion*, ch. 22
11 Lal, *Power and Prejudice*, ch. 7.
12 Scarr, *Politics of Illusion*, ch. 29. *Fiji Times*, 27 June 1987.
13 Lal, *Power and Prejudice*, ch. 8. Sharpham, *Rabuka of Fiji*, 128–32.

but others involved with the Taukei movement were insisting on entrenching Fijian control. A strong influence on the latter group was religious fundamentalism, which had been growing within the Methodist religion, which was dominant among Fijians. Indeed, after the coup the Methodist Church became divided between the fundamentalists who supported Rabuka and broader church people. The influence of this religious fundamentalism was indicated in one of Rabuka's early edicts after the second coup. On 25 September 1987 all work, sport and public transport on Sundays were banned, a rigid sabbatarianism that even forced people who did not own cars to walk to church. The claim was that this law would help to establish a more religious and faithful community, but its effect was socially divisive. Those arrested for breaking the Sunday observance laws often received rough treatment, including a group of seventeen children between the ages of five and twelve who were stripped and beaten until they could no longer stand up. When the Sunday law was lifted in November 1988 on the return of a civilian government led by Mara, Methodist militants set up Sunday roadblocks and were arbitrarily released by Rabuka after they had been arrested. The opposition of some church leaders to the militants caused a split in the Methodist Church that reflected divisions in the Fijian community since the second coup.[14]

By 1989 Fiji's economy was recovering from the effects of the coups, assisted by the granting of tax concessions to foreign investors and by the revival of the tourist trade. A decline of 6.3 per cent in gross domestic product in 1987 became a growth rate of 12.6 per cent in 1989. However, suppression of trade unionists and sweat-shop working conditions were features of the new economic order, and there had been a flight of many well-qualified Indo-Fijians, though that had restored Fijians to a majority in the population.[15]

The first coup in Fiji received wider world condemnation. Australia and New Zealand denounced it vehemently as a blow to democratic values. The anger of the Australian and New Zealand Prime Ministers was sharpened by the overthrow of a government led by a fellow Labour Party premier. Governments in Canberra and Wellington had been taken completely by surprise. People in the Australian Department of Foreign Affairs

---

14 Michael C. Howard, 'State Power and Political Change in Fiji', *Journal of Contemporary Asia*, 21, 1991, 99–100. John Garrett, 'Uncertain Sequel: the Social and Religious Scene in Fiji since the Coups', *The Contemporary Pacific*, 2, 1990, 100–4. Sharpham, *Rabuka of Fiji*, 143.

15 *FEA*, 1991, 763. Satendra Prasad, 'Tax Free Zones and National Development'; Wadam Nasey, 'Privatization and the Poor', in Satendra Prasad (ed.), *Coup and Crisis: Fiji – A Year Later* (Melbourne 1988), chs 6–7. Shireen Lateef, 'Current and Future Implications of the Coups for Women in Fiji', *The Contemporary Pacific*, 2, 1990, 113–19.

'ran round like headless chooks', said one of them to the author. The Australian Prime Minister, 'Bob' Hawke, claimed that a couple of his senior ministers suggested using a naval helicopter 'to pluck' Bavadra to safety but that this idea was scotched by the Chief of the General Staff. Australian troops were flown to join Australian naval ships just outside Fiji's territorial waters in preparedness to rescue Australians and other expatriate citizens from Fiji. But they were under no threat. However, Australia and New Zealand suspended all military and some economic aid to Fiji.[16]

Australia and New Zealand were criticized by the Melanesian group in the South Pacific Forum for not consulting with other Pacific Islands states. The Melanesian states, whose premiers sympathized with the desire of their fellow Melanesians in Fiji to protect their interests, achieved the addition of the words 'recognizing the complexity of the problems' to the resolution expressing 'deep concern and anguish' about Fiji passed by the May 1987 meeting of the South Pacific Forum. There was little support in the forum for the diplomatic attempts by Australia and New Zealand to ensure a return to constitutional rule in Fiji.[17]

After the second coup, Australia and New Zealand further reduced economic aid to Fiji and refused to recognize the Republic of Fiji. However, France started fishing in the troubled waters, offering AUS$16 million in aid, which was eagerly accepted by Rabuka's regime. The prospect of France's supplanting Australia as the provider of most aid and as the main trading partner of Fiji encouraged Canberra to recognize the new Fiji state and restore economic, but not military, aid.[18]

Papua New Guinea (PNG)

PNG faced its own violent problems during the 1980s. On its western border the OPM guerrillas in Irian Jaya were still active. In 1984, as the result of a wave of Indonesian oppression, some 11,000 refugees crossed the border into New Guinea. Though the PNG government insisted that most were local people who traditionally wandered back and forth across the arbitrary boundary line drawn up in colonial days, many of them were

---

16 Roger C. Thompson, *Australia and the Pacific Islands in the Twentieth Century* (Melbourne 1998), 210–12. Bob Hawke, *The Hawke Memoirs* (Melbourne 1994), 329.
17 Roderic Alley, 'The 1987 Military Coups in Fiji: The Regional Implications', *The Contemporary Pacific*, 2, 1990, 37–46.
18 Ibid., 46–56. Stephen Henningham, *France and the South Pacific: A Contemporary History* (Sydney 1992), 216–17.

genuine political refugees. However, there was great resistance from Port Moresby to call for UN assistance, a mark of the government's concern to appease Indonesia. Only reluctantly, after protests from churches and non-government aid agencies about deaths and disease in the refugee camps, was the UN High Commissioner for Refugees allowed to distribute aid to the people there. The government's policy had been influenced by the diplomatic necessity of a country with a small population facing a very populous neighbour with an aggressive reputation. The policy was certainly not in response to public opinion, as the author discovered in 1984 when he raised the question with a large class of first year students at the University of PNG. They unanimously supported their Melanesian cousins in Irian Jaya and expressed vociferous dislike of Indonesia. The PNG government of that time, led by Michael Somare, did protest about Indonesian hot pursuit of OPM guerrillas across the border and was reluctant to send any refugees back. But when a split in the Pangu Parti resulted in a change of government led by Pius Wingti, a former Pangu member of a highlands constituency, Port Moresby became more accommodating to Indonesia. A friendship treaty was signed with Indonesia in 1986, and the PNG army was instructed to cooperate with Indonesian troops in apprehending OPM guerrillas. In 1990 that resistance movement was still active in Irian Jaya, though many of its warriors were armed only with bows and arrows.[19]

The PNG government also faced a rebellion on its own islands of Buka and Bougainville. Despite the concessions of higher copper mining royalties and a provincial government, popular resentment at the much larger profits being derived from the Panguna copper mine by the central government and by the Australia-based mining company, Bougainville Copper, was bubbling away under a surface tranquillity in the islands.

The company had made efforts to conciliate the islanders by employing the American anthropologist, Douglas Oliver, from 1968 to 1979 to advise on how 'to shield Bougainvillians as much as possible from the harms that inevitably accompany such mining'. But neither he nor the company could stop the inevitable impact of the money that was generated for the provincial government, for Bougainvillians who worked at the mine and for landowners in a former sleepy, economically backward and non-Westernized

---

19 Personal knowledge (the author participated in the church pressure on the PNG Government). R.J. May, 'East of the Border' and Alan Smith and Kevin Hewison, '1984: Refugees, "Holiday Camps" and Deaths', in R.J. May (ed.), *Between Two Nations The Indonesian–Papua New Guinea Border and West Papua Nationalism* (Bathurst, NSW 1986), 100–59, 200–17. Beverley Blaskett and Loong Wong, 'Papua New Guinea Under Wingti: Accommodating Indonesia', *Australian Outlook*, 43, 1989, 44–60. 'Rebels of a Forgotten World', Australian Broadcasting Corporation (ABC) television program, 15 March 1992.

cultural society. The result was increased islander demands, not for the tinned food, knives and tobacco that were prized in pre-mine days, but now for refrigerators, video players and automobiles. Western education combined with the cargo cult flavour of traditional islander thinking contributed to such aspirations. The growing population also was placing pressures on land-use, which provoked anger about the area being appropriated by the ever-growing open pit and slag-heaps of the mine. Furthermore, the company failed to check river pollution, which was believed by islanders to cause crop failure and human sickness. The islander clergy of the dominant Catholic Church supported Bougainvillian complaints about the copper mine. Fundamentally, the problem that had encouraged earlier moves for secession remained: the cultural and racial divisions between black Buka-Bougainvillians and brown-skinned Papua New Guineans. The sense of being 'Bougainvillian' had grown with improvements in transport facilities and geographical mobility provided by education, resulting in intermingling of islanders previously living in isolated small hamlets. The presence of 'red-skin' Papua New Guineans as employees at the mine, many holding higher paid jobs than Bougainvillians, was an additional resentment.[20]

There were also political developments encouraging opposition to the mine. Bougainville had been a neglected area for economic development and, despite the revenue generated by the mine for the central and provincial governments, not enough money was being spent in the eyes of many Bougainvillians to improve roads, the distribution of electric power and other improvements. This political discontent was exploited by the Melanesian Alliance led by a Catholic priest, Father John Momis, who actually disliked the rush for Westernized development in PNG and had long opposed the copper mine. A result was the election of Joseph Kabui as provincial premier. His electorate covered the mine area and he had been an industrial relations officer for the Bougainville Mining Workers' Union, but he was no friend of the company. In the 1987 national election Momis pushed 'the Bougainville Initiative', which demanded a 3 per cent royalty from the gross income of the mine to the North Solomons provincial government. The company, bound by an agreement with the PNG government, was unable to comply. Into this confrontation stepped Francis Ona, a neighbour of Kabui, who started dynamiting mining company property. Described by one of his teachers as an unknowable mystic, Ona worked at the company as a mine-pit surveyor and haul-truck operator from 1973 until he resigned in 1988. He now demanded the closing of the mine and

---

20   Douglas Oliver, *Black Islanders: A Personal Perspective on Bougainville* (Melbourne 1991), xi–xviii, 199–200.

ten billion kina from the mining company as compensation for environmental damage. He obviously knew they were impossible demands for the company to meet, because his ultimate aim, as expressed in a letter to the landowners' association, was to 'break away from PNG'.[21]

Such demands were a recipe for confrontation. Four hundred police were sent to Bougainville to stop the sabotage and to arrest Ona and his companions, without success. Charges of police brutality, such as house burnings, looting and rape started to spread among Bougainvillians and whipped up hostility towards the PNG government. It offered to raise payments to the landowners and to the provincial government in a peace package. However, continued acts of sabotage against the mine, especially destruction of electricity transmission lines and attacks on personnel, caused it to cease operations in May 1989 and to close permanently in September. The mood of Ona and his followers was clearly indicated on 11 September, two days before an agreement to implement the peace plan was signed by the provincial government, when the minister who had led the peace initiative, John Bika, was assassinated. The militants also gained the services of some military trained Bougainvillians, especially Sam Kauona, who had been trained in jungle warfare in Australia and became the commander of the Bougainville Revolutionary Army (BRA). Using guerrilla warfare tactics and armed with weapons preserved since the Second World War and captured from their opponents, the BRA was too elusive for a PNG force that had grown to 500 soldiers and 200 police by July 1989. In the mountainous jungle of Bougainville it proved impossible for the nation's army, which was only 3,350 strong in 1989, to defeat the BRA in a bloody struggle, in which atrocities against the local population were committed by both sides. Indeed, the brutality of PNG soldiers further alienated Buka-Bougainvillians who gave the BRA widespread support.[22]

To give into the BRA's secessionist demand was considered impossible by Port Moresby because of the potential domino effect on other regions in the culturally and linguistically diverse country – although Buka-Bougainvillians were a more distinct group in the nation than any other region. Indonesia also was pressing PNG to maintain control of the island because of Jakarta's constant fear of secessions within its own nation. Likewise other Pacific Island states were supporting PNG – even the Solomon Islands government, where there was public sympathy for the BRA, particularly in the ethnically related Western Islands.

---

21   Information from Dr Garry Trompf, Sydney. Ona to members of the Panguna Landowners' Association n.d. [1989] in Peter Polomka (ed.), *Bougainville: Perspectives on a Crisis* (Canberra 1990), 7. Oliver, *Black Islanders*, ch. 10.
22   Oliver, *Black Islanders*, ch. 11.

The government in Port Moresby launched on 12 January 1990 a final unsuccessful military campaign, 'Operation Footloose', to conquer the island. Its failure prompted a cease-fire agreement with the BRA on 28 February and evacuation of PNG military and special police forces from Buka and Bougainville. An international observation team led by a Ghanian diplomat was assembled hastily to supervise the agreement. This was a major victory to the BRA in achieving official recognition and the withdrawal of PNG forces. Disenchanted with the agreement, the government controller of the state of emergency on Bougainville, Police Commissioner Paul Tohian, withdrew all police and prison guards, allowing the BRA to take *de facto* control. It declared the independence of Buka and Bougainville on 17 May 1990.[23]

Port Moresby's response was to withdraw all government services and to impose an economic blockade, resulting in major economic dislocation on Buka and Bougainville. While traditional bush gardening maintained basic food resources, the drying up of medical supplies led to a dramatic rise in infant mortality and other deaths estimated to number more than 2,000 above the normal death rate by the end of the year. But one member of the Port Moresby government, Bernard Narakobi, was maintaining radio contact with Kabui, the Minister for Justice in the BRA government. Consequently, a peace initiative was launched from 29 July to 5 August 1990, assisted by the government of New Zealand, which supplied two frigates supporting its supply ship, *Endeavour*, as a neutral meeting ground for representatives of the BRA and the Port Moresby government. They agreed to an accord that would restore PNG government services to Bougainville and postpone the political issue to a later meeting. But significantly Ona was not present at the talks, and some members of the Port Moresby government led by the Defence Minister Ted Diro, opposed it. After one consignment of medical aid was landed from the *Endeavour*, further assistance was rejected by the BRA when, in breach of the spirit of the accord, PNG troops landed on Buka in response to requests from the local people. With further fighting between BRA guerrillas and government soldiers, PNG troops had established by the end of 1990 tenuous control of Buka and an enclave on the northern coast of Bougainville.[24]

The Australian government supported Port Moresby's attempts to suppress the rebellion. This was not primarily because Bougainville Copper

---

23 Terence Wesley-Smith, 'Papua New Guinea' in 'Political Review–Melanesia', *The Contemporary Pacific*, 2, 1991, 407–9.
24 Ibid., 409–10. Oliver, *Black Islanders*, chs 12–13. Yaw Saffu, 'The Bougainville Crisis and Politics in Papua New Guinea', *The Contemporary Pacific*, 4, 1992, 325–43.

was Australian. Canberra was concerned to maintain the political stability of PNG as a traditional defence shield for Australia. Revenue from the mine also reduced the high degree of Australian financial support for the budget of its former colony which, though it had decreased since independence, was still 19 per cent of total revenue in 1989. The most tangible Australian military support was provision of four helicopters, ostensibly for transport purposes only, but used as gunships by PNG forces.[25]

The Bougainville crisis increased economic and political instability in PNG. The Panguna mine had been contributing 45 per cent of the country's exports and 17 per cent of its national revenue. After increasing by 4.8 per cent in 1988, PNG's GDP declined by 3 per cent in 1989. Resulting government austerity measures increased internal disorder in a country with a rising crime rate. There was a failed coup in March 1990 led by Police Commissioner Tohian, smarting from his reprimand for exceeding government instructions on Bougainville.[26]

New Caledonia

The return of the Socialist Party to power in France in May 1981, for the first time since 1958, provided a more concerted French attempt to reach an accord with the Kanak community in New Caledonia. However, though party spokesmen acknowledged past injustices and the desirability of eventual independence, the Socialist government under President François Mitterrand did not abandon France's middle-power pretensions. So the CEP was retained, and a worldwide chain of small departments and territories, including New Caledonia, continued under French rule. Furthermore, there was an appreciation in Paris that a majority of people in New Caledonia were not supporting independence and that some of them were violently opposed to it. Indeed, in September 1981 the UC Secretary-General, Pierre Declercq, a French-born former schoolteacher, was murdered. This first political assassination in the South Pacific provoked Kanak roadblocks, shots fired at European farmhouses, killing of cattle and rioting in Noumea.[27]

The French government, however, was still determined to implement a reform program in New Caledonia. In December 1981 a prominent Socialist

---

25 Saffu, 'The Bougainville Crisis', 124, 230–1. *FEA*, 1991, 812.
26 James Griffin, 'The Papua New Guinea Elections of 1987', *Journal of Pacific History*, 23, 1988, 106–16. Wesley-Smith, 'Papua New Guinea', 411–14.
27 Henningham, *France and the South Pacific*, 71–2. Robert Aldrich, *France and the South Pacific Since 1940* (London 1993), ch. 7. John Connell, *New Caledonia or Kanaky? The Political History of a French Colony* (Canberra 1987), 286–95.

politician, Christian Nucci, arrived in Noumea as High Commissioner. Three new administrative offices were established to acquire land for Kanaks, to implement economic development for the interior and the Loyalty Islands, and to foster and preserve traditional Melanesian culture. Tjibaou was made director of the cultural office. Furthermore, provision was made for advisors experienced in customary Kanak law to be present in court proceedings involving Kanaks. The Socialist government attempted further to promote moderate political groups in New Caledonia at the expense of extremists on both sides. For a time this strategy worked. In June 1982 the FNSC broke with the RPCR and helped the FI to pass controversial tax legislation. The FI consequently achieved a majority in the government council, headed by the front's leader, Tjibaou. However, in the embittered racial climate right-wing elements reacted with violence to this Kanak majority government, such as an invasion of the Assembly by sixty masked men wielding clubs and assaulting FI and FNSC members. Riot police, tear gas and gaol sentences were necessary to quell such disturbances, though there were continuing brawls between Europeans and Melanesians. The land reform program was a particular object of European anger, and Kanak counter violence grew during 1983. Two gendarmes were killed in a violent struggle over a Kanak blockade of a saw mill, and the post office and five houses in the west coast village of Temala were fire bombed in revenge for the death of a young Kanak.[28]

This poisonous racial climate destroyed the French socialist government's attempt to reach an agreement between Europeans and Kanaks about the territory's future. At a conference of representatives of the main New Caledonian political parties in Paris in July 1983, Secretary of State Georges Lemoine recognized the Kanaks' innate right to independence, but he also acknowledged the right of Europeans to live in New Caledonia. However, the RPCR delegation refused to sign such a statement, and radical Kanaks had reservations. Nevertheless, the French government implemented the Lemoine statute, which called for new elections in 1984, more internal autonomy and a referendum on independence in 1989. The RPCR and other right-wing groups denounced the concessions to the FI, whereas it demanded an earlier referendum date and restrictions on the franchise to people with at least one parent born in New Caledonia.[29]

To place pressure on the French government, the FI re-formed itself in September 1984 into the *Front de Libération Nationale, Kanak et Socialiste*

---

28 Connell, *New Caledonia or Kanaky?*, 286–95, 299–307. Henningham, *France and the South Pacific*, 72–4.

29 Henningham, *France and the South Pacific*, 74–6. Connell, *New Caledonia or Kanaky?*, 306–20.

(FLNKS). The name expressed the front's major aims: to liberate Kanaks from capitalist and colonialist exploitation in a socialist republic in which only second generation Europeans would have the right to vote. To express its rejection of the Lemoine statute, the FLNKS boycotted the November 1984 assembly election, using roadblocks and other pressure to stop Kanaks from voting. However, some Kanaks voted, though only 50 per cent of the whole electorate participated compared with the normal 70 to 80 per cent. After the election Kanak militants in some districts maintained the road-blocks and kept European settlers, including the whole town of Thio, under siege. The FLNKS strategy was to use violence against property rather than people, though the distinction was not always practised. A typical right-wing misrepresentation of the situation was a comment by a visiting *Le Figaro* journalist, who lamented that 40,000 whites in New Caledonia were 'at the mercy of a handful of savages who are ready for a massacre'.[30]

The French government sought negotiation to resolve the escalating conflict. Edgard Pisani, a socialist deputy in the EEC Parliament, arrived as a new High Commissioner and made an agreement on 5 December with Tjibaou for the lifting of the blockades. But that evening, two of Tjibaou's brothers and eight other Kanaks returning from a UC meeting, which agreed to the peace proposal, to their village in the Hienghene district on the east coast were ambushed and massacred by local mixed-race farmers, who feared Kanak claims on their land. Tjibaou demonstrated his states-manship by continuing to support the peace agreement. Pisani responded with a plan that sought to reconcile Kanak and European interests by promising a referendum in July 1985, which would offer a choice between the status quo and 'independence in association' with France. Under the latter choice people could become citizens of the new nation or retain French nationality, non-Kanak land would become lease-hold with rents to traditional Kanak owners, special provisions would be made for Noumea, and France would provide for defence and support the territorial budget.

The main problem with the Pisani Plan was that it was too late. Though FLNKS leaders were willing to consider it, some members, embittered by the violent conflict, denounced it as neo-colonialist. The RPCR and its conservative allies condemned the plan out of hand, though agreeing to support the referendum if there was no change to the existing franchise, which allowed all French citizens to vote, no matter how recently they had arrived in New Caledonia. A peaceful implementation of the plan was

---

30 Connell, *New Caledonia or Kanaky?*, 321–34 (quotation, 332). Aliane Chanter, 'The Media and Politics in New Caledonia in the 1980s', *Journal of Pacific History*, 26, 1991, 316–19. Henningham, *France and the South Pacific*, 82–4.

shattered in January 1985 when one of the FLNKS militants, Eloi Machoro, took a band of armed supporters to settle a score with a right-wing opponent, Roger Galliot, which led to the killing of one of his relatives. In protest at this murder, European opponents of independence rioted in Noumea's streets, firebombing buildings owned by FLNKS supporters. The violence ended only with the news that Machoro and his wife had been killed by police sniper fire. Leading the European militancy were French immigrants, especially ex-army officers. An influx of French troops reduced, but did not eliminate, further violence. Despite the collapse of Pisani's compromise plan, the socialist French Prime Minister, Laurent Fabius, went ahead with another scheme for the election of four regional councils, which would have significant local powers including economic development. The independence referendum was postponed until 1987. With only one of the new regions embracing Noumea, the FLNKS won control of the other three, with less than 40 per cent of the total vote.[31]

This partial Kanak victory in New Caledonia collapsed with the defeat of the French Socialist Party in the parliamentary election of March 1986. The new Prime Minister, Jacques Chirac, leader of the neo-Gaullist *Rassemblement Pour La République*, had visited New Caledonia in 1978 when he made contact with the newly formed RPCR. Since then he had cooperated closely with the RPCR leader, the millionaire Jacques Lafleur, who gave donations to Chirac's party and was one of the two New Caledonian members of the French parliament. Unsurprisingly, Chirac and his Minister for Overseas Territories, Bernard Pons, moved to weaken the power of the FLNKS. The Pons statute reduced the powers of the regional councils and rearranged boundaries to give Europeans control over the west coast. The land reform office was merged with the development office and purchases of properties for Kanaks ceased. More funds were spent in loyalist regions than in FLNKS strongholds. A government propaganda campaign denounced the FLNKS as terrorists who represented only a small minority of Kanaks. Chirac honoured the referendum proposal of the Fabius Plan, but prescribed only three years' residence in New Caledonia as the voting qualification, which effectively ensured an anti-independence majority. Appreciating this reality, the FLNKS called for a boycott of the vote, though the presence of over 8,000 French troops and riot police prevented most of the methods employed in 1984. This time 59 per cent of the electorate voted, with only 2 per cent supporting independence; but more than 70 per cent of Kanaks,

---

31 Henningham, *France and the South Pacific*, 84–90. Connell, *New Caledonia or Kanaky*, 335–68. Frédéric Bobin, 'Caldoches, Metropolitans and the Mother Country', *Journal of Pacific History*, 26, 1991, 310–11.

who formed 43 per cent of the 1983 population, refused to vote. This referendum showed the continuing political polarization in New Caledonia.[32]

In early 1988 violence escalated in New Caledonia. Despite the dispersion of soldiers across the islands, Kanaks employed local knowledge to erect road barricades, to kill one of the perpetrators of the Hienghene massacre, and to harass other opponents of independence. The most serious foray occurred on the almost entirely Kanak populated island of Ouvéa, one of the Loyalty Islands. On 22 April, two days before the first round vote in the French presidential election, a group of armed Kanaks raided the local gendarmerie, killing four gendarmes and transferring twenty-six French hostages to a cave hidden in the mountainous northern section of the island. The captors demanded the revocation of the Pons statute, the cancellation of regional elections, which were to be held in conjunction with the French election, and the withdrawal of all French military forces from the territory. Tjibaou, who had been involved in the planning of this local FLNKS action, declared that the violence on Ouvéa was the consequence 'of the partisan, cynical and despicable policy of the RPCR', which had introduced firearms and Wallis Islander thugs to attack pro-independence Ovéans. The Kanak militants, however, released some of hostages, who guided army special forces to the location. It was successfully raided two days before the second round of votes in the French presidential election. Twenty-three hostages were released unharmed, nineteen Kanak militants were killed, some after they were taken prisoner, at the expense of two dead French soldiers. There is little doubt that Chirac ordered the raid in the hope that a decisive victory over Kanak 'terrorists' would assist him in the election against President Mitterrand. However, he won easily.[33]

The socialists also regained control of the French parliament. Once more a change of government in Paris had a major influence on French policies in New Caledonia. The new socialist prime minister, Michel Rocard, sought an accord to break the cycle of violence. Such was the concern in New Caledonia about the way the colony was lurching towards civil war that he received agreement to participate in talks in Paris from the FLNKS and from loyalist political groups. Exceptions were the extreme right *Front Calédonien* and the *Front National*, whose leader, Guy George, declared: 'In New Caledonia our roots have been irrigated with the blood of our dead . . . and we will not let the FLNKS pull them out.'[34] The result was the Matignon

---

32   Henningham, *France and the South Pacific*, 98–103. Jean Guiart, 'A Drama of Ambiguity: Ouva 1988–89', *Journal of Pacific History*, 32, 1997, 85–102. John Connell, *New Caledonia: The Matignon Accord and the Colonial Future* (Sydney 1988), 9–13.

33   Connell, *New Caledonia*, 13–15.

34   Quoted in ibid., 17.

accord, signed on 26 June 1988 by Lafleur on behalf of the RPCR and by Tjibaou for the FLNKS. This momentous agreement repealed the Pons statute. It placed New Caledonia under direct French rule for a year until new elections for three regions, consisting of the northern and southern portions of the main island and the Loyalty Islands. A referendum was promised in 1998 on a franchise restricted to those living in New Caledonia ten years earlier. Rocard also pledged massive financial assistance to the underdeveloped northern and Loyalty Islands regions, in which the Kanak population was respectively 74 and 98 per cent.

The Matignon accord met with widespread approval in New Caledonia except from extremists on both sides. In November 1988 the accord received an 80 per cent affirmative vote in a referendum in France, though only 37 per cent of the population voted. In New Caledonia the affirmative vote was 57 per cent of the 64 per cent who voted, which reflected extremist dissension. In May 1989 a frustrated militant in Ouvéa, Jubli Wea, assassinated Tjibaou and his deputy, who had provoked Ouvéan anger for distancing themselves from the island during the hostage crisis. This left a leadership gap in the FLNKS, which was not filled until March 1990 when Paul Néaoutyine, the PALIKA leader, was elected as president. The 1989 regional elections displayed broad acceptance of the accord with the RPCR winning power easily in the southern region and the FLNKS in the other two. Assisting this development was a new moderation displayed by the major New Caledonian newspaper, *Les Nouvelles Calédoniennes*, under new French ownership, and by Radio France Outremer.[35]

French Polynesia

There was no violent independence movement in French Polynesia in the 1980s. The conservative, *Tahoeraa Huiraatira* (Rally for the People) Party, which received 30 per cent of the vote in the 1982 election, had switched in 1980 to support for autonomy under French rule, a policy supported by its leader, a part-European former school teacher, Gaston Flosse. Therefore the *Tahoeraa* party, which assumed government in 1982 with the support of independents, welcomed the offer in 1983 of an increase in local autonomy by the French socialist government. However the autonomy statute retained French control over economic, immigration, defence and foreign policy.

---

35 Henningham, *France and the South Pacific*, 105–16. Guiart, 'A Drama of Ambiguity', 99–102. Chanter, 'The Media', 313–39.

Many Polynesians in the territory were happy with restricted self-government and continued economic benefits flowing from the CEP. Flosse's party was able to increase its vote to 40 per cent in the 1986 election, and, with the help of weighted electorates in the outer islands, gained twenty-two of the forty-one seats in the legislature. Chirac enhanced Flosse's prestige in 1986 by making him minister for the South Pacific, the first such devolution of political responsibility in French imperial history. However, allegations started circulating about corruption in his government which, though not unusual in a society with strong family ties and personal patronage, appeared to be on a large scale.

The *Tahoeraa* party also ran into trouble in October 1987 when striking dock workers, protesting at labour reductions and at the intervention against peaceful pickets by riot police sent from France, went on a rampage in central Papeete, causing widespread looting and destruction. Flosse, in Paris at the time, returned to a split in the party. Defectors objected to Flosse's authoritarian style and the use by the government of metropolitan police in the dock strike. A new governing coalition included the three members of the socialist pro-independence *Ia Mana* party.[36]

The dock strike riot in 1987 was a reflection of declining economic and social conditions in French Polynesia in the late 1980s. Unemployed youths gave muscle to the rioters. There were also wide gaps in personal income. Polynesians, many of them seduced from traditional village life by the allure of Western culture, formed the least-advantaged class. Nevertheless, French spending by the 1980s was double that in New Caledonia, despite the fact that New Caledonia's 1989 population of 188,814 was only 24,641 greater than in French Polynesia. The CEP was a major reason for the difference, and it contributed to a higher GNP per head in French Polynesia than in New Zealand. The result was that the *Tahoeraa* party, though expressing moral opposition to atomic weapons, supported the CEP as vital for French Polynesia's economy. Only the small *Ia Mana* and *Tavini Huiraatira No Te Ao Maohi* parties were staunchly opposed to the CEP and were advocates of independence. In 1986 they gained only 15 per cent of the vote and five seats. However, personality and parochial factors influenced elections, and territory-wide support depended on more financial resources than the pro-independence parties possessed. Also the main Protestant church, the Evangelical Church of French Polynesia, which attracts the allegiance of half of the territory's population, was urging 'an end to the nuclear tests'

---

36 Henningham, *France and the South Pacific*, 140–1, 148–55, 242. Aldrich, *France in the South Pacific*, 285–94. Karin von Strokirch, 'The Impact of Nuclear Testing on Politics in French Polynesia', *Journal of Pacific History*, 26, 1991, 330–2.

and was promoting the rights of the Maohi people. A proposal to integrate French Polynesia with the EEC aroused popular fears of being swamped by European immigrants, which caused a 90 per cent boycott of the European Parliament election in the territory in June 1990.[37]

Other Pacific nations and the French presence in the Pacific

The CEP aroused widespread opposition from French Polynesia's Pacific neighbours in the 1980s. The election of Labour Party governments in Australia in 1983 and in New Zealand in 1984 increased the vehemence of those countries' opposition to French nuclear tests. These governments were unimpressed by the French claim that the tests contributed to nuclear deterrence in Europe and argued that if underground testing was as safe at Moruroa as Paris has claimed, it could be conducted in France. Particularly galling to those Pacific nations has been France's rejection of an offer by the US government to use its nuclear testing facilities in Nevada. The CEP had become a symbol of French military independence.[38]

New Zealand's relations with France nose-dived after the sinking in Auckland harbour, on 10 July 1985, of the *Rainbow Warrior*. That Greenpeace ship, which was on its way to monitor nuclear testing at Moruroa, was ripped apart by two explosions, which killed its Spanish photographer. An anti-French furore broke out in New Zealand with the arrest of two French agents, Alain Mafart and Dominique Prieur, who were convicted and jailed for planting the bombs. The French government retaliated with commercial pressure against New Zealand exports of wool to France and of lamb to New Caledonia and threatened to pressure the EEC to reduce the quota for New Zealand butter. New Zealand, which depended on an increasingly vulnerable agricultural economy, was forced to accept a deal of US$7 million compensation and the release of Mafart and Prieur to serve detention for three years on Hao Atoll in French Polynesia. But within two years the Chirac government brought the two agents back to France to resume military

---

37   von Strokirch, 'The Impact of Nuclear Testing', 332–46. 'Memorandum of the 1986 Synod of the Evangelical Church in French Polynesia', *Pacific Conference of Churches News*, January 1987, 4. Bruno Saura, 'The Tahitian Churches and the Problem of the French Presence in 1991', *Journal of Pacific History*, 26, 1991, 347–57. Henningham, *France and the South Pacific*, 158–62.

38   Henningham, *France and the South Pacific*, 169–70, 223. Stewart Firth, *Nuclear Playground* (Sydney 1987), 116–19.

duties. New Zealand took this broken agreement to international arbitration and received a favourable judgement in April 1990. France was directed to pay a further US$2 million to New Zealand citizens, which France honoured.[39]

Australian relations with France declined also when Hawke criticized the Chirac government's confrontationist policies in New Caledonia, though not supporting the Kanak independence movement. The Australian consul in Noumea was expelled. Relations between the two countries remained at a low ebb until the advent of the Rocard Socialist government, which promoted mutual prime ministerial visits between France and Australia in 1989. Rocard also repaired French relations with New Zealand with a public apology for the *Rainbow Warrior* affair. The ironical sequel was France's permission for *Rainbow Warrior II* to carry out the snooping in French Polynesia that France had sought to end with the bombing of its predecessor.[40]

Australasia and the US

New Zealand also was involved in diplomatic conflict with the US in the 1980s. In 1984 the New Zealand Labour Party won office with a platform including opposition to visits of nuclear-armed ships to New Zealand. Effectively this policy banned US warships from New Zealand since the US policy was 'neither to confirm nor to deny' the nuclear arming of its warships. The new prime minister in Wellington, David Lange, was 'puzzled' by the way the New Zealand policy so upset the US. 'Whatever the Russians might be up to in the South Pacific', he wrote, 'it wasn't very much', therefore 'the presence in South Pacific harbours of American nuclear vessels wasn't going to make the least difference. New Zealand itself, a thousand miles distant from its neighbour, was not going to become the focus of Soviet strategic planning.' Yet he found hostile US officials 'unable to talk about events in the South Pacific without framing them in terms of a global struggle between the United States and the Soviet Union'.[41]

With the refusal in January 1985 by Lange's government to allow port access to USS *Buchanan*, the first test case of the anti-nuclear policy, the US cancelled most of the military cooperation with New Zealand that had been part of the 1951 ANZUS treaty. With New Zealand's refusal to submit to

---

39 Henningham, *France and the South Pacific*, 224–6.
40 Ibid., 226–9. Nic Maclellan and Jean Chesneaux, *After Moruroa: France in the South Pacific* (Melbourne 1998), 217.
41 David Lange, *Nuclear Free – The New Zealand Way* (Auckland 1990), 40.

this diplomatic pressure, the American Secretary of State, George Schulz, announced in July 1986 that the US would suspend its ANZUS obligations to defend New Zealand. While that country was of minimal strategic importance, Washington was deeply concerned about the precedent that New Zealand was creating, which might encourage more strategically important Pacific Islands to deny entry to US warships. The New Zealand government's response was to emphasize a self-reliant defence policy. Opponents pointed to the incapacity of the nation's small industrial base and limited financial resources to maintain the stated Labour policy of defending not only New Zealand but also its dependent Pacific Islands states: the Cook Islands, Niue and Tokelau.[42]

Australia, the other partner in ANZUS, also opposed the New Zealand nuclear ship policy. In Lange's view his Australian Labor colleague, Hawke, 'was just the man to encourage his country's infatuation with America'. Occupying a vast under-populated continent, Australians have traditionally looked to great world powers to guarantee their defence, first to Great Britain and, with the British retreat from Asia by the end of the 1960s, to the US. Left-wing members of the Australian Labor Party had advocated banning US warships from Australian ports, but they were a minority within the party, which on assuming office in 1983 conducted a review of the ANZUS policy and fully endorsed the alliance. Whereas New Zealand's geographic isolation encouraged majority popular support for nuclear-free policies, the long-standing public nervousness about potential designs on Australia by foreign powers, which had been reinforced by threatened Japanese invasion in 1942 and postwar fears of Chinese communist expansionism, restricted opponents of the US alliance to a small minority of the Australian community. Australia, however, was willing to continue the traditional close defence cooperation with New Zealand. Australia's Defence Minster, Kim Beasley, stated that there were 'very compelling reasons' to ensure that the rift with the US did not disrupt New Zealand's long-term close relations with Australia. Indeed, since 1983 these neighbouring nations had been developing a 'Closer Economic Relations Trade Agreement' (CER), and free interchange of goods was achieved in 1990. However, on the nuclear ships issue, while suggesting to Washington a less condemnatory policy towards New Zealand, the Australian Labor government was concerned not to upset in any way its treaty relationship with the US. As a

---

42   Peter Jennings, *The Armed Forces of New Zealand and the ANZUS Split: Costs and Consequences* (Wellington 1988), chs 2–3. Ewan Jamieson, *Friend or Ally: New Zealand at Odds with its Past* (Sydney 1990), chs 2–3. Michael McKinley, 'The New Zealand Perspective on ANZUS and Nuclear Weapons', in John Ravenhill (ed.), *No Longer an American Lake?* (Sydney 1989), ch. 2.

major contribution to the alliance Australia hosted a wide range of communication, command, control and intelligence installations supporting wider world US naval operations and military space surveillance.[43]

The US did extend half an olive branch to New Zealand in 1990, offering to renew high-level diplomatic contacts between the two nations. However, there was no revival of the defence alliance. The dying of the Cold War had not thawed US concern to isolate the New Zealand anti-nuclear ship disease. In New Zealand the strength of public support for the policy was such that the opposition National Party, which won a sweeping victory in the October 1990 election, did not promise to abandon the nuclear ships policy.[44]

The US and the Pacific islands

The US use of the Pacific for nuclear ships and weapons engendered diplomatic tension with other Pacific islands in the 1980s, especially Palau. The constitutional ban on the presence of any nuclear weapons in this territory required a 75 per cent vote in a popular referendum to amend it. However, the US administration and its supporters in Palau placed strong pressure on other Palauans to throw out the anti-nuclear clause. From 1983 to 1990 Palauans were subjected to seven such referenda in attempts to secure the requisite majority. It was never reached despite strong American economic cajolery with promises of $430 million in aid if Palau entered a compact of free association with the US without the anti-nuclear clause, as well as violent intimidation against Palauan supporters of the constitution. The chairman of the 1979 constitutional convention and the popular Palauan President, Haruo Remeliik, was murdered on 1 July 1985, the first assassination of a Pacific Islands head of state. Two relatives of Remeliik's former political opponents, Roman Tmetuchl and two associates were charged with the murder but not convicted because of inadequate evidence. Many pro-constitution Palauans believe the CIA murdered him. The real culprit,

---

43   Lange, *Nuclear Free*, 46. Stuart McMillan, *Neither Confirm nor Deny: The Nuclear Ships Dispute between New Zealand and the United States* (Wellington 1987), ch. 13. Andrew Mack, 'Australian Defence Policy and the ANZUS Alliance', in Ravenhill, *American Lake*, ch. 6. P.J. Lloyd, 'Australia–New Zealand Trade Relations: NAFTA to CER', in Keith Sinclair (ed.), *Tasman Relations: New Zealand and Australia 1788–1988* (Auckland 1987), 142–63. P.J. Lloyd, *The Future of CER: A Single Market for Australia and New Zealand* (Wellington 1991), 40. Desmond Ball, *A Suitable Piece of Real Estate: American Installations in Australia* (Sydney 1980), chs 4–10.
44   Jamieson, *Friend or Ally*, chs 11, 13.

who was convicted in 1993 for ordering the murder, was John Ngiraked, whose business interests had been thwarted by Remeliik. The succeeding president, Lazarus Salii, who was facing corruption allegations, committed suicide in 1988. The relentless pressure from the US and its Palauan supporters did achieve a 73 per cent vote in favour of changing the constitution in August 1987, and the same majority was given for a compact agreement with the US without the anti-nuclear provisions, which the American Congress moved to ratify. But in a climate of personal intimidation, including murder and fire-bombings, the Palau Supreme Court declared the compact vote unconstitutional. By February 1990 voter approval for a compact with the US had dropped to 61 per cent.[45]

The strong US interest in Palau devolved principally from its strategic location. This island group is 800 kilometres east of the Philippines where major American bases faced the threat of future prohibition. Palau is a southern anchor for a fallback defensive arc of islands going north through Guam to Tinian in the North Marianas. Palau's good harbours prompted the US to demand of Palauans the reservation of about a third of the biggest island in the group, Babeldaop, for potential base facilities. The other main points of the defensive arc were safely under US control. Guam remained US territory, without any major independence movement; and the North Marianas continued to succumb to the economic attractions of a compact of free association with the US, which gave America full defence rights.[46]

Elsewhere in the Pacific the US was opposing a push by island states for a nuclear free Pacific. In 1985 there was an agreement to implement a Pacific Nuclear Free Zone Treaty at a meeting of the South Pacific Forum at Rarotonga in the Cook Islands. It was the culmination of a gradual development since the 1960s. It had received a fillip from a New Zealand Labour government initiative in 1975 to request UN support for a South Pacific nuclear free zone, which had been granted by a vote of 110 to nil with twenty abstentions, though vigorously opposed by the US. The Rarotonga treaty was pushed by the Australian Labor government, supported by New Zealand and by the Polynesian states except Tonga. In reality it was an Australian move to preserve the Pacific from a more radical proposal being proposed by Vanuatu and supported by the other two Melanesian independent states. The Rarotonga treaty opposed nuclear testing, the dumping of nuclear waste and land-based nuclear weapons. It

45   Arnold H. Leibowitz, *Embattled Island: Palau's Struggle for Independence* (Westport 1996), chs 7, 22. Richard J. Pamentier, 'The Rhetoric of Free Association and Palau's Political Struggle', *The Contemporary Pacific*, 3, 1991, 146–58. David Robie, *Blood on their Banner: Nationalist Struggles in the South Pacific* (London 1989), ch. 9.
46   Robie, *Blood on their Banner*, 163. Firth, *Nuclear Playground*, 60–4.

did not prohibit the transporting of nuclear weapons by air or sea across the Pacific or missile testing. Nauru and the Melanesian states argued that this freedom did not really make the Pacific a nuclear free zone. Australia rejected their attempt to include missile testing in the treaty's prohibitions. New Zealand's support for the Rarotonga treaty reflected its concern to limit diplomatic fall out with the US. Yet the Reagan administration in Washington, lobbied vigorously by France, refused to endorse even this Australian attempt to protect US nuclear activities in the Pacific. Washington argued that 'a proliferation of such [nuclear free] zones in the free world, unmatched by disarmament in the Soviet bloc, is clearly detrimental to Western security'.[47]

Australia, Indonesia and the islands

Australia remained the main metropolitan power in the South Pacific during the 1980s. In 1989 its armed forces numbered 69,600, far more than the rest of the South Pacific, including New Zealand, combined. After using its military transport capacities to support PNG's intervention in Vanuatu in 1980, Australia maintained a generally low profile and moved by the late 1980s to a 'constructive commitment'. As an Australian High Commissioner to PNG confessed, one of his main policies was to ensure that Australia was not seen to be dictating to its former colony. However, while giving equipment and army training support to PNG's attempts to suppress the Bougainville rebellion, the Australian government did protest about abuses of human rights by PNG defence forces in that region. Australia also provided military aid to other South Pacific nations, such as riot-control equipment to Vanuatu when the government there in 1988 faced internal disturbances following a split in the ruling Vanua'aku Party. The Australian government was concerned to keep communist influence out of the South Pacific, and there was a brief scare in 1987 of Libyan intervention to support Kanak and other potential Pacific Islands rebels. But Australia relied on its substantial financial aid, which in the financial year 1988–89 amounted to AUS$1 billion for island states, and retention of good relations with island governments to maintain political stability in the South Pacific. The financial aid was a vital ingredient for the budgets of PNG and also was

---

47   Quoted in Michael Hamel-Green, *The South Pacific Nuclear Free Zone Treaty: A Critical Assessment* (Canberra 1990), 114. For the nuclear free zone see ibid., *passim* and Robie, *Blood on their Banner*, ch. 8.

important for micro states such as Tuvalu, which in 1988–89 received from Australia AUS$1.3 million for developmental aid, which was more than 20 per cent of the island group's annual revenue.[48]

The economic vicissitudes of the 1980s had made many of the island economies more vulnerable than before. Even the wealthiest Pacific state, Nauru, was feeling the effects of declining phosphate production, which was due to die out in 1995. This problem was sharpening the republic's case being prepared at the end of 1990 for a hearing before the International Court of Justice for AUS$72 million compensation for damages caused by phosphate mining during the period of Australian administration. Australia was marshalling its case to resist the claim.[49]

Australia tried to retain good relations with its potentially powerful Southeast Asian neighbour, Indonesia. Canberra was careful to refrain from any support for guerrillas in East Timor and Irian Jaya by muting criticisms of human rights abuses in those territories and other parts of Indonesia. However, the Australian government could not stop a sharp cooling of relations in 1986 when the *Sydney Morning Herald* published an article exposing corruption and nepotism in the ruling Suharto family in Indonesia. However, by 1990 there were signs of the Australia–Indonesia relations improving. Also, while there were some differences in Indonesian–Australian policies in the South Pacific, such as Indonesia's quick establishment of good relations with the post-coup government of Fiji, there was a common concern to preserve the stability of island governments, especially with regard to the secessionist movement in Bougainville.[50]

Conclusions

The greater violence in the Pacific Islands in the 1980s was the result principally of the continuation and the legacy of Euro-American imperialism

---

48 Henningham, *France and the South Pacific*, 221. Information from Mr Michael Wilson. John Connell, 'Vanuatu' in 'Political Review: Melanesia', *The Contemporary Pacific*, 1, 1989, 163–4. Greg Fry (ed.), *Australia's Regional Security* (Sydney 1991), ch. 11. The Parliament of the Commonwealth of Australia, *Australia's Relations with the South Pacific* (Canberra 1989), 57–8. *FEA*, 1991, 833.

49 Stuart Inder, 'Nauru' in 'Political Reviews', *The Contemporary Pacific*, 4, 1982, 188–90. For economic problems of other states see Christopher Browne with Douglas A. Scott, *Economic Development in Seven Pacific Island Countries* (Washington 1989).

50 David Jenkins, 'The Quiet, Bald Moneymaker of Jakarta's Elite', *Sydney Morning Herald*, 19 April 1986. Desmond Ball and Helen Wilson (eds), *Strange Neighbours: The Australia–Indonesia Relationship* (Sydney 1991), chs 1–2, 5–6, 11–16.

in the Pacific. The British Empire had bequeathed to Fiji the racial tensions that underlay the Fiji coups. Moreover, the power of pro-coup eastern Fijian chiefs, which had been threatened by political change, had been entrenched by British colonial policy. France's world power pretensions, which imposed the CEP in the Pacific, and the presence of a large French community in New Caledonia, were the principal causes of the violence inflamed by Kanak aspirations for independence. The US concern to preserve the North Pacific Islands as a wide-ranging security zone created a climate of violence in Palau. The US demand for free passage of nuclear ships caused diplomatic conflict with New Zealand, where there was also an outbreak of violence caused by the presence there of a ship representing wider world opposition to French nuclear testing. France also pressed the US to oppose even the moderate nuclear free Pacific proposal proposed in American interests by the US's firm ally, Australia. Australia needed to provide additional defence assistance to PNG to cope with the violent legacy of Australian and German colonialism, which had separated Buka and Bougainville from the rest of the Solomon Islands. Consequently, during the 1980s Pacific Islands had become a less peaceful region whereas other conflicts in the Pacific Basin were moving towards peaceful resolutions.

CHAPTER NINE

War and Cooperation in the Western Hemisphere, 1980–1990

In the Eastern Pacific Basin in the 1980s the US administration, especially under President Reagan, was still strongly opposed to revolutionary movements with any Marxist flavour. That is the main theme of this chapter, concentrating on the surrogate war fought by the US against the Sandinista government of Nicaragua and support for Latin American governments combating Marxist insurgencies. It demonstrates how the Cold War dominated the Latin American policies of the Reagan administration at the same time when there were improving relations with China and the Soviet Union in the West Pacific Basin. Another theme is the degree to which, in the Cold War cause, American administrations from 1980 to 1990 were willing to tolerate violations of human rights by anti-democratic governments. Another theme is US economic relations with nations of the Western Hemisphere. Also the inter-relations of Latin American governments and relations between the Americas and the rest of the Pacific Basin are discussed.

The US crusade against Nicaragua

Whereas Carter's administration had accepted the coming to power of the Sandinista government in Nicaragua in 1979, the Republican Party National Platform for the 1980 election campaign declared: 'We abhor the Marxist-Sandinista takeover of Nicaragua.' Consequently, this small Central American republic became one of Reagan's prime targets in his worldwide anti-communist crusade. An intense propaganda campaign was launched to convince the US public that Nicaragua was a second Cuba, another domino in the Soviet plot to impose communist dictatorship on the whole of Central America, America's own 'backyard'. The issue was also linked to America's championship of world freedom. Reagan exclaimed: 'If Central America were to fall, what would the consequence be for our position in Asia, Europe, and the alliances such as NATO? If the United States cannot respond to a threat near our own borders, why should Europeans or Asians believe that we are seriously concerned about threats to them?'[1]

The Sandinista regime was not blameless in the confrontation with the US. Concerned about potential threats from right-wing neighbouring countries, the Sandinistas decided in 1979 to build up the Nicaraguan army, which was small under Somoza. Distrust of the US and ideological factors turned the Sandinsitas to Cuba and the USSR for arms, a move that was literally a red rag to wave at the American bull. The Nicaraguan army's size by 1981 was still small – 6,700 troops and another 8,000 paramilitary forces – and it was certainly not overwhelming compared with the 11,200 strong Honduras army and El Salvador's 17,000 troops. But, because of its military ties with Cuba and the USSR, Nicaragua was already a concern to its neighbours and to the US. The most damaging Sandinista policy, in American eyes, was to provide a conduit for Cuban arms for Marxist guerrillas in El Salvador. This was Reagan's excuse to suspend on 1 April 1981 the $15 million remaining from a $75 million aid package for Nicaragua provided by Carter. The Sandinistas, however, expected Reagan to condemn them whatever they did and therefore had no intention of abandoning the rebels in El Salvador, despite denying sending any weapons.[2]

The US did offer a deal to the Sandinista government. If it stopped supporting the El Salvadorian rebels and ceased its military expansion, Washington would be prepared to offer a non-aggression pact with Nicaragua, paramilitary training camps in the US for Cuban and Nicaraguan refugees would be closed, and Congress would be asked to restore economic aid. However, the deeply suspicious Sandinistas were not prepared to barter the El Salvadorian rebels or cuts in military expenditure for Washington's promises to abide by its own Neutrality Act and the Inter-American Treaty of Reciprocal Assistance of 1947, in which the principle of non-intervention in the affairs of other Latin American states had been established.[3]

---

1 Thomas W. Walker (ed.), *Nicaragua: The First Five Years* (New York 1985), 22–4. Edward Best, *US Policy and Regional Security in Central America* (London 1987), 51. Viron Vaky, 'Reagan's Central American Policy: An Isthmus Restored', in Robert S. Leiken (ed.), *Central America: Anatomy of a Conflict* (New York 1984), 233–57.

2 Best, *US Policy and Regional Security*, 51–3. William M. LeoGrande, 'The United States and Nicaragua', in Walker, *Nicaragua*, 425–9. Roger Miranda and William Ratliff, *The Civil War in Nicaragua: Inside the Sandinistas* (New Brunswick 1993), 116–19.

3 Best, *US Policy and Regional Security*, 52–3. LeoGrande, 'The United States and Nicaragua', 429–30.

With the failure of diplomacy, hard-liners within the Washington administration, supported by Reagan, gained the ascendancy over those who still sought to negotiate with the Sandinistas. A strong rebel offensive in El Salvador strengthened the case for military action. Secretary of State Alexander Haig, an ex army general, sought to block the sources of supplies to the rebels without addressing the social conditions inside El Salvador that had spawned the rebellion. Direct US military action in El Salvador and Nicaragua was ruled out in these post-Vietnam War days, when US foreign policy makers feared the political consequences of embroilment in potentially protracted and unpopular warfare. But, as well as a policy of imposing economic isolation on Nicaragua, it was decided to launch covert paramilitary action inside that nation ostensibly to interdict arms flows, but with the ultimate intention of overthrowing the Sandinista government. Reagan signed in December 1981 an authorization for the CIA to spend $19.8 million to create a paramilitary force in Honduras for operations inside Nicaragua.[4]

These rebels, made up of ex-National Guardsmen, other former supporters of Somoza and opponents of the Sandinistas, including some disillusioned early Sandinista supporters, were known as 'contras', who from May 1982 were receiving direct training by the CIA. But though 10,000 strong by 1983, the contras did not have sufficient power or popular support to challenge the Sandinistas in urban areas. The rebels restricted their activities to rural regions, especially in the northwest of the country, and utilized safe havens across the Honduras border. Their operations were mostly attacks on bridges, power generators, state farms, rural health clinics and small villages. The human rights agency, *Americas Watch* reported in 1985 that contras 'systematically engaged in the killing of prisoners and the unarmed, including medical relief personnel; selective targets on civilians, and indiscriminate attacks; torture and other outrages against personal dignity'. Against rapidly expanding Sandinista armed forces, which by mid 1984 were estimated to number 61,800, and which clearly had majority popular support, the contras did not have a wide enough impact.[5]

Realizing that the covert war against Nicaragua was not being won, the CIA in mid 1983 assumed direct command. Using its own people and

---

4 William LeoGrande, *Our Own Backyard: The United States in Central America, 1977–1992* (Chapel Hill 1998), 285–6. Best, *US Policy and Regional Security*, 55–7. William I. Robinson and Kent Norsworthy, *David and Goliath: Washington's War Against Nicaragua* (London 1987), 41–5. Robert A. Pastor, *Condemned to Repetition: The United States and Nicaragua* (Princeton 1987), 230–6.

5 R. Pardo-Maurer, *The Contras, 1980–1989: A Special Kind of Politics* (London 1990), 2–3. Peter Kornbluh, 'The Covert War', in Thomas W. Walker (ed.), *Reagan Versus the Sandinistas: The Undeclared War on Nicaragua* (Boulder 1987), 21–8. Best, *US Policy and Regional Security*, 56–60. Janusz Bugajski, *Sandinista Communism and Rural Nicaragua* (New York 1990), ch. 5.

specially trained Latin Americans, US aircraft bombed selected targets. Fast speedboats, supplied by the US Drugs Enforcement Agency, launched attacks on harbour facilities and oil storages. In January 1984 CIA operatives started to lay mines in Nicaragua's harbours, which by April had sunk or damaged ten commercial ships, one of them Russian. When the USSR delivered a sharp protest, Washington simply replied that the mines and all other attacks were the work of the contras.[6]

However, the CIA was unable to keep secret its involvement in the undeclared war against Nicaragua. The revelation that American-planted mines were sinking ships in Nicaragua's harbours, created a public uproar in the US. Even the Republican-controlled Senate passed a resolution in April 1984 calling for an end to the mining. More seriously for the administration, in the Democrat-controlled House of Representatives the Democrats were angry about misuse of funds that had been restricted by Congress to interdiction of arms supplies and voted to cut off all aid to the contras.[7]

The administration did not accept this House decision. A surrogate network was established to distribute funds to the contras. Money was solicited from overseas allies like Saudi Arabia, from private donations and from the proceeds received from the sale of arms, in violation of US neutrality laws, to Iran for its war against Iraq in exchange for the release of American hostages in Lebanon. Over $60 million was raised by these efforts during the eighteen months of the congressional arms ban for the secret delivery of arms and equipment to the contras.[8]

This covert funding effort kept the contras going, their operations depending almost entirely on American money. Meanwhile, the administration launched a massive propaganda campaign to reverse the congressional decision. Frank McNeil, a senior member of the State Department's Bureau of Intelligence and Research, commented: 'the intelligence process was prostituted to a desire to convince Congress to renew assistance to the contras'. The contras were 'freedom fighters' opposing a Marxist 'tyranny', despite the fact that in 1984 the Sandinistas had held elections in which they received 63 per cent of the vote, in polls that were declared open and fair by international observers. To gain the support of Democrats in Congress, the administration falsely claimed that pressure from the contras was the only way to get the Sandinista government to negotiate for the restoration of democracy. Indeed, the US administration pressured opposition candidates

---

6   Kornbluh, 'The Covert War', 28–31. Robinson and Norsworthy, *David and Goliath*, chs 3–4.

7   LeoGrande, *Our Own Backyard*, 299–314, 320–46. Cynthia J. Arnson, *Crossroads: Congress, the President, and Central America* (New York 1993), 163–80.

8   Kornbluh, 'The Covert War', 31–3.

in Nicaragua to withdraw from the 1984 election in order to discredit it as a one horse race. Contras also took military action to prevent people from voting, though 75 per cent of registered voters participated. Washington harped on Sandinista human rights abuses, which ignored more serious violations by the contras. The Nicaragua government was also charged with smuggling drugs to poison the youth of America. But in 1984 the Sandistas pulled out of drug trafficking, while the contras continued to be involved in drug running and the US was using a known drug runner, General Manuel Antonio Noriega, the dictator of Panama. He provided the contras with information via the Panamanian embassy in Managua and as a source of financial aid.[9]

This intense pressure from Reagan, to whom the downfall of the Sandinistas had become an obsession, reversed the congressional ban. Congressmen had been worn down by the barrage of propaganda about the evils of the Sandinistas and the virtues of the contras. In vain did liberal Democrats legitimately claim that Nicaragua's closeness to Cuba and the USSR was a consequence of the undeclared was waged by the US. While the Sandinistas did receive valuable Soviet arms, including attack helicopters, in reality the over-stretched Soviet Union was unable to extend major financial support to Nicaragua. The estimate was $300 million annually in economic assistance from 1987, which was stopped in 1990. Nor could Democrats gain mileage from the brutality and corruption of the contras against administration denials of the accuracy of the relevant reports. Political threats from party leaders helped switch the votes of Republican opponents of contra aid. In June 1986 a bill providing $100 million aid to the contras was approved in the House of Representatives by 221 votes to 209.[10]

Renewed American financial aid, however, did not save the contras. In the mid-term congressional election in November 1986 the Republicans lost control of the Senate. This defeat rendered the Reagan administration vulnerable to the disclosure, which emerged within the next month, of information concerning the illegal use of money from armaments sales to Iran to fund the contras. The Democrats were able to use their Senate numbers to launch a full investigation of the deals, which quickly became

---

9 Frank McNeil, *War and Peace in Central America* (New York 1988), 218. Eldon Kenworthy, 'Selling the Policy', in Walker (ed.), *Reagan Versus the Sandinistas*, 159–77. LeoGrande, *Our own Backyard*, 367–5, 463–4. Miranda and Ratliff, *Inside the Sandinistas*, 160–1. Frederick Kempe, *Divorcing the Dictator: America's Bungled Affair with Noriega* (New York 1990), ch. 11.

10 LeoGrande, *Our Own Backyard*, 469–75. Bruce D. Larkin (ed.), *Vital Interests: The Soviet Issue in US Central American Policy* (Boulder 1988), parts 2 and 3. Nicola Miller, *Soviet Relations with Latin America* (Cambridge 1989), ch. 7. Miranda and Ratliff, *Inside the Sandinistas*, ch. 8. Arnson, *Crossroads*, 185–217.

known as the Irangate affair, a reference to the Watergate cover-up of illegal government activity. The contras, however, flush with the money voted to them and new equipment, such as Redeye missiles which robbed the Sandinistas of their helicopter advantage, had been carrying out destructive raids deeper into Nicaragua, causing further damage to the badly faltering Nicaraguan economy. But, as a result of Irangate, in February 1988 the administration's request for renewed aid for the contras was defeated in the House of Representatives. Deprived of vital financial assistance and wracked by internal disputes and poor leadership, the contra movement in 1988 rapidly lost effectiveness.[11]

Furthermore, there had been in 1987 a peace agreement between Nicaragua and its Central American neighbours. As early as 1984 a peace plan had been advanced by Mexico, Venezuela, Colombia and Panama, frontline states to the region of Central American conflict. In 1983 they had formed the Contadora group, named after the Panamanian Island where they met, to establish a common approach to regional security. In the next year they forwarded a plan for ending the Nicaraguan conflict. Its major features were: respect for the sovereign rights of all states, mutual demilitarization, reduction in foreign military advisors and no support for insurgencies in other states. Nicaragua assented to the plan if the other Central American states would agree. But the US, alarmed by this move, which would spell the end to its covert war against Nicaragua, placed pressure on the other Central American countries not to sign the treaty.[12]

By 1987 these republics were willing to revive a peace plan put forward by Costa Rica's premier, Oscar Arias. A reason for this change was that the neighbouring countries no longer believed that Nicaragua was a threat to them, despite Reagan's propaganda about the menace of the Soviet-supported military build up there. The actual military balance was much more even because, with US assistance, neighbouring states had been strengthening their own armies. The Arias plan called for a cessation of aid to all insurgent groups and for domestic reconciliation based upon a cease-fire. This time the Central American republics resisted the pressure from the US, Irangate having created, in their view, a 'lame duck' administration. These states were keen to rid their region of insurgency violence, and in August 1987 in Guatemala City Nicaragua signed with them an accord in which the Sandinistas pledged not to support insurgency, to work towards

---

11 Leslie Cockburn, *Out of Control: The Story of the Reagan Administration's Secret War in Nicaragua, the Illegal Arms Pipeline, and the Contra Drug Connection* (New York 1987), 247–9. Pardo-Maurer, *The Contras*, ch. 5. LeoGrande, *Our Own Backyard*, ch. 20.

12 LeoGrande, *Our Own Backyard*, 349–63, 505–25.

national reconciliation with political opponents, and to hold elections in 1990.[13]

Despite this accord, the US did not relax economic sanctions against Nicaragua. In May 1988 Congress also voted for strictly controlled human-itarian aid for the contras, which prevented their dissipation. However, in March 1988 the Sandinista government had signed an agreement with the contras for a sixty-day cease-fire, which was given monthly extensions, though some contra raids recommenced before the end of the year.[14]

The Sandinistas called an election to be held on 26 February 1990. Most of the opposition parties combined in the *Unión Nacional Opositor* (UNO). Its presidential candidate was Violeta Barrios de Chamorro, the owner of the *La Prensa* newspaper, who had a national status as an unflinching opponent of the Sandinistas. She had a Cory Aquino-style stature as the sixty-year old smiling eyed and matronly widow of the country's most famous martyr, Pedro Chamorro Joaquín, the leader of the bourgeois opposition to Somoza, who had been murdered by the dictator's National Guard in 1978. The Bush administration also provided $11.6 million to UNO so as 'to level the playing field' in the contest with the governing Sandinistas, who were fielding as their candidate President Ortega. More effectively for the US cause, the economic blockade and the contra war had produced grave shortages of consumer goods and hyperinflation, and there was a popular belief that the US restrictions would be lifted only if Ortega were defeated. Consequently, Chamorro won with 55 per cent of the vote; and UNO gained fifty-one seats in the ninety-three seat National Assembly. The US had finally achieved the demise of the Sandinistas and promptly restored economic ties as well as supplying financial aid to the Chamorro government.[15]

The US and the long war in El Salvador

El Salvador under the Republican Party administrations in the 1980s was a case of major US support for anti-communist regimes. The El Salvadorian government, which had emerged after the coup of October 1979, was a

13 Dunkerley, *Power in the Isthmus*, 317–18, 324–6. Raúl Benítez Manaut *et al.*, 'Armed Forces, Society, and the People: Cuba and Nicaragua', in Augusto Varas (ed.), *Democracy Under Siege: New Military Power in Latin America* (New York 1989), 152–4. Rico F. Carlos, 'The Contadora Experience and the Future of Collective Security', in Richard J. Bloomfield and Gregory F. Treverton (eds), *Alternative to Intervention: A New US–Latin American Security Relationship* (Boulder 1990), 93–114.
14 LeoGrande, *Our Own Backyard*, ch. 22.
15 LeoGrande, *Our Own Backyard*, 553–63. Arnson, *Crossroads*, 234–9 (quotation 236).

combined military/civilian regime, and in May 1980 it joined in a coalition with the middle-class Christian Democratic Party (PDC). However, the new government had insufficient control over the security services, which continued to carry out acts of violence against perceived enemies of the oligarchy. In January police opened fire on a peaceful march by a working-class opposition group, killing twenty-four marchers. The influential Catholic archbishop of San Salvador, Oscar Romero, wrote to Carter requesting the withdrawal of US military aid to El Salvador. On 24 March Romero was assassinated while saying mass; and police opened fire on a crowd of 30,000 gathering for his funeral killing thirty of them. The government's legitimacy was rapidly disintegrating but, pressured by the US, the PDC stayed in the coalition. The US was hoping that this government would be a democratic bulwark against a leftist take-over as in Nicaragua.[16]

The Carter administration was also concerned about the possibility of a right-wing coup. Its ambassador in San Salvador warned that the US would not tolerate such a move. Washington was placing its faith in the PDC to carry out meaningful reform. However, Carter's patience ran out when three American Catholic nuns and a female lay-worker were killed. On 5 December 1980, US military aid to El Salvador was suspended. Two weeks later, however, the aid was restored after the PDC leader, José Duarte Napoleón, took control of the government and announced that the murders were being thoroughly investigated. Only four National Guard scapegoats were ultimately charged with the crime, which certainly involved higher military officers.[17]

With the advent of the Reagan administration, the emphasis of US policy towards El Salvador changed. This shift was associated with a major offensive launched by Marxist insurgents in mid January. During 1980 separate insurgent groups had combined into a National Liberation Front, the *Farabundo Martí Frente de Liberación Nacional* (FMLN). Assisted by arms from Cuba via Nicaragua, the FMLN was hoping for a general popular uprising, Nicaragua style, provoked by the unpopularity of the government. This was the offensive creating the alarm in Washington that drove Reagan to launch his campaign against Nicaragua as well as to provide large-scale military aid to Duarte's regime in El Salvador.[18]

The FMLN's 1981 offensive did not inspire the anticipated popular uprising. The country was not being governed by an avaricious dictator like

---

16 Arnson, *Crossroads*, 40–8. Hugh Byrne, *El Salvador's Civil War: A Study of Revolution* (Boulder 1996), ch. 3.
17 LeoGrande, *Our Own Backyard*, 105–16. Micheal McClintock, *The American Connection* (London 1985), vol. II, 257–83.
18 Byrne, *El Salvador's Civil War*, 73–80.

Somoza, and the PDC had church support and popularity going back to the days when it led the political opposition to the oligarchy. In addition the government had tried to implement reform, especially a decree in March 1980 for the expropriation of all properties of over 500 hectares in size for the formation of farm cooperatives. The reforms were to face trenchant oligarchic opposition, but initially they preserved the PDC's popular image.[19]

While the FMLN could not overthrow the government, it did attract significant popular support. The government's land reform program did not assist the 60 per cent of peasants who were landless. Declining economic conditions following the Fútbol War, the oligarchy's emphasis on commercial farming, and rising prices for oil and manufactured goods, coupled with falling agricultural prices had greatly reduced the average standard of living. Thus, despite operating in a country far smaller than Nicaragua, with fewer mountainous retreats, and with no cross-border havens as were enjoyed by the contras, the FMLN with some 8,000 insurgents, maintained an effective guerrilla war. They were aided by the government's repressive counter-insurgency policies. The FMLN practice of releasing prisoners of war encouraged many of the press-ganged recruits in the army, which grew to 50,000, to surrender. But US military aid, which increased from $58 million in 1980 to $435 million in 1985, was a crucial factor in preventing a guerrilla victory in the long-running war. Building on false claims of physical Nicaraguan involvement in the opening offensive of the war, Reagan nominated El Salvador as one of the dominoes that would fall into Soviet hands should the guerrillas achieve victory. In fact the Soviet Union had no intention of aiding a guerrilla movement which it did not see as having much chance of success and because such aid would jeopardize its relations with other Latin American countries.[20]

However, there was growing concern among Democrats in Congress about human rights abuses in El Salvador, which created administration fear of a congressional threat to the military funding for El Salvador. After an election in 1982, boycotted by left-wing groups, a new party organized by the oligarchy, the *Alianza Republicana Nacionalista* (ARENA), was in a position to take power. There was intense US pressure to prevent its leader, Roberto D'Aubuisson, the mastermind of the right-wing death squads, from becoming president and to ensure continuation of the PDC's land reforms. A compromise apolitical president, Alvaro Magaña, was appointed. But his

19 Ibid., 80–1. Dunkerley, *Power in the Isthmus*, 367–8, 392–4, 399–400.
20 Dunkerley, *Power in the Isthmus*, 393–404. Miller, *Soviet Relations*, 190–1. LeoGrande, *Our Own Backyard*, 80–9.

Government of National Unity was ineffective, especially in land reform or in reining in the death squads. An intense administration effort was needed in Washington to keep funds flowing to the El Salvadorian military. The US was more comfortable when Duarte again became president after an election in 1984, in which the US spent $2.1 million to defeat D'Aubuisson. Duarte's government acceded to US pressure to promote economic growth with an economic-austerity package that assisted in alienating its popular support. Consequently, in an election in March 1989 ARENA won presidential power. But the new president, Alfredo Cristiani, was less extreme than D'Aubuisson and continued to receive military aid from the Bush administration. However, with the encouragement of other Central American states, peace talks between the government and the FMLN under UN auspices had commenced in Costa Rica in October 1989, though there was a major FMLN offensive in November 1989 to demonstrate its continued potency. One right-wing response on 16 November, which achieved international notoriety, was the murder of six Jesuit priests and two co-workers. Failure to convict any culprits prompted the US Congress in October 1990 to halve US military aid to El Salvador and threaten its end if the government did not negotiate seriously for peace or move to prosecute the murderers of the Jesuits.[21]

US relations with other Central American States and Panama

The Government of Guatemala had become so vicious towards its own people that in 1981 the US Congress refused to sanction a decision by Reagan to rescind the Carter administration's prohibitions on military aid and arms sales to that regime. An internationally scandalous example of its style was when in January 1980 the Spanish embassy in Guatemala City was invaded by troops bent on killing thirty-nine Mayan peasants sheltering there. However, the Reagan administration used another channel to assist the Guatemalan military. With US financial support, Argentina supplied arms and training to the Guatemalan army, which expanded from 15,000 in 1980 to 51,600 in 1985. It also received valuable assistance from Israel. Furthermore, the rebels, the *Unión Revolucionaria Nacional Guatemalteca* (URNG)

---

21 LeoGrande, *Our Own Backyard*, 125–70, 226–60, 566–74. Byrne, *El Salvador's Civil War*, 57–8, 137–41, 152–3, 181. Cynthia McClintock, *Revolutionary Movements in Latin America: El Salvador's FMLN and Peru's Shining Path* (Washington 1998), 222. Dunkerley, *Power in the Isthmus*, 405–12.

made a strategic mistake, like the FMLN in El Salvador, by launching in 1981 a major military offensive in a vain search for a popular uprising. Weakened by a subsequent war of attrition, the guerrillas were unable to prevent the Guatemalan army, with the assistance of civilian defence forces, launching a campaign against Mayan Indians, who were over half the 7.7 million Guatemalan population in 1985. Based on Vietnam War precedents, Mayan peasants, who were not willing to be herded into strategic hamlets, were targets in free fire zones. The grisly nature of the campaign ensured that not even Reagan was willing to restore aid to the Guatemalan army while it remained in control of the country. The US had supported the overthrow in 1982 of the brutal regime of General Romeo Lucas Garcia. But his replacement by General Efraín Ríos Montt did not lead to a better human rights record.[22]

However, in 1986 the Guatamelan army handed power back to civilian control, with the election of the government of Mario Vinicio Cerezo Arévalo, leader of the Christian Democratic Party. Washington seized the chance to restore relations with the Guatemalan army. In 1987 US pilots and helicopters were flying Guatemalan troops into combat zones. The army and right-wing groups in turn assured that radicalism did not get out of hand. In the first six months of 1989, 1,598 Guatemalans were murdered and 906 disappeared. Cerezo admitted that security forces, over which he had no control, were 'creating a climate of terror'. This was a situation which the Bush administration, now no longer ideologically committed to the Cold War, could not tolerate, though it gave the Guatemalan military plenty of warning when in March 1990 the US Ambassador was withdrawn from Guatemala. On 22 December 1990 Washington suspended all military aid because of a failure of the government 'to criticize or exhaustively investigate' continued abuses of human rights. However, the Guatemalan army had also made an error. Most attention in the US official statement about the aid suspension was devoted to the murder of a US citizen and the torturing and rape of an American Catholic nun.[23]

Even Costa Rica, which was proud of its traditions of an independent foreign policy and no army, was driven into the arms of the US in the mid 1980s. In 1983 Premier Luis Alberto Monge tried to distance Costa Rica from the developing crisis in Nicaragua by proclaiming his country's unarmed

---

22   Dunkerley, *Power in the Isthmus*, 480–504. Ariel C. Armory, *Argentina, the United States and the Anti-Communist Crusade in Central America* (Athens, Ohio 1997), 65. McClintock, *American Connection*, vol. II, chs 8–9. Susanne Joans, *The Battle for Guatemala: Rebels, Death Squad, and US Power* (Boulder 1991), 103, 120–3, 146–54, 196–9, 204–6. LeoGrande, *Our Own Backyard*, 528–9.
23   Ibid., 156–9, 161–9, 206. *Keesing's Record of World Events*, vol. XXXVI, 37276, 37311, 37912.

neutrality, though a contra force was operating in the border region. The Reagan administration waged a campaign against this proclamation by suspending aid money. The US also exploited CIA-provoked border skirmishes to sabotage Costa Rica's neutrality and offered to deploy troops there to protect against the alleged threat off a Nicaraguan invasion. The death of two Costa Rican civil guards in 1985, probably due to cross fire between Nicaraguan troops and contras, but blamed on the Sandinistas, was the catalyst for US arming and training a Costa Rica civil guard. Contra controlled airfields in northern Costa Rica also were used as staging posts for drug running from Colombia and Panama to the US. However, in 1986 a peace candidate, Oscar Arias, was elected president of Costa Rica. He switched to a more independent foreign policy as demonstrated by his advocacy in 1987 of the Nicaragua peace plan. Predictably, the US sought to undermine Arias by holding up economic assistance money and funding his political opponents who produced a magazine constantly attacking him and government policies, especially the peace initiative. But Arias and his peace policy survived.[24]

Honduras in the 1980s was known by such names as 'state for sale' and 'Pentagon republic'. Its role as the main base for the contra war against Nicaragua was invaluable to Washington. Nicaragua assisted in locking Honduras into this system in August 1983 by sending there a guerrilla band of about a hundred men, who were quickly rounded up by US troops engaged in military exercises. This 'invasion' was excellent US propaganda material, which was reinforced by subsequent Nicaraguan incursions across the frontier in hot pursuit of contras who were free to use Honduran soil for their murderous raids in the other direction. However, the compliant Honduras President Gustavo Alvarez was overthrown in 1984 by military officers, who demanded more US money for supporting the contras. This demand was resisted. A result was the closing of an El Salvador training camp in Honduras and more restrictions on the contras including at times holding up shipments of arms to them. Also, old enmities between Honduras and El Salvador had re-emerged with Honduran complaints of violation of air space and frontier lines.[25]

One of the Reagan administration's most valuable Latin American supporters, Noriega of Panama, had a less-enduring relationship with the US.

---

24 Dunkerley, *Power in the Isthmus*, 622–48. Martha Honey, *Hostile Acts: US Policy in Costa Rica in the 1980s* (Gainesville 1994), chs 10–11, 14. LeoGrande, *Our Own Backyard*, 528–9, 464. Peter Dale Scott and Jonathon Marshall, *Cocaine Politics: Drugs, Armies and the CIA in Central America* (Berkeley 1991), 65.
25 Dunkerley, *Power in the Isthmus*, 519–21, 577–8. LeoGrande, *Our Own Backyard*, 393–5. *Keesing's Record of World Events*, vol. XXXVI, 37275.

He was an army officer who had been employed by the CIA in the 1960s and who had became the intelligence chief and right-hand man of Panama's dictator, General Omar Torrijos, who seized power from the Panamanian oligarchy in 1968. In that position Noriega had profited from Mafia money laundering, gun running and drug trafficking, for which Panama became a centre after Cuba was sanitized by Castro. After Torrijos's death, Noriega in 1983 became dictator and was used by the US as a source of intelligence, a conduit for arms and money for the contras plus providing secret training grounds for contras and El Salvadorian military. The Reagan administration ignored shootings and beatings of Noriega's opponents in Panama, though its intelligence knew much about them – they tapped a satellite phone line they had provided for him. Panamanian business people and other middle-class citizens, who had no history of such repression in easy-going Panama, started a public agitation in 1987 in the form of a civic crusade. The handkerchief-waving, horn-honking crowds were no real threat to Noriega. But resultant publicity provided an opportunity for one of his Panamanian opponents to attract the attention of Senator Edward Kennedy. He organized a Senate resolution, passed by seventy-five votes to thirteen, calling for a public investigation into charges that Noriega was responsible for murder, for corrupting the 1984 Panamanian election, for drug trafficking and for money laundering. Noriega responded with public demonstrations against the US embassy, which provoked the Ambassador to cut off all aid. The CIA, reluctantly, dropped Noriega from its payroll, a saving of $200,000 per annum. Noriega thought he could count on his friends in the CIA, but the exposure of its secret deals in the Irangate affair and the death of William Casey, its director, had introduced a new regime unprepared to save him. Nevertheless, Reagan was uninterested in doing more. However, US Drug Enforcement Administration officials busily prepared a case for Noriega's indictment in February 1988 by a grand jury for having conspired with the Medellín cartel of Colombia to traffic drugs into the US.[26]

This unprecedented indictment of the head of a foreign power locked the US into a struggle to depose Noriega. In April 1988, Washington imposed partial economic sanctions on Panama, but they hurt the population much more than the dictator. The Panamanian president, Eric Arturo Delvalle, whom Noriega had shunted aside, was recognized as the head of the Panama government so that its assets in the US could be seized. An attempt to bargain for Noriega's resignation in return for dropping the drug

---

26 Kempe, *Divorcing the Dictator*, chs 4–14. LeoGrande, *Our Own Backyard*, 311. Scott and
    Marshall, *Cocaine Politics*, ch. 4. Manuel Noriega and Peter Eisner, *America's Prisoner: The
    Memoirs of Manuel Noriega* (New York 1997), 213. Carlos Guevara Mann, *Panamanian
    Militarism: A Historical Interpretation* (Athens, Ohio 1996), ch. 9.

indictments collapsed when news of it leaked to the American press so that it was considered dangerous for George Bush's election campaign. The Bush administration placed hope on a national election in Panama in May 1989, which was required by the Panama Canal Treaty, and on which Washington spent $10 million to boost opposition candidates. They won easily, but Noriega used military force to overturn the result before it was declared. Bush responded by sending extra troops to the Canal Zone, and ordered US military exercises to be held there. But this military pressure was applied to a dictator who believed the US would not dare use military force. Bush, concerned about a developing indecisive public image caused by the affair, decided to act after Panamanian soldiers on 16 December 1989 mortally wounded a US serviceman who had lost his way and tortured an American naval officer and his wife who witnessed the shooting. On 20 December some 24,000 US troops, who had been making preparations for two months, invaded Panama to depose one man. He fled to the Papal Embassy but was pressured by the Papal Nunciate to leave and was taken as a prisoner to Miami. However, the US invasion of Panama was condemned by the UN and the OAS, though some governments sympathized with Bush's dilemma, and raised fears of continued US military interventionism in Latin America.[27]

The US and other American nations

There were no American invasions, covert wars or even involvement in coup attempts elsewhere in the Pacific Basin states of Latin America. There were revolutionary movements there. One of the most vicious was the *Sendero Luminoso* (Shining Path) movement in Peru. It evolved in the 1960s from the ideas and teaching of Marxist staff members at the University of Huamanga in the city of Ayacucho, who regularly took students to Cuba and who formed a tightly organized Maoist faction. In 1980 it launched a guerrilla war against the bourgeois state. *Sendero*'s first appearance in May was in the burning of presidential election ballot boxes and the appearance of dead dogs hanging from lamp-posts in Ayacucho and Lima bearing signs

---

27 Kempe, *Divorcing the Dictator*, chs 15–22. Michael L. Conniff, *Panama and the United States: The Forced Alliance* (Athens 1992), ch. 9. Ivan Musicant, *A History of United States Military Intervention in Latin America from the Spanish–American War to the Invasion of Panama* (New York 1990), ch. 10. Thomas M. Leonard, *Panama, the Canal and the United States: A Guide to Issues and References* (Claremont, Calif. 1993), ch. 3. Luis E. Murillo, *The Noriega Mess: The Drugs, the Canal, and Why America Invaded* (Berkeley 1995), 881–902.

that read: 'Deng Xiaoping, Son of a Bitch'. From late that year *Sendero* carried out bombings of public buildings and private companies and assassinations of public figures in the area of its greatest strength, around Ayacucho. It fed on the deprived nature of the mostly Indian province of Ayacucho, long neglected by governments. In the 1960s the province had benefited from some economic development, which passed by the Indian peasants but gave them an inkling of a better life.[28]

By 1983 the Peruvian government realized it was facing a serious revolt by a movement with as many as 3,000 armed members. Subsequent strong military pressure drove *Sendero* largely out of its home base area. But there were enough other depressed rural areas in a nation-wide environment of serious economic decline, caused mainly by over borrowing and falling commodity prices, which produced hyperinflation. By 1990 *Sendero* had an estimated 10,000 fighters and controlled 28 per cent of Peruvian municipalities, a higher proportion than the FMLN ever controlled in El Salvador. The US response to this revolution was not as great as in Central America. The Maoist *Sendero* was obviously not an agent of Soviet expansion into Latin America. Nor did it ever launch a major offensive as did the revolutionary movements in El Salvador and Guatemala. So *Sendero* was perceived as less threatening. Furthermore, since the 1960s there had been tense relations between the US and Peru's leftist military regimes. So the total US aid to Peru in the last half of the 1980s was only one sixth of American aid to El Salvador. Only at the beginning of the 1990s, when *Sendero* was linked to drug trafficking, did US aid to Peru increase under the Bush administration's war on drugs.[29]

Chile became a concern to the US for another reason. Though the Reagan administration initially acted to change the Carter administration's human rights-influenced policy towards Chile, it made no attempt to pressure the Democratic Party to lift the arms ban at a time when it was pressing for aid to El Salvador and the contras. Also in Reagan's strong rhetoric about defending the free world, support for democracy was becoming a priority within his administration. Chile was becoming a target for democratic change, which even Republican conservatives were starting to accept with the argument that without it there might be a Sandinista style revolution there.

---

28 David Scott Palmer, 'The Sendero Luminoso Rebellion in Rural Peru', in Georges A. Fauriol (ed.), *Latin American Insurgencies* (Washington 1989), 67–96. Carlos Iván Degregori, 'Return to the Past', in David Scott Palmer, *The Shining Path of Peru* (New York 1992), ch. 3. Iván Hinojasa, 'On Poor Relations and the Nouveau Riche: Shining Path and the Radical Peruvian Left', in Steven J. Stern (ed.), *Shining and Other Paths: War and Society in Peru, 1980–1995* (Durham 1998), 60–83.

29 Lawrence A. Clayton, *Peru and the United States: The Condor and the Eagle* (Athens, Ga. 1999), 262–4. McClintock, *Revolutionary Movements in Latin America*, chs 2, 5.

Certainly, there was in the 1980s a ground swell of public opposition in Chile to Pinochet's regime, despite repressive government responses. The US pressure on Pinochet was still mild, such as cultivation of opposition groups by the US ambassador in Santiago and US abstentions on World Bank loans for Chile. The most important pressure was provision of money through non-government organizations to assist in voter education and opposition campaigning in the plebiscite in 1989 on Pinochet's presidency, which he expected to win, as he had in 1980. But, despite the alternative of an uncertain future, 55 per cent of Chileans voted 'no'. Pinochet accepted the result and the call for elections in the next year in a deal that left him commander of the armed forces for the next eight years and a Senator for life.[30]

The US was also pleased when Ecuador returned to democracy in the 1980s after a period of military rule. Democratic government, however, was plagued by political contests between the President and a congress controlled by his political opponents, which did not help a badly faltering economy. That year the conservative President of Ecuador, León Febres Cordero, was praised on a visit to Washington by Reagan as 'an articulate champion of free enterprise' who had pursued a free market economy. But an Ecuadorian human rights activist accused Febres' government of brutal treatment of opponents: 'Barracks were transformed into prisons, hooded men entered people's houses, people were detained without reason, tortured and disappeared.' There was also economic decline in Ecuador with the world trade slump in the mid 1980s, and Febres lost office in 1988. The new left-wing president conducted a more independent foreign policy, especially in cooperation with other Andean republics. In 1990 Febres was arrested and charged with embezzling US$150,000 of public funds while he was in office.[31]

By the end of the 1980s Ecuador was cooperating with the Andean Pact republics in discussions about free trade. Earlier in the decade there had been armed clashes between Ecuador and Peru over a long-standing border dispute over Ecuador's wish to have access to the Amazon River. In January 1981 the fighting lasted for five days before a cease-fire was established. There were further briefer clashes in 1983 and 1984 in a still unresolved dispute.[32]

In Colombia in 1989–90 there was a vicious war waged by the Colombian government against the Medellín drug cartels. An agreement in 1979 to

---

30   Paul E. Sigmund, *The United States and Democracy in Chile* (Baltimore 1993), ch. 8.

31   David Corkill and David Cubitt, *Ecuador: Fragile Democracy* (London 1988), chs 3–5. Anita Isaacs, *Military Rule and Transition in Ecquador, 1972–92* (Pittsburgh 1993), 136 (quotation). *Keesing's Record of World Events*, vol. XXXVI, 37482.

32   James D. Rudolph, *Peru: The Evolution of a Crisis* (Westport 1992), 85.

extradite drug bosses to the US had not been enforced until the Colombian Minister of Justice was murdered in 1984, and even then only a small number of traffickers were sent to the US. In Colombia many drug bosses went free because of bribery and intimidation. Police officers, judges, government officials, journalists and any others thought to be in the way of Medellín operations were assassinated, and public buildings were bombed. Colombians were unaware of the extent of the Medellín operations until the publication in 1987 in the *Miami Herald* of details about the cartel, which reputedly earned $8 billion and was the source of 80 per cent of the cocaine imported into the US. Washington poured financial aid into a Colombian army campaign to crush the cartel, which had become a state within a state. The appointment of a government of national unity in August 1990, resulted in halting the military offensive against the cartel, waiving extradition to the US and offering reduced prison sentences.[33]

The discussion about free trade in the Andean Pact states was succeeded by conclusion of a free trade agreement between the US and Canada, which was implemented on 1 January 1989. The aim was to improve bilateral trade between the two nations, which exceeded US$129 billion in 1987, the most valuable commerce between any two nations in the world. The agreement was initially a Canadian move supported by a Conservative Party government elected in 1984, by economists wedded to market forces and by a business community enthused by visions of freer access to the huge American market. Significant latter-day fear was generated by the opposition parties in Canada about an American take-over of the country, with Canada already enjoying a healthy trade balance with the US that was worth US$12.38 billion in 1988.[34]

The US had a different kind of economic problem with its southern neighbour, Mexico, the Latin American nation most dominated by American commerce and investment. The US controlled about two-thirds of Mexico's foreign trade and direct foreign investment there. In 1982 Mexico shocked the financial world by freezing all its US dollar accounts, closing its foreign exchange market and declaring a moratorium on repayments of its US$100 billion external debt, the largest in the world except for Brazil. The

---

33 Jorge P. Osterling, *Democracy in Columbia: Clientalist Politics and Guerrilla Warfare* (New Brunswick 1989), ch. 7. Bruce Michael Bagley, 'The New Hundred Years War? US National Security and the War on Drugs in Latin America', in Donald J. Mabry, *The Latin American Narcotics Trade and U.S. National Security* (New York 1989), ch. 4. *Keesing's Record of World Events*, vol. XXXVI, 37482–4; vol. XXXVII, 38245; vol. XXXVIII, 38717.

34 Robert Bothwell, *Canada and the United States: The Politics of Partnership* (New York 1992), 142–53. Dorothy Robinson-Mowry, *Canada–U.S. Relations: Perceptions and Misconceptions* (Latham, Md. 1988), chs 2, 5. *YTTS*, 1988, 140. *OECD Economic Outlook*, 51, June 1992, 83–7.

Mexican economy had been booming in the late 1970s, driven by rising prices for oil, which earned about 70 per cent of the country's foreign exchange and 45 per cent of government revenue. But the boom masked deep structural inadequacies in the Mexican economy, which had relied for too long on increasing injections of foreign capital. Hence there was a crisis when oil prices fell in the early 1980s.[35]

At least Reagan did not take the attitude of the conservative Republican US Senator Jesse Helms, who opened a Senate enquiry into Mexico's problems and declared: 'If Mexico wants United States help, the Mexican people have no choice, it seems to me, but to bring about fundamental political reform.' Reagan and his advisors knew how sensitive Mexican citizens were. The Helms enquiry threw them into a frenzy, with public demonstrations against the US embassy and formal protests to the State Department. So Reagan did not press the ruling party to open up the Mexican political system. He also was willing to discard his free trade ideology sufficiently to provide Mexico with a US$9.45 billion financial aid and credit package, a case of pragmatic necessity to assist a country of vital interest to the US. But in the rescheduling of its debt repayments, Mexico was subjected to an austerity program imposed by the IMF, which decreased wages and the general standard of living of the Mexican people. The economy also was bleeding from a flight abroad of Mexican capital and a devastating earthquake in Mexico City in 1985. A re-negotiated IMF plan, which provided US$7.7 billion from the fund and US$6 billion in commercial bank loans, was applied in 1986 to a still sick economy. However, the economy was improving because of more efficient taxation, trade liberalization and other economic reforms, which were partly a result of American pressure. A US-assisted debt-scheduling program, known as the Brady Plan, was implemented in April 1990. It greatly assisted in restoring overseas investor confidence in Mexico and assisted an average annual growth rate in GDP of 4 per cent in the years after 1989, compared with an average of only 0.6 per cent from 1982 to 1988.[36]

During the 1980s the Reagan administration also had problems with Mexico's refusal to join his campaigns against Nicaragua and the rebels in El Salvador. The Mexican government considered that revolutionary change in Central America was inevitable and that to support the US policies to

---

35 Miguel D. Ramírez, *Mexico's Economic Crisis: Its Origins and Consequences* (New York 1989), *passim.*

36 Robert A. Pastor and Jorge G. Castañeda, *Limits to Friendship: The United States and Mexico* (New York 1988), chs 4–7 (quotation 119). *OECD Economic Surveys: Mexico*, 1991/1992, 14, 36–43. W. Dirk Raat, *Mexico and the United States: Ambivalent Vistas* (Athens, Ga. 1992), ch. 8.

stem the tide would prevent its ability to mediate in disputes there and would provoke denunciations from left-wing Mexicans. Another source of tension in US–Mexico relations was the growth of the country as a source of drugs and illegal immigrants entering the US, which resulted in tightening of American border controls.[37]

The economic problems of the 1980s did not assist Latin American republics to escape from US economic dominance. The spread of neo-conservative economic policies served to facilitate American and other overseas direct investment. The US was still the principal source of imports for each of the Pacific Basin Latin American states and their principle market, except Nicaragua, on which there was a US trade ban. By 1988 the average standard of living in Latin America was 6.6 per cent below the level of 1980. The American-imposed debt rescheduling programs had contributed to an even greater debt burden with a net transfer of capital out of Latin America from 1982 to 1988 of $178.7 billion plus an estimated flight from the region of at least another $100 billion. The only comfort to Latin Americans was that from 1982 to the end of 1986 the US national debt had trebled to $2,217 billion, with about 11 per cent of it owed to foreigners, especially the Japanese.[38]

The Americas and the Pacific Basin

Japanese trade with Latin America had its vicissitudes in the 1980s reflecting the economic downturn in Latin American republics in the 1980s. US$10.5 billion worth of Japanese exports to that region in 1981 fell to US$6.4 billion in 1983 and did not pass the 1981 level for the rest of the 1980s. Japanese imports were also significantly higher than Latin American exports to Japan. The big increase in Japanese imports from Latin America in the 1970s had slackened with a shift in Japanese raw materials purchasing to Asia. But Japan remained the second most important source of supply and market for Latin America after the US, though only at a level of

---

37 Ibid., Lesler D. Langley, *Mexico and the United States: The Fragile Relationship* (Boston 1991), chs 6–7.

38 Bailey, 'Foreign Investment in Mexico' in Langley, *Mexico and the United States*, ch. 2. Joseph Ramos, *Neoconservative Economics in the Southern Cone of Latin America, 1973–1983* (Baltimore 1986), chs 7–9. *YTTS*, 1981, 1989, *passim*. Ronald A. Pastor, 'The Centrality of Central America', in Larry Berman (ed.), *Looking Back on the Reagan Presidency* (Baltimore 1990), 43–4. Akira Iriye, 'US–Asian Relations in the 1980s', in David E. Kyvig (ed.), *Reagan and the World* (New York 1990), 144–5.

6 per cent for imports and 7.5 per cent for exports and not far ahead of Germany. Also some US exports to Latin America by 1990 were from Japanese subsidiary companies in the US.[39]

Japanese direct foreign investment declined in Latin America in the 1980s as Japanese capitalists sought more profitable regions. Pacific Basin exceptions were Chile and especially Mexico. The nature of Japanese investment was changing from mining developments to financial and commercial enterprises, but with little attention to manufacturing, with the exception of Mexico, which was second only to Brazil as a Latin American location for Japanese capital. Mexico was offering incentives for foreign capitalists in bonded industrial zones along the US–Mexican border, called *maquiladoras*. Only ten Japanese firms had taken advantage of these opportunities by 1986, mostly electrical companies such as Sanyo and Sony. But by late 1987 twenty-one other Japanese firms had joined them or were planning to do so. For example, in 1988 Mitsubishi was making in Mexico parts for assembling forklifts in the US in order to escape American penalty duties and to exploit Mexican wage rates that were only 10 per cent of those in the US. This investment helped increase the contribution of manufactured goods to Mexico's imports from 30 per cent in 1983 to 56 per cent in 1989. Direct Japanese investment in Mexico jumped sharply from US$87 million in 1988–89 to $168 million in 1990–91.[40]

However, the government of Japan did not see Latin America as a major field for trade and investment. It was recognized in Tokyo that this was a region of primary US strategic and economic interest and therefore there should be minimal economic friction there, particularly in view of the emerging trade conflicts between those two economic superpowers. Consequently, Japan had acknowledged American diplomatic leadership in the region, which continued in the 1980s, for example by refusing any government aid to Nicaragua. American–Japanese cooperation in Latin America continued when the Bush administration exhibited more keenness to promote Latin American economic growth, in 'A New Partnership for Trade, Investment and Growth'. At a time of huge budget deficits, this American policy could not be carried out by government aid as in the Alliance for Progress in the 1960s. The emphasis was on free trade and foreign investment, which the debt crises of the 1980s had forced most Latin American governments to

39 A. Blake Friscia, 'Japanese Economic Relations with Latin America: An Overview', in Susan Kaufman Purcell and Robert M. Immerman (eds), *Japan and Latin America in the New Global Order* (Boulder 1992), 8–16.

40 Ibid., 18–26. *YTTS*, 1980, 578; 1989, 572. A. Blake Friscia, 'Japanese Economic Relations with Latin America: An Overview' and Luis Rubio, 'Japan in Mexico: A Changing Pattern' in Purcell and Immerman, *Japan and Latin America*, 15, 20, 69–100.

accept. In this process the Bush administration looked to Japan to play a role, which received a ready response from Tokyo. Japan has also cooperated with the US in debt rescheduling strategies in Latin America.[41]

To 1990 in the Latin American region of the Pacific Basin Japan was willing to concede the importance of US political and economic hegemony. Indeed, the US empire in the region was much more paternalist than Japan's economic empire in the Western Pacific Basin, which at this stage had not sought, or indeed needed, any assertions of even informal Japanese political control. However, the difference has been significantly influenced by the Cold War, which on the one hand allowed Japan to shelter under the American defence umbrella and on the other provoked US governments to oppose radical political movements in Latin America.

Latin American countries bordering the Pacific Ocean were also taking more interest in the wider Pacific Basin. Diplomatically, Chile's Pinochet had more success in the 1980s with his 'Pacific drive'. After breaking off relations with the Philippines after Marcos refused him entry, he received an apology from Manila and established good relations with that ASEAN nation. Chile also established good relations with an Asian nation in the opposite ideological camp, communist China, demonstrating pragmatic attempts to increase Chile's influence in the Pacific. Such initiatives contributed to a growth from 1980 to 1988 in the non-Soviet Asian proportion of Chile's export trade from 18.8 to 23.1 per cent. Peru was more inward looking in the 1980s with its serious economic problems and the *Sendero* insurgency. But another left-leaning government elected in 1985 looked across the Pacific to the Soviet Union for support. Not to be outdone by the USSR, China maintained in the 1980s good relations with Peru. Mexico had an ambition to play a greater role in the Pacific Basin. With its new free market economy, Mexico was starting to look for more Pacific Basin trading opportunities and to model its future development on the East Asian NICs.[42]

But the Latin American nations had not contributed greatly to the growing economic importance of the Pacific Basin in the 1980s. By 1986 Pacific Basin economies constituted almost 50 per cent of world GNP compared

---

41 Friscia, 'Japanese Economic Relations' and Susan Kaufman Purcell and Robert M. Immerman, 'Japan, Latin America, and the United States: Prospects for Cooperation and Conflict' in Purcell and Immerman, *Japan and Latin America*, 34, 122–32.
42 Virginia Gamba-Stonehouse, *Strategy in Southern Oceans: A South American View* (New York 1989), 40, 54, 62–3. *YTTS*, 1989, 162. Rubio, 'Japan in Mexico', 87–8. Teritomo Ozawa, 'The Dynamics of Pacific Rim Industrialization: How Mexico Can Join the Asian Flock of "Flying Geese" ', in Riordan Roett (ed.), *Mexico's External Relations in the 1990s* (Boulder 1991), 129–54.

with less than 35 per cent in 1965. In 1986 Mexico, the largest Pacific rim Latin American economy, contributed only 2.1 per cent of Pacific Basin GNP, and the Pacific rim nations of Latin America only 4 per cent, compared with Australia's 3.1 per cent and Japan's 34 per cent, which had almost caught up to the US's 36 per cent. Nor were Latin American countries much involved in the growth of trade across the North Pacific, which during the 1980s became more extensive in volume and value than trade across the North Atlantic. Furthermore, the Latin American states south of Panama were not strategically important since only local shipping used the sea-lanes down the west coast of South America. Nor were Latin American countries involved in the nuclear free Pacific campaign, having established an earlier nuclear free zone in Latin America, the Tlatelolco Treaty, signed by all Pacific rim states, except Chile. That treaty in fact was one of the inspirations for the nuclear free movement in the South Pacific.[43]

The US contribution to economic growth in the Pacific Basin was much greater. During the 1980s Japan, the East Asian NICs and the newer developing ASEAN economies benefited from relative peace under an American strategic umbrella. Also Japan and the East Asian Tigers, in particular, benefited from trade with the US which swung increasingly in their favour during the 1980s. Moreover, US investments helped give kick-starts to their economic growth. Reagan spent most of his adult years and all his political life in California and showed appreciation of the growing importance of the Pacific Basin. In 1984 he publicized the fact the Pacific region had become more important than Europe for American trade. He and other members of his administration often spoke of the coming Pacific age. However, Reagan's initial primary foreign policy interest was to strengthen the US crusade against Soviet Union-backed communism, which created his obsession with combating alleged communist threats in Nicaragua and El Salvador, and to pursue an arms build up which greatly increased the US public debt. One of the main emphases in Reagan's East Asia policies was pressure on Japan and other allies to spend more on their own defence to make their trading policies more acceptable to the US. However, he also presided over the growing détente with China and with the USSR.[44]

---

43 Gerald Segal, *Rethinking the Pacific* (Oxford 1990), 286-8. Gavin Boyd, *Pacific Trade, Investment and Politics* (New York 1989), ch. 1. Gamba-Stonehouse, *Strategy in Southern Oceans*, 64-5. Michael Hamel-Green, *The South Pacific Nuclear Free Zone Treaty: A Critical Assessment* (Canberra 1990), ch. 2.

44 David E. Kyvig, 'The Foreign Relations of the Reagan Administration'; Iriye, 'US–Asian Relations in the 1980s' and 'Reagan and the World: A Roundtable Discussion', in Kyvig, *Reagan and the World*, chs 1, 7, 8. John Lewis Gaddis, *The United States and the End of the Cold War: Implications, Reconsiderations, Provocations* (New York 1992), ch. 7. Samuel P. Huntington, 'America's Changing Strategic Interests', *Survival* 23, 1991, 3-17.

Conclusions

The US government demonstrated in the 1980s its strong opposition to any Marxist expansion in Latin America. The consequence was continued support for oligarchic control in El Salvador, compromising the demilitarization of Costa Rica, maintenance of a military regime in Honduras, and support for a drug trafficking dictator in Panama, until his oppressive reign gained the attention of American senators and drug enforcement administrators. Only military governments in Guatemala, where human rights abuses were notorious, were abandoned by the Reagan and Bush administrations.

The overthrow of the Sandinista government of Nicaragua became an obsession for Reagan. It justified any means, including gross violations of human rights by contra guerrillas, direct CIA acts of war, and the use of a known drug trafficker, Noriega. Despite the winding down of the Cold War, the Bush administration still imposed economic sanctions on Nicaragua and provided financial aid to political opponents of the Sandinistas in a final successful attempt to depose that government.

The attention placed by the US on military opposition to insurgencies in Central and South America ignored even the advice of a bipartisan commission of enquiry on Central America headed by Henry Kissinger. Its report recognized that: 'Widespread hunger and malnutrition, illiteracy, poor educational and training opportunities, poor health conditions, and inadequate housing are unstable foundations on which to encourage the growth of viable democratic institutions.'[45] Furthermore, the neo-conservative economic policies favoured by the US administration and the International Monetary Fund did not take into account structural weaknesses, such as inequitable distributions of income and widespread poverty in Latin America. A consequence was the persistence of revolutionary guerrilla movements. US free trade policies always have been a reflection of American economic strength, and, even though the US economy had weakened, it was still dominant in Latin America.

---

45 *The Report of the President's National Bipartisan Commission* (New York 1984), 81.

CHAPTER TEN

The Post-Cold War Pacific Basin since 1991

The post-Cold War era of the 1990s witnessed major changes in international relations in the Pacific Basin. There were continuing unresolved tensions in East Asia at the end of the decade. By contrast there were outbreaks of peace elsewhere in the Pacific Basin, though not completely in Latin America. Also in East Asia the economic miracle of the previous decade collapsed in the last years of the 1990s with foreign policy implications. The other main theme of this chapter is the development of economic cooperation between members of existing and new international organizations in the Pacific Basin.

Japan's relations with the US and Russia

A prediction in 1991 that there would be a war between the US and Japan did not eventuate in the 1990s.[1] However, there were still trade disputes. In February 1991 in a review of the 1989–90 SII trade negotiations, US negotiators perceived no positive changes in Japan's restrictions against foreign imports. The US again requested the removal of Japanese structural barriers, especially anti-competitive practices, but the US trade deficit with Japan increased from 1992 to 1993 by 14 per cent to $43.6 billion. In 1993 a new Democratic Party US President, William (Bill) Clinton, adopted a more aggressive approach in 'economic framework talks' with the Japanese Prime Minister, Miyazawa Kiichi.[2]

---

1 George Friedman and Meredith Lebard, *The Coming War with Japan* (New York 1991).
2 Michael Schaller, *Altered States: The United States and Japan since the Occupation* (New York 1997), 258. Mayumi Itoh, *Globalization of Japan: Japanese Sakoku Mentality and US Efforts to Open Japan* (New York 1998), 28–30.

Subsequently, in June 1995 Clinton claimed 'a great victory for the American people' in an agreement about automobiles and auto parts exports to Japan, which followed a previous 'breakthrough' in areas of government procurements and insurance. But this was much less than he had demanded originally in the framework talks. Therefore, there was further American pressure for deregulation reform in Japan. But a survey of American businessmen in 1998 revealed that a big majority considered Japanese non-tariff trade barriers as bad as China's. Also an academic assessment that year concluded that 'the regulatory reform measures implemented so far have had a relatively small, marginal effect' on increasing competition and the role of market forces in the Japanese economy. Indeed, after a fall from 1994 to 1996, the deficit in the US trade with Japan had increased by 1999 to $73.9 billion, though a strengthening US dollar was also a factor.[3]

The resistance to open market reform in Japan had deep roots. In the process of Japanese modernization both formal and informal government economic regulation were integral features of the Japanese economy in which business cartels thrived. American pressure for liberalization of the Japanese economy since the mid 1980s had been strongly resisted. Only in a few areas where American pressure had some internal Japanese support was there any notable progress. Established interests in the old economy were too politically powerful for most reform efforts, even after 1993 when the LDP, for the first time, lost sole political power.[4]

However, American anger in the late 1990s about Japanese trade restrictions was less intense than a decade previously. The comparative economic fortunes of the two countries had changed. In 1991 the economic boom in Japan collapsed under the weight of an overheated domestic economy and wider world recession. Political instability and the exposure of major structural problems in Japan's economy did not assist economic recovery during the 1990s. GNP growth rate slumped to an average increase of 1.7 per cent from 1991 to 1997 compared with 4 per cent in the previous decade, and Japan's GDP declined by 0.7 per cent in 1997 and by 1.8 per cent in 1998. There were also some staggering reversals in the performance of Japanese capital penetration of the US that had upset many Americans in the 1980s.

---

3 Leonard J. Schoppa, *Bargaining with Japan: What American Pressure Can and Cannot Do* (New York 1997), 254. *OECD Economic Surveys: Japan 1997–1998* (Paris 1998), 137. Lonny E. Carlile and Mark C. Tilton, 'Is Japan Really Changing?', in Lonny E. Carlile and Mark C. Tilton (eds), *Is Japan really Changing its Ways?: Regulatory Reform and the Japanese Economy* (Washington 1988), 206. 'US Posts Trade Deficits with Japan, China, EU in 1999', Reuter's Information Service, 23 February 2000.
4 Carlile and Tilton, 'Is Japan Really Changing?', 198–203. Schoppa, *Bargaining with Japan*, ch. 8.

Examples in 1995 were Sony's loss of $3 billion on its Columbia Pictures purchase and Matsushita's sale of MCA, the owner of Universal Studios, at a loss of nearly $400 million. By contrast, after the recession of the early 1990s, the American economy moved into a sustained period of strong economic growth.[5]

Another new reality about the 1990s was the changed US–Japan security position in the post-Cold War world. Although there was no longer a Soviet Union to threaten the US or Japan, the Northeast Asian region was still unstable with tension on the Korean Peninsula and a growth in Chinese military power. US forces were moved from more visible presence in the Japanese main islands and concentrated on the island of Okinawa, which had been restored to Japanese rule in 1972, but on which the US had military base rights. The presence of a large military force on that island received unpleasant publicity in 1995 when two US marines and a naval rating abducted and raped a thirteen-year-old local girl. This incident brought home to many Japanese the unwelcome continued presence of large US forces within their nation. However, the US–Japan Security Treaty was reconfirmed in 1996. On a visit to Japan in November 1998 Clinton announced that this alliance was 'the cornerstone of stability and prosperity in the Asia-Pacific region'. Indeed, the revised Guidelines for US–Japan Defense Cooperation, issued in September 1997 and passed by the Japanese Diet in May 1999, outlined a more active partnership role for Japan with the US in any future crisis in East Asia.[6]

Japan's relations with Russia, which inherited the USSR territory facing the Pacific Ocean, were less profitable. After a long delay, in October 1993, the Russian President Boris Yeltsin visited Japan and, after negotiations with the Japanese Prime Minister, Hosokawa Morihiro, they signed the Tokyo Declaration. It advocated negotiations toward an early conclusion of a peace treaty between Russia and Japan, but only after a settlement to the dispute about Russian occupation of the southern Kurile Islands. Yeltsin

5   Rob Steven, *Japan in the New World Order: Global Investments, Trade and Finance* (Basingstoke 1996), ch. 2. *OECD Economic Surveys: Japan 1997–1998*, 22. L.M. Destler, 'Political Change in the United States and Its Impact on US–Japan Relations', in Chihiro Hosoya and Tomohito Shinoda (eds), *Redefining the Partnership: The United States and Japan in East Asia* (Lanham 1998), 40. Robert Uriu, 'Japan in 1998', *Asian Survey*, 39, 1999, 114. Kazuo John Fukuda, *Japan and China: The Meeting of Asia's Economic Giants* (New York 1998), 16.
6   Schaller, *Altered States*, 259–60. W. Lee Howard, 'The Alliance and Post-Cold War Political Realignment in Japan', in Michael J. Green and Patrick M. Cronin (eds), *The US Japan Alliance: Past, Present and Future* (New York 1999), 210–12. Robert A. Scalapino, 'The United States and Asia in 1998: Summitry Amid Crisis', *Asian Survey*, 30, 1999, 6. Tsuneo Akaha, 'Beyond Self Defense: Japan's Elusive Security Role under the New Guidelines for US–Japan Defense Cooperation', *The Pacific Review*, 11, 1998, 461–83.

also announced that there would be a withdrawal of Russian troops from those islands, leaving only border guards. In Moscow in April 1996 Japan's Prime Minister, Hashimoto Ryutaro, and Yeltsin confirmed the Tokyo Declaration. But there were still Russian troops on the islands. The Russian military considered those islands strategically important for unfettered Russian access to the Pacific Ocean. There was also wider opposition in Russia to handing back any territory, which could be a dangerous precedent. However, in June 1997 Yeltsin and Hashimoto agreed to make the utmost efforts by 2000 to conclude a peace treaty on the basis of the 1993 Tokyo Declaration. In April 2000 new national leaders of Russia and Japan, Vladimir Putin and Yoshiro Mori, met in Russia and confirmed the need for a peace treaty by the year's end. But Russian control of the Southern Kuriles remained a difficult issue for negotiation.[7]

There were also problems in Japan's economic relations with Russia. Trade was adversely affected by economic troubles in Russia, which created indebtedness to Japanese companies, declining volumes of trade, and decreasing confidence. Japan's Russian imports, which from 1995 to 1998 were over three times the value of Japanese exports to Russia, were mainly raw materials. In fact in 1998 Japanese exports to Russia were less than half the value they were in 1991. Nor was there much Japanese investment in Russia. By June 1996 it was worth only $0.42 billion, which was 8.1 per cent of all foreign direct investment in Russia, compared with the leading source of capital, the US, with investments worth $1.66 billion, 31.5 per cent of the total. The investments by Japanese capitalists in Russia were also a mere 0.5 per cent of world-wide Japanese investment.[8]

The two Koreas and international powers

The most dangerous potential flash point along the western rim of the Pacific Basin in the 1990s was the Korean peninsula where South and

---

7   Tsuyoshi Hasegawa, *The Northern Territories Dispute and Russo–Japanese Relations*, vol. II, (Berkeley 1998), 482–3, 492–7. Robert Valliant, 'Main Events of a New Era', in Vladimir I. Ivanov and Karala S. Smith (eds), *Japan and Russia in Northeast Asia: Partners in the 21st Century* (Westport 1999), 155–64. Robert H. Donaldson and Joseph L. Nogee, *The Foreign Policy of Russia: Changing Systems, Enduring Interests* (Armonk 1998), 245–8. Kimie Hara, *Japanese–Soviet/ Russian Relations since 1945: A Difficult Peace* (London 1998), 192–223. *Canberra Times*, 1 May 2000.

8   Andrei P. Rodionov, 'The Russian View of Economic Links' and Susumu Yoshida, 'Economic Links from a Japanese Viewpoint', in Ivanov and Smith (eds), *Japan and Russia*, 218–30, 233–4. OECD, *Monthly Statistics of International Trade, January 2000 (OMSIT)* (Paris 2000), 62–3.

North Korea were still technically in a state of war. However, in December 1991 there was an agreement between the two Koreas, which aimed to promote reconciliation and non-aggression; and there was another agreement that month for mutual renunciation of nuclear weapons. These pacts were probably influenced by a greater sense of diplomatic isolation in North Korea marked by China's decision in 1991 not to block South Korea's application to join the UN after the Soviet recognition of the ROK in 1990.[9]

The US played a significant role in subsequent events. In January 1992 there was a high-level meeting between North Korean and US officials in New York. North Korea was interested in improving relations with the US, which could upstage the ROK and compensate for the loss of former powerful communist friends. In return North Korea agreed to permit inspection of its nuclear facilities, which had been developed with Soviet assistance, by the International Atomic Energy Agency (IAEA). But the DRPK did not allow for the scientific sophistication of the IAEA. Its investigators discovered that the small amount of plutonium given to them was not just from one old source, as had been claimed. Its constituent parts pointed to a significantly greater, but unknown, amount of plutonium in North Korean hands. There were deep suspicions in Washington that there might be enough to manufacture nuclear weapons, which was true according to Russian nuclear scientists who had been involved in North Korea's nuclear program. Pyongyang also rejected Seoul's demand for snap inspections of DPRK nuclear facilities by South Koreans that were projected in the December 1991 nuclear agreement.[10]

The consequence was a sharp deterioration in North/South Korean relations. ROKA generals reacted by pressing for the revival in 1993 of the annual 'Team Spirit' joint US/South Korean military exercise, which had been cancelled in 1992 as a good will gesture to North Korea. The DPRK responded by cancelling all the recently established contacts with South Korea. The IAEA nuclear inspection program also ran into trouble when North Korea refused entry into two suspect sites. Furthermore, on 8 March 1993, the day before the start of Team Spirit, North Korea declared a high military alert. Claiming a potential war situation as justification, the DRPK on 12 March withdrew from the UN Nuclear Proliferation Treaty, the first country to do so, citing an alleged US nuclear threat against North Korea.

---

9   James Cotton, 'The Two Koreas and Rapprochement: Foundations for Progress?', *The Pacific Review*, 5, 1992, 162–9. Don Oberdorfer, *The Two Koreas: A Contemporary History* (London 1997), 260–5.

10   Oberdorfer, *The Two Koreas*, 265–72. Doug Bandow, *Tripwire: Korea and US Foreign Policy in a Changed World* (Washington 1996), 103–7.

However, the terms of the treaty meant that the withdrawal would not take effect for three months, which allowed time for diplomacy.[11]

Hence the DRPK sought negotiations with the US before the withdrawal deadline, which achieved its postponement. But US negotiators became frustrated with the North Korean tactics that constantly avoided conceding complete freedom for IAEA inspectors. A catalyst for the next crisis was the removal of irradiated fuel rods from a North Korean nuclear reactor, which could potentially provide enough plutonium for atomic weapons production. Consequently, in late 1993 and early 1994 there was a build up of American forces in and around the Korean peninsula and activity at UN level to impose on the DPRK an escalating program of economic sanctions. Russia, which had established good relations with South Korea, was annoyed about the threat of nuclear development in North Korea. Moscow had suspended all nuclear cooperation with the DRPK and supported UN sanctions if necessary, though recommending first an international conference to solve the crisis. Also, according to a Chinese source, Beijing, though having restored good relations with North Korea, warned Pyongyang not to count on a Chinese veto. The DPRK was urged to come to an accommodation with the US.[12]

Indeed, North Korea defused this explosive situation. Kim Il Sung greeted a special envoy from the US, ex-President Jimmy Carter. He returned with the outline of an agreement whereby North Korea would freeze its nuclear energy developments and keep IAEA inspection in place. In turn the US would agree to facilitate a request for light water nuclear reactors. Furthermore, Kim Il Sung agreed to a potentially momentous event. His South Korean counterpart, Kim Young Sam, accepted an invitation to visit North Korea on 25 July 1994 for the first-ever meeting between the presidents of the two Koreas. But, as he was making preparations for this visit, Kim Il Sung died on 7 July.[13]

This death sparked another downturn in North/South Korean relations. It provoked a controversy in South Korea after an opposition spokesman

---

11 Oberdorfer, *The Two Koreas*, 274–80. Michael J. Mazarr, *North Korea and the Bomb: A Case for Nonproliferation* (New York 1995), chs 5–6. Evgeniy P. Bazhanov, 'Military-Strategic Aspects of the North Korean Nuclear Program', in James Clay Moltz and Alexandre Y. Mansourov (eds), *The North Korean Nuclear Program: Security, Strategy, and New Perspectives from Russia* (New York 2000), 102.

12 Oberdorfer, *The Two Koreas*, 281–321. Larry A. Niksch, 'North Korea's Negotiating Behaviour', in Samuel S. Kim, *North Korean Foreign Relations in the Post-Cold War Era* (Oxford 1998), 58–60. Evgeniy P. Bazhanov, 'Russian Views of the Agreed Framework and the Four-Party Talks', in Moltz and Mansourov (eds), *The North Korean Nuclear Program*, 222–5, 227–8. For China-North Korean relations see Taeho Kim, 'Strategic Relations Between Beijing and Pyongyang: Growing Strains amid Lingering Ties', in James R. Lilley and David Shambaugh (eds), *China's Military Faces the Future* (Washington 1999), 295–321.

13 Oberdorfer, *The Two Koreas*, 326–38. Mazarr, *North Korea and the Bomb*, 159–65.

suggested official ROK condolences to grieving North Koreans. Angry conservatives went on a counter-attack, and Kim Young Sam denounced any condolence expressions. He made further inflammatory anti-North Korea statements, which earned bitter resentment in the DRPK and a renewal of virulent anti-South propaganda by the new regime led by Kim Il Sung's son, Kim Jong Il. He had been for years a right-hand advisor to his father and was an intelligent film-producer and playwright. But in public he was an enigmatic recluse. However, his government signed on 21 October 1994 a 'Framework Agreement' with the US at a conference in Geneva, in which the US promised provision of the light water reactors – to be largely funded by South Korea and Japan – and 500,000 tons of heavy fuel oil. In return North Korea accepted IAEA inspection and promised to resume dialogue with South Korea. But South Korea, which had not been included in the negotiations, denounced the agreement with a country facing economic ruin.[14]

Indeed, the North Korean economy soon was collapsing. The catalyst was a deluge of rainfall from 26 July 1995 until mid August, creating disastrous floods. The impact was worsened by agricultural policies that allowed denuded hillsides and over-used farmland with resultant declining productivity. Also North Korea no longer could import cheap food from communist allies and lacked capital to purchase it on international markets. The result was a massive food shortage that created widespread malnutrition and starvation. For the first time the DRPK was forced to plead for international assistance. A reluctant contributor was South Korea other than an initial gift of 150,000 tons of emergency food. Its government objected to sustaining an economy on the point of a collapse that might force North–South unification on Southern terms. Japan sent 500,000 tons of food aid, and the US committed $2 million to a UN emergency appeal. Heavier than normal rain in 1996 compounded the North Korean problems, such as flooded coal mines that cut power supplies.[15]

There were still, however, tensions between North and South. The worst was the beaching of a North Korean submarine near Kangnung on the east coast of the ROK on 18 September 1996. One of its few survivors confessed its aim had been to spy on US/ROKA military facilities and to land infiltrators. US–South Korean relations were soured by Kim Young Sam's bellicose response and his outrage at US soft-pedalling on the issue, which impacted on the relationship with North Korea that Washington was

---

14   Oberdorfer, *The Two Koreas*, 344–68. Bandow, *Tripwire*, 112–13. Adrian Buzo, *The Guerrilla Dynasty: Political Leadership in North Korea* (Sydney 1999), 206–14.

15   Oberdorfer, *The Two Koreas*, 369–73.

carefully cultivating. Eventually North Korea apologized, and there was a renewal of negotiations to provide the DRPK with more economic aid.[16]

However, there were still difficulties in delivering assistance as North Korea tried to use aid as a bargaining tool about peace negotiations. Also continued DPRK military exercises raised fears of a North Korean invasion of the South as an act of desperation. Japan's generosity in aid was compromised by revelations of North Korean kidnapping of Japanese civilians. The US Administration faced difficulties with a Republican dominated Congress where Clinton was being accused of appeasing a devious dictator. China was contributing most to North Korean relief. Also another dramatic incident occurred on 12 February 1997 when a senior DPRK official, Hwang Jang Yop, walked into the ROK consulate in Beijing seeking political asylum. Before he defected he had written on 21 August 1996 that the DRPK 'is developing nuclear, rocket and chemical weapons' and 'believes it would win in a war' against the South, even though in 1995 the ROK had as much as twice the military power of the DRPK. Hwang's defection was uncomfortable for China in terms of its good relations with North Korea. But China struck a deal with South Korea whereby Hwang was allowed to travel to the Philippines before arriving in Seoul on 20 April. A brighter note was the beginning of long sought peace talks between the two Koreas in Geneva in December 1997.[17]

A positive development for the peace talks was the election on 18 December 1997 of a new South Korean president, Kim Dae Jung, a former political prisoner, who announced a 'sunshine' policy of more openness towards North Korea. However, in the two years after he took office in February 1998, there was no significant progress. Indeed, North Korea was still creating a rogue-nation image by developing, with probable Chinese assistance, long-range missiles, and on 31 August 1998 test flew one over Japan's island of Honshu to the great annoyance of the Japanese government. That incident spurred US–Japan research into theatre missile defences. However, there was one ray of hope with a simultaneous announcement in Pyongyang and Seoul on 10 April 2000 of a meeting from 12 to 14 June in Pyongyang between Kim Dae Jung and Kim Jong Il.[18]

---

16 Ibid., 387–9.
17 Ibid., 393–408 (quotation 404). Taik-young Hamm, *Arming the Two Koreas: State, Capital and Military Power* (London 1999), 115. Chae-Jin Lee, 'The Evolution of China's Two-Korea Policy', in Bae Ho Hahn and Chae-Jin Lee (eds), *The Korean Peninsula and the Major Powers* (Sungham, Korea 1998), 124–5.
18 David G. Brown, 'North Korea in 1988: A Year of Foreboding Developments', *Asian Survey*, 39, 1999, 129–30. *Keesing's Record of World Events*, 1998, 42446. Bazhanov, 'Military Strategic Aspects', 108. Melbourne, *Age*, 11 April 2000.

China, the US and Taiwan

For Clinton, relations with China were not plain sailing. In the 1992 presidential election campaign he had inveighed against the Bush administration's accommodation of the 'butchers of Beijing' whose army had murdered pro-democracy Chinese citizens in Tiananmen Square. On the other hand, China was an emerging economic giant, possessing veto rights in the UN Security Council and wielding major military power.

Indeed, in the early 1990s many American businessmen were enthusiastic about economic prospects in China. Robert Allen, the Chief Executive Officer of the giant American telephone company AT&T enthused: 'next to China, all other opportunities around the world pale'. Indeed, some Americans were profiting well from China. The mobile phone company, Motorola, after a few years there, considered business in China more profitable than in Japan.[19]

However, Clinton initially tried to link the continuation of most favoured nation (MFN) trading status for China with improvement in human rights and regulation of armaments exports, having condemned Bush for extending MFN benefits to China without any attached conditions. But Clinton received no evidence that China was responding to his policy. Also he was under pressure from sections of American business and from the Pentagon, which was concerned about rising tension with North Korea, to be more conciliatory towards China. So Clinton in September 1993 changed his policy to one of engagement with China on a wide range of levels. Then in May 1994 he cut the link between MFN and human rights issues.[20]

On the trading front Clinton also pushed for more Chinese liberalization of trade, in an environment of a growing American trade deficit with China, which in 1993 had increased to $22.7 billion. In 1992 the Bush administration had threatened steep punitive tariffs if China did not agree to trade reform measures. In 1995 the US Government Accounting Office declared that China had taken significant trade reform steps. But there were still contentious trade issues centring on mushrooming Chinese textile exports to the US and Chinese piracy of US entertainment and computer software products. In these cases the US was able to achieve some success with agreed quotas for textile imports and better enforcement in China of intellectual property rights. However, such measures did not stop the trade deficit from

---

19   Daniel Burstein and Arne De Keijzer, *Big Dragon. China's Future: What it Means for Business, the Economy, and the Global Order* (New York 1998), 14–15.

20   James Mann, *About Face: A History of America's Curious Relationship with China, from Nixon to Clinton* (New York 1999), ch. 16.

ballooning to $69.7 billion in 1998. Nevertheless, this trade created a Chinese dependency on the US, which had become China's second most important market. American investments in China were also worth $21 billion in 1998 creating a significant Chinese dependence on American capital for its economic modernization.[21]

Diplomatic relations between the US and China became more tense because of Taiwan. Since 1979 US administrations had maintained a one China policy. Even though continuing to provide military assistance to Taiwan, the refusal of visas to official representatives of Taiwan to visit the US was a means of maintaining good relations with China. But in November 1994 the Republican Party won a majority in both Houses of Congress, for the first time since 1948. A result was a significant increase in the number of supporters of non-communist Taiwan. Their leader was the Republican Party Speaker of the House of Representatives, Newt Gingrich, who had little understanding of how seriously China treated the issue of its 'renegade province'. The other agent of US policy change was Lee Teng-hui, a Presbyterian Church minister who became leader of the KMT and President of Taiwan in 1988. The KMT, which had held continuous power in Taiwan since 1945, had supported the concept of one China in pursuit of the hopeless dream of restoration of KMT rule over the whole of China. But among the Taiwanese population there was growing support for independence. Lee, who was the first Taiwanese-born KMT leader, though not supporting independence, was concerned to promote the status of Taiwan. Hence, with the new political development in the US, he was eager to make a visit there. Indeed, Lee received strong Republican Party and wider public support for a private trip to Cornell University, where he had gained a doctorate in agricultural economics in 1968. Clinton, faced with enough trouble with the Republican dominated congress, did not want a fight about Taiwan. So on 19 May 1995 Lee was informed that he could make a strictly private visit to the US, where he would receive no official welcome.[22]

Apart from propaganda about American treachery, China's initial reactions to Lee's arrival in the US on 7 June were diplomatic jabs, such as postponing official US–China meetings and recalling the Chinese ambassador from Washington. But this was followed on 19 July with a week-long

---

21   Le He, 'North American Free Trade Agreement (NAFTA) and Economic Impact on China', in Yu Bin and Chung Tsungting (eds), *Dynamics and Dilemma: Mainland, Taiwan and Hong Kong in a Changing World* (New York 1996), 156. Robert S. Ross, 'Engagement in US China Policy', in Alistair Iain Johnston and Robert R. Ross (eds), *Engaging China: The Management of an Emerging Power* (London 1999), 185–7 190–1. *OMSIT*, 58–9.

22   John W. Garver, *Face Off: China, the United States and Taiwan's Democratization* (Seattle 1997), 67–71. Mann, *About Face*, 319–26.

series of Chinese naval exercises using live ammunition in the Taiwan Strait and the firing of four missiles into waters to the north of Taiwan that were the result of significant recent Chinese missile development.[23]

Contributing to that provocation had been a previous decline in relations between Taiwan and China. Lee had angered China with moves to enhance Taiwan's international status, such as pressing countries to grant diplomatic recognition to Taiwan. There was also a fundamental difference between two definitions of 'one China'. To Beijing it meant Taiwan's subordination to the mainland. To Lee it was a partnership of equals, reflected by the enormous economic growth in Taiwan. Indeed, Taiwanese economic involvement in China was booming, with investments there worth $31.62 billion in 1995, the second largest external investment in China behind Hong Kong. Also the value of Taiwan's indirect trade with China had increased from $5.17 billion in 1990 to $20.99 billion in 1995.[24]

Another factor in China's new military posture towards Taiwan was political change in China. It has been argued that in the last days of Deng Xiaoping, who had Parkinson's disease and died on 19 February 1997, contenders for future power were vying to outdo each other as defenders of Chinese nationalism. An alternative argument is that Deng's policy of pursuing a peaceful policy towards Taiwan was collapsing under the weight of Lee Teng-hui's actions, especially an interview with a Japanese writer in March 1994, when he likened himself to Moses leading the Israelites to freedom across the Red Sea, followed by his visit to the US. Lee seemed to be heading along the path of Taiwanese independence. The Chinese naval exercises were a warning for him to back off. But Lee responded with a large military parade in Taipei to show off new weapons.[25]

The Chinese military action aroused more concerted attention to China by Clinton's administration, which had been concentrating more on domestic policy and other foreign policy issues. Consequently, at a meeting

---

23 Mann, *About Face*, 327–8. Garver, *Face Off*, 71–5. For the missile development see Mark A. Stokes, *China's Strategic Modernization: Implications for the United States* (Carlisle, Pa. 1999), ch. 4.

24 Stephen M. Goldstein, 'Terms of Engagement: Taiwan's Mainland Policy', in Johnston and Ross (eds), *Engaging China*, 70–2. T. Wang, *The Dust that Never Settles: The Taiwan Independence Campaign and US–China Relations* (Lanham NY, 1999), 314–21. Suisheng Zhao, 'Economic Interdependence and Political Divergence: A Background Analysis of the Taiwan Strait Crisis', in Suisheng Zhao (ed.), *Across the Taiwan Strait: Mainland China, Taiwan, and the 1995–1996 Crisis* (New York 1999), 24–5.

25 Suisheng Zhao, 'Introduction', John F. Copper, 'The Origins of Conflict Across the Taiwan Strait: The problem of Differences in Perception', You Ji, 'Changing Leadership Consensus: The Domestic Context of War Games', Edward Friedman, 'The Prospects of a Larger War: Chinese Nationalism and the Taiwan Strait Conflict', in Zhao (ed.), *Across the Taiwan Strait*, 4–8, 41–4, 60–1, 77–94, 243–72.

in Brunei, Secretary of State Warren Christopher handed to the Chinese Foreign Minister, a secret letter from Clinton to President Jiang Zemin in which a new policy was stated, later known as the 'three noes'. The US would oppose independence for Taiwan, would not support 'two Chinas' and would vote against Taiwan's admission to the UN. Soon China expressed its satisfaction with this development by returning its ambassador to Washington.[26]

However, the Taiwan crisis was not over. Lee's defiance and his candidacy in Taiwan's first democratic presidential election to be held on 23 March 1996 provoked a more deadly Chinese military response, the greatest since the bombardment of Jinmen in 1958. From 8 to 15 March 1996, China fired missiles that landed 19 and 28 nautical miles from Taiwan's two major ports, Keelung and Kaohsiung, which handled 70 per cent of Taiwan's trade. Later the PLA conducted live-ammunition amphibious landings in the islands near Mazu. Taiwan went on to high military alert. This time the US militarily responded. Two aircraft carriers, one withdrawn from the Persian Gulf, with accompanying warships, were sent to waters near Taiwan, the largest US naval fleet action in the Western Pacific Basin since the Vietnam War. However, the US ships were careful not to enter the Taiwan Strait, which China had declared would be an act of war. China had not intended to invade Taiwan. Indeed, its main purpose was defeated when Lee won the election with 54 per cent of the vote, after which the Chinese military exercises ceased. But China had given a blunt warning that a military response would be the answer to any declaration of independence by Taiwan.[27]

Throughout the Taiwan crises of 1995–96, the Clinton administration was careful to issue no guarantee that the US would defend Taiwan, despite many calls within the US Congress to do so. While continuing to contribute to Taiwan's defence capabilities, Washington refused to supply advance anti-missile systems. This ambiguous strategic policy was governed by the requirement for good relations with Beijing. Indeed, China responded positively during Clinton's presidential re-election campaign in 1996 by agreeing to the clamp down on the piracy of American products; and after the election there were accusations that Chinese money had increased Clinton's campaign fund. He was a better bet for Beijing than the pro-Taiwan policy of his Republican Party challenger. After his election victory, Clinton set in motion arrangements for Jiang Zemin to achieve his previously expressed

---

26 Mann, *About Face*, 329–30.
27 Mann, *About Face*, 335–8. Qimao Chen, 'The Taiwan Strait Crisis: Causes, Scenarios, and Solutions', Dennis Van Vranken Hickey, 'The Taiwan Strait Crisis of 1996: Implications for US Security Policy', in Suisheng (ed.), *Across the Taiwan Strait*, 127–8, 277–80.

wish to visit the US. He arrived in October 1997 for a summit that only resolved a few of the trade, arms sales and human rights issues between the two countries. In June 1998 Clinton made his first-ever visit to China, where he pleased his hosts by publicly acknowledging the 'three noes' policy about Taiwan. These two summit meetings had restored US–China policy to its pre-Tiananmen level. But there were still troubles during 1999, such as the revelation of a Chinese spy in an American nuclear laboratory and rock-throwing crowd attacks on the US embassy in Beijing after American aircraft accidentally bombed the Chinese embassy in Serbia. However, when there was the threat of the pro-independence leader of the opposition Democratic Progressive Party, Chen Shui-ban, winning the next presidential election on 18 March 2000 in Taiwan, China bombarded the island only with threatening words. That action diminished after Chen's electoral victory – the first defeat of the KMT – and his soft-pedalling on the independence issue.[28]

China, Hong Kong and Macau

The ceremony on 1 July 1997 for the hand-over of Hong Kong Island and the New Territories by Britain to China, attended by CCP leaders, British royalty and the PRC's newly appointed Hong Kong elite, was a gala event spoiled only by soaking rain. Hong Kong was a rich prize for China. Its average annual GDP growth rate from 1980 to 1993 was 6.5 per cent. Its domestic exports to China had expanded from $21.9 billion in 1989 to $35.98 billion in 1995. Hong Kong was the source of nearly half of the direct foreign investment in China in 1996. A democratically elected legislative assembly introduced by Britain's last governor of Hong Kong, Chris Patten, had now been replaced with a provisional legislative body selected by the CCP in Beijing; and the CCP had appointed the chief executive officer, Tung Chee-hwa for the Hong Kong Special Administrative Region (SAR).[29]

---

28 Mann, *About Face*, ch. 18. Tyler, *A Great Wall*, 419–30. Peter Koehn and Joseph Y.S. Cheng (eds), *The Outlook for US–China Relations Following the 1997–1998 Summits: Chinese and American Perspectives on Security, Trade and Cultural Exchange* (Hong Kong 1999), *passim*. Melbourne, *Age*, 4, 20 March 2000.

29 Avery Goldstein, 'China in 1997: A Year of Transitions', *Asian Survey*, 38, 1998, 39. Chaangqui Wu, 'Hong Kong and Greater China: An Economic Perspective', in Warren I. Cohen and Li Zhao (eds), *Hong Kong Under Chinese Rule: The Economic and Political Implications of Reversion* (Cambridge 1997), 121. Alice H. Amsden, 'Manufacturing Capabilities: Hong Kong's New Engine of Growth?', in Suzanne Berger and Richard K. Lester (eds), *Made by Hong Kong* (Hong Kong 1997), 334. Yanrui Wu, *Foreign Direct Investment and Economic Growth in China* (Cheltenham, UK 1999), 60.

Tung promised to abide by the Basic Law agreed to by Britain and China for the future government of Hong Kong, which in Chinese terms created 'one country, two systems'. Two years after the hand-over, the international community was praising China for adhering to the Basic Law in Hong Kong with a resultant high degree of autonomy for the SAR. But within the region there was increasing criticism that Tung's governing style was becoming too autocratic. The level of public satisfaction in his government's perform-ance had declined from 66 per cent in June 1997 to 42 per cent in October 1998, and a survey in April 1999 found that 68 per cent of people were 'somewhat' or 'very' worried about the SAR government's efficiency. But the fact that such surveys could be taken and published indicated the higher level of public freedom in Hong Kong than in the rest of China.[30]

Macau was less of an economic prize for China. It depended significantly on its thriving gambling industry, which in 1990 contributed 60 per cent of total government revenue. There had been some economic develop-ment, which had transformed a manufacturing industry which in the 1960s consisted mainly of fireworks and matches to one dominated in the 1980s and early 1990s by textiles and garments. This had been facilitated by the economic growth of Hong Kong. Garments comprised 64 per cent of Macau's exports in 1994. Also in 1992–93 there was a GDP growth of 4 per cent. In this development China played a major role, especially the dominance of the Bank of China in the financial sector. But there was little dissent in Macau when on 18 December 1999 Portuguese rule ended and Macau became a Chinese SAR like Hong Kong.[31]

China's relations with Russia and Japan

In the 1990s China was able to improve its relations with its former es-tranged communist neighbour, Russia. Initially, China was displeased about the political changes in Russia, which had inspired pro-democracy demon-strators in China in 1989, and there was barely disguised Chinese support in 1991 for an abortive procommunist coup against Yeltsin. But in Decem-ber 1991 he sent an emissary to Beijing to reassure China about the border accords signed by Gorbachev, which was confirmed when the Russian Foreign Minister, Andrei Kozyrev, visited Beijing in March 1992. He also

---

30   Goldstein, 'China in 1997', 39–40. Eliza W.Y. Lee, 'Governing Post-Colonial Hong Kong', *Asian Survey*, 39, 1999, 940–59. 'Hong Kong Transition Project', 1, accessed 21 April 2000 on the world wide web at <www.hkbu.edu.hk/òhtkp/do/dopquestion>.
31   Gunn, *Encountering Macau: A Portuguese City-State on the Periphery of China, 1557–1999* (Boulder 1996), 136–50.

signed a trade agreement. But China was upset about Russian relations with Taiwan. Russia acted to mollify this concern by decreeing that such relations could only be on a non-official level. Yeltsin visited Beijing in December 1992 and further agreements were signed including a mutual promise not to enter into a military alliance directed at either party. The Chinese described the talks as 'friendly, open and constructive'. Russian and Chinese descriptions of subsequent presidential meetings in Beijing and Moscow became increasingly glowing, reflecting a growing warmth in Russo-Chinese relations. Yeltsin during his visit to Beijing in April 1996 declared the relationship, which though not a military alliance, was a 'partnership directed towards the twenty-first century' and better than any 'such pair in the world'. Such statements were also addressed to other countries, especially the US. Both China and Russia were concerned about American hegemonic trends: the expansion of NATO into eastern Europe for Russia and Taiwan for China. Russian trade with China also boomed to a value of $7.8 billion in 1993. But it fell to $5 billion in 1994 because Russia responded to complaints in Siberia about illegal Chinese migrants and set up border controls, which stifled a profitable cross-border trade. However, Russia's trade with China rose again to $6.8 billion in 1996, $3 billion of which was a Russian surplus. A major component of Russian exports to China were weapons, such as missile destroyers, multiple rocket launchers and especially aircraft. To criticisms in Russia that China was becoming better armed than Russian forces, the former defence minister, Pavel Grachev, retorted in 1995: 'China poses no threat to Russian security.'[32]

China's relations with Japan were less warm in the 1990s. After the sharp cooling of the relationship caused by the Tiananmen massacre, there were significant divisive issues between the two countries. Japan was still refusing to apologize for its wartime atrocities in China. A survey of readers of the *China Youth Daily* in December 1996 found that among its readers, who were nearly all too young to remember the Second World War, 84 per cent of respondents associated Japan with the 1938 Nanjing massacre. The renewal of the Japan–US security alliance in 1996 also was resented in China. On the Japanese side there was resentment about China's claim to the Senkaku (Diaoyu) Islands northeast of Taiwan. Also China's underground nuclear test in August 1995 provoked calls in the Japanese Diet for suspension of financial aid to China. As a result Japanese grant assistance to China, but not loans, were frozen and not renewed until China announced an end to nuclear testing in July 1996. In November 1998 Jiang visited Tokyo, the first-ever such visit by a Chinese Head of State. But he was disappointed in

---

32   Donaldson and Nogee, *The Foreign Policy of Russia*, 240–5 (quotations 240, 244).

his hope that Japan would give an apology to China for past wrongs, as had been given recently to Korea, or that Japan would endorse the American 'three noes' policy about Taiwan.[33]

However, Japanese capitalists viewed China in the early 1990s as a potential economic bonanza. In early 1990 there were only about 700 Japanese-invested projects in China. Two years later there were nearly 1,900, and by 1996 Japan was the biggest foreign investor in China, apart from Hong Kong, and Japanese firms were moving aggressively into newly opened areas for foreign investment in China, such as transport, real estate and finance. Japan's trade with China was also growing. Worth $20.28 billion in 1991, it grew to $64.37 billion in 1997, though it slipped to $57.08 billion in 1998 with the impact of economic downturn in Japan and elsewhere in East Asia. China enjoyed the lion's share of its trade with Japan in 1997–98 with exports worth nearly two times the value of imports. By contrast, in 1998 Japan's exports to Taiwan were worth two and half times its imports from Taiwan in a trade worth $35.83 billion.[34]

The ASEAN states

A feature of ASEAN in the 1990s was expansion of its membership. In July 1995 Vietnam was admitted. That was a very significant event, given the previous enmity between ASEAN and Vietnam but, though still a communist state, Vietnam had withdrawn from Cambodia, after which an international Cambodian peace agreement had been signed in Paris in October 1991, and the Cold War had ended. Vietnam's major motives for applying for ASEAN membership in 1994 were to link its national security with the rest of Southeast Asia and to enhance its economic development. Vietnam also hoped to resolve demarcation and territorial issues with Malaysia, the Philippines and Thailand. Furthermore, ASEAN membership would enhance Vietnam's diplomatic relations with other nations, especially with China and the US.[35]

---

33 Osaki Yuji 'China and Japan in Asia Pacific: Looking Ahead', in Wakisaka Noriyuki, 'Japanese Development Cooperation for China', in Kokubun Ryosei, *Challenges for China–Japan–US Cooperation* (Tokyo 1998), 92–3, 119–20. Allen S. Whiting, 'Chinese Foreign Policy: Retrospect and Prospect', in *China and the World: Chinese Foreign Policy Faces the New Millenium* (4th edition, Boulder 1998), 293–5. Joseph Fewsmith. 'China in 1998: Tacking to Stay the Course', *Asian Survey*, 39, 1999, 111.

34 Fukuda, *Japan and China*, 108. Yanrui, *Foreign Direct Investment*, 60. *OMSIT* (Paris 2000), 62–3.

35 Carlyle A. Thayre, 'Vietnam and ASEAN: A First Anniversary Assessment', in Daljit Singh (ed.), *Southeast Asian Affairs 1997* (Singapore 1997), 366–9.

The other new members of ASEAN completed its original goal of covering all of Southeast Asia. Myanmar (Burma) was admitted in 1997, a controversial decision because of the appalling human rights record of its dictatorial military government. It was hoped that ASEAN membership would encourage more openness in Myanmar's society, but with no perceivable success by the end of 1999. Laos was admitted in 1997. Cambodia's admission was planned for that year but postponed because of a coup by Hun Sen, the Vietnamese-appointed ruler of Cambodia in the 1980s. There was a concern within ASEAN that admitting Cambodia at the same time as Myanmar could have damaged too much the organization's reputation in the West. There was some Western pressure on ASEAN to lead diplomatic opposition to the coup. That was divisive among its members because of the non-interference principle; but postponement of Cambodia's admission was a compromise that did not upset that tradition. A return to a democratically elected coalition government was ASEAN's condition for Cambodia's membership, and ASEAN reluctantly offered mediation to the disputant Cambodian political parties. Hun Sen initially rejected this offer, but accepted it when Japan, Vietnam's major aid donor, proposed a peace plan. The result was an election in July 1998, which a UN monitoring group declared as fair. Hun Sen stayed in power but leading a coalition government including a royalist party. Consequently, Cambodia in April 1999 became the tenth member of ASEAN. It was one of the poorest members with a per capita GNP in 1998 of only $320 compared with $32,940 in the wealthiest ASEAN country, Singapore.[36]

Diplomatically, ASEAN's biggest challenge in the 1990s was Chinese expansionism in the Spratly Islands. During the 1980s Vietnam, the Philippines and Malaysia acted to strengthen their claims to separate islands, such as building airstrips, developing tourism and setting up oil rigs. China's opposition to these developments, based on a Chinese claim to the whole of the Spratly group, hardened after 1987; and in 1988 Chinese naval ships clashed separately with Vietnamese and Philippines ships. Influencing the change was the demise of the USSR–Vietnam alliance that had been a major obstacle to the Chinese claim. Also China had significantly expanded and modernized its navy. However, in the more difficult international environment after the Tiananmen massacre in 1989, China offered to solve the issue diplomatically with negotiations for joint development of the islands. But at the ASEAN Ministers' Meeting in 1992 in Manila the Philippines raised strong objections to Chinese activities in islands claimed by them. The Philippines had the weakest navy in ASEAN and in 1991 had rejected

---

36 Jeannie Henderson, *Reassessing ASEAN* (Oxford 1999), 24–6, 33–40.

a new treaty for the American bases there, with consequent withdrawal of US forces. China rejected the offer to negotiate with ASEAN, preferring to deal with individual nations, which caused ASEAN disunity on the issue. But there were further Chinese incursions in 1994–95 into islands claimed by the Philippines. Manila's loud protest produced a unified ASEAN response, an unpleasant surprise for China. While not recanting its claim to all the islands, Beijing did not wish to upset good relations with ASEAN.[37]

An ASEAN response to the growing power of China and the end of the Cold War was a first venture into wider regional security by establishing the ASEAN Regional Forum (ARF) in 1994. The ARF initially included, as well as the ASEAN states, China, Japan, Russia, South Korea, Laos, Australia, New Zealand, PNG, Canada, the US and the EEC. This wide-scale agreement to join ARF demonstrated ASEAN's prestige in the 1990s as well as the new multi-polar post-Cold War world. Myanmar and India were included in 1995–96 and Mongolia in 1998. The hope was that future disputes between ARF states would be resolved peacefully, not by signing treaties, but by the kind of dialogue and conflict resolution that had characterized ASEAN. ARF had no secretariat. There was a standing committee and meetings tacked on to the annual meetings of ASEAN foreign ministers. ARF's limitations were that Taiwan was out of bounds – a condition of Chinese membership – and North Korea was not a member. ARF's deliberations also were weakened by a lowest common denominator factor, especially because of the touchiness of China. Nevertheless, it was a step towards establishing an environment of peace in the western Pacific Basin.[38]

Certainly, peace was maintained within ASEAN. There were some disputes in the 1990s. Examples were Thai accusations in 1998 of Malaysian support for a Muslim separatist movement in southern Thailand, Malaysian concerns about illegal Indonesian immigrants, Malay–Philippines contention about Spratly islands and squabbles between Malaysia and Singapore about inflammatory public statements. But most of these disputes were resolved by negotiations.[39]

---

37 Sheng Lijun, *China's Policy Towards the Spratly Islands in the 1990s* (Canberra 1995), 9–19. Chris Roberts, *Chinese Strategy and the Spratly Dispute* (Canberra 1996), 13–25. Jianwei Wang, 'Managing Conflict: Chinese Perspectives on Multilateral Diplomacy and Collective Security', in Yong Deng and Fei-Ling Wang (eds), *In the Eyes of the Dragon: China Views the World* (Lanham, Md. 1999), 84–8.

38 Michael Leifer, *The ASEAN Regional Forum. A Model for Cooperative Security in the Middle East* (Canberra 1998), 1–16. Jeffrey Winters, 'The Risks and Limits of a Corporate Foreign Policy', in Selig S. Harrison and Clyde V. Prestowitz (eds), *Asia After the 'Miracle': Redefining US Economic and Security Priorities* (Washington 1998), 226–8. Jianwei, 'Managing Conflict', in Yong and Fei-Ling (eds), *In the Eyes of the Dragon*, 86–7.

39 N. Ganesan, *Bilateral Tensions in Post-Cold War ASEAN* (Singapore 1999), 11–57.

Another major commitment by ASEAN states in the 1990s was to strive for more economic unity. In 1992 the ASEAN Free Trade Agreement (AFTA) was signed at the Fourth ASEAN Summit in Singapore. The objective was free trade within ASEAN by 2008, later brought forward to 2003. The agreement reflected a greater maturity among the industrializing economies of most of the ASEAN states, reducing the need for previous protectionist policies and creating greater opportunities for inter-regional trade. An objective of AFTA was to increase the international competitiveness of ASEAN products and to enhance the region as a location for foreign investments. At the time of this agreement the economies of the original ASEAN members were mostly continuing to boom. Average annual GDP growth rates from 1990 to 1995, except for 2.3 per cent in the Philippines, ranged from 8.7 per cent in Malaysia to 8 per cent in Indonesia. However, the economic boom collapsed in 1997.[40]

The East Asian economic crisis

On 2 July 1997 the government of Thailand floated the Thai baht after costly attempts to defend it against speculative capital outflows. Promptly the baht's value plunged by 20 per cent and by mid December it had fallen by about 77 per cent. A major reason was the Thai economy's poorly regulated and growing dependence on foreign capital, mostly from Japan and the Asian Tigers. Also the pegging of the baht to the US dollar, which had been a blessing for Thai traders when the dollar was weak, became a curse when it rose in value from 1995. Thai exports become over-priced, and their growth rate plunged from 38.7 per cent in 1995 to −0.35 per cent in 1996.[41]

The virulent financial disease in Thailand quickly infected other East Asian economies. Within three weeks there was a dramatic slump in the value of the Malaysian ringgit, the Philippine peso and, especially, the

40 Jose L. Tongzon, *The Economies of Southeast Asia: The Growth and Development of ASEAN Economies* (Cheltenham UK 1998), 161–2. Ross Garnaut, 'The East Asian Crisis', in Ross H. McLeod and Ross Garnaut (eds), *East Asia in Crisis: From being a Miracle to Needing One?* (London 1998), 22.

41 Peter G. Warr, 'Thailand', in ibid., 49–60. Suchitra Punyaratabandhu, 'Thailand in 1997', *Asian Survey*, 38, 1998, 161–4. Jeffrey A. Winters, 'The Financial Crisis in Southeast Asia', in Richard Robinson, Mark Beeson, Kanishka Jarasuriya and Hyuk-Rae Kim (eds), *Politics and Markets in the Wake of the Asian Crisis* (London 2000), 34–42. Pasuk Phongpaichit and Chris Baker, *Thailand's Boom and Bust* (Chiang Mai 1998), 39–43, 94–126.

Indonesian rupiah, which in January 1998 was worth only 30 per cent of its pre-crisis value. The stronger economies of Singapore and Taiwan, under the impact of this spreading financial hurricane, also experienced currency devaluation though not nearly as much as in the ASEAN Tigercubs; but it was stronger in South Korea, blowing away 44 per cent of the value of the won.[42]

The worst affected East Asian countries had economic problems similar to Thailand's. Malaysia, the Philippines and Indonesia all suffered from over-borrowing and worsening terms of trade for their US dollar-based currency caused by the strength of the American economy. There was also a common weakness of political corruption. For example, in Thailand early in 1997 the awarding of five new banking licences to strong government supporters was the final trigger for the capital flight. In Indonesia an announcement in August 1997 that the world's largest bridge would be built across the Straits of Malacca to Malaysia by a company belonging to one of Suharto's daughters suggested an air of unreality towards the crisis within the Indonesian government. That helped sink the value of the rupiah. In Malaysia a stock deal that bailed out a company linked to the government political party tumbled the ringgit to its lowest level. Malaysia's Prime Minister Mohamad Mahathir blamed the whole crisis on a conspiracy of international speculators. Certainly, wider world currency traders had an effect on the spreading crisis, but Mahathir ignored the fact that his fellow citizens were busy off-loading ringgits. His irrational response along with other government mistakes, such as the raising of interest rates in Indonesia to protect the rupiah, only deepened the crisis in those countries. South Korea's economy was stronger, but it too suffered from over-borrowing, some of which was used for overseas investments, which rose by 33 per cent in 1995. Many of the loans provided low returns in an economy that began to slow with the emergence of a high trade deficit in 1996. Seven of the thirty large industrial corporations, the *chaebols*, became bankrupt with consequent serious pressure on the banking sector, which had significant structural weakness.[43]

Another common factor influencing the spread of the financial crisis in East Asia was the economic slow down in Japan. The result was that in

---

42 Henderson, *Reassessing ASEAN*, 40–1. Hal Hill, *The Indonesian Economy in Crisis: Causes, Consequences and Lessons* (Sydney 1999), 34. Australian Department of Foreign Affairs and Trade (ADFAT), *Korea Rebuilds: From Crisis to Opportunity* (Canberra 1999), 35.

43 *Korea Rebuilds*, 32–4. Winters, 'The Financial Crisis', 42–8. Heather Smith, 'Korea', in Mcleod and Garnaut, *East Asia in Crisis*, 66–76. Panicos O. Demetriades and Bassam M. Fattouh, 'The South Korean Financial Crisis: Competing Explanations and Policy Lessons for Financial Liberalization', *International Affairs*, 75, 1999, 779–92.

1995 there was a 50 per cent devaluation of the yen compared with the US dollar and consequent trade difficulties in the East Asian economies that had linked their currency to it. For example an estimated 50 per cent of South Korea's exports competed with Japanese goods, consequently impacting on wider South Korean trade let alone exports to Japan. Indeed, Japan in 1995 absorbed 28 per cent of the value of Indonesia's exports and 17 per cent of Thailand's. Japan therefore was no longer a market for the over-production caused by the inflow of Japanese and other capital.[44]

International responses to the East Asian economic crisis also made it worse. The world's greatest economic power, the US, was slow to act even to help its former protégé, South Korea. In the post-Cold War world South Korea was no longer a special case for US assistance, as had happened in earlier economic crises. This time, economic motives prevailed in the American preference for IMF pressure on the ROK to provide a more open economy, instead of responding to its pleas for financial backing for its stricken financial sector that probably would have prevented the roller coaster collapse of the won. An offer by Japan to provide $100 billion for an Asian monetary fund to bolster the ailing economies of the region also was scuttled by the US in favour of drastic IMF medicine that suited the American open markets economic agenda. Not that the IMF was under US control, as the South Koreans accused. But there was a community of interest between the IMF and the US. The American delayed response significantly worsened the crisis. So too did IMF actions. For example, pressure on Indonesia to reform its banking system provoked the sudden closure of fifteen banks with links to the Suharto family and consequent greater haemorrhage of the sickening Indonesian economy. Also the traditional IMF medicine of reduced government spending and higher interest rates damaged the social and economic fabrics of Asian societies to the extent that later in 1997 the IMF itself scaled back its austerity requirements. But that relief was too late to stem rising popular discontent which had major political consequences. Indeed, the crisis continued into 1999, with only small signs of recovery by that year's end.[45]

The economic collapse in East Asia also helped topple most of its governments, with some foreign policy results. One was the electoral victory in South Korea in 1998 of Chen Shui-ban with his new 'sunshine' policy towards North Korea. In Thailand, after the electoral win in 1997 of the

44 ADFAT, *Korea Rebuilds*, 33. Tongzon, *The Economies of Southeast Asia*, 119. Richard Higgott, 'The International Relations of the Asian Economic Crisis', in Robinson *et al.* (eds), *Politics and Markets*, 263–4.
45 Linda Weiss and Johm M. Hobson, 'State Power and Economic Strength: What's so Special about the Asian Crisis', in Robinson *et al.* (eds), *Politics and Markets*, 67–73.

Democrat leader Chuan Leekpai, his government in 1998 pushed for more flexibility in ASEAN's policy of non-intervention in internal affairs. But Thailand received support only from the new government in the Philippines led by the populist film actor Joseph Estrada. Political change was resisted in Malaysia but at a cost of growing authoritarianism by Mahathir's government. The jailing of his main political rival, Deputy Prime Minister Anwar Ibrahim, provoked open criticism from Thailand and the Philippines; Anwar was one of Estrada's friends. Such criticism infuriated Mahathir. The most momentous political change was in Indonesia in May 1998 with the fall of Suharto and the end to his thirty-two years of authoritarian rule after waves of popular protests. His replacement by the vice president, B.J. Habibe, was to have a major impact on Indonesia's policies about East Timor and relations with Australia.

Indonesia, East Timor and Australia

On 27 January 1999, Habibe offered a referendum in which East Timor's people could opt for either improved autonomy within Indonesia or for independence. This was a surprising decision given the resolute refusal of Suharto's government to any suggestion of independence for East Timor.

However, there had been more international pressure on Indonesia about East Timor in the 1990s than before. By the end of the 1980s, Suharto believed that Indonesia had won the war against Fretilin, which had encouraged him to open East Timor to the outside world starting with a visit there by Pope John Paul II in October 1989. But Suharto did not appreciate the emergence of a strong East Timorese youth revolt against Indonesian oppression. This movement received international attention when on 21 November 1991 Indonesian soldiers opened fire indiscriminately on a crowd of at least 3,000 mostly young people who had marched to the Santa Cruz Cemetery in Dili to honour the grave of a young man who had been killed by Indonesians two weeks previously. Their only crime was to carry banners with slogans such as 'Vive Independence'. But, in the more open climate in East Timor, an English eyewitness filmed the scene, which became known as the Dili massacre. His pictures provoked wider world shock. Canada and the Netherlands suspended aid to Indonesia, an action not followed by the US, though Washington issued a public condemnation. Australia protested, which aroused anger in Jakarta. However, this dent in previously improving Australia–Indonesia relations was repaired when the Australian Prime Minister, Paul Keating, visited Jakarta in April 1992. There was a further improvement in the relationship in 1995 with the signing of a mutual security agreement between Indonesia and Australia.[46]

Another measure of wider world concern about East Timor was an invitation by American bishops to East Timor's Bishop Belo, who had publicly protested at the brutal oppression of East Timorese, to visit the US. A result was the successful nomination in 1996 of Belo along with Ramos Horta, East Timor's unofficial ambassador at large, for the Nobel Peace prize, which provoked strong anger in Indonesia. Also Fretilin guerrillas, now known as Falintal, were still at large. Though their leader, Xanana Gusmao, had been captured in 1992, and they were only a few hundred strong, Falintal still carried out some successful ambushes of Indonesian soldiers. An Indonesian response by the late 1990s was to arm 'home defence units' to terrorize people accused of supporting Falintal. After the Indonesian government's announcement of the independence ballot, to be conducted by the UN, these units were incorporated into a militia to conduct 'a dirty war' against pro-independence groups and to intimidate East Timorese to vote against independence. But Catholic priests knew they only had to tell the big majority of the East Timorese people, who attended church services on Sunday 29 August, to go out and vote. The result on 30 August was a 78.5 per cent majority for independence, in a poll of an extraordinary 98.6 per cent of East Timor's adult population. Significantly, during the ballot there was minimal militia violence, a measure of militia subjection to military control. With the territory swarming with reporters and UN officials and other observers from around the world, Indonesia did not want any international embarrassment. Also the Indonesian government had not perceived the counter-effect of the militia intimidation. Its foreign secretary, Ali Alatas, said later that 'the overwhelming vote for independence came as a shock to the government'.[47]

However, following the ballot, and especially after the announcement of its result on 4 September, the militia, with police and military assistance,

---

46   Australian Department of Foreign Affairs and Trade, 'East Timor – 12 November 1991 Killings: Composite Chronology of Events', 26 November 1991. Bob Catley and Vinsensio Dugis, *Australia and Indonesia since 1945: The Garuda and the Kangaroo* (Aldershot 1998), 224–6, 292–7. Paul Keating, *Engagement: Australia Faces the Asia-Pacific* (Sydney 2000), 129–34, 138–40.

47   Arnold S. Kohen, *From the Place of the Dead: The Epic Struggles of Bishop Belo of East Timor* (New York 1999), 224–6. Helene van Klinken, 'Taking the Risk, and Paying the Price: East Timorese Vote in Ermera District', Damien Kingsbury, 'The TNI and the Militias' and Peter Bartu, 'The Militia, the Military, and the People of Bonboro District', in Damien Kingsbury (ed.), *Guns and Ballot Boxes: East Timor's Vote for Independence* (Melbourne 2000), 43–98. 'Alatas Blames PM on Timor', Melbourne, *Age*, 3 November 1999.

enacted their revenge. First, the press reporters and many of the UN officials were scared away with acts of intimidation. Then there was a massive
destruction of the territory's houses and infrastructure with widespread killings, targeting especially pro-independence leaders and church personnel,
and mass deportation of people to West Timor. Belo, who escaped from
East Timor during the mayhem, said to an American reporter: 'A cyclone
of violence orchestrated by Indonesian army elements has swept East Timor
from end to end. This is a monstrous effort to annul the people's choice.'[48]
A militia leader, John Marquez, later admitted: 'the order came from Jakarta
to kill unarmed civilians after East Timor's ballot'. Ultimate responsibility
for the devastation, according to a human rights report in Jakarta in February 2000, extended to the commander-in-chief of the Indonesian army at
the time, General Wiranto.[49]

There was intense international pressure on Jakarta to agree to a UN
military intervention to stop the violence. Probably most effective was action by the US to cut military contacts with Indonesia and a threat to veto
vital IMF money for the ailing Indonesian economy. Consequently, a UN
authorized peace-enforcement military force, mainly consisting of Australian troops, landed in East Timor on 20 September. This was remarkably
speedy action compared with previous UN military interventions on human
rights issues, which was helped by the fact that Australia already had a
force on standby. But it was fortunate that the militia were easily scared away
by a few skirmishes, because the hasty Australian deployment included
insufficient ammunition for any major conflict. Though Australian led and
dominated the force included personnel from many other Pacific Basin
countries: New Zealand, Canada, the US, South Korea, Thailand, the
Philippines, Singapore and Malaysia. Japan offered financial assistance
and China offered civilian police. There were also military personnel from
other countries, such as Britain, Portugal and Brazil.[50]

Australia's pressure for UN military intervention in East Timor, strong
government criticism of Indonesia over the East Timor violence and widespread community protests, including trade union bans, provoked great
anger in Jakarta. Alatas responded by abrogating the 1995 Indonesia–
Australia Security treaty. The Australia–Indonesia relationship had sunk to

48 *Washington Post*, 16 September 1999. Hidayat Djajajmihardja, 'A Reporter's View' in
    Kingsbury (ed.), *Guns and Ballot Boxes*, 110–15.
49 'Militiaman Implicates Jakarta', Melbourne, *Age*, 1 December 1999. ABC, 'East Timor
    Referendum', 14 February 2000.
50 William Shawcross, *Deliver Us from Evil: Warlords and Peacekeepers in a World of Endless
    Conflict* (London 2000), 354–61. ABC, 'East Timor Referendum', 21 September 1999.
    Information supplied by Al Palazzo.

its lowest level since 1965. But on 19 October 1999 the newly elected Indonesian People's Assembly voted to relinquish Indonesian control of East Timor. The UN now had the task to prepare East Timor for independence.[51]

Australasia, the US and the Pacific Islands

The close relations between New Zealand and Australia continued in the 1990s. There were further extensions of the CER agreement beyond the free trade in goods established in 1990. By 1996 anti-dumping regulations, joint food standards and a free labour market had been achieved. But more work was needed on free trade in services and free movement of capital. Also, though Australia was New Zealand's largest trading partner and New Zealand, Australia's third, this interchange in 1998 accounted for 21 per cent of New Zealand's trade but only 5 per cent of Australia's. From 1991 there were also moves for a 'closer defence relationship'. A barrier though was the continuation of New Zealand's legislation banning nuclear powered or armed ships, which kept New Zealand outside the ANZUS alliance. Australia could not share US intelligence information or invite New Zealand to participate in joint military exercises with the US. Australia regarded its alliance with the US as more important than its relationship with New Zealand.[52]

The US viewed Australia as a useful partner, especially in terms of Australian defence responsibility in the South Pacific. Secretary of State Christopher described it as a 'very close and productive relationship in the post-Cold War era'. However, this did not extend to the US government overriding the interests of its farming community in disputes about Australian agricultural exports to the US, in a trade heavily weighted in American favour. In 1998 US exports to Australia were worth over two times more than imports from Australia.[53]

For Australia's South Pacific islands policy, although there was no longer a need to counter Soviet influence, there were still problems for the islands about external influences such as violation of fishing rights. Australia responded with the provision of twenty patrol boats to island states by 1995.

---

51 Scott Burchall, 'East Timor, Australia and Indonesia', in Kingsbury (ed.), *Guns and Ballot Boxes*, 176, 181. ABC, 'East Timor Referendum', 20 October 1999.

52 P.J. Lloyd, 'Completing CER: Report of a CEDA/Australian APEC Study Centre Roundtable on the Closer Economic Relations Trade Agreement' (Melbourne 1997), 1–3. *OMSIT*, 61–2, 66–7. James Rolfe, *The Armed Forces of New Zealand* (Sydney 1999), 75–6.

53 Joseph M. Siracusa and Yeong-Han Cheong, *America's Australia. Australia's America* (Claremont, Calif. 1997), ch. 5 (quotation 102). *OMSIT*, 59–60.

Australia's defence cooperation funds provided significant other assistance, such as a communications network in Tonga. Other Australian aid money continued to be supplied to fragile island economies, such as a rural water supply project in the Solomon Islands. But in this new post-Cold War environment Australian governments demanded more accountability from island counterparts. For example, when a new Solomon Islands government abandoned Australian-sponsored restrictions on over-exploitation of timber resources by foreign companies, Australia reduced its annual aid for the Solomons from AUS\$14.2 million in 1994–95 to AUS\$11.6 million in the next year. Furthermore, Australia enjoyed the lion's share of its trade with the islands. From 1996 to 1998 Australia's exports to the islands were worth nearly four times its Pacific Islands imports. Also Japan had replaced Australia as the major aid provider in the South Pacific, except for PNG.[54]

The most dramatic case of Australian pressure on a Pacific Islands government in the 1990s occurred in March 1997 when there was a storm of Australian criticism about the revelation that the PNG government had hired a British-based mercenary army, Executive Outcomes. Its mercenary soldiers, mostly black veterans of civil war in Angola commanded by white South African officers, had been used for military intervention in strife-torn African countries. The PNG Prime Minister, Julius Chan, hoped they could solve the problem of the rebellion on Bougainville, which was still continuing despite PNG occupation of significant proportion of the island, helped by BRA defections. In a four-hour conversation with Chan in Canberra on 9 March, the Australian Prime Minister, John Howard, firmly told him that negotiations were the only solution to the Bougainville crisis, and there was a threat to reduce Australia's substantial aid to PNG if the mercenaries were used in Bougainville. Chan resisted. But when he sacked his Australian-trained army commander, Brigadier-General Jerry Singirok, for publicly condemning the Sandline contract, there was a mutiny by soldiers and public rioting in Port Moresby. A shaken Chan cancelled the contract.[55]

Indeed, a truce was declared in Bougainville in November 1997. After Chan's electoral defeat in June 1997, New Zealand, which had participated in the first of five abortive Bougainville peace plans in the 1990s, invited war-weary BRA leaders and representatives of PNG's Bougainville

---

54   Roger C. Thompson, *Australia and the Pacific Islands in the Twentieth Century* (Melbourne 1998), 228–30. Sandra Tarte, *Japan's Aid Diplomacy and the Pacific Islands* (Canberra 1998), 28–36, 194–219.

55   Thompson, *Australia and the Pacific Islands*, 221–3. For more detail see Sinclair Dinnen, Ron May and Anthony J. Bergan (eds), *Challenging the State: The Sandline Affair in Papua New Guinea* (Canberra 1997), and Sean Dorny, *The Sandline Affair: Politics and Mercenaries and the Bougainville Crisis* (Sydney 1998).

administration for peace talks at Burnham army camp near Christchurch. A result was a 250-strong military and civilian force established in Bougainville to monitor the truce. Its personnel were supplied chiefly by Australia, but also by New Zealand, Fiji, Tonga and Vanuatu. Ironically, personnel from each of these nations had arrived on Bougainville once before, in 1994, as part of a peace plan that collapsed at the point of their arrival. This time the truce was upgraded to a cease-fire in April 1998 and was holding firm two years later. However, there was still the problem of the BRA's ultimate objective of independence, which PNG has not been prepared to concede.[56]

The Bougainville crisis had produced international tension. In 1992 relations between Australia and the Solomon Islands became strained after incursions by Australian-supplied PNG troops across the Solomon Islands border bent on destroying sources of supply to the BRA, especially a raid on 12 September which resulted in the deaths of two local people. A serious crisis in Papua New Guinea–Solomons relations was defused by a promise from Port Moresby to put the offending troops on trial and to pay financial compensation. Ironically, Australia then provided assistance to equip the Solomon Islands to patrol the border in order to stop any further incursions by the Australian-supported PNG army.[57]

One issue in the mid 1990s uniting all South Pacific Islands nations was more French nuclear testing, despite President Mitterrand's announcement in 1992 of the end of all testing. After the right-wing Chirac became President of France in May 1995, he gave notice on 13 June of a program of six more nuclear tests at Moruroa to upgrade French nuclear weapons capability. This provoked outrage across the South Pacific region, such as large public anti-French demonstrations in Australia and New Zealand. The other Pacific Islands states were pleased to endorse an Australian-worded protest statement to France, and there was unanimous support for a motion at the Forum meeting in PNG in September, which expressed 'extreme outrage' at the tests. Predictably, this pressure failed to budge Chirac. Nuclear tests continued until the end of the program in January 1996. However, then France joined Britain and the US in March 1996 in signing the Rarotonga treaty that had been rejected by those nuclear powers in the 1980s.[58]

---

56 Karl Claxton, *Bougainville 1988–98: Five Searches for Security in the North Solomons Province of Papua New Guinea* (Canberra 1998), 18–20. Dorny, *The Sandline Affair*, 47–56. Anthony J. Regan, 'Causes and Course of the Bougainville Conflict', *Journal of Pacific History*, 33, 1998, 270–85.

57 Greg Fry, *South Pacific Security and Global Change: The New Agenda* (Canberra 1999), 8–9. Thompson, *Australia and the Pacific Islands*, 214.

58 Thompson, *Australia and the Pacific Islands*, 214–15. Ramesh Thakur, *The Last Bang Before a Total Ban: French Nuclear Testing in the Pacific* (Canberra 1995), 12–17. N.C. Maclellan and Jean Chesneaux, *After Moruroa: France in the South Pacific* (Melbourne 1998), 208.

The South Pacific Forum was a useful means for small island nations to address major regional issues. It facilitated the regional peace-monitoring contributions in 1994 and 1997 for Bougainville. After the end of the French nuclear tests the greatest Forum interest was to support wider world action on greenhouse gas emissions because of a fear of rising sea levels for low-lying atoll states such as Kiribati and Tuvalu. On this issue there was conflict with Australia, the world's fourth largest emitter of greenhouse gases per capita. At the Forum meeting in the Cook Islands in September 1997 Prime Minister Howard of Australia belittled the islanders' fears, and the meeting was forced into an unprecedented long search for a bland joint statement on the issue. One peace-making contribution from outside the region was when in June 1999 the Commonwealth of former British nations, at the request of the Solomon Islands government, sent a peace mission to the Solomon Islands led by former Fijian Prime Minister, Sitiveni Rabuka. The target was a violent campaign by indigenous people in Guadalcanal to expel from their island all Malaitans, killing a number and creating 10,000 refugees. A background to this violence was serious economic decline, influenced by the East Asian crisis, which ruined the Malaysian dominated logging industry that had provided the Solomons' most valuable exports. A twenty-four-man Fijian and Vanuatan police team arrived to monitor the resultant peace agreement.[59]

Rabuka as peacemaker was a remarkable transition from former military coup leader. Indeed in 1992, to become Prime Minister of Fiji, he had been supported by the Labour Party, which in 1987 he had arrested at gun point. He then promoted a democratic constitution to replace the pro-Fijian one of 1990 that had followed his overthrowing of democracy in 1987 in the cause of Fijian paramountcy. Under the new constitution in the election in May 1999 the Labour Party defeated Rabuka's government. Fiji now had its first Indo-Fijian prime minister, Mahendra Chaudhary. A year later, however, this government was overthrown by Fijian extremists.[60]

Another notable transformation after the violent 1980s was peaceful New Caledonia in the 1990s. Though more of the development money supplied by the French government under the terms of the Matignon Accord was spent in the European dominated southern region of New Caledonia, Kanaks had received some benefit, and there was a new Kanak confidence expressed

59   Fry, *South Pacific Security*, 22–3, 31–2. Thompson, *Australia and the Pacific Islands*, 231–2. Tarcisius tara Kabutaulaka, 'Melanesia in Review: Issues and Events, 1998', *The Contemporary Pacific*, 11, 1999, 440–1. John Sharpham, *Rabuka of Fiji: The Authorised Biography of Major-General Sitiveric Rabuka* (Rockhampton, 2000), 307–8. *Age*, 24 January 2000.
60   Brij V. Lal, *Another Way: The Politics of Constitutional Reform in Post-Coup Fiji* (Canberra 1998), 30–100. Sharpham, *Rabuku of Fiji*, 170–1, 210–32, 261–302. *Age*, 18 May 2000.

in indigenous cultural activities. But in 1998 with further European immigration, the proportion of Kanaks in the colony's population declined by 0.7 per cent from 44.8 per cent in 1988 despite a higher Kanak birth rate. Indeed, FLNKS leaders appreciated that independence would not be achieved in the referendum promised in the Matignon Accord for 1998. Therefore they agreed to negotiate for a lesser deal. The result was the Noumea Accord signed by the French government, the FLNKS and the RPCR on 5 May 1998. This agreement 'gave a new status for New Caledonia within the French Republic – no longer an overseas territory – with 'shared sovereignty' and a new citizenship based on ten years' residence. There would be an 'irreversible' transfer of local administrative powers to a new elected congress and local authorities. There would be measures to recognize Kanak culture, including a preamble to the accord acknowledging the 'shadows' of the colonial past. There was to be a fifteen to twenty year period of transition before a future referendum on possible independence. The agreement was ratified by nearly 72 per cent of New Caledonia's population in a referendum in November 1998 and implemented by the French Parliament in March 1999. France, however, retained powers over justice, public order, defence, finance and currency, a fact that assisted European support in New Caledonia for the accord. Assisting the achievement of significant self-government had been the election in France of a left-wing coalition government in 1997.[61]

In French Polynesia there was a movement in 1999 by the government of Gaston Flosse to seek a similar autonomy accord as in New Caledonia, which received a positive response from France. But Flosse was not seeking independence, which still had only minority support in the territory. There had been a riotous protest demonstration in Papeete in 1995 following the first of the new nuclear tests. But all it achieved were later jail terms for its organizers.[62]

The US also retained strategic influence in North Pacific Islands. The North Marianas remained a self-governing Commonwealth within the US. The Federation of Micronesia and the Marshall Islands had become virtually independent states in free association with the US. They were admitted to the UN in 1991 and maintained their own diplomatic relations. But the US retained military access rights in return for financial aid. Palau, no longer strategically important to the US in the post-Cold War era, became

61 Nick Maclellan, 'The Noumea Accord and Decolonisation in New Caledonia', *The Contemporary Pacific 209*, 245–52.
62 Karin von Strokirch, 'French Polynesia' in 'Polynesia in Review: Issues and Events, 1 July 1998 to 30 June 1999', *The Contemporary Pacific*, 12, 2000, 221–6. Maclellan and Chesneaux, *After Moruroa*, 135.

independent in 1994 also in free association with the US. All have significant dependence on the US for economic viability but have also sought other sources of assistance. Here they benefited from the competition for diplomatic influence between China and Taiwan. For example, when in November 1998 the Marshall Islands recognized Taiwan, better economic returns were received than previous Chinese aid. But for the North Marianas close contacts with East Asia became economically disastrous when the East Asian crisis dried up a previously lucrative tourist trade.[63]

North America and APEC

On the North American side of the Pacific Basin there was more economic cooperation in the 1990s with the commencement on 1 January 1994 of the North American Free Trade Agreement (NAFTA), a widening of the Canada–US free trade region to include Mexico. As well as free trade, this agreement aimed for freedom of interchange of services and capital. It was achieved after intense opposition in the US to the inclusion of Mexico, a country with socio-economic and political differences with the US that were of much greater extent than between the US and Canada. There was also a fear of a threat to lower skilled jobs from poorly paid Mexican workers. On the contrary side of the debate were the arguments that the US had a $1.7 billion favourable trade balance with Mexico with exports in 1993 worth $42 billion. Also American direct investments in Mexico were worth $13 billion, the greatest of any Latin American country except Brazil.[64] Nor was there Mexican unity about NAFTA. While there was good support in commercial, middle class and government sectors of Mexico, which saw NAFTA as means for Mexico to join the developed world, there was discontent in the Third World peasant sector of the country. That surfaced dramatically in the southern state of Chiapas on the day of the NAFTA commencement. An armed guerrilla band, calling themselves Zapatistas, took over the town of San Christobal shouting 'Stop NAFTA!' That was the beginning of an irritating revolt for the Mexican government. Also Mexico suffered from a financial crisis in December 1994 caused principally by over-borrowing and an over-valued currency. NAFTA probably helped in ameliorating the crisis when the Clinton administration acted to support the

63 Julianne M. Walsh, 'Marshall Islands' and Samuel F. McPhetres, 'Northern Mariana Islands' in 'Micronesia in Review: Issues and Events, 1 July 1998 to 30 June 1999', *The Contemporary Pacific*, 209, 212–13. Arnold H. Leibowitz, *Embattled Island, Palau's Struggle for Independence* (Westport 1996), chs 23–6.
64 Sydney Weintraub, *NAFTA What Comes Next?* (Westport 1994), xxi–xxii, 1–3, 36–45.

plunging Mexican peso. There were other problems in Mexico–US relations with political violence and revelations of corruption in Mexico that soured American views about their new free trade partner and constant complaints in the US about illegal Mexican immigrants. Also the trade balance changed to a surplus in Mexico's favour of $8.6 billion in 1998.[65]

As in the US there was opposition in Canada to the negotiations for NAFTA from organized labour. Its arguments were bolstered by declining terms of trade between the US and Canada, Canadian business collapses and employment losses after the 1989 free trade agreement with the US, but this was probably mainly the result of a world-wide recession. Indeed, by 1998 there was a favourable Canadian trade balance with the US worth $206 billion. In the post-Cold War era, Canada had also become less Eurocentric in its foreign policy. Apart from involvement in UN peace-keeping in Cambodia and East Timor, the Canadian government was paying more attention to its small Pacific navy in an era when Canada did not have to concentrate so much on its NATO commitments. Canada has also been a keen member of ARF and the Asia–Pacific Economic Conference (APEC). But such involvement did not lead to any great Canadian trade expansion. For example the Japanese proportion of Canada's exports fell from 4.5 per cent in 1993 to 3.7 per cent in 1997, a result of the Japanese economic decline. In the same time period South Korea's proportion of Canada's exports increased only slightly to 1 per cent and China's fell from 0.9 per cent to 0.8 per cent.[66]

APEC, an Australian initiative supported by Japan, was inaugurated in Canberra, Australia, in November 1989 with the aim of promoting the region's economic dynamism. It was launched at the first inter-government meeting of an original non-government body to promote economic cooperation, the Pacific Trade and Development Conference representing the US, Canada, Japan, South Korea, Australia, New Zealand and the ASEAN nations. Annual APEC foreign ministers meetings commenced in Singapore in 1990. There were also meetings of trade, finance and environment ministers, and an APEC secretariat was established in Singapore in 1993.

---

65   Hertmann von Bertrab, *Negotiating NAFTA: A Mexican Envoy's Account* (Westport 1997), 145–54. Tom Barry, *Zapata's Revenge: Free Trade and the Farm Crisis in Mexico* (Boston 1995), *passim. OMSIT*, 57–8.

66   John Herd and Stephen J. Randall, *Canada and the United States: Ambivalent Allies* (Athens, Ga. 1994), 294–5. Brian Job and Frank Langdon, 'Convergence and Divergence of Interests in the Changing Asia-Pacific Security Setting', in Charles F. Doran, *et al.* (eds), *Pacific Partners: Canada and the United States* (Washington 1994), 110–16. Glen Norcliffe, 'Foreign Trade in Goods and Services', in John N.H. Britton (ed.), *Canada and the Global Economy: The Geography of Structural and Technological Change* (Montreal 1996), 29. *OMSIT*, 55–6.

Membership was widened to include China, Hong Kong and Taiwan in 1991; Mexico and PNG in 1993; Chile in 1994; Peru, Russia and Vietnam in 1998. APEC's prestige was enhanced when in Seattle in 1993 Clinton inaugurated the first annual meeting of APEC heads of state. A significant US motive for belonging to APEC was expressed by his Under Secretary of State for Economic Affairs, Joan Spero. She told Congress in 1993: 'APEC is another way for us to engage in the region and promote, not necessarily trade negotiations in the classical sense, but trade facilitation and the removal of barriers.' For ASEAN members virtues of APEC were its loose organization, consultative framework and conservative aims that would not impinge on their independent action. For Australia and other small Pacific Basin nations it was a body in which they could attract the attention of bigger powers to economic issues of their concern. China was keen to join because its economy was closely linked with other Pacific Basin countries.[67]

APEC did make an early significant joint declaration, at Bogor, Indonesia in 1994. This was a commitment by all leaders to a goal of free trade and investment in the Pacific Basin by 2010 for industrialized nations and 2020 for developing countries. There was further agreement at the Manila meeting in 1996 on a need to improve individual action plans to achieve the free trade goals. Also, by the end of the 1990s APEC had become the dominant organization for Pacific Basin cooperation with activities ranging from organizing trade fairs – the fourth to be held in Indonesia in October 2000 – to offering Master of Business Administration scholarships at Nanyang Technological University in Singapore.[68]

Central and South America

New features in the 1990s in Central and South America were outbreaks of peace after the violent 1980s. The most significant was a peace agreement signed in Mexico City on 16 January 1992, which ended the long war in El Salvador that had cost 75,000 lives. A major reason for this development

---

67 Gareth Evans and Bruce Grant, *Australia's Foreign Relations in the World of the 1990s* (2nd edition, Melbourne 1995), 128–34. Anthony Grew and Christopher Brook, *Asia Pacific in the New World Order* (London 1998), 181. Hadi Sowesastro, 'APEC: An ASEAN Perspective' and Zhang Yunling, 'China and APEC: Interests, Opportunities, and Challenges', in Donald C. Hellman and Kenneth B. Pyle (eds), *From APEC to Xanadu: Creating a Viable Community in the Post-Cold War Pacific* (Armonk, NY 1997), 174–6, 195–6. M. Dutta, *Economic Regionalization in the Asia-Pacific* (Cheltenham, UK 1999), chs 8, 22–5.

68 Philippa Dee, Chris Geisler and Greg Watts, *The Impact of APEC's Free Trade Commitment* (Canberra 1996), 1. APEC Secretariat home page, world wide web accessed 5 May 2000: www1.apecsec.org.sg.

was the emerging impossibility of victory for both sides of the conflict. The FMLN offensive of November 1989, and a second one in November–December 1990, dispelled the myth perpetrated by the El Salvador government and its US ally that the FMLN was a dying force. However, the FMLN's inability to defeat the US-supported government was also becoming apparent. The rebels during 1990 had gained a new military advantage with the purchase from Nicaragua of Soviet-made surface to air missiles, which negated the government's air advantage. But this was achieved because of the end of the contra war in Nicaragua. After the peace deal there, the USSR, at Washington's behest, pressured Cuba and the Sandinistas to stop providing the FMLN with Soviet-supplied arms, and the subsequent electoral defeat of the Sandinistas denied the FMLN any future support from Nicaragua. US pressure on the other side of the conflict was even more influential. First was Congress's threat to cut all US military aid. This threat and the Bush administration's support for President Cristiani's struggle with hardliners in ARENA and the military over the need for major concessions helped achieve a breakthrough in the peace process. Also hardliners were on a back foot because of the Jesuit murders, and the army was pressured to hand over a colonel and a lieutenant, who were convicted in September 1991 of ordering the murders. The final peace agreement was a compromise. The army and the ARENA government survived and the FMLN was to be gradually disarmed. But the army was to be reduced in size and its special forces and paramilitary groups were to be disbanded; FMLN fighters were to be incorporated into the police, full democracy would be restored, land would be redistributed and human rights abuses would be investigated. While there were disputes about carrying out the agreement's provisions, the peace settlement was assured by mid 1993 ahead of internationally acknowledged fair elections in 1994, which ARENA won.[69]

The peace process in Guatemala was more protracted. The military situation there was less balanced than in El Salvador. In the early 1990s the URNG was only about 2,000 strong, its membership and influence having been reduced severely by the brutal tactics of the Guatemalan army and absence of outside support. The army saw no need for a negotiated peace, and its actions were largely outside the control of the weak civilian government. However, there was also US pressure. The army-perpetrated human rights abuses resulted in the December 1990 freezing of US military aid followed by congressional action early in 1991 to cut the larger US economic aid to Guatemala. Consequently, peace negotiations started in Mexico

---

69 James Dunkerley, *The Pacification of Central America: Political Change in the Isthmus, 1987–1993* (London 1994), 65–76. LeoGrande, *Our Own Backyard*, 568–78. Byrne, *El Salvador's Civil War*, 169–204.

City in mid 1991 but stalled over the URNG's demands about human rights and reductions in army size and activity. A constitutional crisis in Guatemala in 1993, which installed a technocratic administration led by the ombudsman, León Carpio, pressure from the Clinton administration and involvement of the UN and other Latin American states, especially Mexico, finally achieved a peace agreement on 29 December 1996. It implemented fundamental army and constitutional reforms and established a Human Rights Truth Commission. However, a year after that commission produced a comprehensive report in February 1999 nothing had been done to implement its recommendations, and there were still human rights abuses in the country.[70]

The Shining Path insurrection was solved in a different way in Peru. It depended far more than other guerrilla movements on a charismatic leader, Abimael Guzmán Reynoso, whose career had been shaped by a time in China during the cultural revolution. He was captured in Lima on 12 September 1992. But already Shining Path's influence was declining because of its brutality that matched Peruvian army tactics. By 1992 many rural villages had organized armed patrols to fight Shining Path in alliance with the military. By 1995 Shining Path was no longer a threat to the political stability of Peru. A new president in 1990, Alberto Fujimori, a descendant of Japanese immigrants to Peru, contributed to the defeat of Shining Path with his *autogolpe* (self-coup) in 1992 when he overthrew Peru's Congress and the judiciary, to provide a freer hand for the military. The US responded by suspending all but humanitarian aid, but only for a time. Washington had supported the campaign against Shining Path as part of its war on drugs. Fujimori also had clear public support. In December 1996 another small rebel force, the Marxist Túpac Amaru Revolutionary Movement, achieved wider Pacific Basin notoriety by seizing the Japanese Ambassador's residence in Lima and holding seventy-two people hostage for four months. However, Fujimori then won wider world plaudits when a Peruvian anti-terrorist force stormed the embassy and freed the hostages.[71]

Peru was also cooperating with the other Andean Pact nations in an agreement in 1991 to create a free trade region. But peace between two

---

70 Dunkerley, *The Pacification of Central America*, 76–88. Chronology of the Peace Talks' Accord Guatemala, world wide web accessed 6 May 2000 www.c-r.org/acc_guat/chronol.html. 'Truth Commission One Year Later', Harbury Archive, world wide web accessed 6 May 2000 www.eecs.umich.edu/~pavr/harbury/archive.html.

71 Lawrence A Clayton, *Peru and the United States: The Condor and the Eagle* (Athens, Ga. 1999), 9, 265–85. Ponciano del Pino H., 'Family, Culture and "Revolution", Everyday Life with Sendero Luminoso' and Orin Starn, 'Villagers at Arms: War and Counterrevolution in the Southern Andes', in Steven J. Stern (ed.), *Shining and Other Paths: War and Society in Peru, 1890–1995* (Durham 1998), 159–89, 224–60.

members of the pact was broken in February 1995 with more fighting between Peru and Ecuador over their disputed border. Peace was soon re-established with the help of the US, Brazil, Argentina and Chile. With their encouragement, there was an agreement about demarcation of the border signed by Ecuador and Peru in Brazil's capital on 26 October 1998.[72]

There was also wider Latin American economic cooperation. In 1998 there was an agreement between the nations of the Andean Pact, the Central American Common Market and the Brazil-led Mercosur customs union to work towards free trade. This decision preceded a summit meeting in Santiago, Chile, in April 1998 of thirty-eight North and South American countries for free trade between them by 2005. This process had commenced at a meeting between those countries in Miami in the US in 1994. The membership qualification was 'democracy', defined as countries with elected presidents, not all of whom, as in Peru, ruled in full democratic fashion.

The conclusion of an earlier international agreement completed the final US withdrawal from Central America on 31 December 1999 when the Panama Canal was handed over to the Republic of Panama. Meanwhile, Panama's Manuel Noriega languished in jail in the US. There he had been convicted in 1992 for drug-trafficking, though continuing to protest his innocence.[73]

Drugs were continuing to be at the centre of US relations with Colombia, where drug barons and Marxist guerrillas were maintaining a continuous climate of violence. Colombia was the Latin American country receiving the most military aid, in a dirty war that had a wide impact on civilians. Five million of them in October 1999 poured on to Colombian streets to protest against the violence and call for peaceful negotiations.[74]

In the 1990s Latin America also was being integrated more into the wider Pacific Basin. An indication was the involvement of Mexico, Peru and Chile in APEC. On the other side, Japan, which had 15 per cent of its investments in Latin America in 1991, saw the election of Fujimori in Peru, with its significant colony Japanese-heritage citizens, as an economic opening. That year 10.1 per cent of Peru's exports, and 19.4 per cent of Chile's went to Japan. However, the subsequent economic crisis in Japan meant that there was a decline in that trade. The proportion of Chile's exports going to Japan in 1996 was 16.4 per cent and Peru's was 6.6 per cent.[75]

---

72 Clayton, *The United States and Peru*, 296. CNN News 26 October 1998.
73 See Noriega and Eisner, *America's Prisoner.*
74 Gary M. Leech, 'Fifty Years of Violence', Amnesty International, Colombia Report, world wide web, accessed 8 May 2000, www.colombiareport.org.
75 Alvaro Vargas Llosa, *The Madness of Things Peruvian: Democracy Under Siege* (New Brunswick 1994), 139. *YTTS 1996*, 203, 812.

Conclusions

It has been recently argued that the Cold War has not really ended in the Pacific Basin because of on-going tensions there that are the result of the survival of old Cold War issues.[76] Certainly, as this chapter has shown there were on-going tensions over the status of Taiwan and on the Korean Peninsula and unresolved issues about the status of the Kurile, Senkaku and Spratly Islands. But only one of those issues, the Kuriles, was a carry-over from the Cold War between the Soviet Union and the West. The most obvious Cold War relic was the two Koreas, but a post-Cold War reality was an absence of Russian support for North Korea. Survival of communism in China was a carry-over from the Cold War era, but the American relationship with China with mutual presidential visits were continuations of the earlier US–China détente era. Also, despite the continuing tension over Taiwan, the US support for one China was a continuation of détente not the Cold War. China's foreign policy in the 1990s was also as much the flexing of new national power as survival of a communist regime. A classic case of a new era for a communist survivor, Vietnam, was its admission into ASEAN. There was a continuation of issues from previous decades, notably the US trade dispute with Japan. But that issue was less contentious with the change in relative Japanese and American economic fortunes in the 1990s.

On the other hand the 1990s were notable for an outbreak of peace agreements in regions of previous conflict in the Pacific Basin. The end of the Cold War was influential for the peace agreements in Central America and Cambodia. Also the end of the Cold War facilitated the development of new regional organizations in the Pacific Basin involving China, Russia and the US, especially ARF and APEC. The drive for free trade that influenced other economic cooperation was influenced by the new dominance of the US in the post-Cold War era. The new era was also reflected in Australia's emphasis on Pacific Islands government accountability. One very new feature of the 1990s was the collapse of the Asian economic miracle with the overthrow of some old regime governments, notably Suharto's in Indonesia, with a resultant very post-Cold War outcome in independence for East Timor.

---

76 Kimie Hara, 'Rethinking the "Cold War" in the Asia-Pacific', *The Pacific Review*, 12, 1999, 515–35.

CONCLUSION

The Pacific Basin by the end of the 1990s had undergone a dramatic transformation since 1945. From a region devastated by the Pacific War, with European powers attempting to revive colonial empires, and with Japan crushed by defeat and under military occupation, the Pacific Basin by 1990 had become the region of the world's greatest economic activity. Japan had recovered more than its pre-war economic dominance to become a feared economic rival of the US, which had been the world's dominant economic power in 1945. Two of Japan's former colonies, South Korea and Taiwan, and two island states of the old British Empire, Singapore and Hong Kong, had become 'Asian Tigers' with booming industrialized economies. Other Southeast Asian countries, especially Malaysia and Thailand, were following their industrializing path. Indonesia, China and Mexico on the other side of the Pacific Basin were showing signs of future great potential economic growth. By contrast, the US was suffering economic decline. During the 1990s these roles were reversed with economic recession in Japan and the East Asian economic crisis, while the US economy experienced steady economic growth. In this post-Cold War era, the US, with its regained economic strength, was keen on movements for free trade, achieved with NAFTA, developing in the new Pacific Basin group APEC and projected in talks with Latin American states. Even ASEAN nations were committing themselves to internal free trade as well as expanding their numbers to include Vietnam and the rest of Southeast Asia.

Many of the events in the Pacific Basin in the intervening years were influenced by the contest between the superpowers, the US and the USSR. Important consequences of the Cold War were the restructuring of Japan, the freezing of relations between the US and China, the division of Korea and the Korean War, the division of Vietnam and the long Vietnam War, the survival of US and French colonialism in the Pacific Islands and US support for right-wing governments in Latin America. The Cold War also induced Soviet support for North Korea, froze relations between the USSR and Japan and encouraged Soviet support for newly independent nations in Southeast Asia, especially North Vietnam.

However, the growing split between the Soviet Union and China caused a competition for influence between those powers, which in turn influenced further warfare in Indochina after the US withdrawal. The Soviet–China split, as well as the experience of the Korean War, removed the danger of any new war between the US and China and encouraged a search for détente between those major Pacific Basin powers by the end of the 1960s. Similarly the USSR had no interest in provoking a war with the US, so postwar Pacific Basin conflicts never grew into wider wars.

The post-Cold War era also inaugurated an outbreak of peace agreements in the 1990s ending most of the violent conflicts in Latin America and in Cambodia. However, there were still tensions about the status of Taiwan, over ownership of the Senkaku, Spratly and Kurile Islands and on the Korean Peninsula, though early in 2000 there was a glimmer of hope for future peace there.

Another major force shaping the destinies of postwar Pacific Basin nations was indigenous nationalism. French and Dutch pretensions to restore their colonial empires in Southeast Asia unleashed nationalist revolutions, whose outcomes were influenced by the Cold War. The defeat of communism in Indonesia gained US support for the revolution there, while the spectre of communism sucked the US into opposing nationalism in Vietnam. The easy postwar achievement of independence in the Philippines assisted the defeat of a communist revolution, but the dominance of the socio-economic elite bequeathed further revolutionary violence to that republic. Malay nationalism was a factor in the defeat of the Chinese-based revolution in Malaya. Conversely, the earlier British colonial policy of importing immigrant labour forces to protect indigenous communities created conditions for the Malayan Emergency and also for the later military coups in Fiji.

In the Pacific the cultural diversity of islanders and pre-war paternalistic colonialism delayed independence movements in most island groups. The absence of major economic resources in the islands also encouraged a generally non-violent transference of colonial power in the British and Australasian territories. There was even significant British and Australian pressure on islanders, in the interests of shedding economic burdens and avoiding UN criticism, to become independent. Conversely, the strategic interests of the US in the North Pacific and France's world power pretensions by the 1980s were provoking violence in territories still under their control. However in the 1990s the North Pacific islands had gained virtual independence and in Palau's case, full independence. Also there was a new accord in French New Caledonia. The legacy of colonial boundaries produced violent conflict in regions of ethnic diversity, as Indonesia discovered after seizing power in East Timor and Irian Jaya, and as Papua New Guinea experienced in Bougainville. However, by the end of the 1990s Indonesia had relinquished East Timor and there was peace in Bougainville, though new ethnic tensions had developed in Indonesia and were continuing in the Philippines.

The Cold War in the Pacific Basin also encouraged the revival of the Japanese economic empire, which lay in ashes in 1945. Stimulated by 'reverse course' American policies and its use as an arsenal during the Korean War, the trade-driven Japanese economy was booming by the 1960s. Ripples of Japanese trade and investment in East Asia were becoming rolling waves in the Pacific Basin by the 1970s. The Asian Tigers received a major boost from Japanese investment and trade, and more lately Japan was financing emerging industrial countries of Southeast Asia and Latin America. More seriously, the growing trade imbalance with the US engendered commercial conflict between the two strategic allies. But those tensions weakened with changing economic fortunes in the 1990s, with the Japanese recession influencing the East Asian economic crisis, and with only hesitant signs of recovery at the end of the decade. The US economic hegemony in Latin America was preserving inequitable social systems, which provoked violent conflicts in that region, though the end of the Cold War influenced the subsequent peace movements there. There was also an outbreak of democracy in the 1990s, with elected presidents in all Pacific Basin Latin American governments, though there were still some limits on full democracy. There was also some continuing violence in South America and an outbreak of violent protest about the new economic order in Mexico.

Indeed, the Pacific Basin world, despite APEC, still is not as united as the North Atlantic community. Religious, cultural and linguistic diversities in the Pacific Basin are much greater. The Christian background of the North Atlantic nations is shared in the Pacific Basin with the other great religions of Islam and Buddhism, the philosophy of Confucianism and a host of lesser non-Christian religions. The Asian and Pacific Island languages have far less common roots than those of Western Europe, though English has become the language of the new Pacific Basin organizations. Political ideology is also more diverse in the Pacific Basin. Communism was a greater and more growing force than in Europe, though it also displayed less unity with communists killing each other in Indochina. Even with the collapse of communism in the former Soviet Union, it survived a democratic challenge in China, is defiantly alive in North Korea and remains dominant in Indochina. Also, despite the demise of Shining Path in Peru there are still Marxist guerrillas there and in Colombia. Democratic ideology, so promoted by the US, had spread to other Latin American states by 1999 though it is still shaky in Guatemala, Colombia and Peru. Fiji's experience demonstrated the frailty of democracy in the Pacific Islands, where cultural influences mutated democratic institutions, as in Tonga and in West Samoa until 1990. Fiji returned to the democratic fold in the 1990s, but only temporarily. Democracy is strongly entrenched in Australasia. In Asia, Malaysia, Singapore and Japan were democracies that were dominated, like Mexico, by one political party, and in Singapore and Malaysia there were restrictions on free speech. In the 1990s there was new political instability in Japan and Mexico and growing authoritarianism in Malaysia. Democracy has revived in the Philippines and Thailand, and has been newly established in South Korea and Taiwan. Even Indonesia has newly installed democracy. How well some of these new democratic developments will survive is a question for the future.

The new cooperative and free trade movements in the Pacific Basin are still only pale shadows of the developing European community. However in the Pacific Basin the new emphasis on cooperation and negotiation, as demonstrated in ASEAN and promised in ARF and APEC, is a foretaste of potential new unity in the region in the twenty-first century.

This is a guide to major publications for readers who wish to delve more deeply into topic areas of this book. For further publications consult the footnotes for each chapter.

The Reconstruction of Japan

A valuable book on the American occupation of Japan is Robert E. Ward and Sakamoto Yoshikazu (eds), *Democratizing Japan: The Allied Occupation* (Honolulu 1987). An earlier good survey of the literature, including theses that later became books, is Carol Gluck, 'Entangling Illusions – Japanese and American Views of the Occupation', in Warren I. Cohen (ed.), *New Frontiers in American East Asian Relations: Essays Presented to Dorothy Borg* (New York 1983). The best book by a participant is Theodore Cohen, *Remaking Japan: The American Occupation As New Deal* (New York 1987). For a Japanese view see Masumi Junnosuke, *Postwar Politics in Japan, 1945–1955* (Berkeley 1985). A more recent study using some Japanese sources and covering the whole occupation era is Richard B. Finn, *Winners in Peace: MacArthur, Yoshida, and Postwar Japan* (Berkely 1992). The most recent book is John Dower, *Embracing Defeat: Japan in the Wake of World War II* (London 1999).

China and the Cold War

A good interpretation of the Cold War in Asia is Marc S. Gallicchio, *The Cold War Begins in Asia: American Policy and the Fall of the Japanese Empire* (New York 1988), and there is a useful historiographical essay by Robert L. Messer in Akira Iriye and Warren Cohen (eds), *American, Chinese and Japanese Perspectives on Wartime Asia 1931–1949* (Wilmington 1990). For an overview of US policy towards China that is very critical of US policies see Bevin Alexander, *The Strange Connection: US Intervention in China, 1944–1972* (New

York 1992). For detailed scholarly studies of aspects of the 1945–49 period, see especially William Stueck, *The Wedemeyer Mission: American Politics and Foreign Policy During the Cold War* (Athens, Ga. 1984); June M. Grasso, *Truman's Two-China Policy 1948–1950* (Armonk 1987) and Thomas J. Christensen, *Useful Adversaries: Grand Strategy, Domestic Mobilization, and Sino-American Conflict, 1947–1958* (Princeton 1996). For Soviet–Chinese relations see the valuable new book, Odd Arne Westad (ed.), *Brothers In Arms: The Rise and Fall of the Sino-Soviet Alliance, 1945–1963* (Stanford 1998) and Brian Murray, *Stalin, the Cold War and the Division of China: A Multi-Archival Mystery* (Washington 1995). A good book with a useful bibliography on the Chinese Civil War is E.R. Hooton, *The Greatest Tumult: The Chinese Civil War 1936–49* (London 1991).

The Division of Korea and the Korean War

For the division of Korea and the causes of the Korean War, an influential revisionist book is Bruce Cumings, *The Origins of the Korean War*, 2 vols (Princeton 1981, 1990). A good shorter overview is Peter Lowe, *The Origins of the Korean War* (2nd edition, London 1997). A more specialized study of American policy is James Irving Matray, *The Reluctant Crusade: American Foreign Policy in Korea, 1941–1950* (Honolulu 1985). An analysis of the Korean origins of the war is John Merrill, *Korea: The Peninsular Origins of the War* (Newark 1989). A newer interpretation of USSR policy is Kathryn Weathersby, *Soviet Aims in Korea and the Origins of the Korean War, 1945–1950: New Evidence from Russian Archives* (Washington 1993); and for North Korea see A. Seiler, *Kim Il-song 1941–1948: The Creation of a Legend, The Building of A Dream* (Lanham 1994). For Chinese policy see Shuguang Zhang and Jian Chen (eds), *Chinese Communist Foreign Policy and the Cold War in Asia: New Documentary Evidence, 1944–1950* (Chicago 1996). Also valuable for Soviet and Chinese policy in the coming of the war is Sergei N. Goncharov, John L. Lewis and Xue Liai, *Uncertain Partners: Stalin, Mao and the Korean War* (Stanford 1993).

The Korean War has become a new historiographical growth area. The best short history of the war is still Burton I. Kaufman, *The Korean War: Challenges in Crisis, Credibility and Command* (Philadelphia 1986). A good diplomatic history of the war is William Stueck, *The Korean War: An International History* (Princeton 1995). Also valuable is Richard Whelan, *Drawing the Line: The Korean War, 1950–1953* (Boston 1990). For the Chinese intervention see Shuguang Zhang, *Mao's Military Romanticism: China and the Korean War, 1950–*

1953 (Lawrence 1995) and Jian Chen, *China's Road to the Korean War* (New York, 1993). For a recent bibliography of literature on the war, see Paul M. Edwards, *The Korean War: An Annotated Bibliography* (Westport 1998). For USSR policies see William J. Williams (ed.), *A Revolutionary War: Korea and the Transformation of the Postwar World* (Chicago 1993) and Odd Arne Westad (ed.), *Brothers In Arms: The Rise and Fall of the Sino-Soviet Alliance, 1945–1963* (Stanford 1998).

The Indonesian Revolution

The best overall survey of the Indonesian revolution is still Anthony Reid, *The Indonesian National Revolution 1945–50* (Melbourne 1974). For a more recent general overview see Robert Cribb and Colin Brown, *Modern Indonesia: A History since 1945* (London 1995). Good studies of aspects of the revolution are William H. Frederick, *Visions and Heat: The Making of the Indonesian Revolution* (Athens, Ohio 1988); Robert Cribb, *Gangsters and Revolutionaries: The Jakarta People's Militia and the Indonesian Revolution 1945–1949* (Sydney 1991) and Shigeru Sato, *War, Nationalism and Peasants: Java under the Japanese Occupation 1942–1945* (St Leonards, NSW 1994). For Britain and the revolution see Peter Dennis, *Troubled Days of Peace: Mountbatten and South East Asia Command, 1945–46* (Manchester 1987). For US policy towards Indonesia, see Robert J. McMahon, *Colonialism and Cold War: The United States and the Struggle for Indonesian Independence, 1945–49* (Ithaca 1981). For an Indonesian view see Salim Said, *Genesis of Power: General Sudirman and the Indonesian Military in Politics 1945–49* (Singapore 1991).

The Malayan Emergency

The authoritative study of the Malayan Emergency is Anthony Short, *The Communist Insurrection in Malaya 1848–1960* (London 1975). More recent military studies are Robert Jackson, *The Malayan Emergency: The Commonwealth's Wars 1948–1966* (London 1991) and John Coates, *Suppressing Emergency: An Analysis of the Malayan Emergency, 1948–1954* (Boulder 1992). The impact of the emergency on the peoples of Malaya is analyzed well in Richard Stubbs, *Hearts and Minds in Guerrilla Warfare: The Malayan Emergency 1948–1960* (Singapore 1989). For the Malayan background, with a good bibliography, see Albert Lau, *The Malayan Union Controversy 1942–1948* (Singapore 1991).

The Huk Rebellion, the US and the Philippines

The best study of the Huk rebellion and its origins is still Benedict J. Kerkvliet, *The Huk Rebellion: A Study of Peasant Revolt in the Philippines* (Berkeley 1977). See also John A. Larkin, *Sugar and the Origins of Modern Philippine Society* (Berkeley 1993). Lawrence M. Greenberg, *The Hukbalahap Insurrection: A Case Study of a Successful Anti-Insurgency Operation in the Philippines, 1946–1955* (Washington 1987) provides an analysis of the defeat of the rebellion. US policy towards the Philippines in the era is covered by Stanley Karnow, *In Our Image: America's Empire in the Philippines* (New York 1989) and by H.W. Brands, *Bound to Empire: The United States and the Philippines* (New York 1992).

The Vietnam Wars

Jaques Dalloz, *The War in Indo-China 1945–54* (Dublin 1990) provides a good survey from the French viewpoint of the first Vietnam War. For French policy, see also Martin Shipway, *The Road to War: France and Vietnam, 1944–1947* (Providence, RI 1996). For early US involvement in Vietnam, see David G. Marr, *Vietnam 1945: The Quest for Power* (Berkeley 1995). A good study, using Vietnamese language sources, of the evolution of the Vietminh army is Greg Lockhart, *Nation in Arms: The Origins of the People's Army of Vietnam* (Sydney 1989). Carl Thayer, *War by Other Means: National Liberation and Revolution in Viet-Nam 1954–1960* (Sydney 1989) is an another valuable study based on Vietnamese sources. A good survey of the causes of the war is Anthony Short, *The Origins of the Vietnam War* (London 1989). A more extensive study of causation is George McT. Kahin, *Intervention: How America Became Involved in Vietnam* (New York 1986). For a new challenging view of reasons for American military intervention in the war see Frederick Logevall, *Choosing War: The Lost Chance for Peace and the Escalation of War in Vietnam* (Berkeley 1999).

A very good short history of the whole war from the American perspective is George C. Herring, *America's Longest War: The United States and Vietnam 1950–1975* (3rd edition, New York 1996). Another good recent overview is Robert D. Schulzinger, *A Time of War: The United States and Vietnam, 1941–1975* (New York 1997). Good military histories of the war are William S. Turley, *A Short Political and Military History, 1964–1975* (Boulder 1986) and Andrew Krepenivich, *The Army and Vietnam* (Baltimore 1986). A good set of readings about the war, which includes Soviet, Vietnamese and Chinese policies, is Peter Lowe (ed.), *The Vietnam War* (New York 1998). For the

Vietnamese side of the war see also Robert S. McNamara, James G. Blight and Robert K. Brigham, *Argument Without End: In Search of Answers to the Vietnam Tragedy* (New York 1999) and Robert K. Brigham, *Guerrilla Diplomacy: The NLF's Foreign Policy and the Vietnam War* (Ithaca 1999). For USSR policy see also Ilya V. Gaiduk, *The Soviet Union and the Vietnam War* (Chicago 1996).

It is invidious to single out the many good specialized studies of the war, but ones especially useful for the writing of this book were Thomas C. Thayer, *War Without Fronts: The American Experience in Vietnam* (Boulder 1985), which is full of carefully compiled statistics; Eric M. Bergerud, *The Dynamics of Defeat: The Vietnam War in Hau Nghia Province* (Boulder 1991), which admirably complements Jeffrey Race's much earlier local study, *War Comes to Long An: Revolutionary Conflict in a Vietnam Province* (Berkeley 1972); Larry E. Cable, *Conflict of Myths: The Development of American Counterinsurgency Doctrine and the Vietnam War* (New York 1986), which places the war in the context of preceding guerrilla wars; Neil Sheehan, *A Bright Shining Lie: John Paul Vann and America in Vietnam* (New York 1988), which is the one of the best of the many biographies of Americans in the war, and Richard A. Hunt, *Pacification: The American Struggle for Vietnam's Hearts and Minds* (Boulder 1995), which analyzes why the Americans did not win the struggle for popular support.

Indonesia, Malaysia and Confrontation

A good study of the origins and course of Confrontation is still J.A.C. Mackie, *Konfrontasi: The Indonesia-Malaysia Dispute 1963–1966* (Kuala Lumpur 1974). A more recent longer view of the causes of the conflict is Greg Poulgrain, *The Genesis of Konfrontasi: Malaysia Brunei Indonesia 1945–1965* (Bathurst 1998). A good book on Australia's involvement in the West New Guinea dispute and the Confrontation is Peter Edwards, *Crises and Commitments: The Politics and Diplomacy of Australia's Involvement in Southeast Asian Conflicts 1948–1965* (Sydney 1992). Christopher J. McMullen, *Mediation of the West New Guinea Dispute, 1962: A Case Study* (Washington 1981) provides a comprehensive account of the international negotiations. A new study of US involvement in rebellions in Indonesia in the late 1950s is Audrey R. and George McT. Kahin, *Subversion as Foreign Policy: The Secret Eisenhower and Dulles Debacle in Indonesia* (Seattle 1995). Pamela Sodhy, 'Malaysian-American Relations during Indonesia's Confrontation against Malaysia, 1963–66', *Journal of Southeast Asian Studies*, 19, 1988, 111–36 is a good study of US policy towards Confrontation. B. Weinstein, *Indonesia's Foreign Policy and the Dilemma of Dependence: From Sukarno to Suharto* (Ithaca 1976) is a study of the making of Indonesian foreign policy in the period. English language books which analyze the attempted coup and fall of Sukarno are Harold Crouch, *The Army and Politics in Indonesia* (revised edition, Ithaca 1988) and Robert Cribb (ed.), *The Indonesian Killings* (Clayton, Victoria 1990).

For the Indonesian invasion of Timor and its aftermath John G. Taylor, *Indonesia's Forgotten War: The Hidden History of East Timor* (London 1991) is the best overall account. A good recent book on Australia and East Timor is James Cotton (ed.), *East Timor and Australia* (Canberra 1999). A new valuable book that throws light on the East Timorese struggle against Indonesian rule is Arnold S. Kohen, *From the Place of the Dead: The Epic Struggles of Bishop Belo of East Timor* (New York 1999). A good introduction to Indonesia's problems in Irian Jaya is Robin Osborne, *Indonesia's Secret War: The Guerrilla Struggle in Irian Jaya* (Sydney 1985). For Australia's relations with Indonesia see Desmond Ball and Helen Wilson (eds), *Strange Neighbours: The Australian-Indonesia Relationship* (Sydney 1991) and Bob Catley and Vinsensio Dugis, *Australia and Indonesia since 1945: The Garuda and the Kangaroo* (Aldershot 1998).

The US, USSR and China

A good study of this topic to 1972 is Gordon H. Chang, *The United States, China, and the Soviet Union* (Stanford 1990). A competent overview of US–Chinese relations from 1972 to 1990 is Harry Harding, *A Fragile relationship: The United States and China Since 1972* (Washington 1992). A revisionist study of early US–Communist China relations is David Allan Mayers, *Cracking the Monolith: US Policy Against the Sino-Soviet Alliance, 1949–1955* (Baton Rouge 1986). For a new good book on more recent relations between the US and China see James Mann, *About Face: A History of America's Curious Relationship with China, from Nixon to Clinton* (New York 1999). For early USSR–China relations see especially Odd Arne Westad (ed.), *Brothers In Arms: The Rise and Fall of the Sino-Soviet Alliance, 1945–1963* (Stanford 1998). Other more specialized studies are Michael R. Beschloss, *The Crisis Years: Kennedy and Krushchev 1960–1963* (New York 1991) and John W. Lewis and Xue Lital, *China Builds the Bomb* (Stanford 1988).

The New Japanese Economic Order

A Marxist, but well-researched study of Japanese economic expansionism is Rob Steven, *Japan's New Imperialism* (London 1990). See also William R. Nestor, *Japan's Growing Power over East Asia and the World Economy* (London 1990). For a Japanese view see Masataka Kosaka (ed.), *Japan's Choices: New*

Globalism and Cultural Orientations in an Industrial States (London 1989). For a critical analysis of where the Japanese economic empire was heading see Bill Emmott, *The Sun Also Sets: The Limits to Japan's Economic Power* (New York 1989). For its world role in the early 1990s see Rob Steven, *Japan in the New World Order: Global Investments, Trade and Finance* (Basingstoke 1996). For economic conflict between the US and Japan see Edward J. Lincoln, *Japan's Unequal Trade* (Washington 1990); Leonard J. Schoppa, *Bargaining with Japan: What American Pressure Can and Cannot Do* (New York 1997) and Mayumi Itoh, *Globalization of Japan: Japanese Sakoku Mentality and US Efforts to Open Japan* (New York 1998).

East Asian Tigers

A critical overview of the economic progress of South Korea, Taiwan and Singapore at the end of the 1980s is Walden Bello and Stephanie Rosenfeld, *Dragons in Distress: Asia's Miracle Economies in Crisis* (San Francisco 1990). For the economic development of South Korea see Alice H. Amsden, *Asia's Next Giant: South Korea and Late Industrialization* (New York 1989) and Robert Castley, *Korea's Economic Miracle: The Crucial Role of Japan* (London 1997). For relations between the two Koreas see especially Don Oberdorfer, *The Two Koreas: A Contemporary History* (London 1997). For Taiwan's economic performance and diplomatic relations see Gary Klintworth (ed.), *Modern Taiwan in the 1990s* (Canberra 1991); Mei-ling T. Wang, *The Dust that Never Settles: The Taiwan Independence Campaign and US–China Relations* (Lanham, NY 1999) and John W. Garver, *Face Off: China, the United States and Taiwan's Democratization* (Seattle 1997). Good accounts of Hong Kong's development are Felix Patrikeeff, *Mouldering Pearl: Hong Kong at the Crossroads* (London 1989) and Kevin P. Lane, *Sovereignty and the Status Quo: The Historical Roots of China's Hong Kong Policy* (Boulder 1990). A good history of Singapore is C.M. Turnbull, *A History of Singapore 1819–1980* (Singapore 1989). For the collapse of East Asian economies in the late 1990s see especially Ross H. McLeod and Ross Garnaut (eds), *East Asia in Crisis: From being a Miracle to Needing One?* (London 1998) and Richard Robison, Mark Beeson, Kanishka Jarasuriya and Hyuk-Rae Kim (eds), *Politics and Markets in the Wake of the Asian Crisis* (London 2000).

Southeast Asia

For the development of ASEAN see Alison Broinowski (ed.), *Understanding ASEAN* (London 1983) and Michael Leifer, *ASEAN and the Security of*

South-East Asia (London 1989). A very good study of conflict in Indochina after the conquest of South Vietnam is Grant Evans and Kelvin Rowley, *Red Brotherhood at War: Vietnam, Cambodia and Laos since 1975* (revised edition, London 1990). For Pol Pot's Kampuchea see especially Elizabeth Becker, *When the War was Over: Cambodia's Revolution and the Voices of its People* (New York 1986). For the Sino-Vietnamese War of 1979 see King C. Chen, *China's War with Vietnam, 1979* (Stanford, 1987) and Stephen J. Morris, *Why Vietnam Invaded Cambodia: Political Culture and the Causes of War* (Stanford 1999). For ASEAN and Vietnam's occupation of Cambodia see K.K. Nair, *Words and Bayonets: ASEAN and Indochina* (Selangor 1986). For recent developments in ASEAN see N. Ganesan, *Bilateral Tensions in Post-Cold War ASEAN* (Singapore 1999) and articles in relevant journals. For economic developments in ASEAN states see Alison Broinowski (ed.), *ASEAN into the 1990s* (New York 1990) and Jose L. Tongzon, *The Economies of Southeast Asia: The Growth and Development of ASEAN Economies* (Cheltenham UK 1998).

The Pacific Islands

A general history of the islands with a good bibliography is Deryck Scarr, *The History of the Pacific Islands: Kingdoms of the Reefs* (Canberra 1990). A new history of the Pacific in the twentieth century with a historiographical bent is Robert Kiste, Kerry Howe and Brij Lal (eds), *Waves of History: The Pacific Islands in the Twentieth Century* (Honolulu 1994). A good history of France in the Pacific since 1945 is Stephen Henningham, *France and the South Pacific: A Contemporary History* (Sydney 1992). For Australia and the Pacific see Roger C. Thompson, *Australia and the Pacific Islands in the Twentieth Century* (Melbourne 1998). For some good books about specific Pacific islands groups see Ian Downs, *The Australian Trusteeship, Papua New Guinea 1945–75* (Canberra 1980); Judith Bennett, *Wealth of the Solomons: A History of a Pacific Archipelago* (Honolulu 1987); Howard Van Trease, *The Politics of Land in Vanuatu: From Colony to Independence* (Suva 1987); Brij V. Lal, *Broken Waves: A History of the Fiji Islands in the Twentieth Century* (Honolulu 1992); Malama Meleisea, *The Making of Modern Samoa: Traditional Authority and Colonial Administration in the Modern History of Western Samoa* (Suva 1987); Barrie Macdonald, *In Pursuit of Sacred Trust: Trusteeship and Independence in Nauru* (Wellington 1988); Barrie Macdonald, *Cinderallas of the Empire: Towards a History of Kiribati and Tuvalu* (Canberra 1982) and Arnold H. Leibowitz, *Embattled Island: Palau's Struggle for Independence* (Westport 1996).

For islanders' struggles for independence and a nuclear free Pacific see Stewart Firth, *Nuclear Playground* (Sydney 1987) and David Robie, *Blood on their Banner: Nationalist Struggles in the South Pacific* (London 1989). For a competent historical analysis of the rebellion on Bougainville see Douglas Oliver, *Black Islanders: A Personal Perspective of Bougainville 1937–1991* (Melbourne 1991), and for more recent developments there see Karl Claxton, *Bougainville 1988–98: Five Searches for Security in the North Solomons Province of Papua New Guinea* (Canberra 1998). For the Fiji coups see especially Brij V. Lal, *Power and Prejudice: The Making of the Fiji Crisis* (Honolulu 1988) and John Sharpham, *Rabuka of Fiji: The Authorized Biography of Major-General Sitiveni Rabuka* (Rockhampton 2000).

Latin America

There is a comprehensive bibliography relating to Central America in Thomas M. Leonard, *Central America and United States Policies, 1820s–1980s: A Guide to Issues and Reference* (Claremont, California 1985). An excellent survey of history and the nature of the political systems in Central America in the 1980s is James Dunkerley, *Power in the Isthmus: A Political History of Modern Central America* (London 1988). A very good new survey is William LeoGrande, *Our Own Backyard: The United States in Central America, 1977–1992* (Chapel Hill 1998); and for peace movements there see James Dunkerley, *The Pacification of Central America: Political Change in the Isthmus, 1987–1993* (London 1994). More specific studies of Central America and the US are Susanne Joans, *The Battle for Guatemala: Rebels, Death Squad, and US Power* (Boulder 1991); Tommie Sue Mongomery, *Revolution in El Salvador: From Civil Strife to Civil Peace* (2nd edition, Boulder 1995); Martha Honey, *Hostile Acts: US Policy in Costa Rica in the 1980s* (Gainesville 1994) and Michael L. Conniff, *Panama and the United States: The Forced Alliance* (Athens 1992).

A good analysis of US policy towards Nicaragua is Robert A. Pastor, *Condemned to Repetition: The United States and Nicaragua* (Princeton 1987). For the Sandinista era see especially Dennis Gilbert, *Sandinistas: The Party and the Revolution* (New York 1988); Thomas W. Walker (ed.), *Reagan Versus the Sandinistas: The Undeclared War on Nicaragua* (Boulder 1987) and Cynthia J. Arnson, *Crossroads: Congress, the President, and Central America* (New York 1993).

Valuable studies of the Eisenhower era are Stephen G. Rabe, *Eisenhower and Latin America: The Foreign Policy of Anticommunism* (Chapel Hill 1988); Richard H. Immerman, *The CIA in Guatemala: The Foreign Policy of Intervention* (Austin 1982) and Nick Cullather, *Secret History: The CIA's Classified Account of its Operations in Guatemala* (Stanford 1999). For discussions of the Alliance for Progress see Stephen G. Rabe, *The Most Dangerous Area in the World: John F. Kennedy Confronts Communist Revolution in Latin America* (Chapel Hill 1999).

For other good books on the Pacific Basin states of Latin America and their relations with the United States see Lester D. Langley, *Mexico and the United States: A Fragile Relationship* (Boston 1991); Augusto Varas (ed.), *Democracy Under Siege: New Military Power in Latin America* (New York 1989); David Corkill and David Cubitt, *Ecuador: Fragile Democracy* (London 1988); Lawrence A. Clayton, *Peru and the United States: The Condor and the Eagle* (Athens 1999); Mark Falcoff, *Modern Chile 1970–1989: A Critical History* (New Brunswick 1989); Paul E. Sigmund, *The United States and Democracy in Chile* (Baltimore 1993). For an analysis of Japanese economic interests in Latin America see Susan Kaufman Purcell and Robert M. Immerman (eds), *Japan and Latin America in the New Global Order* (Boulder 1992).

The Pacific Basin

A book analyzing the concept of the Pacific Basin is Gerald Segal, *Rethinking the Pacific* (Oxford 1990). Two other useful books discussing contemporary aspects of the Pacific Basin are Gavin Boyd, *Pacific Trade, Investment and Politics* (London 1989); and Janos Radvanji (ed.), *The Pacific in the 1990s: Economic and Strategic Change* (Lanham, Maryland 1990). For more recent developments in the Pacific Basin see Donald C. Hellman and Kenneth B. Pyle (eds), *From APEC to Xanadu: Creating a Viable Community in the Post-Cold War Pacific* (Armonk, NY 1997) and M. Dutta, *Economic Regionalization in the Asia-Pacific* (Cheltenham, UK 1999).

MAPS

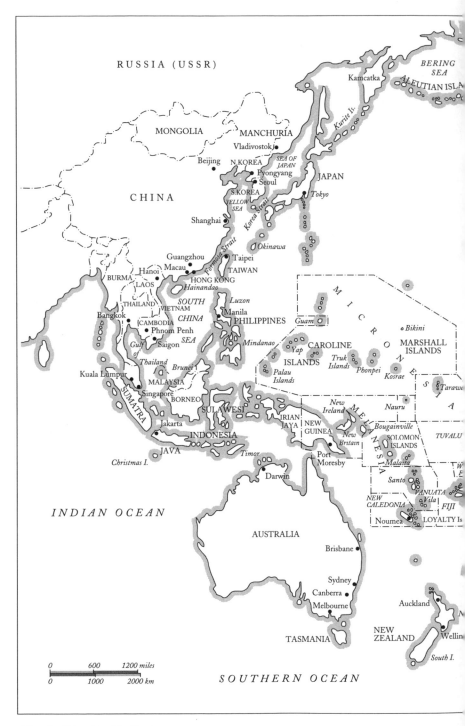

Map 1   The Pacific Basin

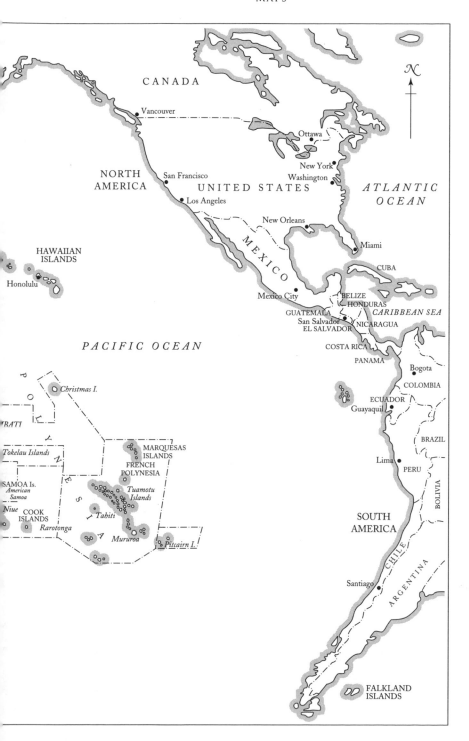

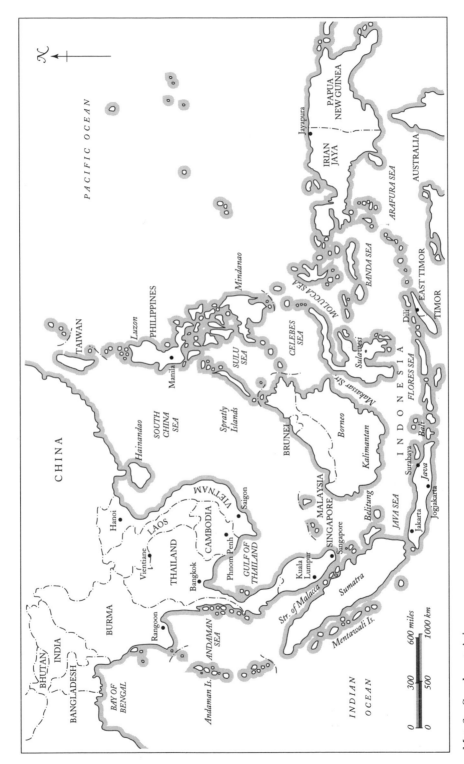

Map 2 Southeast Asia

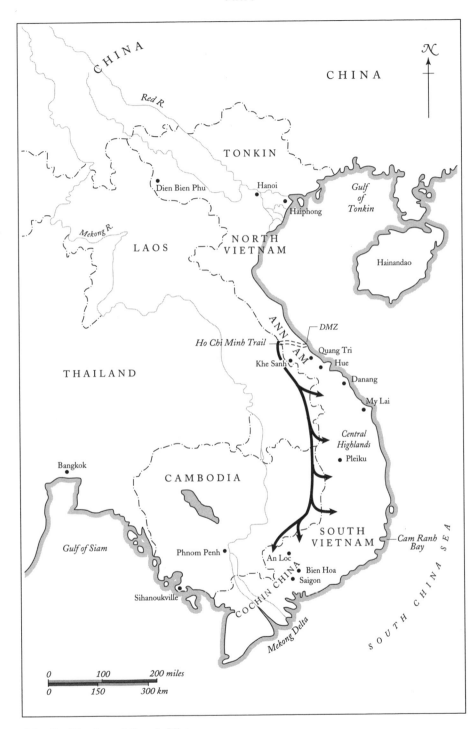

Map 3 North and South Vietnam

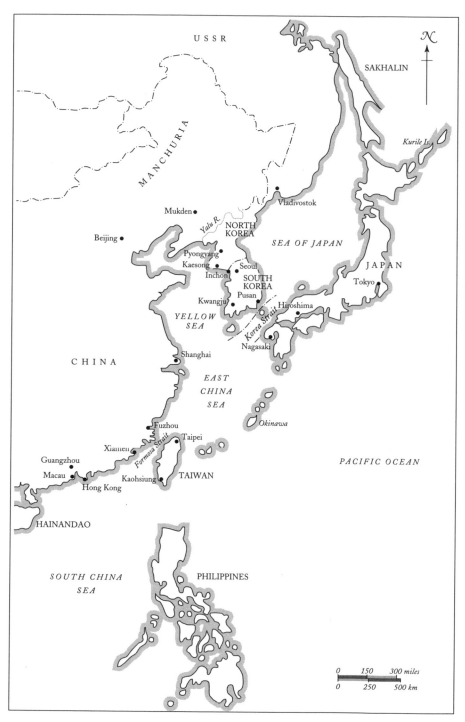

Map 4   Eastern China, Korea and Japan

Map 5 Central America

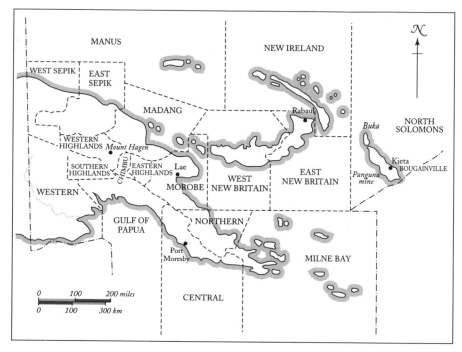

Map 6 Papua New Guinea

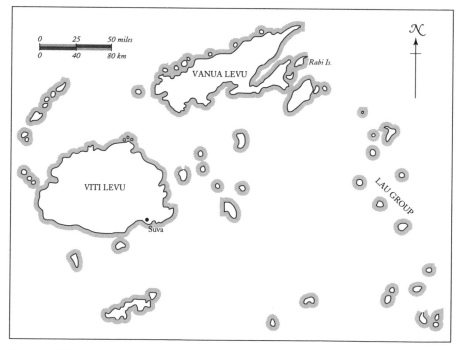

Map 7 Fiji

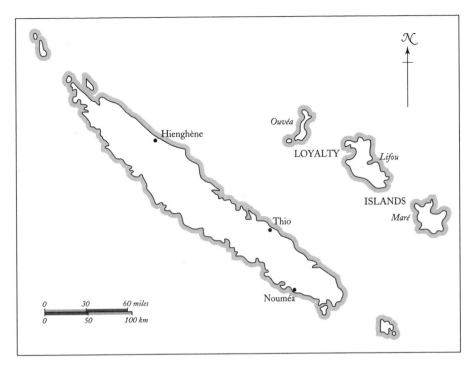

Map 8 New Caledonia

INDEX

Afghanistan, 134, 210, 213, 222
Alatas, Ali, 223, 299, 300
Allende Gossens, Salvador, 177, 181–5, 188, 190, 192
Alliance for Progress, 176–8, 183, 192, 273
Andean Pact, 186, 269, 311
ANZUS Treaty, 56, 247–9, 301
Aquino, Corazon, 225–6, 260
Argentina, 185, 263, 311
Arias, Oscar, 259, 265
ASEAN Regional Forum (ARF), 294, 307, 312
Asia-Pacific Economic Conference (APEC), 307–8, 311, 312, 313, 315, 316
Association of Southeast Asian Nations (ASEAN), 104–5, 126, 127, 194, 224–7, 274, 275, 294–5, 296, 298, 307–8, 316
  and Cambodia, 128, 130, 132–3, 138, 221–4, 293
  and Japan, 127, 137, 195, 202–3, 205, 206, 228
  and US, 128, 222, 225, 226, 275, 294
  expansion of, 227, 292–3, 312, 313
Australia, 2, 316
  and APEC, 294, 307, 308
  and China, 99, 170, 248
  and Fiji, 142, 160, 161, 165, 170, 172, 173, 231, 233–4
  and Indonesia, 27, 28–9, 71, 81, 84, 99, 124–7, 168, 252, 298–301
  and Japan, 5, 56, 136, 204
  and Malaya/Malaysia, 69, 84, 87, 128
  and Nauru, 143–4, 170, 252
  and New Zealand, 56, 128, 143, 171–3, 233–4, 238, 248, 301
  and nuclear-free Pacific, 172, 238, 250–1, 303
  and Pacific Islands, 170–1, 172, 203, 229, 251–2, 302, 304, 312, 314
  and PNG, 81, 140–1, 148–51, 155, 170–1, 172, 235, 237, 238, 251, 253, 302–3

  and South Korea, 22, 43
  and US, 56, 60, 126, 128, 144, 248–9, 251, 253, 301
  and Vanuatu, 155, 172, 250, 251
  and Vietnam, 99–100, 223, 252

Bao Dai, 24–5, 57, 61, 62
Belo, Carlos Ximenes, 299, 300
Bikini Atoll, 63, 163, 166
Bolivia, 2, 186, 190
Bougainville, 148, 151, 170, 229, 235–9, 251, 252, 253, 302–3, 304, 315
Brazil, 191, 270, 273, 300, 306, 311
Brezhnev, Leonid, 114, 115, 132
Britain, *see* Great Britain
Brunei, 82, 83, 84, 137, 227, 288
Bui Diem, 91, 110
Burma (Myanmar), 33, 41, 57, 64, 293
Bush, George, 213
  and East Asia, 197, 216–17, 274, 285
  and Latin America, 260, 263, 264, 267–8, 273, 276, 309

Cambodia, 60, 120, 194, 307, 312
  and ASEAN, 132–3, 138, 221, 223, 224, 226, 293
  and China, 108, 112, 129, 130–1, 132–3, 222, 223
  and Vietnam, 64, 111–12, 116, 122, 129–31, 132, 133, 138, 220–3, 227, 292
  and US, 107, 108, 111–12, 120, 122, 132, 133, 222
Canada, 19, 136, 298, 300
  and Pacific region, 2, 294, 307
  and US, 270, 306–7
  and Vietnam, 60, 101
Carter, Jimmy
  and Asia, 132, 133, 134–5, 214, 225, 282
  and Latin America, 188–90, 192, 254, 255, 261, 263, 268
Castro, Fidel, 177, 181, 187, 188, 266

Chan, Julius, 168, 169, 172, 302
Chiang Kai-shek, 11, 12, 13, 14, 15, 39, 50, 51, 100
Chile, 183–4, 185, 275
  and Pacific region, 191–2, 273, 308, 311
  and Peru, 190, 311
  and Mexico, 188
  and US, 177, 181–2, 184–5, 190, 192, 268–9, 274
China, 2, 192, 202, 307, 312, 315
  and APEC, 307, 308, 313
  and ASEAN, 104, 132, 224, 293–4
  and Cambodia, 108, 112, 129, 130–1, 132–3, 222, 223
  and Hong Kong, 53–4, 54–5, 104, 136, 201, 209, 217–19, 287, 289–90
  and Indonesia, 80, 84, 86, 124, 132, 217, 224, 300
  and Japan, 11, 70, 136, 203, 206, 211, 217, 291–2
  and Korea, 20, 41–9, 135, 214, 281, 284
  and Latin America, 268, 274, 310
  and Macau, 53, 54–5, 290
  and Malaya/Malaysia, 32, 33, 34, 84, 132, 224
  and Pacific Islands, 170, 306
  and Russia, 290–1
  and Taiwan, 13, 43, 44, 45, 50–2, 53, 55, 72, 114, 134, 209, 217, 286–9, 291, 294, 306
  and Soviet Union, 79
    civil war, 10–11, 12, 14, 15
    détente, 210–11, 216, 219, 222, 223, 227
    Korean War, 40–1, 42–3, 44–5, 47–8, 49
    Sino-Soviet split, 50, 51–3, 59, 72, 74, 80, 90, 102, 108, 114–15, 170, 314
  and US
    1940s, 8, 10, 11–15, 25, 38
    1950s, 40, 41, 44–8, 49, 50, 51–3, 59, 72, 313
    1960s, 74, 76, 79, 80, 88, 95, 102, 105, 114
    1970s, 106, 114–15, 118, 132, 133, 134, 135, 136, 138, 181, 314
    1980s, 194, 209–10, 216, 219, 222, 227, 254, 275
    1990s, 216, 216–17, 278, 285–9, 291, 312
  and Vietnam, 21, 23, 44, 57, 58, 59, 63, 64, 79–80, 89–90, 96, 102, 105, 114–15, 118, 130–2, 133, 138, 223, 292, 293

China, Nationalist, see Taiwan
Chirac, Jacques, 242, 243, 245, 246, 303
Christopher, Warren, 288, 301
Clinton, William (Bill), 284, 306, 308, 310
  and Japan, 277–8, 279
  and China, 285–9, 306
Colby, William, 177, 181
Colombia, 186, 259, 265, 266, 269–70, 311, 315
Colonial Sugar Refining Company (CSR), 142, 144
Cook Islands, 171, 248, 250, 304
Costa Rica, 180, 263
  and Nicaragua, 179, 259, 264–5, 259
  and US, 264–5, 276
Cuba, 73, 80, 177
  and Central America, 178, 180, 254, 255, 258, 261, 266, 309
  and Mexico, 187, 188
  and South America, 178, 180, 186, 192, 267

Deng Xiaoping, 129, 131, 203, 209, 216, 218, 268, 287
  and Soviet Union, 132, 134, 210, 215, 222
DeRoburt, Hammer, 143, 169
Diem, Ngo Dinh, 2, 61–3, 64–5, 74–5, 76–8, 79, 88, 122
Dijoud, Paul, 154, 162
Duarte, José Napoleón, 261, 263
Dulles, John Foster, 51, 56, 60, 62, 175
Duong Van Minh, 88, 90

East Timor, 106, 123–7, 138, 167, 226, 252, 298–301, 307, 312, 314–15
Ecuador, 178, 186, 269, 311
Eisenhower, Dwight, 73, 80, 163
  and Asia, 48, 49, 51–2, 59, 60, 65, 70, 71, 74, 92
  and Latin America, 174, 175–6, 179
El Salvador, 175, 264, 308
  and Honduras, 186–7, 192, 265
  and Nicaragua, 255, 261, 262, 309
  and US, 180, 189, 255, 256, 260–3, 266, 268, 271, 275, 276, 309
Europe (Eastern), 38, 46, 71, 215, 291
European Economic Community (EEC), 127, 171, 172, 216, 241, 246, 294

Federated States of Micronesia (FSM), 166, 305

Fiji, 139, 169, 192, 229–33, 252, 314, 316
  and Australia, 142, 170, 172, 261, 265,
    170, 173, 231, 232, 233–4
  and Great Britain, 69, 142, 144–5, 253,
    314
  and other Pacific Islands, 143, 172, 234,
    303, 304
Flosse, Gaston, 244–5, 305
Ford, Gerald, 121, 125, 126, 181, 186,
  188
France, 3, 28, 49, 75, 129, 251
  and French Polynesia, 156–7, 244–7,
    253, 303, 305
  and New Caledonia, 141, 157–62,
    173, 239–44, 247, 253, 304–5,
    314
  and other Pacific Islands, 153–5, 172,
    234, 246, 303
  and Vietnam, 20–5, 40, 57–60, 69, 72,
    88, 99, 102, 114, 118
Fraser, Malcolm, 126, 172
French Polynesia, 155–7, 159, 244–6, 247,
  305
Fujimori, Alberto, 310, 311

Gaulle, Charles de., 88, 114, 156, 158–9
Geneva, 49, 59–60, 63, 74, 283, 284
Geneva Agreement(s), 60, 61, 113, 119
Giap, Vo Nguyen, 21, 23, 24, 58, 97
Gilbert and Ellice Islands (*see also* Kiribati,
  Tuvalu), 146–7
Gorbachev, Mikhail, 210, 211, 212, 213,
  215, 219, 222, 290
Great Britain, 3, 10, 25, 60, 96, 216, 246,
  300
  and Australia, 2, 84, 87, 144, 204, 248
  and Hong Kong, 43, 53–5, 72, 104, 136,
    201, 218–19, 289, 290, 313
  and Indonesia, 27–8, 81, 82–5
  and Korea, 15, 17, 43, 44, 46, 49
  and Malaya, 28, 31–4, 57, 67–9, 72, 82,
    84
  and Malaysia, 82–5, 87, 128, 202, 226
  and Pacific Islands, 140, 141, 142,
    144–7, 148, 151–4, 164, 170, 171,
    253, 303, 314
  and Singapore, 86, 87, 128, 313
  and Vietnam, 21, 22, 56–7, 59
Gromyko, Andrei, 52, 212
Guam, 127, 165, 166, 203, 205, 250
Guatemala, 259, 268, 315
  and Mexico, 187, 309–10
  and US, 174–6, 178, 180, 187, 189,
    192, 263–4, 276, 309–10

Hasluck, Paul, 147, 148, 150
Hatta, Muhammed, 26, 30
Hawaii, 126, 162, 164, 166, 226
Hawke, Robert, 234, 247, 248
Helms, Richard, 181, 185
Hirohito, Emperor, 1, 6
Ho Chi Minh, 20, 21, 22–4, 25, 59, 61,
  64, 102
Hodge, John, 16, 17, 18, 19
Holland, *see* Netherlands
Honduras, 2, 175, 180, 255
  and El Salvador, 186–7, 192, 265
  and US, 178, 256, 265, 276
Hong Kong, 43, 105, 202, 308
  and China, 53–4, 54–5, 104, 136, 201,
    209, 217–19, 287, 289–90
  and Great Britain, 43, 53–5, 72, 104,
    136, 201, 218–19, 289, 290,
    313
  and Japan, 137, 138, 198, 200, 201, 203,
    292
  and Vietnam, 24, 104, 219
Hukbalahap (Huk) movement, 36–8, 40,
  65–7, 69
Hun Sen, 223, 293
Hurley, Patrick, 11, 12, 15

India, 28, 60, 64, 111, 169, 294
Indonesia, 33, 38, 202, 237, 295, 296–7,
  308, 313, 316
  and ASEAN, 104–5, 126, 127, 132, 223,
    224, 225, 227
  and Australia, 27, 28–9, 71, 81, 84, 99,
    124–7, 168, 252, 298–301
  and China, 80, 84, 86, 124, 132, 217,
    224, 300
  and East Timor, 4, 106, 123–7, 138,
    226, 298–301, 312, 314–15
  and Irian Jaya, 73, 80, 138, 166–8, 173,
    234–5, 314
  and Japan, 137, 195, 201–3, 206, 297
  and Malaya/Malaysia, 31, 32, 71, 73,
    82–6, 105, 128, 294, 296
  and Netherlands, 25–30, 31, 71, 73, 81,
    82, 167, 298
  and Singapore, 71, 82, 87, 126, 128,
    217, 227
  and Soviet Union, 71, 80–1, 128
  and US, 25, 27, 29, 30, 38, 70, 71, 75,
    81, 84–5, 125, 126, 128, 167, 168,
    226, 298, 299, 300, 314
  and Vietnam, 132, 223, 224
International Monetary Fund (IMF), 226,
  227, 271, 297, 300

Irian Jaya, 30, 71, 80–2, 84, 138, 166, 229,
    234, 235, 252, 314

Japan, 50, 73, 201, 292, 296, 300, 307,
    316
  and ASEAN, 127, 294
  and Australia, 5, 56, 136, 137, 204, 248,
    307
  and China, 11, 53, 70, 136, 203, 206,
    209, 211, 216–17, 291–2
  and Korea, 16, 17, 41, 43, 55–6, 135,
    137, 138, 198, 199–200, 202,
    205–6, 215, 283, 284, 297
  and Latin America, 174, 191, 193, 194,
    272–4, 310, 311, 314
  and Pacific Islands, 139–40, 143, 163,
    164, 165, 203–4, 205, 302
  and Russia, 279–80
  and Southeast Asia,
    1940s, 3, 20, 21, 24, 26–7, 31, 32, 33,
      36, 61, 67
    1950s, 56, 57
    1960s, 100–1, 103, 105, 135
    1970s, 137, 138, 314
    1980s, 194, 195, 200, 202–3, 206,
      227–8
    1990s, 293, 294, 295, 297
  and Soviet Union, 1, 10, 56, 70, 136,
    196, 211–12, 220, 313
  and US
    1940s, 1, 3–9, 10, 13, 16, 38, 67, 140,
      313, 314
    1950s, 41, 43, 46, 51, 55–6, 72, 163
    1960s, 69–70, 75, 100–1, 103, 106
    1970s, 127, 135–6, 138, 165
    1980s, 194, 195–8, 205, 206–9, 228,
      273, 275
    1990s, 220, 277–9, 284, 285, 312
Jiang Zemin, 288–9, 291
Johnson, Lyndon, 87
  and Latin America, 178, 179
  and Vietnam, 75, 79, 88, 89–99, 107,
    113, 122

Kabui, Joseph, 236, 238
Kennedy, Edward, 117, 266
Kennedy, John F., 83–4, 87–8
  and Latin America, 176, 177–9
  and Vietnam, 74–8, 79, 88, 92, 100,
    113
  and Soviet Union, 72–3, 80
Khanh, Nguyen, 88, 89–90
Khmer Rouge, 108, 112, 120, 128–30,
    132, 220–3, 227

Khrushchev, Nikita, 51, 52–3, 59, 71, 74,
    80
Kim Il Sung, 18–19, 42–3, 135, 213, 214,
    215, 282–3
Kim Jong Il, 283, 284
Kim Young Sam, 282, 283
Kiribati, 147, 304
Kissinger, Henry,
  and China, 114–15
  and Latin America, 181, 185, 186,
    276
  and Vietnam, 106–7, 108, 109, 111,
    114, 116, 118–19, 225
Korea (see also Korean War, North Korea,
    South Korea), 10, 15–18, 20, 38,
    39, 47, 114, 135, 220, 279, 312,
    313, 314
Korean War, 40–8, 60, 72, 94, 131, 214,
    313
  influences of, 40, 48–50, 54, 55–6, 58,
    59, 65, 68, 69, 100, 105, 314, 315
Kurile Islands, 10, 211–12, 279–80, 312,
    314
Kuwait, 207, 220

Laos, 2, 58, 60, 64, 74, 102, 112, 122, 129,
    131, 293, 294
Le Duan, 90, 97
Lee Kuan Yew, 86–7, 132, 200, 201
Lee Teng-hui, 286–8
Lenormand, Maurice, 157–8, 159, 161
Lini, Walter, 153, 154–5, 172
Lodge, Henry Cabot, 78, 88
Lon Nol, 111, 112, 120, 128, 221

MacArthur, Douglas, 4–5, 6, 7–8, 9, 36,
    43–4, 45, 46, 55
Macau, 53, 54, 290
McNamara, Robert, 75, 94
Magsaysay, Ramon, 66–7, 77
Mahathir, Mohamad, 296, 298
Malaya, 37, 40, 41, 84, 142
  and Britain, 28, 31–4, 57, 67–9, 72, 82,
    84
  and Indonesia, 31, 32, 71, 82, 85
  and Singapore, 32, 86, 87
Malayan emergency, 31–4, 40, 41, 67–9,
    84, 314
  and Vietnam wars, 69, 72, 75, 77, 99
Malaysia, 300, 304, 313, 316
  and ASEAN, 104, 105, 128, 132, 224,
    225, 227, 292, 294, 295
  and Australia, 84, 87, 128
  and Britain, 82–5, 87, 128, 202, 226

and China, 132, 224, 293
and Indonesia, 73, 82–6, 105, 128, 294, 296
and Japan, 137, 202, 206
and Singapore, 82, 86–7, 128, 225, 294
and Thailand, 86, 225, 294, 295, 298
and US, 84–5, 128, 226, 296
and Vietnam, 224, 292
Mao Zedong, 13, 51, 128, 129, 131
and Soviet Union, 15, 42–3, 44, 47, 52–3
and Vietnam, 90–1, 102
Mara, Ratu Kamisese, 169, 230, 231, 232, 233
Marcos, Ferdinand, 100, 138, 192, 214, 225–6, 274
Mariana Islands, 164–5, 250, 305, 306
Marshall, George, 12, 13, 14
Marshall Islands, 163–4, 165, 305, 306
Marshall Plan, 25, 30
Melanesia (Melanesian), 81, 123, 138, 139, 140, 142, 147, 151, 152, 155, 161, 166, 172, 173, 234, 235, 326, 240, 250–1
Mexico, 313, 315, 316
and El Salvador, 271, 308
and Guatemala, 187, 309–10
and Japan, 191, 273
and Nicaragua, 188, 259, 271
and Pacific Basin, 274, 275, 308, 311
and US, 187–8, 270–2, 306–7
Micronesia (Micronesian), 139, 140, 146, 164, 165, 166, 173, 204
Mindanao, 66, 195, 225
Mitterrand, François, 239, 243, 303
Mook, Hubertus van, 27, 29
Moruroa Atoll, 155, 246, 303

Nauru, 143–4, 169–70, 172, 251, 252
Netherlands, 3
and Australia, 28, 81
and Indonesia, 25–30, 31, 71, 73, 81, 82, 167, 298
Netherlands East Indies, see Indonesia
New Caledonia, 139, 150, 153, 229, 245
and Australasia, 172, 246, 247
and France, 141, 157–62, 173, 239–44, 247, 253, 304–5, 314
New Hebrides, see Vanuatu
New Zealand, 229, 245, 307
and Australia, 56, 100, 128, 144, 171–3, 233–4, 238, 248, 301
and France, 246–7, 253

and Pacific Islands, 141, 142–3, 144, 170, 171–2, 232, 233–4, 238, 246, 250, 251, 302–3
and Southeast Asia, 60, 99, 100, 124, 128, 294, 300
and US, 56, 247–9, 301
Nhu, Ngo Dinh, 2, 62, 64, 78
Nicaragua, 175
and Costa Rica, 179, 259, 264–5, 259
and Cuba, 178, 180, 254, 255, 258
and El Salvador, 255, 261, 262, 309
and Honduras, 256, 265
and Soviet Union, 254, 255, 257, 258, 309
and US, 178, 180, 186, 188–9, 254–60, 261, 265, 271, 272, 273, 275, 276, 309
Niue, 171, 248
Nixon, Richard, 127–8
and Cambodia, 107–8, 111–12
and China, 14, 114–15
and Latin America, 176, 181–2, 183, 185, 186
and Vietnam, 99, 106–7, 108–9, 112–14, 115–18, 118–21, 225
Nixon doctrine, 127–8, 135, 138
Noriega, Manuel, 258, 265–7, 276, 311
North American Free Trade Agreement (NAFTA), 306–7, 313
North Korea, 49, 294, 315
and China, 19, 42–3, 44–8, 214, 215, 281, 282, 284
and Japan, 55–6, 135, 206, 215, 283, 284
and Russia, 282, 312
and South Korea, 40–3, 102–3, 135, 214, 219, 281, 282–4, 297
and Soviet Union, 18–19, 42–4, 47–8, 212–13, 215, 219, 281, 313
and US, 40–1, 43–5, 47–8, 49, 101–2, 135, 219–20, 281–4
North Marianas, see Mariana Islands
North Vietnam, see Vietnam
nuclear/atomic weapons, 70, 190
advocated, discussed use of, 45, 51, 52, 59, 103
development of, 53, 74, 281–3, 289
fear, suspicion of, 1, 101, 115, 127, 220, 281–2
limitation, banning of, 80, 108, 213, 249–50, 281
nuclear armed ships, 126, 247–8, 249, 251, 253, 301
nuclear-free Pacific, 250–1, 253, 275, 303

possession of, 10, 19, 25, 42, 48, 80, 135, 284
testing of, 15, 80, 115, 155–7, 163–6, 172, 229, 245–6, 253, 291, 303, 304, 305

Ocean Island, 143, 146, 147
Okinawa, 13, 100, 279
Ona, Francis, 236–7, 238
Organization of American States (OAS), 187, 267

Palau, 164, 165, 229, 249–50, 253, 304–5, 314
Panama, 275
  and Nicaragua, 258, 259
  and US, 179–80, 189–90, 258, 265–7, 276, 311
Papua New Guinea (PNG), 167, 168–9, 173, 236–9, 294, 308
  and Australia, 81, 140–1, 148–51, 155, 170–1, 172, 235, 237, 238, 251, 253, 302–3
  and Indonesia, 168, 234–5, 237
  and other Pacific Islands, 155, 172, 237, 251, 303
Paracel Islands, 130
Park Chung Hee, 103–4, 105
Peru, 308, 311, 315
  and Chile, 190, 311
  and Ecuador, 269, 311
  and Japan, 191, 310, 311
  and Soviet Union, 186, 190, 274
  and US, 180, 185–6, 190, 192, 268
Philippines, 40, 69, 130, 138, 202, 227, 228, 250, 274, 300, 314, 315, 316
  and ASEAN, 104, 132, 294, 295
  and China, 132, 284, 293–4
  and Indonesia, 71, 225
  and Japan, 137, 195, 203
  and Malaysia, 84, 105, 225, 294, 298
  and Vietnam, 77, 99, 100, 132, 224, 292
  and US, 4, 13, 14–15, 35–8, 41, 60, 65–7, 75, 84, 100, 128, 190, 192, 214, 225–6, 294, 296
Phonpei, 165, 166
Pinochet Ugarte, Augusto, 185, 190, 191–2, 269, 274
Pol Pot, 128, 129, 130, 133, 221, 223
Polynesia (Polynesian), 139, 142, 144, 146, 147, 155, 156, 159, 161, 171, 172, 173, 204, 245, 250
Portugal, 53–4, 123–4, 125, 290, 300
Pouvanaa a Oopa, 155, 156

Rabuka, Sitiveni, 231, 232–3, 234, 304
Rahman, Tunku Abdul, 82, 85, 86–7
Rarotonga treaty, 250–1, 303
Reagan, Ronald, 251
  and Central America, 254–6, 258–9, 261–6, 275, 276
  and Japan, 196, 207, 275
  and other American states, 261–2, 268–9
  and Southeast Asia, 222, 225–6
  and Soviet Union, 213, 254–5, 275
Remeliik, Haruo, 249–50
Rhee, Syngman, 17, 18–20, 41, 43, 48–9, 103
Rocard, Michel, 243, 244, 247
Roosevelt, Franklin, 4, 10, 11, 12, 15, 21, 140, 176
Russia, 294, 308, 312
  and China, 290–1
  and Japan, 279–80
  and Korea, 282

Saipan, 165
Samoa, Eastern, 162
Samoa, Western, 141–3, 144, 162, 169, 170, 172, 173, 316
Sendero Luminoso (Shining Path), 267–8, 310, 315
Sihanouk, Norodom, 107–8, 111–12, 221–2
Singapore, 3, 72, 201, 296, 300, 313, 316
  and APEC, 307, 308
  and ASEAN, 104, 127, 132, 224, 227, 293, 295
  and Australia, 87, 128
  and Indonesia, 71, 82, 87, 126, 128, 217, 227
  and Japan, 105, 137, 138, 195, 198, 200, 202, 205, 206
  and Malaya/Malaysia, 32, 82, 86–7, 128, 202, 225, 294
  and Soviet Union, 128, 132, 224
  and US, 128, 132, 200, 226
Solomon Islands, 203, 304
  and Australia, 253, 302, 303
  and Great Britain, 140, 151–2
  and PNG, 151, 237, 253, 303
Somare, Michael, 150, 151, 168–9, 235
Somoza family, 178, 179, 180, 186, 188–9, 192, 255, 256, 260, 262
South East Asia Command (SEAC), 22, 27, 28, 39
South East Asia Treaty Organization (SEATO), 60–1, 89, 100, 107, 128

South Korea, 201, 215, 307, 316
  and China, 43, 46, 214, 281, 284
  and Japan, 55–6, 137, 138, 198–9, 200,
    202, 206, 209, 297, 313
  and North Korea, 40–3, 102–3, 135,
    213–14, 219, 281, 282–4, 297
  and Soviet Union/Russia, 17, 18, 42–3,
    209, 212–13, 281, 282
  and Southeast Asia, 61, 294, 296, 300
  and US, 16–20, 40–1, 43–5, 48–9, 99,
    100, 103, 134–5, 138, 199–200,
    213, 214–5, 219, 281, 283, 297
  and Vietnam, 99, 100, 103, 105
South Pacific Forum, 172, 173, 234, 250,
  304
South Vietnam, see Vietnam
Soviet Union (USSR), 170
  and China
    1940s, 10–11, 12, 14, 15
    1950s, 40–1, 42–3, 44–5, 47–8,
      49–50, 51–3, 59, 72
    1960s, 74, 79, 90–1, 101–2, 114,
      115
    1970s, 130, 131–2, 135
    1980s, 194, 210–11, 219, 222, 223
  and Japan, 1, 10, 56, 70, 136, 196,
    211–12, 220, 313
  and Korea, 16, 17, 18–19, 20, 42–4,
    47–8, 49, 135, 209, 212–13,
    214–15, 219, 313
  and Mexico/Central America, 188, 254,
    255, 257, 258, 309
  and other South East Asia, 33, 41, 71,
    80–1, 132, 128, 224
  and South America, 186, 190, 274
  and US, 313, 314
    1940s, 1, 11, 14, 16, 18, 25, 39
    1950s, 41, 42, 43–4, 45, 47–8, 49–50,
      51–2, 57
    1960s, 70, 73–4, 80, 101, 108, 115,
      164
    1970s, 116, 118, 132, 134, 135
    1980s, 194, 196, 210, 213, 222, 227,
      255, 257, 258, 275
  and Vietnam, 23, 24, 41, 57, 59, 63, 64,
    74, 79, 80, 90–1, 96, 101–2, 105,
    108, 111, 116, 130, 131–2, 222,
    223, 293, 313
Spratly Islands, 130, 132, 293, 294, 312
Stalin, Joseph, 33, 50
  and China, 10, 11, 12, 14, 15, 40, 42,
    44, 47, 48
  and Korea, 15, 16, 18, 42, 44, 47, 48
  and US, 10, 15, 16, 42, 44, 47

Suharto, Raden, 85, 86, 125, 126, 168,
  226, 252, 296, 297, 298, 312
Sukarno, Achmed, 26, 30, 70–1, 81, 82–3,
  85, 105

Tahiti, 155, 156
Taiwan, 104, 105, 201, 296, 308, 314,
  316
  and China, 13, 43, 44, 45, 50–2, 53, 55,
    72, 114, 134, 209, 217, 286–9, 291,
    294, 306
  and Japan, 50, 136, 137, 198, 199, 202,
    206, 209, 292, 313
  and US, 44, 45, 46, 50, 51–2, 53, 72,
    80, 85, 114, 134, 136, 138, 199,
    286–9, 312
Taruc, Louis, 36, 37, 65
Thailand, 86, 295–6, 313, 316
  and ASEAN, 104, 105, 128, 132, 225,
    227, 297–8
  and Cambodia, 128, 132, 133, 220, 224,
    226
  and Japan, 202, 297
  and Malaysia, 86, 225, 294, 295, 298
  and US, 57, 60–1, 71, 75, 100, 128,
    132, 226
  and Vietnam, 75, 99, 100, 132, 224,
    226, 292
Thieu, Nguyen Van, 91, 99, 108, 109, 110,
  118, 119, 120, 121
Tjibaou, Jean-Marie, 161, 240, 241, 243,
  244
Tokelau, 171, 248
Tonga, 145–6, 169, 170, 173, 250, 302,
  303, 316
Tran Van Don, 62, 76
Truk Islands, 165, 166
Truman, Harry, 21, 38, 51, 60, 65, 140,
  175
  and China, 10, 11, 12, 13–14, 15, 25,
    41, 45, 57, 80, 106
  and Japan, 4, 8
  and Korea, 14–15, 16, 17, 18, 45, 46,
    49
  and Soviet Union, 10, 14, 16, 17, 18, 25,
    41
Tung Chee-hwa, 289–90
Tuvalu, 147, 170, 172, 252, 304

United Nations (UN), 99, 220
  and Cambodia, 132, 133, 223–4, 293,
    307
  and China, 41, 46, 54, 134, 217, 281,
    285, 288

and Indonesia, 28, 71, 81, 84, 126, 127,
    167, 299–301
and Korea, 18, 19, 40, 41, 42–7, 60,
    281, 282, 283
and Latin America, 182, 263, 267, 310
and Pacific Islands, 140, 141, 144, 147,
    148, 154, 163, 164, 235, 250, 305,
    314
United States (US),
  and Australasia, 56, 60, 126, 128, 144,
    247–9, 251, 253
  and Canada/Mexico, 270–2, 187–8,
    306–7
  and Central America, 276, 308–10, 275,
    276, 309, 311
    1950s and 60s, 174–6, 178–80
    1970s, 186–7, 188–90, 192
    1980s, 254–60, 260–7, 271, 273, 276
    1990s, 260, 309
  and China, 59
    civil war, 8, 10, 11–15, 25, 38
    détente, 106, 114–15, 134, 135, 136,
      138, 181, 194, 209–10, 219, 222,
      254, 275, 314
    Korean War, 40, 41, 44–8, 49, 72, 313
    Taiwan, 44, 45, 50, 51–3, 72, 80, 114,
      134, 136, 138, 286–9, 312
    Vietnam War, 76, 79, 80, 88, 95, 102,
      114–15, 118, 122
  and Japan, 41, 51, 163, 165
    occupation of, 3–9, 10, 38, 313
    defence relations, 13, 43, 46, 51,
      55–6, 72, 69–70, 75, 100–1, 103,
      135, 138, 194, 206–9, 275, 220,
      279, 284
    Second World War, 1, 16, 17, 67, 140
    trade tensions, 106, 127, 135–6,
      195–8, 205, 228, 273, 220, 277–9,
      285, 312
  and Indonesia, 25, 27, 29, 30, 38, 70,
    71, 75, 81, 84–5, 125, 126, 128,
    167, 168, 226, 298, 299, 300, 314
  and Korea, 15–20, 40–9, 100–3, 134–5,
    138, 199–200, 213, 214–15,
    219–20, 281–4, 297
  and other Southeast Asia, 57, 60–1, 71,
    75, 84–5, 100, 128, 132, 226, 296
    200
  and Pacific Islands, 139, 140, 144,
    163–6, 170, 173, 246, 249–51, 253,
    301, 303, 305–6, 313, 314
  and Philippines, 4, 13, 14–15, 35–8, 41,
    60, 65–7, 75, 84, 100, 128, 190,
    192, 214, 225–6, 294, 296

and South America, 177–8, 180, 181–2,
    184–6, 190, 192, 268–70, 274, 311
and Soviet Union, 25, 73–4, 164, 227,
    255, 257, 258, 275
  and China, 11, 14, 39, 41, 44, 45,
    47–8, 49–50, 51–2, 80, 115, 132,
    134, 210
  and Japan, 1, 70, 194, 196
  and Korea, 16, 18, 39, 41, 42, 43–4,
    45, 135, 213
  and Vietnam, 57, 74, 101–2, 108, 115,
    116, 118, 132, 213, 222, 223
and Taiwan, 44, 45, 46, 50, 51–2, 53,
    72, 80, 85, 114, 134, 136, 138, 199,
    286–9, 312
and Vietnam, 21, 25, 41, 57, 58, 59–61,
    62, 64–5, 72, 73, 74–9, 85, 87–90,
    91–101, 103, 105, 106–7, 108–23,
    127, 128, 132, 133, 138, 181, 213,
    222, 225, 226
United States Central Intelligence Agency
    (CIA), 249
  and Central America, 174–6, 178,
    256–7, 265, 266, 276
  and Indochina, 62, 74, 95, 110, 111, 112
  and Indonesia, 71, 86
  and South America, 177, 178, 181–2,
    185

Vann, John Paul, 77, 93, 94
Vanuatu, 139, 151, 303, 308
  and Australia, 155, 172, 250, 251
  and France, 140, 152–5, 172
Venezuela, 175, 186, 259
Vietnam, 2, 38, 227
  and ASEAN, 132–3, 221, 222, 223–4,
    292, 312, 313
  and China, 21, 23, 44, 57, 58, 59, 63,
    64, 79–80, 89–90, 96, 102, 105,
    114–15, 118, 130–2, 133, 138, 223,
    292, 293
  and Cambodia, 64, 111–12, 116, 122,
    129–31, 132, 133, 138, 220–3, 227,
    292
  and France, 20–5, 40, 57–60, 69, 72,
    88, 99, 102, 114, 118
  and Soviet Union, 23, 24, 41, 57, 59, 63,
    64, 74, 105, 130, 131–2, 222, 223,
    293, 313
  and US, 21, 25, 41, 57, 58, 59–61, 62,
    64–5, 72, 73, 74–9, 85, 87–90,
    91–101, 103, 105, 106–7, 108–23,
    127, 128, 132, 133, 138, 181, 213,
    222, 225, 226

Vietnam wars
  First Vietnam War, 24–5, 57–60, 62,
    76
  Second Vietnam War, 2, 63–5, 73–80,
    87–102, 105, 106–14, 115–23, 313
  influences of, 98–9, 102–4, 105–6,
    107–8, 109, 112, 113–15, 117,
    120–2, 128, 134, 135, 136, 159,
    183, 188, 200, 223, 256, 264, 313

Wallis and Futuna Islands, 159, 243
Wedemeyer, Albert, 11, 14
Westmoreland, William, 93, 98, 122

Whitlam, Gough, 125, 126, 149, 150
women, 5, 6, 7, 8–9, 95, 125, 145, 177,
    184, 225–6, 260, 261, 264, 308
World Bank, 182, 208, 226, 269
World War, Second, 1, 3, 27, 48, 66, 95,
    96, 119, 139, 141, 142, 164, 165,
    166, 167, 207, 237, 291

Yalta Agreement, 10, 15, 211
Yeltsin, Boris, 279–80, 290, 291
Yŏ Un-hyŏng, 16, 17

Zhou Enlai, 12, 15, 52, 55, 60